Jesuits

Menology of the Society of Jesus

Jesuits

Menology of the Society of Jesus

ISBN/EAN: 9783744646796

Printed in Europe, USA, Canada, Australia, Japan

Cover: Foto ©ninafisch / pixelio.de

More available books at **www.hansebooks.com**

MENOLOGY

OF THE

SOCIETY OF JESUS.

ROÉHAMPTON:
PRINTED AT ST. JOSEPH'S PRESS.

1874.

MENOLOGY

OF THE

SOCIETY OF JESUS.

JANUARY.

JANUARY 1.

1. At Toulouse, in France, in the year 1564, the happy death of Father John Pelletier, the first Rector of the Roman College; surnamed by Saint Ignatius the "Saintly Rector," and by the people of Pamiers and elsewhere the "Doctor of Mary," on account of his constant exhortations, both public and private, in honour of the Mother of God. When an image of Our Lady had been thrown down, he caused it to be replaced with solemn prayers, in spite of the Iconoclast Calvinists. They put him in chains, which he bore with the same constancy with which he refused to accept the Bishopric of Cahors.

2. At Cuzco, in Peru, in the year 1598, Father Alphonsus Barréna, surnamed the "Apostle of Peru." He was one of the most cherished disciples of that great master of spiritual life, John of Avila. After his entrance into the Society, he was sent by St. Francis Borgia to labour in Peru, where he converted to Christ the last of the native monarchs with a number of his people. He did much both by word and example; and his memory was so powerful, that he knew by heart all the Epistles of St. Paul, and was master of eleven languages. He often underwent

great labours, for the space of five or six days, without any nourishment except the Holy Eucharist; and sometimes accomplished in a few hours a journey which was ordinarily performed in eight days. He was very devout to the Infant JESES, and once in a severe sickness when he could not reach the image of the holy Infant, it came of its own accord to him and pressing itself to his breast said; "See me, here I am, you need not be so distressed." He died at the age of seventy years, forty of which he spent in the Society.

3. In the Philippine Isles, in the year 1617, Father Gabriel Sanchez, an Apostolic man, so addicted to prayer, that amid the greatest labours he used to spend seven hours daily in it; so attached to the Vows of Religion and observant of them, that he daily renewed the formula sixty times; so careful of his angelic purity, that once when shipwrecked he would not allow his clothes to be removed that he might swim more easily ashore.

4. At Treves, in the year 1607, Father Luke Elleniz, a successful labourer in preparing for their last end sorcerers condemned to die. He assisted at least two hundred of them, to the great benefit of their souls, passing days and nights with them in their prison, praying and exhorting them to attend to their salvation, in spite of the opposition of the demons, and although his life was demanded in the sorcerers' assembly.

JANUARY 2.

1. At Cape Comorin, in India, in the year 1549, Adam Francisco, not as yet admitted to the Priesthood, who, by the testimony of St. Francis Xavier, was a truly devout man, of a generous and fervent zeal for the conversion of the heathen. "For my part," says Xavier, "I rather recommend myself to him, than him to God."

2. At Manilla, in the Philippine Isles, in the year 1632, Father Francis de Enzinas, an active missioner in the Indies for thirty years. When he applied himself to the recital of the Office, after the day and a great part of the night spent in the confessional, he lit up his Breviary with the light which shone from his face in such a manner as to need no lamp or candle.

3. At Hamburg, in Germany, in the year 1654, Father Henry Schacht, an indefatigable and energetic missioner in the German camp and amongst

heretics. When he was in Sweden, he concealed himself, in order to assist the Catholics secretly, in the disguise of a rat-catcher and man-servant, and rocked the child's cradle in the house of the Catholic Consul at Upsal. He was at last betrayed, and dragged almost naked from his bed to a horrible prison, where he heroically endured cold, filth, and chains, and, three times, the tortures of the rack. When the Consul, Anthel, and his Secretary, Gregory Ursin, were beheaded for the Faith, Father Henry escaped the same sentence, as not being a native of Sweden. Returning into Germany, he became a most useful labourer in the Catholic army.

4. At Alcala, in Spain, Father Peter Balbas, a Novice. He lived but three months in the Society. Having long resisted an interior call, he at last exchanged his Abbey of St. Just and the dignity of Chancellor of the University for the humble position of a Novice. Throwing himself upon his knees, with the most admirable candour he disclosed to the Rector the most intimate secrets of his heart. The Canons of St. Just came in a body to congratulate him upon the resolution he had taken to journey to Heaven by the shortest and safest road. They assured him that by trampling under foot honours of which the world was so ambitious, he had edified not only the City of Alcala, but all Spain. Father Balbas thanked them for their attention, and assured them that it was his intimate conviction that had he renounced the Episcopal rank and the Archbishopric of Toledo, the sacrifice would have seemed to him as nothing in comparison of the joy which he found in being in the Society. At the approach of Christmas, he said that it was his intention to ask the Infant JESUS to bestow on him the gift of a painful sickness, for as he had nothing else to suffer, it would be a satisfaction to be able to make an offering of his sufferings. His prayer was heard, for on the very night of the Nativity, and immediately after he had said his third Mass, he was attacked by the disease of which he died. He breathed his last in sentiments of intense joy, repeating again and again: "To Heaven—I am going to Heaven. I go at last to the enjoyment of eternal glory—what happiness!"

JANUARY 3.

1. At Cagliari, in Sardinia, in the year 1624, James de Alagona, a Temporal Coadjutor of the Society, illustrious for his contempt of his rank

of Marquis, and the world. He preferred the drudgery of the kitchen and refectory, and similar offices, to rank and power. But God raised him to intimate union with Himself in ecstatic contemplations, and refreshed his soul with heavenly delights, which, however, he would have preferred not to have, as he considered the present life a time not of rejoicing but of suffering.

2. At Verdun, in Lorraine, in the year 1634, Father Peter le Cames, who having asked for great crosses, when influenced by an ardent desire of suffering for the sake of Christ, received an evident answer to his prayer, and, like holy Job, for the space of three years, was tried with exceedingly bitter sufferings.

3. At Tournay, in Belgium, in the year 1592, Baldwin Cuvillon, in his childhood an anchorite, and in his youth a perfect Novice of the Society. When but nine years old, having heard of the Hermits of old, he retired with a companion of the same age to a mount near the city, to imitate the Fathers of the Desert. Later, he left a noble and rich inheritance to join the Society, and led a life worthy of such beginnings. He used to repeat those words of the Gospel: "Wo to you rich!"—and, "It is difficult to pass from earthly pleasures to heavenly: it is well to whet our appetite here by poverty, fasting, and other austerities; there we shall feast without satiety, and enjoy pleasures that surpass man's understanding."

JANUARY 4.

1. At Valencia, in Spain, in the year 1609, Father Michael de Fuentes. As he lay wearied out with Apostolical labours in India, the Blessed Mother of God, whom he honoured with special devotion, appeared to him, and promised him that he should go to Heaven without suffering the pains of Purgatory. To keep up the remembrance of this favour, which he received on a Monday, he devoted that day in each week to humble offices, taking his food on the ground, and serving in the kitchen. A learned and holy Franciscan saw his soul immediately after death ascending into Heaven, where the Blessed Virgin, St. John, and St. Ignatius, coming to meet him, honoured their servant by placing on his head the crown of eternal life.

2. At Evora, in Portugal, in the year 1610, Vincent de Rocha, a youth pious from his birth. Before lying down to rest he paid a visit

to each of the pictures in the room, to reverence the Saints depicted in them and wish them good night. He embraced the bearer of the news of his approaching death, and made him a present of the hairshirt he used to wear. Amid the pains and sufferings of sickness, he exclaimed: *Non satis est, Domine,*—It is not enough, O Lord, it is not enough."

3. At Gandia, in Spain, in the year 1576, died Father Diego Puellas, a man remarkable for his angelical modesty, which was owing to his constant recollection of the presence of God. He gave a singular proof of his obedience, when for a whole year he punctually and with alacrity attended school and gave lessons to only one scholar. It is not the number of scholars that make the Professor, but learning and diligence; and Heaven will give the same reward for attention to one as to many.

4. At the Noviceship, in Naples, the anniversary of Brother Mary Joseph de Geronimo, Temporal Coadjutor, who from humility chose this state, though nothing was wanting to admit of his being raised to the Priesthood. In his novitiate he showed the finished virtues of an advanced Religious, so much so that scarcely were the two years of his novitiate ended, than he was appointed Socius to the Master of Novices, so great were the piety, modesty, and prudence, which were happily united in him. In this office he continued for forty years, assisting not only the Novices, but the Master of them by his advice. He was most fervent in prayer and in practices of charity and mortification. For many years he never slept on a bed, ate no fruit, and never laid aside his hairshirt. He was constant in his long continued disciplines, watchings, and other penances. But his virtue shone most conspicuously in his self-restraint and self-command. He showed no resentment when wronged, nor made excuse when blamed, nor resisted those who opposed him. In the midst of his varied duties he was always self-possessed, and showed the constant serenity of his mind by his cheerful countenance. He was always the same, without change, without disturbance; always occupied, and ready for labour without weariness or depression; mindful of the wants of others and regardless of his own. In his last sickness nothing grieved him more than that his pains should be alleviated at the expense of the labours of others, desiring rather that their pains, and more, should be added to his own. He foretold the day and hour of his death, which took place in the year 1713, in the fifty-eighth year of his age, and the forty-second

from his entrance into the Society. His death was revealed at the moment it took place to St. Francis de Geronimo, his brother in the flesh and still more in the spirit, though he was far distant from him.

January 5.

1. At Rome, in the year 1583, Father John Maldonado, a Spaniard, a learned commentator on Holy Scripture, especially the Gospels, distinguished for his talent and zeal in confuting and convincing heretics. He was listened to with such eagerness when lecturing on theology and Holy Scripture, that Preachers, Parish Priests, Abbots, and Bishops, nay even heterodox ministers, thronged to hear him, and came an hour or two before the time to secure places—the concourse was often so great that he was obliged to give his lecture outside of the schools in the open air. He was summoned from France to Rome by Gregory XIII. that he might assist in bringing out a new edition of the Septuagint, which the Pontiff proposed to publish, but did not long survive, dying, as he had lived, a holy death, and well prepared.

2. At Granada, in Spain, in the year 1632, Father James Granada, who for prudence, learning and sanctity, may be justly reckoned among the greatest lights of the Society. He taught philosophy and theology thirty years, and published the whole of theology in eight volumes. He was a perfect model of Religious Life, and was honoured with many supernatural favours both before and after death. He was exceedingly reverent to churches, and when near to one he walked with his head uncovered. He esteemed so much the grace of his Religious vocation that he kept the anniversaries of his entrance into the Society, of the taking of his first Vows, and of his Religious Profession, by special exercises and practices of piety for eight days. He received the message of his death with the words of David, "I rejoiced at the things that were said to me, we will go into the house of the Lord."

3. At Jacasco, in Japan, in the year 1564, Edward de Silva, a Portuguese, the Apostolical Coadjutor and most faithful companion of St. Francis Xavier. He was the first to publish a copious lexicon and grammar in Japanese, which were of great service to the Society. At Funasi he baptized thirty nobles. He was a man of great energy in action and fortitude in suffering, which are the characteristic virtues of Apostolic men.

January 6.

1. In the Molucca Isles, in the East Indies, in the year 1558, Father Alphonso de Castro, a Portuguese. Being taken by the Mahometans, in whose district he laboured, he was stripped and fastened to a cross, like St. Andrew the Apostle, and thus exposed to the heat of the sun and the stings of insects. He was tied to a tree and scourged, and left without food for eight days, after which he was invited to embrace the creed of Mahomet with offers of high advancement, but with undaunted spirit and astonishing cheerfulness of countenance amid his torments, he stood faithful to God and the Society. At last being beheaded, he died a glorious martyr. His body was cast into the sea, and for some days was seen resting on a rock, with the waters arching over it. Afterwards it came on shore, and was found with heavenly light shining round it, and wounds fresh bleeding. So that he was held in great veneration by the very Mahometans themselves.

2. In the Isle of Majorca, in the year 1580, John Meseguer, Temporal Coadjutor. Being previously in perfect health, at a late hour of the night, urged by a strong impulse, he went to the Rector and asked for the last Sacraments. The Doctor being sent for, pronounced it to be nothing but a diseased imagination. However Brother John prepared himself carefully for death, and, having received the last Sacraments, died, with no apparent previous sickness. As he had learned in life to obey the inspirations of grace, so he recognised its call in death.

January 7.

1. In the Kingdom of Manado, in the East Indies, Father Peter Mascaregnas, a Portuguese, poisoned for the Faith. He was the first missioner who by his labours converted sixty-six towns of the Salsettans: preached to the people of Ternate and Celebes, and other savage tribes. He made converts of the Princes of the Sionese and Manadese, and of the King and Queen, and many nobles of the Saugies. When he was once with much compassion looking down from a mountain upon a village of Idol-worshippers lying at his feet, he suddenly heard the voice of a child coming

up from the valley below distinctly saying, "In the name of the Father, and of the Son, and of the Holy Ghost." By which, being greatly comforted, as a presage foretelling the Faith in the Holy Trinity, he was encouraged to do and suffer all things for the glory of God and the good of souls.

2. At Omura, in Japan, in the year 1620, the glorious departure to liberty and eternal life of Ambrose Fernandez, Temporal Coadjutor, after a year's horrible imprisonment for the Faith. The other Confessors of Christ incarcerated in the same prison, in honour of his holy death, sang the Psalm, *Laudate Dominum omnes gentes,*—"Praise the Lord all ye nations."

3. At Courtrai, in Belgium, in the year 1579, Father John Francisci died a holy death—a man most solicitous for his perseverance in the Society. He often asked those with whom he lived, saying, "Pray for me that I may not lose my vocation." This petition he fervently repeated in his agony; for he used to say, that when a Novice he heard a voice saying these words: "John, if you persevere in the Society you will be saved; if you are dismissed from it, by your own fault, you will be lost." He went to confession every day. After the celebration of Mass he heard three other Masses most devoutly. He parted out his room into seven Stations of the Passion, and daily visited them with never failing devotion; and yet, with such fervent piety, he feared lest he should fall from his vocation.

4. At Burgos, in Spain, the anniversary of Brother John Carrera, noted for his devotion to his Angel Guardian, with whom he enjoyed extraordinary familiarity. He consulted him on all occasions, and received immediate answers. Every night he was awakened by him to prayer, and when once through weariness he yielded to sleep, he was deprived of his friendly intercourse for several days, until by much prayer and fasting he obtained a reconciliation. For as all the Angels are ministering spirits, they love the diligent in the service of God, and shun the slothful.

5. At Bahia, in Brazil, Brother Louis Manuel, a Temporal Coadjutor. He was indebted for his vocation to an accident that nearly proved fatal. He was fired at, and received several balls in the body. He escaped death by a kind of miracle, and was carried to one of our Houses close at hand. Every assistance was rendered him which charity could bestow, and he ultimately recovered. His feelings of gratitude made him resolve to consecrate to God the remainder of a life preserved by so singular a benefit,

January 7, 8.

and enter the Society. During the ninety-two years he survived he was always an example of extraordinary virtue. Though habituated to the freedom of an independent life, he became in Religion docile and obedient as a child. He not only devoted to prayer the time prescribed by the Rule, but every evening withdrew to the Church, and remained for hours before the Blessed Sacrament, where he found the only repose he desired after the fatigues of the day. On Sundays and Holidays he passed the greater part of the morning in hearing Masses. In temper he was naturally passionate, but by the practice of abnegation he became a model of patience and meekness. He used great corporal austerities, frequent disciplines, and the hairshirt, and took but little sleep, and that on the bare boards. He was full of the spirit of Poverty, seeking always for himself the worst things in the house, especially in food and clothing.

January 8.

1. At Mexico, in America, in the year 1599, Francis de Ciudad Real, a Temporal Coadjutor, endowed with a singular gift of prayer and tears. His constant exclamation was, "Praised be our Lord JESUS CHRIST,"—*Laudetur Dominus noster Jesus Christus*. With this ejaculation he honoured the Birth of the Infant JESUS in a stable, and the thought filled him with heavenly joys. He was often found rapt in ecstasy with his eyes fixed on Heaven. He washed a poor Indian's lothsome and putrid sores, and even wiped them with his tongue.

2. At Palermo, in Sicily, in the year 1627, Father Joseph Scamacca, of singular innocence of life, which he never stained by mortal sin, and honoured by God with miraculous favours. He was a preacher of great fame and fruit, by choice rather plain and solid in discourse than elegant. As he spoke, sometimes a dove was seen resting on his head, at another time he appeared all radiant with heavenly light.

3. At Horasdowitz, in Bohemia, in 1610, Father Wenceslaus Swihowsky, a descendant of the ancient kings of Bohemia; but still more illustrious for the virtue of humility, for his skill in reconciling those at variance, and successful zeal in the conversion of heretics. For besides a number of citizens and men of rank, he received into the Church many noble ladies; so that he may well be called an Apostolic man, deservedly

renowned not only for his active zeal, but for his reserve and prudence in dealing with the other sex.

January 9.

1. At Madrid, in Spain, in the year 1556, Father John Ruiz, a man of admirable innocence. An act of Christian generosity was the beginning of his sanctity and the occasion of his vocation to the Religious life. When a youth he received a blow on the face in a quarrel, and was on the point of taking vengeance for the insult, when the offender fell at his feet, and in the name of JESUS CHRIST, Who forgave His enemies, asked his pardon. Ruiz, touched by the grace of God, flung himself upon his knees and freely forgave him. For this act of virtue God gave him a desire of quitting the world: he was faithful to the grace and entered the Society. His two special safeguards for the preservation of his chastity, were great devotion to the Blessed Virgin Mother of God, and implacable hatred to his flesh, which he subdued by continual hairshirts, disciplines, fastings, short sleep upon a bed filled with stones, and long prayer. He brought some eatables, offered him in a journey, to the Rector of the College, saying, that he could not refuse to receive them, but he could leave them untouched.

2. At Naples, in the year 1598, Father Gaspar Haywood, an Englishman, who died in exile, after many glorious labours and sufferings, and painful imprisonments. By his admirable skill and force of reasoning he brought back to the bosom of the Church a great number of heretics, and among them were even earls and lords. After a severe struggle in his last agony he exclaimed, " Thanks dearest Lady, Mother of my God, for thy mercy in coming to my aid, and driving the enemy far from me."

3. At Almonacid, in Spain, in the year 1623, Father Francis de Ubierna. When a Student in Theology he was seized with a dangerous malady, and being at the point of death he greatly grieved that he was about to be snatched away before he had laboured for God. Turning to an image of the Mother of God, he fervently asked for a longer life that he might spend it in the salvation of souls. He received an answer, and the event proved that his prayer was heard. Recovering from sickness, he devoted the whole fifteen years he survived to unwearied labour in the saving of souls.

4. At Munich, in Bavaria, in the year 1611, Father Jerome Torres,

of Catalonia. He was honoured with this rare eulogy, "That he was never known to do anything which the Society forbade, or leave undone anything it commanded." In this short encomium all is contained, since on these two things hang all our perfection and sanctity in Religion.

JANUARY 10.

1. At Madrid, in Spain, in the year 1605, Father Louis Gusman, who was Provincial once of Andalusia, and twice of Toledo. Although his mode of life was a model of religious exactness, yet neither his piety, nor eminent services, nor prayer, often continued for twelve hours, could shield him from a grievous calumny and being cited before the ecclesiastical court. But gold is only made brighter by the fire. After a strict examination the Apostolic Nuncio declared that not only was Father Louis proved innocent, but that evidence had come out to entitle him to be ranked among the Saints. The good Father obtained for his calumniators an acquittal before an earthly tribunal, but the punishment of God came upon them.

2. At Grün, in Styria, in the year 1619, Father John Decker, a Belgian. In his last agony he said softly, "Come Lord Jesus—come." Then pausing a moment he added, "I come"; and so departed. A man illustrious no less for his perfect life in Religion than for his great learning. He used to fast from the eve of Maunday Thursday to Easter Sunday at noon. His noble chronological work of three folios was the work of forty years; and when some asked for its publication, and others thought it should be suppressed, he said that he would throw it into the fire without being at all disquieted if Superiors desired it. Father John was the first to employ the method of teaching philosophy and theology which is now adopted everywhere as most convenient in the schools.

3. At Brussels, in Belgium, in the year 1663, Father William Stanihurst, a Belgian. He was a man of virginal innocence of life and purity of mind. It is said that in his youth an attempt was made upon his chastity similar to that of St. Thomas of Aquin, and by his victory he obtained a similar reward, freedom from temptations of the flesh. His countenance breathed such an air of purity, telling of the brightness of his soul within, that the very heretics themselves held him in veneration. Amongst them was a countess very bigoted in her sect, who at the first sight of Father

William was so changed, that she exclaimed, "Certainly if there is a Saint in the world this man is one." She then received from him instruction in the Catholic Faith with good will, and without difficulty surrendered to the truths he taught, for nothing so clearly and powerfully recommends them as a holy life.

January 11.

1. In Brazil, in the year 1608, Father Francis Pinto was cruelly murdered by the Abipon savages, on account of the Faith. He was afterwards held in veneration by them, because, they said, he had obtained rain for them when their country was suffering from drought. Father Joseph Anchieta, the Thaumaturgus of Brazil, when he visited him in sickness, foretold the time of his death to him, then cured him, and bid him prepare himself for greater labours for God. He added, "that he would have to wash his hands well before he sat down to dinner in Heaven"—intimating that it would not be in water but in blood. Then giving him his clothes to put on, he said, "Come, get up, and make a visit to the Blessed Sacrament, to return thanks to God for your recovery." Francis obeyed, arose suddenly cured, and went to the church as he was commanded. Afterwards he was sent to the Tapoian Savages, and from these he made his way amid hunger, thirst, and cold, to the Abipons, through a country almost impassable. While with industry and labour he was winning them to Christ, a band of these savages rushing in upon him as he was saying his Office, slaughtered him, breaking his jaws, thrusting out his eyes, and shattering his skull, and then plundered the holy vestments and sacred things belonging to the altar.

2. At Ceuta, in Morocco, in the year 1580, Father Alexander Villareggio, renowned for his labours in the salvation of souls and the glory of God in Europe, Asia, and Africa. Once when at the point of death he received Extreme Unction, and immediately recovered. Afterwards going to India and Japan he laboured there with the greatest fruit, until he was recalled to Europe by Father Francis Borgia, General of the Society, his constitution being entirely broken, but supported by his indomitable spirit. Nothing in his Apostolical career was so hard for him to bear as this recall. With heroic obedience he returned, and arrived safely

in Europe. Being sent from Rome to Portugal, he accompanied Don Sebastian in his expedition to Africa, carrying before the army the Crucifix worked upon a banner. The battle was lost, and he was taken by the Moors, and endured captivity for a year; then being ransomed returned to Portugal. From thence he was sent again by Don Henry to Africa for the redemption of the captives, and there, while he was attending those infected with the plague, he was seized with it, and was summoned to his reward.

3. At Loreto, in Italy, Father Januarius Cavalieri. After his Noviceship he taught a low class of grammar at Naples and Nola for seventeen years, and was ready to do so for the rest of his life, but our Lord, as if to recompense his humility, inspired his Superiors to send him to Loreto to hear confessions. He spent thirty years in this employment, and often passed entire days in the confessional without any sign of weariness. He especially exhorted his penitents to love purity as a homage to the Queen of Angels. He crowned his zeal and devotion by an admirable act of obedience. The Provincial having said to him that a master was wanting in one of our Houses to take a lower class of grammar, and having half expressed a wish that he should undertake it, Father Cavalieri did not wait for an express order, and in an hour was on the road. Warned by serious infirmities of his approaching end, he begged to be allowed to return to Loreto, where he had passed nearly half his life, and where, as he said, he had left his heart. Before he expired he told those around him, that having had the happiness to spend such a number of years in the service of the Mother of God, he felt full of the greatest hope of his eternal salvation.

JANUARY 12.

1. At Alcala, in Spain, in the year 1563, Father Antony Madrid, an Apostolic Preacher. From a shepherd's life he passed to College, and having gained honours in theology entered the Society. He preached with such spirit and ardour that he was called "The Burning Coal," and with so great fruit that in one discourse he brought to true and lasting penitence all the persons of abandoned character who heard him, and not a few were present. Before his sermon he used to take a severe discipline, as he said, "to strike the fire from the flint," until Father Francis Borgia

January 12.

on account of his health limited him to fifteen strokes, and bid him give the rest to obedience. He often said to himself: "Die daily to yourself—let your life be a perpetual praise of God."

2. Also at Alcala, in the year 1577, Father Peter Manrique, who had left great prospects and fortune in the world. He had composed for his own use a little book of select passages from the Psalms and the holy Fathers, which he had read to him when death approached, the time of which he had foretold. Dominic Fernandez, a Coadjutor, beholding him dying, begged of him that when he got to Heaven he would get for him the grace to follow him speedily. Father Peter promised that he would, and in four months Brother Dominic followed him.

3. In the Mission of Mexico, in the year 1621, Father Jerome Ramirez, a most zealous labourer in the vineyard of Christ. He was the first to carry the light of the Gospel to the Jepegnans and the Parras. When Rector of a college of boarders he is believed to have had the hearts of the young people completely open to him, so that he often discovered their secret thoughts, and sent them to confession; hence those who had any bad designs were afraid to come into his presence. When he was doubting about the state of life he should embrace, a man of venerable aspect stood before him, and told him it was the will of God that he should enter the Society.

4. In the Kingdom of Tonkin, in the year 1737, Fathers Bartholomew Alvarez, Emmanuel de Alven, Vincent d'Accentra, Portuguese; and Gaspar Cratz, a German, received the crown of martyrdom. They had been sent to preach the Gospel at a time when the King was putting the Christians to death, and Priests especially, with frightful tortures. They fell into the hands of the tyrant the very day they entered his dominions. With memorable courage they endured every imaginable torment, and were finally beheaded. Thus they sealed with their blood the testimony which their lives had given to the Christian Faith. The only reason alleged for their condemnation by their iniquitous judges was their avowal that the object of their visit to Tonkin was to announce to the inhabitants of that kingdom the law of Christ.

JANUARY 13.

1. At Genoa, in Italy, in the year 1606, Father Francis Adorno, who having been Confessor to St. Charles Borromeo, was always much beloved and honoured by him. The holy Cardinal appeared to him after his death, and told him that "all was well with him," and then added, "you too will be summoned soon." To remove an unchaste affection of a person towards him he smeared his face with filth, and as a reward for this act his countenance became singularly beautiful in death.

2. At Potosi, in the West Indies, in the year 1589, Father Bartholomew Jacobi, who fell a victim to his charity while assisting the infected with the plague. He was the Nestor of India for his eloquence, and was called by the Indians "*Misqui Simi*," or "Honey Tongue."

3. At Rome, in the year 1685, Father Daniel Bartoli, an Italian. After he had filled the office of Preacher in the principal cities of Italy, with no less zeal than eloquence, he was employed in writing the Annals of the Society, which he did in many beautifully written volumes. He was Rector of the Roman College. Southwell in his *Bibliotheca Societatis* reckons twenty books on various subjects written by him, remarkable for learning, elegance, and grandeur of style, so that he is equally delightful and full of information. He had planned the composition of a very extensive work on Questions of Philosophy, when in the distribution of the monthly Patron Saints he received the following warning: "So arrange your employments that death may find you engaged in some holy work." He took the admonition, abandoned his design, and devoted himself to a work of piety, "*Pensieri Sacri*—Pious Thoughts." As he foresaw that this would be the last production of his pen, he laboured at it with particular care, and as soon as it was finished he was seized with the sickness which brought him to the grave.

JANUARY 14.

1. At Douay, in Belgium, in the year 1614, Father John de la Haye, a Servian, of lively and much-obtaining trust in God. So great an observer of Poverty that he would not use a little needle he had found until he

had very humbly asked leave for it. He had pictures of the Stations round his room, that he might make them more frequently, and this he did with great devotion.

2. At Evora, in Portugal, in the year 1617, Father Martin de Mello. When Rector or Provincial his sweetness without pretence, and his readiness to forget all faults when corrected, endeared him to all. He was most observant of his Vows and all his Rules, but especially of Poverty, using the same soutane for thirty years, if indeed it could be called one, for it was more like a piece of patchwork of bits without number. His love for the Society was so tender that he could scarce hear it spoken of without being affected to tears. He seemed the natural protector of the reputation of others, and no one dared to utter an uncharitable remark in his presence.

3. At Warsaw, in Poland, in the year 1695, Father Albert Tylkowsky, a Pole. He had talent and application for literature of every kind, which he so perfected by constant study and diligent research in libraries, that he had the erudition sufficient for writing any kind of work. In the houses of Bishops and Prelates, whom he was ordered to wait upon, he found leisure for study; and if the time of meals was much prolonged, with the Prelate's leave he betook himself to his study. He wrote books on various subjects, and several smaller treatises, nineteen of which Southwell reckons in his *Bibliotheca Societatis*, but many more were afterwards published.

January 15.

1. At Louvain, in Belgium, in the year 1623, Father Leonard Lessius, a man who on many accounts has claims to immortal memory. It may be said that he rather ceased to die than to live: for he was so grievously afflicted with pains of the bowels, colic, stone, complicated hernia, and other diseases, from his youth to his sixty-ninth year, that, as he owned himself, they were worse than death, and that what he suffered was less endurable than being buried alive. Yet all these pains he bore with incredible patience, and comforted himself chiefly by the remembrance of the Passion, ejaculating often, "My Love is crucified." It seems then like a miracle, that in the midst of so many and such incessant pains he could have composed so many and such learned treatises on a variety

of subjects held in very high estimation by theologians and canonists. His doctrine of predestination and the aids of grace was unjustly censured by the rigorous Schools of Louvain and Douay, but this censure was shortly after done away with by Pope Sixtus V. through the Nuncio Apostolic, and thus the doctrine of Lessius was held in higher esteem than before.

2. In New Spain, at Yamorita, in the year 1635, died Father Peter Cravina, leaving behind him the reputation of sanctity and great zeal for souls. Among other wonderful things it is related of him, that while the Christians fought with the Indian Savages, Suarez, the Christian captain, saw Father Peter, then at a great distance, present at the battle, with a crucifix aloft in one hand and taking the discipline with the other. The victory was won by the Christians, as Father Peter had promised.

3. At Vilna, in Lithuania, in the year 1657, Father James Brent took his triumphant departure after a severe conflict with the devil in his last agony. Though he was conscious of no mortal sin in his whole life, he was attacked so violently by the tempter, that he was heard to exclaim: "Lord I suffer violence; answer for me!—how foul, wicked, and detestible is the devil." To a Father who visited him he said, "What a combat I have had with the devil; he would have persuaded me to entertain blasphemy, but by the grace of God I have overcome!" As Master of Novices he showed great prudence and tact. It was a saying of his to the Novices: "The more you are absent from yourselves the more you will be present with God."

4. At St. Omers, Brother Andrew Wilson, an Englishman. From the time of his entrance into the Society he desired ardently to imitate the zeal of the Missionary Priests who had laboured to restore the Faith in England, and sealed their efforts with their blood. It pleased God to give him another kind of martyrdom by a painful disease during his study of philosophy. In the whole course of this visitation he was a model of patience and resignation. He often expressed his thanks to God for permitting him in his early years to partake in the sufferings of His Passion. During the most violent pains of sickness his cry ever was: "More patience, O Lord; more patience—and more pain." The more he suffered, the more he desired to suffer. He offered himself to continue

not only many days, many months, many years, but even for centuries, were it possible, in the same sufferings, exclaiming always, "Blessed be God—Blessed be Thou, my God." The Fathers who visited him seeing such courage and constancy in one of such tender years could not restrain their tears. Having received the Viaticum, he shortly after expired in sentiments of great peace, with the Holy Names of Jesus, Mary, and Joseph, on his lips.

January 16.

1. At Rome, in the year 1620, of a pestilential fever, caught in charitably attending the convicts in the Pope's Galleys, Father Stephen Benassai. He died in sentiments of extreme joy. "What happiness, my Fathers," he repeated; "What happiness!—to Heaven!—to Heaven!" At the hour in which he died in the Roman College he appeared to one of the Society in the Noviceship in bright white garments, with a smiling countenance, and surrounded with much light. Before he entered Religion the Pope, Paul V., purposed to raise him to the Archiepiscopal dignity; but he chose rather to be the humblest in the least Society of Jesus. In this Society, at the age of fifty years, he learned the Illyrian tongue from its first elements, that he might be capable of instructing that people. His great charity displayed itself at Rome in teaching Gipsies their catechism and bringing them into the Church.

2. At Ebersburg, in Germany, in the year 1621, Father George Hoffer. Among other pious customs he had a habit of saying after Office those words from the Litanies, "From a sudden and unprovided death, O Lord deliver us"; and whilst the Litanies were being said as usual in our house, he breathed his last by a death certainly not unprovided, as he daily so earnestly prayed.

3. At Meliapor, in the year 1656, Father Robert Nobili, or de Nobili, an Italian, nephew of Cardinal Bellarmine, and grand nephew of Pope Marcellus II. Sent upon the Madura mission, he learned the three chief languages spoken by those nations so accurately, that to the amazement of all he spoke the Tamul, Bagadese, and Grandonese, with the greatest fluency. Afterwards to gain to Christ some of the Brahmins of the highest caste, he assumed their most austere mode of life and dress,

January 16, 17.

perpetually abstaining not only from all meat but also from fish. His conformity to their practices, though so advantageous for religion, seemed to many (amongst whom were some of our Fathers, and even Cardinal Bellarmine) to be unbecoming his character—and thus the good Father had no slight occasion of suffering. But being a profound theologian, he satisfactorily explained his course of proceeding, upon which his cause was taken up not only by Archbishops, but by His Holiness Pope Gregory XV. Thus Apostolical men have always something both to do and to suffer. After forty-five years on the mission, the infirmities contracted by his labours and fatigues forced him to abandon his dear flock. He retired by order of Superiors to Meliapor, and there spent the last five years of his life in composing works in Tamul for the use of those who should succeed him. Ripe in years and merits, he passed to Heaven at the age of eighty.

JANUARY 17.

1. At Potosi, in Peru, in the year 1620, Father James Alvarez de Paz, a name well known among the most famous writers on ascetics. Additional weight was added to his works, which in themselves are of the most solid kind, by the interposition of Heaven, for while in the act of writing he was seen surrounded with light and listening to the dictation of a man of majestic form who stood beside him. He bound himself by vow never to give full deliberate consent to venial sin. He went daily to confession before saying Mass, and he was seen at the altar to receive an embrace from our Lord. He is thought to have preserved unsullied his baptismal innocence. His body remained incorrupt.

2. In Paraguay, in the year 1559, Father D—— de Alfaro nobly fell a victim for the Faith and the salvation of souls. For this death, which he foreknew and had foretold to a friend, he prepared himself by a month's spiritual exercises in the strictest retirement.

3. At Rome, in the year 1559, a premature death carried off a noble young Roman, Robert Cardinal de Nobili. He had engaged himself to enter the Society, but was not permitted to leave the Court for the Novitiate. He therefore most exactly regulated his life at Court by the Rules of the Roman College and the Society, and with admirable humility

and obedience put himself under the direction of the Father General. He completed a short life of but eighteen years by an illness borne with heroic patience. His last dying words were a memento which all both high and low should bear in mind, " Humility! humility! humility!"

4. At Vienna, in Austria, in the year 1653, Father Charles Musart, a Belgian. He was a man who, though he had received the degree of Doctor in theology, seemed made for waiting upon all, especially those of the humbler sort. He possessed singular power and zeal in dealing with the young, and instilling into them the love of virtue. For this end he composed several little works of piety. Southwell in his *Bibliotheca Societatis* enumerates above twenty.

5. At Rome, in the year 1687, Father Silvester Moro, an Italian, a man of great modesty, and also of great subtlety of mind. He was a close follower of Aristotle in philosophy, and of St. Thomas in theology. Accordingly he edited all the works of Aristotle with a paraphrase, in six volumes quarto; and wrote many theological treatises in strict accordance with the doctrine of St. Thomas. But his love of Religious perfection surpassed the greatness of his learning.

JANUARY 18.

1. At the City of Dabul, in the East Indies, in the year 1606, Vincent Alvarez, who on his way to Goa to complete his studies, was taken captive by Mahometan pirates. For the other captives they accepted ransom, but for him they refused it, saying, that men of this sort were the most hostile to Mahomet and his law. Being sentenced to die, in the transports of his soul he was not unmindful of penance, and sang the *Miserere*. His body was cast into the sea.

2. At Vienna, in Austria, in the year 1627, Father John Coloneel, a native of Carniola, died in great sentiments of piety. He was so far from being burdened by the prayers of the Daily Office, that he said besides, one Office of the Holy Ghost or of the Blessed Sacrament, and another of St. Barbara, Virgin and Martyr. Besides the Mass, which he said daily, he assisted at two others. At the hour of his death he appeared to a person twenty-six leagues distant from Vienna visible in the clear light of day, somewhat before noon, with his hat and stick, as if prepared for his journey to eternity, and with a sweet and smiling countenance.

3. In England, in the year 1648, Father Francis Gardiner, an Englishman, beloved for his piety and sincerity. He had great devotion to prayer for the souls in Purgatory, and he had great confidence of obtaining assistance from them in all dangers and difficulties: nor was he disappointed. He happened to fall into the hands of the pursuivants while carrying the Holy Viaticum to the sick. The officers searched him so closely that they stripped him to his shirt. Thereupon he said to our Lord: "My God, save Thyself; for I can now do no more." At the same time he held the small pyx closed in his hand, and no one noticed it. Thus it is that sometimes what is most open is least suspected.

January 19.

1. At Rome, in the year 1565, Father James Laynez, a Spaniard. He was the second General of the Society, a man of talent of the highest order, of consummate prudence and learning, of singular innocence and sanctity, and in his manner more modest and sweet than can be expressed. He was the chief assistant of St. Ignatius in founding and modelling the Society. He traversed nearly the whole of Italy, preaching with the greatest zeal and fruit. Nor did he cease from the duty of preaching even when General of the Society. Sent by Pius IV. with Cardinal D'Este into France, he confounded and put to silence the champions of the heretics, Beza and Peter Martyr, in the public national assembly called the *Colloque de Poissy*. Appointed theologian of the Apostolic See by three Popes three several times at the Holy Council of Trent, he held the first place among the theologians, and spoke with so much approbation, admiration, and applause of that august assembly, that he was generally lauded as the chief of theologians, the mouth-piece of the Holy Ghost, and the ark of theological science in all its branches. With profound humility he refused the Cardinal's Hat, offered him by Paul IV., and after the death of that Pope he was voted, by many of the most influential Cardinals, worthy of the Pontificate. Laynez was content with deserving their votes.

2. At Novocomo, in Italy, Father Edmund Auger, a Frenchman, a preacher of Apostolic zeal, and confessor to the two Kings of France, Charles IX. and Henry III. He passed to heavenly glory in the year

1591, celebrated for his triumphant success in the conversion of heretics, forty thousand of whom, some say seventy thousand, together with forty heterodox ministers, he reconciled to the Church, and confirmed many more who were wavering in the Faith: so that he was justly called the Father of his Country, the Preserver of the Faith, Restorer of the people to the way of salvation, the Flood of French eloquence. The source of his eloquent discourse was from the pages of Isaias and St. Paul. For four centuries France was said to have had no preacher like him. On his death-bed he heard heavenly music, and exclaimed, "Come then, let us go—let us go"; and he took his departure, as was shown to a certain person by revelation, surrounded by a glorious company of Angels, and a great train of children singing before him, a sodality of whom he had established in France.

JANUARY 20.

1. At Macao, an island off China, in the year 1606, Father Alexander Valignani, Provincial and Visitor of the Indies for thirty-three years, distinguished for his zeal. He was born of a noble family at Feate. By him the embassy of three Japanese Princes was sent to Rome, to Pope Gregory XIII. With immense fatigues in journeys, perils, and unwearied anxiety, he advanced the Chinese and Indian missions, and filled the annals of that infant Church with his name and labours. He was armed with continual prayer and mortification against all the dangers and pains that he endured.

2. Also at Macao, in the year 1615, Mancien Tai-chieu, Temporal Coadjutor, a Japanese. He was expelled from his country for the Faith, which he promoted by painting holy pictures, and being put on ship-board, although in a weak state of health, died from the hardships of the voyage.

3. At Pekin, in China, in the year 1688, Father John Verbiest, a Belgian. He succeeded Father John Adam Schall in the Professorship of Mathematics, and the government of the Society in that Empire, like an Atlas to a Hercules. He made a very prudent use of the favour he enjoyed with the Emperor, and the authority which his office gave him of strengthening and spreading the Christian interests. He returned kindness for the injuries of his enemies, and thus gained many advantages through the evident sanctity of the law of Christ.

January 21.

1. At Rome, in the year of 1612. Paulinus Cecotti, a Temporal Coadjutor. Among other religious virtues he so excelled in the gift of prayer that it was commonly believed he could easily obtain whatever he asked. For this reason when the life of Father Mutius Vitelleschi was despaired of by physicians, Paulinus was ordered by the Father General, Claudius Acquaviva, to continue in prayer until the sick man should be out of danger. He obeyed, and after eight hours of fervent prayer rose with joy. At the same moment Father Mutius, who was lying ill at Frascati, experienced a sensible relief, and afterwards recovered. Brother Paulinus cured many diseases by the application of relics of St. Ignatius, and was asked by one Biondo, who had left the Society, and was blind of one eye, to apply the relics to him for a cure, but the contrary happened through the justice of God, for upon their application the apostate lost the other eye. A sick person upon whom Brother Cecotti attended, having vomited and thrown up the Sacred Host, conquering all repugnance he himself received it.

2. At Louvain, in Belgium, in the year 1658, Jodocus Schatelinch, a Belgian, who deserved the rare eulogy, "that he never offended in word." He never spoke well of himself nor ill of another, and weighed all his words in the balance of prudence, humility, and charity, living always rather in the spirit than in the flesh.

3. At Huesca, in Spain, in the year 1646, Father Raymond de Funes, a man ever marvellously the same in look and in mind whether in prosperity or adversity, never even in the tone of his voice shewing any sign of elevation or depression. There is a saying of his, worthy of record—"that a truly virtuous man ought to be ready to take ten years from his life, or to let them be taken."

January 22.

1. At Granada, in Spain, in the year 1585, James de Yevenez, a Temporal Coadjutor, who had been a disciple of St. John of God and his companion in ministering to the poor. He was remarkable for innocence

of life, love of prayer, and blind obedience. Being ordered to draw water in a sieve, he did so, and not a drop fell through. He was more than once seen raised into the air while praying in a corner of the kitchen.

2. In the same year, at Bilboa in Spain, Father Matthew Albenosa, a man of most sweet temper and tender charity to all. In his last sickness he was visited and consoled by the Virgin Mother of God, whom he had always sedulously honoured, in company with St Peter; and as he expired he uttered these words—which he sang—" May mine eyes behold Thee, sweet Jesus, good Jesus, may mine eyes behold thee; and lo, I die;" and as he sang he passed to eternal life.

3. At Warsaw, in Poland, in the year 1614, Father Martin Costens, a Pole, called to receive the crown of justice for a life most religiously spent, and in recompense for an iron crown of sixteen pounds weight which was placed upon his head by the heretics who had taken him prisoner. There where two iron bands in this crown, which could be drawn together by a pin and so compress the head. He bravely endured the inclemencies of wind and snow, rain and cold, for six entire months, amid suffering and insult.

4. At Lima, in Peru, God crowned the apostolic labours of Father John Almeida, a native of Brazil. To the Indians, he was master, physician, servant and brother—he was their all in all. He accomplished very many long and difficult journeys, with nothing but his staff. Sometimes when he was on his way to visit the sick, the rain which fell around him did not touch him but left him dry. He astonished men with his gift of prophecy, and gave joy to the Angels, who beheld him after the fatigues of the day spending the night in prayer, from which continued holy exercise callosities formed upon his knees.

JANUARY 23.

1. At Ategnes, in Spain, in the year 1646, Father John Cassarribios, whose funeral was attended by an immense concourse of people, on account of the great opinion of his sanctity, acquired by the long practice of religious virtues during a life of ninety-seven years, sixty-four of which he had spent in religion, and also by extraordinary gifts and graces. He was most remarkable for his mortification and prayer, in which he

spent four hours daily in his old age. He slept little, and in his clothes, that he might rise more readily to prayer. He showed profound respect and reverence to all, and used to say that in this matter there was no "*parvitas materiæ.*"

2. At Innspruck, Gaspar Geloso, a Temporal Coadjutor, who, amongst other excellent gifts, was most remarkable for the guard over his tongue. To restrain it, before joining recreation after meals he used to gaze steadfastly on a picture of the judgment, and reflect upon the strict account he would have to give hereafter of every word and each moment of time.

3. At the College of Naro, in Sicily, in the year 1624, Father Gaspar Paranympho, a Sicilian, much beloved. He was a great and laborious missioner and preacher, and the Blessed Virgin herself spoke of him to a third person with praise for his exact observance of Poverty. He used to say that he could not preach without his hairshirt, in addition to which he took a severe discipline. As he discoursed, a ray of light was seen to dart from the crucifix and illumine his face. In his sermons he always said something on the Passion of Christ. On his death-bed he was consoled with heavenly music, and his soul was seen by more than one carried in glory to Heaven.

4. At Antwerp, in the year 1629, Father Andrew Schott, a Belgian, remarkable for his solid virtue and great learning, which last gained him much praise even among heretics. He spent a long life, nearly all in writing books. Southwell in his *Bibliotheca* mentions fifty-seven published on various subjects. He threw light on many works of the Holy Fathers and other ancient authors by his learned notes.

5. At Paris, in the year 1640, Father James Salian, a Frenchman, celebrated as an historian. He contributed to ecclesiastical history six elaborate volumes of annals, from the Creation to the Death of Christ, and added a compendium of all in a seventh volume. He published besides a treatise of the love and fear of God, another on the art of pleasing God, and a manual of chronology. He was conspicuous throughout his life for modesty, meekness, contempt of self, love of Religious dicipline, and indefatigable labour.

6. In the Isle of St. Vincent, in the year 1654, Fathers William Aubergeon and Francis Gueymen, Frenchmen, cruelly beaten to death

by the Caribbee Indians, to whose salvation they had devoted their apostolic labours. At the moment of the attack upon them, one was saying Mass, and the other preparing to celebrate. It was owing to their love of prayer and ardent zeal for the glory of God, that they were thus chosen to be the first fruits of the mission of that people.

January 24.

1. At Forli, in Italy, in the year 1608, Father Laurence Bresciani, full of days, and commonly esteemed a Saint. When he was incapable in his old age of other work, he read at table and prepared the refectory, performing the offices of a Temporal Coadjutor with great cheerfulness for fifteen years. He was never known to break the rule of silence.

2. At Baston, in France, the year 1639, Father Thomas Cornier, an Englishman, was called to receive the reward of his apostolic labours. Having been sent away from the noviciate of the Society on account of a serious incurable malady, he received the signal favour of being cured by the Blessed Virgin, and of being again admitted into the Society; in which after labouring as a most zealous missioner until his seventy-seventh year, the same disease returned on account of which he had been sent from the noviciate, and he died a holy death, professed of three Vows, having refused the fourth Vow through profound humility.

3. At Vienna, in Austria, in the year 1624, Father Martin Becan, a Belgian. He was celebrated for the facility, brevity, and solidity with which he interpreted St. Thomas of Aquin, and for elucidating knotty points of faith: and these gifts were enhanced by his singular religious modesty. On this account he was called by the Emperor Matthias to adorn the University of Vienna. Being chosen by the Emperor Ferdinand to be his confessor, he gave great satisfaction to him and his whole Court, and to the nobility in general, some of whom were not Catholics, because he never meddled with politics. He was brief in his conversation with externs, thinking it more desirable to leave them still unsatisfied than weary of him, and better to gain time than beguile it. He published many little works against heretics, which were afterwards collected in two volumes. His manual of controversies of the Faith, with its compendium, is the most famous.

4. At Paris, in the year 1692, Father Crasset, a native of Dieppe. When twelve years old, being alone by the side of the death-bed of his father, he took a crucifix in hand, and addressed his father with so much energy, and in so affecting a manner, on that momentous occasion, that the dying man, collecting the little remains of his strength, exclaimed, "My dear child, you will one day be a great servant of God!" He preached with great success in the chief towns of France, and was director of the Congregation of Nobles established in the Professed House in Paris. In his latter years, when his infirmities prevented him from preaching, he devoted himself to the composition of works of piety; thus continuing after death the good he had done in his life. For works of this character he received an especial grace from God. He died at the age of seventy-five.

January 25.

1. In England, in the year 1621, Father Robert Peckham, an Englishman. After several times enduring with constancy imprisonment and its pains for the Faith, being in his last conflict, and having received the last Sacraments, he asked if the Priest who was then saying Mass had already consecrated. When told that he had, he said, "Then the time of my death is come; Jesus and Mary bid me come," and calmly expired.

2. Also in England, Father John Worthing, an Englishman, an illustrious champion of the Faith, called from the confinement of prison, which for several years he had endured with constancy, to the liberty of the children of God. He had laboured for forty-six years in that most perilous mission, with admirable prudence, dexterity, and zeal.

3. At Gandia, in Spain, in the year 1570, Francis Fernandez, a Temporal Coadjutor, died a holy death, the hour of which he had foreseen and foretold. The Blessed Virgin appeared to him while he was feeding a flock of sheep, and bade him enter the Society. He joined the Society in Murcia, and left a great example of Religious perfection, especially to Lay-brothers.

January 26.

1. At Oropesa, in Spain, in the year 1567, Father Antony Córdova, a man still more famous for his profound and true humility than for his noble birth. Through it he not only resigned the Rectorship of a

college of the Society, and devoted himself to teaching the lowest class of grammar, but he contrived to escape the Cardinal's hat, to which the Emperor Charles V. endeavoured to promote him. He gave such continual proofs of contempt of himself, that it was a matter of astonishment not only to seculars but also to Religious. He appeared after death surrounded with great glory.

2. At Ingoldstadt, in Germany, in the year 1647, Ignatius Soier, a Scholastic of Germany, who heroically offered himself to die that God might spare the college in a pestilence. His charity was accepted: he alone died, and the college was spared.

3. At Quebec, in Canada, in the year 1673, Father Jerome Lallemant, a Frenchman. The zeal with which he sought the mission of Canada was great, and equally great his preparation for it when he had obtained his Superior's permission. On the very day on which he received notice that leave had been granted, he resigned the Rectorship of the College of La Flèche, which he then held, after having governed with success the College of Blois, and hastened to the coast, lest the opportunity might slip of passing over into Canada. He spent more than twenty years in that field of labour, and used to animate his companion in apostolic toil with these words, "Courage, Father, let us work for God while we live; for we shall rest for all eternity." He went at length to his rest at the age of eighty, a confessor of the Faith, leaving the crown of Martyrdom, for which he so ardently longed, for his nephew, Gabriel Lallemant, of whom we shall speak on the 17th of March.

JANUARY 27.

1. At Rome, in the year 1597, Father Stephen Tucci, born at Messina in Sicily, a man whose desire of afflicting himself and of suffering was amazing. He took short sleep on the bare boards, and never took off his clothes, except to discipline himself. To his voluntary chastisements, was added a tumour which grew upon his neck to the size of his head, which so contracted the nerves of his throat and mouth that he could only take a little bread and meat burning hot. Yet he never spoke of his sufferings, and desired to suffer not only these, but the very pains of Purgatory for the love of Jesus. He spent every day five hours in

prayer, kneeling without any support, and he never retrenched these notwithstanding his duties of professor of theology and philosophy, which he taught with great reputation, or as director of a large number of souls, or for the solution of innumerable cases submitted to him. Pope Clement VIII., when he heard of his death, exclaimed: "So then, the Saint is dead at last."

2. At Seville, in Spain, in the year 1600, Father Jerome de Zara went to reap the fruit of his labours, distinguished by the splendour of his religious virtues, but especially by his great humility and virtue in teaching grammar for thirty-six years.

3. At Naples, in the year 1644, Father Bernard de Ponte. When saying Mass either his face or his whole form was seen surrounded with glory, or he was raised in the air. As he was on his way on foot to Loreto, and was reposing weary in a grot, the Virgin Mother appeared to him, and gave him a handkerchief to wipe his face.

4. In the Isle of Mindanão, in the year 1621, Father John del Campo, a Spaniard, suffered martyrdom for the Faith. By his great eloquence, unwearied diligence, and pleasing conversation, he gained a great multitude of souls. While he was engaged in the erection of a church the savages pierced him with their spears and arrows.

JANUARY 28.

1. At Nancy, in Lorraine, in the year 1643, Father John Bonvet, died in the manner he had prayed for. Every week for twenty-five years, when the Rubrics permitted it, he said a Votive Mass of the Blessed Virgin, that he might die, having received the Holy Sacraments and giving trouble to no one. For the same intention, for many years before his death, he spent daily an hour in prayer before the Blessed Sacrament. He was taken suddenly ill after having said Mass, and then having received the Viaticum, within eight hours he expired. He was a man of a countenance always the same, neither elated by joy nor dejected by sadness.

2. At Naos, an isle of the Mediterranean Sea, in the year 1651, and in the month of January, but on what day is uncertain, Father Francis Albert, a Frenchman, sacrificed his life a martyr of charity. He was a man of distinguished learning and virtue, and deeply skilled in the Oriental

January 28.

languages. A Greek Priest having refused to assist a person dying of an infectious disease, Father Francis fearlessly attended her, gave her the last Sacraments, and received in reward of his charity a death precious in the sight of God. Heavenly light shone round him, while dying, for the space of an hour, and his body after death breathed forth a most sweet odour, as a proof that his soul was in Heaven.

3. At Plerin, a village of Brittany, in the year 1683, Father Julian Maunoir. His birth, which took place at Rennes in the year 1606, had been foretold by Monseigneur le Nobletz, to whom it was revealed that this child would be his successor in the missions of Brittany. From his infancy he was remarkable for an angelic modesty, which inspired devotion in all that saw him. When he first entered the Society, at the age of twenty, he was remarkable for a great spirit of mortification. At this time also he made a resolution to aim at perfection in charity by an entire renunciation of creatures. Shortly after his ordination he fell sick, and received the last Sacraments. The next morning he awoke perfectly cured, having had a remarkable dream similar to that of St. Francis Xavier, in which he thought he carried a poor peasant of Brittany. This convinced him of his call to the missions of Brittany, although he had previously had a strong desire for those of Canada. In spite of the difficulty of the Breton tongue, by the aid of the Blessed Virgin he acquired it so rapidly that in eight days he was able to catechise in it, and in two months to preach *extempore*. During the forty-two years of his active life he gave missions each year, God assisting him by more than three hundred well attested miracles. Wherever he gave a mission he established some exercises of piety in honour of the Holy Trinity, of the Blessed Virgin, and St. Joachim and St. Anne; and he was constant in invoking the protection of the holy Angels of France, of Brittany, and of each particular parish, from whom he received great help for the conversion of sinners. In his preaching he could move every passion in turn, and by his admirable sweetness won the hearts of those most opposed to him. In men, he saw the children of God, His friends, His images, the price of the Blood of Jesus Christ; and to his last moment he continued to exhort those around him to live and die for Jesus. The favours he received from Heaven served only to confirm him in humility, and he often seemed to hear our Lord say: "Learn of Me, for I am meek and humble of Heart." He

January 29. 31

was insensible alike to praise or blame, success or failure, as also to heat and cold, travelling on foot both summer and winter with his knapsack on his back. He treated his body hardly and as a mere instrument of the soul. Like all zealous servants of God, he did not escape persecution, and was occasionally misunderstood by his Superiors, by which his admirable obedience was made conspicuous. Once in the midst of his most brilliant success, the Provincial accused him of imprudence, and threatened to send him away from Brittany. Father Julian left the room, and shortly returned with hat, staff, and bag, and on his knees begged to be sent to any part of the world the Provincial wished.

JANUARY 29.

1. At Bivona, in Sicily, in the year 1619, Father Salvator Susa, famous for his victory over himself. Although he was a prey to disease, he would admit of no peculiarity in food. After the example of St. Francis Xavier, he overcame his repugnance so far as to suck the matter from the wound of a man with a cancer, by which heroic act the man was cured.

2. At Ingoldstadt, in Germany, in the year 1625, Father James Gretser, went to receive the reward of his glorious labours. He was a most valiant defender of the Catholic Faith, and vanquisher of heretics, whom he utterly confuted in many most erudite works with great diligence and constancy through the whole of his life. Alegambe reckons more than a hundred and twelve works, large and small, on different subjects, but chiefly against heretics. He had time enough to write so many books, and at the same time to instruct the ignorant in the villages, because he lost none, being of few words and sleeping little. His very great erudition was equalled by his humility in refusing the request of his townfolk, who asked to have a picture of him to hang in their town-hall for the veneration of posterity. Gretser replied with some warmth, that if they wanted his likeness "they could have it perfectly by taking a jackass."

3. In Mindanao, one of the Philippine Isles, in the year 1648, Father Francis Paliola, an Italian, cruelly slain by the savages in hatred of the Faith. He was pierced with swords and spears at the instigation of an apostate whom he was endeavouring to reclaim. In hatred of the Faith the savages seized upon the altar-furniture, and tying a Crucifix to a pillar, beat it to pieces with staves, showing thereby the true cause of their fury.

4. At Lisbon, in the year 1706, Father Francis de la Cruz, a Portuguese. Adorned with every quality calculated to make a good Superior, he used to say that nothing gave him so much pain as to be so employed. He spent at least six hours a-day in hearing the confessions of the poor. During a sickness which hindered the Confessor of the Queen from his duty, Father Francis was requested by her Majesty to come every Sunday morning to hear her confession. He refused with respectful liberty, saying, "I beg your Majesty to consider that you have at your disposal every day of the week; at the least indication of your wishes I am at your service on these, but on Sundays and Holidays I require every moment of the day to hear the confessions of my poor, who are compelled to labour all the week for their subsistence." The Queen, instead of taking offence, was much edified by the charity of the good Father.

January 30.

1. At Madrid, in Spain, in the year 1573, Father Antony Araoz, related to our Holy Father Ignatius no less by virtue than by blood. He earned a high reputation in the Society as Provincial, Commissary, Assistant, and also as a preacher. When he preached to the people he was accounted an Angel. He possessed wonderful grace and zeal in assisting those who were at the point of death. He was most eagerly listened to by Philip II. and all the Court of Spain. He was known to give sometimes fourteen hours of the day and night to prayer.

2. At Avignon, in France, in the year 1633, Father John Pujol, a Frenchman, famous as a Master of Novices. He ordered one of them, by name Sebastian Davin, in order to practice him in blind obedience, to water a withered branch in the garden until it should put out green leaves. Sebastian obeyed, and "God gave the increase," for the branch sprouted and grew into a tree of an unknown kind. It remained a long time, and was called the tree of obedience, until it was cut down to make room for some building. It well deserved to grow not only in the garden but in the hearts of all Religious.

3. At Manchester, in England, in the year 1645, Father Richard Bradley, an Englishman, a laborious missioner, worn out by the sufferings endured in prison for the Catholic Faith, he passed to the liberty of the children of God.

4. At Cork, in the year 1580, Father Edmund Dunn, an Irishman, after much suffering in prison for the same reason as above, and the rack, because he refused to acknowledge the Queen as the head of the Church, was hanged and drawn, and so from the gibbet flew to Heaven, to receive his crown from the Head of the whole Church, JESUS CHRIST.

5. At Messina, in Sicily, in the year 1576, Father Louis Nuñez. Before his entrance into the Society he was attached to the Court of the Duke of Bivona, and had abandoned himself to the pleasures of the world without thought of his salvation. Being one day present at a sermon of one of our Fathers, though he had entered the Church with a design of ridiculing what he should hear, he was so touched by the grace of God, that he resolved to quit the world and enter the Society. In going by sea from Messina to Palermo, he was insulted by one of the passengers. All present entreated him to avenge his honour. But he made answer in words worthy of a disciple of our Lord: "JESUS, whom I have chosen as captain, forbids me, and commands that I forgive this insult." From his entrance into the noviceship he was completely transformed, and devoted himself to the practice of mortification and self-contempt. Ordained Priest, he laboured with zeal and success in the conversion of sinners, and his confessional was frequented by persons of the highest rank. When advanced in years he was employed in teaching little children, in which work, more painful on account of his infirmities, his zeal gave great edification both to ours and to seculars. The Society is indebted to him for many excellent Novices whom he formed to the spiritual life. The plague having visited Messina, he asked as a special favour to be allowed to devote himself to the service of the infected, and he died a martyr of charity.

JANUARY 31.

1. At Rome, in the year 1615, Father Claudius Aquaviva, the fifth General of the Society, given to it by God and His Blessed Mother, to defend, propagate, and govern it by his most wholesome instructions and letters in most trying times. He governed the Society for the space of thirty-four years amid numberless violent attacks with unflinching courage and consummate prudence. Once as he prayed during the night Christ consoled him saying, "Be not afraid, for I am with thee." He firmly refused the

Archbishopric of Naples, which was offered him by Clement VIII. St. Philip Neri asserted that he had seen him surrounded with a flood of heavenly light, others saw him whilst at prayer raised in the air for the space of an hour. On receiving the news of his approaching death from Cardinal Bellarmine he quoted the words of St. Ambrose: "*Mori non timeo, nec vivere erubesco, quia bonum Dominum habemus*—I do not fear to die, and to live I am not afraid, for we have a good Master." His funeral obsequies were attended by an immense concourse of noblemen, Religious, and of the people.

2. At Cadiz, in Spain, in the year 1649, Father Sanchez de Mendoza, a Spaniard, a martyr of charity in service of the plague stricken, a man of illustrious birth, and notable for his humility in teaching little boys for many years the rudiments of grammar. He was also memorable for the missions he established, and for his heroic charity.

3. At Liege, in the year 1643, Edmund Renart, a Temporal Coadjutor, likewise a martyr of charity, who twenty times exposed his life in waiting upon the plague stricken, twenty times escaped the infection, and at last took it and died.

4. At Gran, in Styria, in the year 1651, Father Francis Amico, an Italian, went to receive his crown, merited by his learned volumes on theology which he published. He was a man as candid and simple as he was learned, and seemed to know nothing but God and his matters of study.

5. At Munster, in Germany, in the year 1668, Father Herman Busenbaum, a German. He was occupied a long time in carefully teaching the schools of humanities, philosophy, and theology, both dogmatic and moral. Being appointed confessor to his Highness the Prince Bishop of Munster, he adorned the Court by the rare ornament of his virtues, nor was it with less edification and fruit that he governed the college of Hildesheim, and twice that of Munster. But nothing gained him so much renown in the literary world as the book which he published, entitled *Medulla Theologiæ Moralis*, small in size but great in learning, upon moral questions, which perhaps no one has reduced to so small a compass with such great success. The value of it is proved by the number of editions it has gone through in different countries. Southwell says that in his time forty-five editions had been issued.

6. At Toulouse, in the year 1754, Father Peter John Cayron, a native

of Rhodes, in France. His parents opposed his entrance into the Society, and imprisoned him in their house for a year, that so in solitude he might come to a more reasonable frame of mind. God rewarded his constancy by giving him from the commencement of his Religious life a profound contempt of himself and of the world, and an ardent desire of suffering. He several times asked for the foreign missions, but he was destined to satisfy his zeal for souls by other means, namely, in training up zealous and efficient labourers, and during twenty-one years as Master of Novices at Toulouse he was eminently successful in leading them to the perfection required by the Institute. A declared enemy of his body, he incessantly strove to subdue it by fasts, hairshirts, chains, and disciplines to blood, and by this austere life he gained a perfect empire over himself, and complete tranquillity and conformity to God's will in the most trying circumstances. He signalised himself by his zeal in promoting the canonisation of Father John Francis Regis, and the beatification of Cardinal Bellarmine. He was favoured by God with an extraordinary gift of prayer and spirit of prophecy, and after his death he was honoured with many miracles. He is believed to have preserved his baptismal innocence unsullied to his eighty-third year. His life is published.

7. At Cremona, in Italy, in the year 1608, Jerome Cenardi, an Italian Scholastic, aged eighteen, who both in his exterior and interior gave proof of such detachment from self and union with God, that in the judgment of many prudent persons he had attained a high degree of sanctity. After a long and painful sickness, borne with admirable patience, he died holily. Immediately after his death he appeared in glory to one of our Fathers at Milan, and predicted that the Father would go to the Indies and there remain a long time, which came to pass as he had foretold.

FEBRUARY.

February 1.

1. At Gaudaloupe, in South America, in the year 1632, died Father Julius Pasquale, an Italian, and Father Emanuel Martinez, a Portuguese, shot by the savages with poisoned arrows in hatred of the faith, and because they restrained them by the law of Christ from their brutish pleasures. Both had disposed themselves for the glory of martyrdom by their religious virtues. Father Julius even in his lifetime seems to have been favoured by miraculous graces.

2. At London, in England, in the year 1645, Father Henry Morse, an Englishman, who after three years at a time of painful imprisonment, and more than once banishment from England, still returned to renew his apostolic labours and seek death for the faith. He at last obtained his desire, being taken, hanged, and quartered. On receiving the announcement of his death, he exclaimed, exulting in God his Saviour, "Come, most sweet Jesus, that I may be bound for ever to Thee and never turn from Thee! Come chains, come hurdle to drag me to death, come torments and butchery; you are welcome for my Jesus' sake!" Thus, *morsu mortem*, he bid death defiance to the teeth, and conquered.

3. In America, in the year 1619, Peter de Vega, a Spaniard, a Temporal Coadjutor, who at the age of sixty in order to be useful to the Society learned the trade of a shoemaker and most skilfully practised it. Having predicted that he would not take to his bed until the last day of his life, he went to receive the reward of his labours in the manner he had foretold.

4. At Cuidad Real, in Spain, in the year 1606, Father John Ponce, a Spaniard, son of the Duke d'Arcos; but so regardless of former rank that he never spoke of it. He loved to repeat to the last the words of the Royal Prophet—"I have chosen to be an abject in the house of my God, rather

than to dwell in the tabernacles of sinners." He waited on the sick with the most tender solicitude and attentive care, and prepared their food. He made ready for his death, which he had predicted, in such a manner that an Abbot of a Religious Order who was present at it declared he had never witnessed anything like it and took occasion from thence of preaching a long panegyric at his funeral.

5. In Japan, in the year 1600, Father Peter Gomez, a Spaniard. He was remarkable for a most tender devotion to the Blessed Virgin, and never refused anything which was asked of him in her name. One of our Fathers availed himself of this means to obtain possession of his discipline and hairshirt, with which request Father Gomez at first was loth to comply, the more so as they were saturated with his blood. But the efficacy of the holy name of Mary triumphed over the repugnance of his humility. After he had founded the college of Terceira in one of the Azores, he was recalled to Portugal to the great grief of the inhabitants of the island, who revered him as a Saint. He afterwards obtained leave to go on the mission of Japan and there laboured the remainder of his life, striving to follow in the footsteps of St. Francis Xavier. After his death it was found that he had traced with a hot iron on his body the instruments of the Passion— the cross, nails, lance, scourges and crown. Thus with St. Paul he might have exclaimed? "*Ego stigmata Domini Jesu in corpore meo porto*—I bear in my body the marks of the Lord Jesus."

FEBRUARY 2.

1. At Lima in Peru, in the year 1577, died Father John de Zuniga, singing hymns as he died. He was of such mature and solid virtue that whilst yet young and not a Priest he was made Rector of the College of Lima. He himself required a director to prevent him treating too harshly his own body, which he had preserved in its virginal purity. In his last illness, which lasted forty days, supplication was made throughout the city in all the Religious Houses for the preservation of his life both by prayers and corporal austerities. The petition was so far heard that he somewhat recovered, at which he was much grieved; and the Blessed Virgin visited him with the promise that he should die on her next festival, as accordingly he did.

2. In the arduous mission of Guinea, in the year 1612, Father Baltassar Bareirà, a Portuguese, broken down with apostolic labours, rested in God, on the anniversary of the day on which in 1583 he was the means of obtaining a glorious victory to the Portuguese. In this apostolic man it pleased God to renew the miracle of Moses routing the Amalekites by prayer. For when Paul Diaz with only three hundred Portuguese and a few negro bands to help him, engaged with twelve hundred thousand men of Angola, a fierce battle ensuing, the Father was praying in a tent apart for the success of the combatants with heart and hands lifted up to Heaven, and as he prayed more fervently the Portuguese prevailed, as he slackened in prayer the enemy prevailed. Philip II. sent for Father Baltassar to Spain and bestowed on him great honours and privileges for the good of the natives for whose salvation he laboured.

3. At Rome, in the year 1652, Father Jerome Auseld, a Sardinian, died a holy death. He was once admonished by the Blessed Virgin that he should not be so sparing and modest in asking favours but thenceforward be more bold in asking. During the Holy Sacrifice he was seen raised from the ground, surrounded by a bright cloud, while our Lord opening his breast placed within it His own Heart.

4. At Valencia, in Spain, in the year 1658, Father Jerome Lopez happily finished his course, an indefatigable and truly apostolic missioner throughout Spain, and the Balearic Isles, which he traversed with incredible zeal and immense fruit, everywhere as in time of jubilee, receiving general confessions and exciting contrition, God assisting him with miracles even to the raising of one who was dead. His life is published and contains many things worthy of imitation and practice.

5. In Canada, in the year 1646, Father Anne de Nove Chaupenois, after eighteen years spent in most painful labours for the conversion of the savages, was found frozen to death in the snow. He died kneeling, his head bare, his eyes raised to Heaven, and his hands crossed upon his breast.

6. At Lima, in Peru of South America, in the year 1592, Father Jerome Ruiz, a native of Logroño in Castile. St. Francis Borgia by a special inspiration of God sent him with seven others to labour in the Indies for the conversion of the natives. He afterwards founded the Province of Peru and presided over its infancy, to the edification and satisfaction of all with whom he lived. His venerable appearance inspired

respect, his courage and strength of mind were indomitable, and he proved himself a true Apostle of Jesus Christ, full of zeal for the glory of God and the salvation of souls. He possessed a singular talent of touching the hearts, and one word of his worked the most wonderful conversions. His humility was most profound. Even when Provincial he loved to assist those who made the bricks for the building of the church. From such employments he ascended the pulpit to effect the conversion of souls. He died at the age of seventy-two in the college of Lima, where he had laid the foundations of the Province of Peru. He left behind him in his Province the memory of his apostolic labours, and the example of his most heroic virtue.

February 3.

1. At Florida, in North America, in the year 1571, died Father Louis Quiros together with John Baptist Mendez and Gabriel Solis, Novices, slain by the arrows of an apostate cacique named Louis, who had received baptism in Spain under false pretence, and whom Father Louis in his zeal was endeavouring to bring back to the faith.

2. At Ferrara, in Italy, in the year 1607, John Peter Davitia, a Temporal Coadjutor, was released from his worn-out macerated body, noted for his labour and prayer. He passed the hour of recreation after dinner, with leave of his Superiors, prostrate before the Blessed Sacrament. This was permitted him thrice a week. He never approached a fire, nor allowed himself a pillow or sheets for sleeping, nor took more than one kind of food.

3. At Novellāra, in Italy, in the year 1620, Joseph Bracco, Temporal Coadjutor, an Italian. He daily prayed for indifference to any office and ready obedience, saying that without this "the Paradise of Religion was hell." He said moreover that the voice of God was audible in Superiors; that it came to us in those who held minor offices through wooden pipes; in Rectors, through silver; and in Provincials, through golden pipes; in the General through a pipe of gold set with jewels. He gave all the pains of his last sickness to the souls in Purgatory, and bore with great joy the sufferings of the erysipelas with which his whole body was covered.

FEBRUARY 4.

1. At Ezega, in Spain, in the year 1638, died Father D'Espinosa. Death put an end to the torments with which he unceasingly with cruel ingenuity afflicted his body. He showed great wisdom in directing to perfection those engaged in the occupations of the world, especially he advised diligent and daily perusal of pious books, and by this means led whole families to very exalted virtue. The deceased also received assistance from him. Amongst others, an extern whose confession he had heard before death, who had been buried some days, came to him in his room at midnight, and led him with the Rector's leave, from the college to his house, where he gave a list to Father Augustine of the creditors' names whose claims he had not satisfied in his life; he then supplied the Father with money sufficient, begging him to satisfy these claims, and apply the remainder to pious purposes. After a lapse of eight days the deceased returned to thank the Father for the fidelity with which he had discharged the commission. When Father Augustine was suffering from an attack in the eyes, and the medical man said that if he went out of the house he would lose the use of them entirely, he chanced to be ordered soon after by his Superior to transact some business out of the college, and he mentioned what the physician had said, adding that he was ready to go if the Superior wished it. As the Superior persisted in his wish, he obeyed, and returned blind, and so continued for three years after, rejoicing however that he had lost the light of day and his eye-sight for obedience' sake.

2. At Le Puy, in France, in 1623, Father Marcelline Bompar, a Frenchman, who in reward for his great and many virtues obtained the happiness of dying a martyr of charity. He caught the plague while assisting the soldiers suffering from it, and so died.

3. In the Residence of Walz, in Germany, in the year 1646, Father Matthew Kuber, a German. When as yet a youth, and suffering from a grievous malady, the Blessed Mother of God appeared to him in sleep, and said, "My child, you will recover; my Son will work much good by your means." Having entered the Society, the zealous young man restored to the Church his father, who was a heretic, and his three brothers, and whole villages, fully proving himself such a one as the Mother of God had predicted.

February 5.

1. At Nangasachi, in Japan, in the year 1597, the three holy Japanese Martyrs, Paul Miki, John de Goto, and James Kysai. They dyed red with their blood the triumphal chariot of the cross, being pierced from side to side with spears. Paul, a Scholastic of noble birth, was conspicuous for his virtues, zeal for preaching, and powerful eloquence, which he exerted with admirable ardour in prison, and on the cross itself not without signal effect. John, in the flower of his youth, nineteen years of age, also about to be admitted among the Scholastics, and then a Catechist, gave to his own father who was beside him, and who was bedewed with the blood of his martyred son, as a last present, his rosary beads of the Blessed Virgin. James, a Temporal Coadjutor, sixty-four years old, and full of merit, was filled with incredible joy at the participation of Christ's Cross. He had always carried with him a meditation book on the Passion, and had daily made devout use of it. God honoured the death of his Saints by many miracles, and Pope Urban VIII. juridically placed them on the list of the Martyrs. They were canonized by Pope Pius IX in 1862.

2. At Punchal, in the East Indies, in the year 1552, Father Paul Valli, mentioned by St. Francis Xavier as "a man of exalted perfection and virtue." Whilst preaching he was taken prisoner by the Badagese savages, and died of starvation and the hardships of captivity.

3. At Bourdeaux, in France, in the year 1662, Father John Martinon, a Frenchman, a distinguished theologian of great abilities, learning, and virtue. He gave to the world the whole course of dogmatic theology in five volumes. In his statements he is careful and accurate, concise and clear in exposition, acute and discreet in his theological distinctions. He was so little wedded to the productions of his own genius, although some looked on them with suspicion, that when a work of much labour was lost, he took it with the greatest calmness, and said, "No man should care for the loss of any thing but the loss of his soul."

4. At Douay, in France, in the year 1640, Father Francis de Montmorency, a Frenchman. To prepare for his admission into the Society, and bind himself in a manner to perseverance, he renounced various ecclesiastical dignities from which he drew considerable revenues. On

entering the novitiate he kissed the feet of all the Novices, to dispose his heart by this act of humility for religious perfection. Day by day he advanced in the practice of mortification and self-contempt, so that although accustomed to a life of refinement, he regarded as an excess of delicacy the better kind of food provided for him in sickness. Compelled by numerous infirmities to keep his room during twenty years, he was beloved and venerated by all for his admirable example of patience, resignation, and unalterable calmness. In his last days he often repeated the words: "Had I remained in the world, I should not have died in such peace and contentment. I owe this happiness to the grace of my vocation." He expired with the words on his lips, "May God be blessed for ever."

FEBRUARY 6.

1. At Rome, in the year 1612, died Father Christopher Clavius, a German, the Euclid of his age. He defended the reform of the Church Calendar made by Pope Gregory XIII. Great as was his genius, which his five learned volumes on mathematics prove, he displayed no less virtue, especially in solid humility, holding himself superior to none, but inferior to all. He was as careful in the custody of his eyes, as in watching the luminaries of Heaven. Once his eye chanced to wander through his open window upon a person in the street; to punish himself he fastened down the window and never looked out into the street again during the whole of his life.

2. At Punchal, in the East Indies, in the year 1600, Father Henry Henriguez a Portuguese, rich in souls gathered during thirteen years labour on the coast of the pearl-fisheries. By his immense labours he merited the title of Apostle of Comorin. The delights of Heaven poured in upon his soul in proportion to the miseries which pressed upon him on earth. His tomb was hung around with lamps and votive offerings in testimony of the graces received through him from Almighty God.

3. At La Flêche, in France, in the year 1654, Father John de La Chaussée, a Frenchman. A strange circumstance led him to the Society. Whilst engaged in a masquerade in time of Carnival, with

eleven other companions of high birth, in the midst of the dance he saw a thirteenth dancer on a sudden mix with the rest. No small alarm seized upon the company, especially when on the following day an evil spirit being exorcised exclaimed, pointing to John, "That fine fop is mine: he is mine if he does not look to it—I was the cause of the fright of yesterday, I made the thirteenth in the dance." To take measures for his safety Father John entered the Society, and put on Christ in the character of saintly patience.

FEBRUARY 7.

1. At Punchal, in the East Indies, in the year 1549, Father Antonio Criminale, an Italian, born at Pisa, died the first victim of the faith of our Society. He was pierced with lances by the savage Badagese Brahmins who could not brook the breaking of their idols. The exact day is not known, but the day of his entering into life immortal is kept on that upon which he was born. He is praised by St. Francis Xavier in a letter to St. Ignatius as a man of sanctity, beloved by all, and he wished that he had many like him for the Indies. Every month he traversed barefoot the whole province of Comorin which had been assigned to him, a distance of more than 200 miles, such was his wonderful zeal for souls. He daily prayed thirty or forty times on his knees, and upon the bare ground.

2. At Aubenas, in France, in the year 1593, also out of hatred of the faith, died Father James de Sales and William Saltemouche, a Temporal Coadjutor. Falling into the hands of heretics they were for many days tortured with hunger, thirst, and other pains, and then put to death. Father James was first shot through the body, and then as he prayed for his murderers run through the heart with a sword; William embracing the father as he fell was stabbed with daggers. Their bodies lay six days unburied. Both had made good preparation to deserve this their crown. Father de Sales, though subject to many infirmities laboured as if in strong health. Wherever he was he chose some one to admonish him of his faults. When any one knocked at the door of his room he used to kneel and say, "Come in my God, come into my soul." He adored the Blessed Sacrament hourly, and

asked for the grace of martyrdom from the King of Martyrs, the good JESUS, whose Name was ever in his heart and on his lips.

3. In France, in the year 1610, Father Simon Riviere, a Frenchman, a lover of humility and a hater of vainglory. For the last seven years of his life he lived as a Temporal Coadjutor. As he lay dying, he still repeated "Let us fly from vainglory." He loved to hear the words of the Apostle "God forbid that I should glory save in the Cross of our Lord JESUS CHRIST." He predicted the time of his death eight days before he died.

FEBRUARY 8.

1. At Ozaca, in Japan, in the year 1636, died Father Diego Yuki, a Japanese. He endured the martyrdom of the pit, being hung for three days with his head downwards in it until he died, victorious over death in a form so terrible. The Society being banished from Japan by an edict of the Emperor Daifusama, he remained in his own country in disguise, travelling much and labouring greatly for full twenty years. He never lodged in any house for fear of injuring the inmates, but wandered in the woods from which, from time to time, he sallied to give the aids of religion to the Christians, living only upon wild roots.

2. In Florida of America, in the year 1571, Father John Baptist Segura, a Spaniard, was killed and cut in pieces by an apostate and by the savages, together with four companions, Gabriel Gomez, Peter de Linares, Sanchez Saballio, and Christopher Rotundo. The fury with which they fell upon the altar furniture, and especially the Crucifix, plainly showed their motive to be intense hatred to the Faith.

3. At Triguera, in Spain, in the year 1566, Father John Leon, a Spaniard, who received notice to prepare for death with such great joy that he asked to kiss the hand of the medical man who gave it. For the sweetness of his disposition he was called "The Lamb"; but his voice in the pulpit was the voice of a lion to rouse souls to repentance.

4. Alegambe in the *Bibliotheca Societatis* makes mention of another Father John Leon, a Belgian, who to promote the devotion to our Blessed Lady, and inspire in the minds of the young a tender love towards her, was the first to establish at Rome the Sodality of the Blessed Virgin, in

the year 1563. This he afterwards established at Paris, and now we see it everywhere spread throughout the houses and colleges of the Society with immense fruit, and the approbation of the Holy See. He died at Turin; the year and day of his death are unknown.

5. At Prague, in Bohemia, in the year 1692, Father Matthias Tanner, a Bohemian, renowned for virtue and learning and as a Doctor in theology. Besides other works he published two remarkable ones, *The Society waging war to the Shedding of its Blood*, and *The Society, the Follower of the Apostles*. Both volumes are adorned with elegant engravings, and in a great measure depict the author's own likeness.

FEBRUARY 9.

1. At Rome, in the year 1645, died Father Mutius Vitelleschi, an Italian, eminent for the nobility of his birth, but much more for his virtues, and happy government as General of the Society. Of all the Father Generals, he was the most gentle, and that to a wonderful degree; in temper he was most equable, a great consoler of the afflicted, and of great perspicacity. His ears were ever open to give audience to all, his patience in listening was wonderful, considering the multiplicity of affairs to which he had to attend; his courage great; and his indulgence to the extreme that the Constitutions would permit. It was his nature to give honour to all, and thus he was universally beloved. He was great in all he did, as a Student and Scholastic of singular innocence, as a Professor of philosophy and theology, as a Preacher, as Assistant of Italy, as Provincial of Rome and of Naples, and lastly as General of the Society for thirty-five years. We may guess the esteem he had of his vocation, from his custom of observing the 15th of August, the day on which he entered the Society, by a discipline in public the night before, and the reception of some one on that day into the Society.

2. At Cadiz, in Spain, in the year 1649, Father John Havelland, an Englishman, a martyr of charity taken with the plague from attending on the sick. His countenance and modesty of eyes betokened his angelic innocence. Externs sought to be present at his Mass, so holily did he offer that most Holy Sacrifice. In the same year, seventeen of the Society died in different places in the same service of the sick.

3. At Tournon, in France, in the year 1617, Father Jaspar Masic, a Frenchman, so well prepared for death, that to the question, what he would do if he were told when going to the schools or recreation, that within the hour he would die, replied, "that he would go to the schools or recreation, as obedience enjoined."

4. At Alcala, in Spain, in the year 1651, by an untimely death, Father Francis de Oviedo, renowned for piety and solid learning, as his philosophical and theological works testify. Having said Mass with more than usual fervour, and given his lecture in school, he returned to his chamber, fell down and expired.

February 10.

1. At Novocomi, in Italy, in the year 1610, died Father Charles Carlantini, powerful in words, but still more by his tears, when he sat in the sacred tribunal of penance. By these he softened and inflamed the hearts of his spiritual children, the sons of his tears. On one occasion as he entered the church he met a man armed with a gun and other weapons for the murder of his enemy. Father Charles, knowing by secret inspiration his bloody intention, said to him, "What do you wait here for, unhappy man, what purpose is this? come, follow me, and make your confession", so taking him by the hand he led him to the confessional. The man amazed, and almost beside himself, when he came to himself, made a good confession, forgave his enemy, and entered Religious life. God honoured his servant with graces of healing the sick and powers against evil spirits and witchcraft; and so great was the opinion of his sanctity that learned men and noblemen asked to have pieces of the sole of his shoe.

2. At Besançon, in Lorraine, in the year 1638, Father Leonard Perin, a native of Lorraine. So great was the opinion of his sanctity, that as he came out of a certain city the people fell down upon their knees as he passed to ask for his blessing. He was of such ready obedience, that he undertook without demur or excuse to give discourses each day in Advent without preparation. From the chair of theology he came down with the utmost willingness to teach a class in rhetoric, and having many years discharged this duty with much credit, he again returned to preaching, and then again to theology.

3. At Lyons, in France, in the year 1656, Father Francis D'Aix, a Frenchman, was called away, as we may well believe, to enjoy the presence of the Holy Trinity, to Whose worship during life he had been most devout, as also to the Blessed Eucharist, to which he made continual visits both day and night; and as often as he was called to the gate he made a visit before he returned to his chamber. He was most constant in practising bodily austerities, and used to say that "it would be a sad day to him on which he should not have shed some of his blood for Christ; and that if he could not be a martyr, at least he ought in some way to partake in Christ's passion. Every day he read on his knees and with his head uncovered some chapters of Holy Scripture. God bestowed upon him the gift of prophecy and other favours. On one occasion a Temporal Coadjutor who had been dead some days appeared to him, having his body clothed in a hairshirt, and in great suffering, on account of some faults of sensuality, and having begged the Father's prayers disappeared.*

FEBRUARY 11.

1. At Namur, in Belgium, Father John de Renesse died, remarkable for love of the Society and pity for the souls in Purgatory. It pleased the Divine Goodness to show in him an example of the patience of holy Job. For with most admirable fortitude he bore the calamitous and utter ruin of his noble family, and his brother's sad end, long and excruciating pains of a sickly body, and torturing scruples of mind accompanied with fears of death and judgment. But towards the end of his life he enjoyed great tranquillity and peace of mind, desiring nothing but to be dissolved, and died with such signs of joy and gladness, that God seems to have recompensed even in this life his past sorrows.

2. In the year 1599, when a terrible pestilence was depopulating Lisbon, the capital of Portugal, many members of the Society of different nations were employed in comforting and assisting the sick. Six of these died martyrs of charity in that holy service.

3. On this day is the memory of Father Calixtus a Motta, a man of great ardour, toil, and zeal for souls.

February 12.

1. At Lisbon, in Portugal, in the year 1571, died Father Alphonse Nunhez Barrett, first the Rector of the college of of Evora and afterwards of that of Lisbon, though scarcely twenty-seven years of age. In the noviceship, from an ardent desire of self-abasement, he went forth into the market-place of Coimbra in poor clothes and barefoot, and there tied himself to the whipping-post, and implored aloud mercy of JESUS bound to the pillar of shame—a spectacle which amazed the people. That he might make familiar acquaintance with the public porters, a low class of men and extremely ignorant, and so better instruct them, he lived amongst them like one of them, and so brought them well prepared to confession. He waited as a servant on a priest who was leading a scandalous life, to bring him if possible to a better state of mind, but finding it useless, he turned his efforts to the partner of his guilt, and pleaded so effectually as to induce her to expiate her past life by penance, and persevere in amendment of life.

2. At Naples, in the year 1581, Father Christopher Rodriguez, a Portuguese, concluded his perilous missions by a happy death. He was renowned for his travels and labours undertaken for the propagation of the faith. He was sent by Pope Pius V. on important negociations to Cairo; and in the naval expedition led by Don John of Austria against the Turks, he boldly carried the Crucifix aloft amid the balls of the enemy, and with frequent disciplines to blood implored a blessing on the Christian arms. As Provincial he used to visit the colleges on foot, carrying his knapsack at his back, and living only on alms.

3. At Riga, in Polish Russia, in the year 1611, a young Scholastic of Poland, James Mlocki, perfected in a short time was carried off to Heaven by the Queen of Angels in a chariot of glory. He had been exceedingly devout to her, and received from her notice of his early death. In his last sickness he said to the Infirmarian, "We have some great visitors here; see the glorious Queen of Heaven in her chariot of splendour, in which she carries souls to Heaven." Fixing his eyes upon the Crucifix, and pointing to the Holy Mother of God who was to take him away, he departed as we may well believe to the realms of bliss.

February 13.

1. At Naples, in the year 1585, died Father Alphonsus Salmeron, a Spaniard, one of the first ten foundation stones of the Society. He was employed by the Sovereign Pontiffs on many important missions. He was sent by Pope Paul III. to Ireland, and by Paul IV. as Apostolical Nuncio to Belgium and Poland. He was thrice called to the Council of Trent as the Pope's theologian, and there gave proofs of the greatest abilities and astonishing learning. He preached the Lent before Pius V. to his great satisfaction. He was the Founder of the Province of Naples, of which he was appointed the first Provincial, and by his writings and discourses prevented the spread of the errors of Luther. Sixteen volumes on the Gospels and New Testament, of which numerous editions have issued from the press, attest his theological erudition. Distinguished for his piety, zeal, and wisdom, he died lamented by the whole people of Naples.

2. At the College of Theate, in Italy, in the year 1626, Father Ignatius de Juliis, previously warned of death. Two days before his last sickness, as he was kneeling in fervent prayer before the Blessed Sacrament, he heard a voice distinctly say: "Haste, haste. Ignatius, for you have but few days more." The offices, which he filled when in health, sufficed at his death to give full employment to three Priests. He had a great talent for preparing persons for death, so that he was much sought for at that momentous hour even by those who had no love for the Society. No cold of winter drove him to a fire, no heat of summer made him seek refreshment, no bodily weariness could force him to his bed.

3. At Valladolid, in Spain, in the year 1585, Brother Sancho de Ausa, a Novice of Spain. During an illness of eighty days, though parched with thirst, and with cooling draughts at hand, he never refreshed his tongue with them, but offered his burning thirst in union with the thirst of our Lord upon the Cross. Two days before his death our Lord appeared to him as he was when he hung in thirst upon the Cross; Sancho exclaimed, "Lord, am I among Thy elect?" On our Lord assuring him that he was, he continued: "Lord, wilt Thou take me with Thee?" Then Christ replied, "Yes, my child; I will take thee with me." And so after his long suffering of thirst he went to drink of the torrent of delights for ever.

February 14.

1. At Louvain, in Belgium, in the year 1589, died Father John Hamel, a Belgian, the colleague of Father Lessius in the chair of theology, reputed one of the luminaries of his time. He was carried off by an infectious sickness caught in attending a dying person. On his death-bed an angel appeared to comfort him. In the same year the Society lost six of her members at Barcelona in Spain, while ministering to the victims of the plague; and two at Wilna in Poland.

2. At Zebu, one of the Philippine Isles, in the year 1627, Gaspar de Caray, a Temporal Coadjutor, a Spaniard, expired sweetly after a life of great austerity. Three days a week he went without food, and daily disciplines stained his linen with blood. Even in his last sickness he used neither pillow nor sheets, though in the world he had lived in comfort, and had attained the rank of captain in the navy. The last twelve years of his life he was blind, but he satisfied his devotion by hearing most devoutly all the Masses said in our Church.

3. At Cologne, in the year 1656, Father Herman Baving, a German. When Provincial of the Lower Rhine, he exhorted the masters to promote among their scholars the devotion to their Angel Guardians. In modesty and peace of soul he seemed an Angel. He used to say his beads three times a day, and the Litany of our Lady whenever he had a spare moment.

4. At Paray-le-Monial, in France, in the year 1682, Father Claude de la Colombière, a native of St. Symphorian, near Lyons. This holy man was endowed with a rare talent for the direction of souls, and his sermons and other works breathe a spirit of heavenly unction. According to the testimony of all who lived with him he kept inviolate the vow by which he had bound himself to observe all the Rules of the Society. After a sojourn of two years in London as preacher to the Duchess of York, afterwards Queen, he was arrested and thrown into prison, and having in consideration of his chaplaincy escaped the death, which five of his brethren suffered, he was banished to France. His labours and sufferings had exhausted his strength, and three years later he died at Paray-le-Monial. It was during a previous abode in that town that by the disposition of God he became the Director of the Blessed Margaret Mary Alacoque, to aid by his advice this holy soul in the

propagation of the devotion to the Sacred Heart. He laboured for this object with great success, and received from the adorable Heart most signal favours.

5. At Liège, in Belgium, in the year 1693, after a long and painful illness, Father Robert Dicconson, of Lincolnshire in England. He is believed to have made his studies at the University of Oxford, preserving his faith and morals unimpaired in the midst of heresy. At the age of twenty-one he entered the Society in Belgium, and after finishing his studies returned to England and laboured zealously for many years, braving all dangers and courting martyrdom. He was universally esteemed for his sanctity and zeal. Amid all the distractions of a life spent in perpetual journeying to and fro, he was an exact observer of our Rule and a man of prayer. He was recalled to Belgium to profess theology, and was afterwards made Rector of the College of Ghent, ending his days in the office of Spiritual Father. He was a pattern of obedience to all.

FEBRUARY 15.

1. On this day is kept the feast of BB. John Baptist Machado and his Companions, viz., Father Peter of the Assumption, a Franciscan, Leo Tanaca, Matthias of Arima, and Simon Quiota—with the wife and three friends of the last named. Father Machado was born at Tavora in the Azores, and joined the Society in Portugal, ardently desiring to be sent to Japan. His hopes were fulfilled, and for many years he laboured zealously at Nangasachi. He was captured at length in the island of Goto and thrown into prison at Omura, where he found awaiting him Father Peter of the Assumption, who had been arrested just before. Both received sentence of death together, and when they arrived at the place of execution, they embraced each other, and joyfully bent their heads to the scimitar on the 21st day of May in the year 1617 at Nangasachi. Leo Tanaca followed his beloved master within ten days by the same kind of death. The remaining companions of Father Machado suffered martyrdom three years later—Matthias at Nangasachi on the same day, the 21st of May, cruelly tortured to death—the rest at Cocura on the 15th August, crucified head downwards.

2. At Salamanca, in the year 1599, died Father Joseph Acosta, a Spaniard. He was the last of five brothers who entered the Society,

but though in age the youngest he was by no means the least in talent and virtue. Whilst he was preparing a theological lecture an Angel appeared to him in his room with a lighted torch in his hand saying, "Thus shalt thou shine in the Indies." While Father Joseph with desires enkindled by the Angel's torch was offering himself a holocaust to the will of God, the letter of St. Francis Borgia, General of the Society, arrived appointing him to the Indian mission. He proceeded accordingly to South America and there laboured so zealously in teaching, preaching, writing books, giving counsel in the government of provinces, that he gained the respect and admiration of all of the highest rank both in the Indies and in Spain, whither he was afterwards recalled.

3. At Paris, in the year 1626, on his return from Rome, Father Anthony Sucquet, a Belgian; praised for his prudent government as Rector of colleges, Master of Novices, and Provincial, and for his modesty and piety. So great a lover of poverty was he, that whenever he received a new soutane he used to inaugurate the wearing of it by going to the kitchen to wash dishes.

4. At Ruffach, in Alsace, in the year 1634, Father James Mayering, and Brother Andrew Martin, a Temporal Coadjutor, both Germans, slain for the Faith. They were dragged out of a church, shot through and stabbed by heretics.

5. At the Noviceship in Madrid, in the year 1601, Father Francis Antonio, a native of Lisbon in Portugal. After having taught law for two years in the University of Coimbra, he entered the Society at the age of twenty-three. Sent to assist in founding the College of Sassari in Sardinia, he made many journeys, and suffered from cold and hunger in reforming the corrupt morals of that island. Afterwards he was Master of Novices at Rome, and from thence was sent to Germany, where he had under his direction Father Edmund Campian and St. Stanislaus Kostka. The Empress, whose adviser and confessor he was, sent him to Spain to her brother the King, and there Father Francis ended his life in the house in which he had always desired to die.

6. The same day, at Nangasachi, in the year 1614, died Father Louis de Cerqueyra, consecrated in 1594 Coadjutor of Father Peter Martius, and four years later made fifth titular Bishop of Japan. He was teaching theology at the University of Evora, when there came to him from Rome

February 15.

in virtue of holy obedience, the order to receive without delay the episcopal anointing; and the Archbishop of Evora, Don Theotonio de Braganza, to testify his joy at this election, called together all the Bishops of his Province to a grand festivity, of which he himself with kingly generosity wished to defray all the expenses. Louis de Cerqueyra governed for sixteen years, amidst difficulties ever springing up afresh, the church committed to his charge. Exalted and persecuted by turns, almost raised to the honours of a triumph by the Kings of Japan, and then condemned to the last ignominy of punishment, he visited the most distant communities of this vast empire, setting in order, with a rare prudence, all that the misfortune of the times up to that period had not allowed his predecessors to reduce to unity. "In this good Prelate," says the old French account of his death, "there were found many great and rare virtues, and, first and greatest of them all, a supreme fear of offending God even in the most trivial matters." Hence it was that he never decided any affair except after mature deliberation. He loved exceedingly the virtue of chastity, having always hated more than a pestilence the contrary vice. He never spoke rashly and without having well weighed his words beforehand. He treated with consideration and respect all who came to him, and offended no one, however low his rank in life might be. In comforting the afflicted he showed all the kindness of a father, and willingly interrupted for this purpose every other occupation even of importance. He was wonderfully beloved not only by Ours, but by all the Religious of other Orders in Japan, although he was opposed to their entrance into these kingdoms, until the express prohibition of the Sovereign Pontiffs had been recalled. But he expressed his opposition with so much moderation and humility, that his behaviour in this respect only made him seem still more friendly to them. His charity went so far that, when he visited the Christian communities scattered along the coast, every evening he withdrew himself to a boat, where he passed the night, in order as far as possible to cause no expense to any one. "When he was suffering," adds Father de Mattos, "from the long malady of which he died, he never could be induced to lie down on a bed before the day of the Purification, when he celebrated his last Mass. All his ambition was to die and be at rest with JESUS CHRIST; and when he was warned that his last hour was drawing near, raising his hands to Heaven, "Blessed," said he, "be our good God and Lord, and let His will alone be done, as seems good to Him!"

February 16.

1. At Valladolid, in Spain, in the year 1624, died Father Louis du Ponte, a Spaniard, renowned for his ascetical writings, at once pious, copious, and solid. In his life-time he was often seen surrounded with light, or with a bright halo round his head as he prayed; and after death he appeared in glory, arrayed as a Doctor of the Church. He was excessively severe to his body, tearing it open with cruel and frequent disciplines, and the Angels would sometimes bring balsam for his wounds. He often kept watch all night before the Blessed Sacrament, and visited It frequently by day. Such an abundance of divine light was shed upon his soul that he would rise and walk about, exclaiming as if weary: "Enough, O Lord, enough of light—no more, O Lord, it is enough." He bound himself by vow for the last twenty years never to commit a deliberate venial sin, and that he kept his vow is proved by his great sanctity and the singular graces he received from God.

2. At Cracow, in Poland, in the year 1612, Father Gaspar Petkoroski, a Pole, closed his life of constant and unwearied labour. His food was scanty, and, if the pressure of work caused him to lose his dinner, he refused all compensation, and was contented with the usual supper. When he was aappointed confessor to the Bishop of Cracow, he so fulfilled his duties at the Court as not to dim the lustre of his virtues by the least worldliness or laxity, and he gained from all the character of a Saint.

3. At Montelimar, in France, in the year 1630, Father Louis Bovillet, a Frenchman, fell a martyr of charity, full of joy that he died in the Society and in service of the plague stricken. Twenty-two others also died in similar service of the sick in different cities of France.

4. At the College of Coimbra, in the year 1569, at the age of seventeen years, died Brother Francis de Andrada, a Scholastic, the Angel and the Stanislaus of the Province of Portugal, where his memory at the end of a century and a half was still in benediction. The most weighty authorities of this first generation, which may be called the heroic age of the Society, affirmed after his death that they had never seen anything comparable to the perfection of this holy youth. "And I do not believe," wrote his Master of Novices, "that I have read in the life of even the greatest servants

of JESUS CHRIST anything so astonishing as the peace of his soul in circumstances the most difficult, in which he considered nothing but the good pleasure of God." As for the rest, long before his entrance into the Noviceship, dating from the age of ten or twelve years, the young Francis de Andrada had given proof of a zeal and a fervour which rose superior to the weaknesses of tender years. If he heard that a poor sick man was in his agony, he went to him immediately, taking a crucifix and two tapers, and placing these near the dying man, he often stayed with him for many hours, to encourage him and pray with him. It was a sight so charming and so edifying, say the authors of his life, that throughout the whole neighbourhood those who were dangerously ill rivalled each other in calling for the holy child, as the Priests themselves named him, who engaged their penitents to have him sent for. A Novice at the age of fourteen years, Francis de Andrada, in less than three years spent in Religious life, succeeded in raising upon solid foundations the edifice of an incomparable sanctity. At all places and at all times he thought of our Lord and His most holy Mother as standing near him, on the right hand and on the left, and he strove to regulate according to these most perfect models his deportment, his words, his conduct, all his thoughts, and the most transient movements of his heart. Beholding in his Superiors and his Brothers only the image of God who deigned to guide him, and to hold intercourse with him, he testified for them a love and respect so tender and at the same time so humble, that they were quite enraptured with him. Thanks to his unceasing solicitude to please God, never had he to be admonished twice of a fault however small. Was it not enough, he used to repeat, that the Lord had sent him word to correct himself? Every hour he offered to the Eternal Father one of the sorrowful mysteries of His Divine Son; and he likewise invited all creatures, after the example of the three children in the Babylonian furnace, to bless the Lord for the graces with which he had replenished the most holy Virgin, in order to make her the Queen of Heaven. From these pious practices, and many others of the like nature, there flowed, as from their source, into the soul of Francis de Andrada, the plenitude of all virtues:—a longing truly insatiable to crucify his body, and to imprint upon it the marks of the Passion:—an openness of heart so perfect that the Master of Novices was wont to say, "The soul of Brother Francis is as transparent to my eyes as the clearest crystal in the rays of the sun : "—a conformity to the will of God so wonderful, that in the space of a full year he did not remember to have passed a single quarter of an hour in the day without renewing it. And yet upon his death-bed, when he was asked repeatedly, what recollection of his Religious life gave him the greatest joy and confidence in the mercy of God—"After the merits of my Saviour, my sweetest consolation," he replied, "is to have loved above all, obedience." And the earliest account of his death adds, "When any one among us now-a-days is desirous of animating himself more effectually to the practice of obedience, he has only to place before his eyes Francis de Andrada in the act of obeying."

February 17.

1. At Manilla, in the Philippine Isles, in the year 1605, died Father Jerome de Prado, a man whose mind was ever tranquil and fixed in God. Once when he was lying prostrate on the ground, wearied with a long journey on foot, and disabled by a heavy and dangerous fall, the Infant JESUS, to whom he was tenderly devout, appeared to him, bearing His cross, and the sight not only restored his strength, but filled him with incredible joy. At another time he saw St. Francis of Assisi protecting the city of Manilla against the inroads of the Chinese. Out of humility, and in imitation of St. Austin, he wrote and published the sins of his life.

2. Also at Manilla, in the year 1615, Paul Rion, a Temporal Coadjutor, a Japanese, a great and eloquent propagator of the Faith, who had been banished from Japan by the Emperor Cubosama, worn out by the hardships of the voyage, reached the haven of his Heavenly country.

3. At Pultowa, in Poland, in the year 1611, Father George Skarsinski, a Pole, an indefatigable missioner, died suddenly but happily while engaged in an act of charity. Being sent by the Rector of the college to attend a dying man, and feeling himself at the time quite well in body and mind, as he was preparing to hear the sick man's confession he complained of a sudden pain in his head, and resting it upon the breast of his companion who sat beside him, calmly expired, fulfilling the words of the Book of Wisdom : "The just man if he be prevented with death shall be in rest."

FEBRUARY 18.

1. In the Straits of Malacca, in the year 1598, Father Peter Martinez, a Portuguese, Bishop of Japan. He had previously accompanied the army of Don Sebastian to Africa, and when the King had been defeated and slain he was taken captive and kept for a time in cruel slavery. After this he suffered shipwreck, and at last by order of the Pope was made Bishop of Japan. He went to the vineyard alloted to him and laboured in it cheerfully and successfully, living upon alms amid dangers and anxieties, until a terrible persecution arose against the Christians, and he was banished. His shattered strength could not sustain the sufferings of the passage, and he died on the voyage. He was a Priest illustrious for his heroic virtue, and not less distinguished by his humbleness of mind than by his high dignity in the Church.

2. At Braga, in the year 1615, Father John Cardim. A crucifix was given to the dying man to kiss, and it was seen with the hands stretched forward from the cross to embrace him. He never said Mass except in his hairshirt. He carried his book of particular examen suspended from his neck with the formula of his vows written in his own blood. He took such scanty sustenance that he seemed to be fasting all the week. His sacred body was found seven years later breathing a heavenly fragrance. Authentic documents of miracles wrought by his invocation have been procured.

3. At Evora, in Portugal, in the year 1555, died Father Emmanuel Fernandez, an African. The apostle was murdered by ruffians in the pay of a rich man whose resentment he had incurred by converting a woman of scandalous life. The assassins waylaid him and beat him so cruelly that he died shortly afterwards. When he was brought back to the city the Cardinal Henry visited him; the whole city lamented his death, and honoured him with solemn funeral rites. Father Emmanuel could not be induced to name his murderers, but one of them of his own accord surrendered himself and disclosed the whole affair. This man had been moved by the weighty words of the Father, who even while receiving their blows exhorted them to repentance, and when his companions fled away, had confessed his sins to the dying Priest. So great was the industry of this holy man, and so wonderful his success in bringing to peace and

concord those who had been at variance, that on one occasion he reconciled to each other and to God fifty persons in one day. His words seemed, as he spoke, to flame like a torch, which he had enkindled with the Precious Blood received in Holy Mass, for it was his custom to celebrate before he preached.

4. At Seville, in Spain, in the year 1673, Father Francis de Sylva, a Spaniard, piously departed this life—a man gifted with a wonderful discernment of spirits, and with the art of governing consciences, although himself a constant prey to fear and anguish of soul. In public discourses he mastered men's minds by the wonderful energy of his words. No one ever wearied of listening to him, and he seemed not only to be dear to Christ but to dwell in His Sacred Heart.

February 19.

1. At Seville, in Spain, in the year 1688, died Father James Sanchez. Whilst undecided as to the choice of a state of life, he was one day praying earnestly in the presence of the Adorable Sacrament of the Altar, when a voice issuing from the tabernacle distinctly uttered these words: "Be of the Society of My Name." In the Society the object of all his prayers, the end of all his actions, was to *love* and *suffer*.

2. In the Island of Majorca, in the year 1621, Father Raphael Oller, a Spaniard, closed his earthly career and rested from labours which after his death furnished sufficient occupation to three indefatigable missionaries. He was revered by all as a Saint and Apostle. He was so austere that though obliged to preach daily to the people, he fasted most rigorously not only during Lent, but also during the holy season of Advent. An ardent lover of chastity, he strove by every means in his power to preserve his virginity unsullied; and for this purpose he macerated his body, devoting himself to unremitting toil, he was exceedingly harsh and severe to himself, and he honoured in a special manner the Blessed Eucharist and the Immaculate Virgin Mother of God. In recompense for these works of piety God granted His servant the grace of living and dying a virgin.

3. At Cologne, in Germany, in the year 1622, died Father Arnold Boecop, a Belgian. Taken by the heretics and thrust into prison, he fell into a lingering illness, and died in the most exquisite torture. His death,

as the physicians testified, was hastened, if not entirely caused, by poison administered by the heretics, who were enraged at being unable to find a pretext for putting him to an ignominious death. Father Boccop preserved alike his faith untainted by the breath of heresy and his virginity intact, although exposed to temptations which might have proved fatal to many others; for he was heir to a magnificent estate in Bavaria, and for many years member of, and in constant communication with, the academy of that country.

4. At Frezenal, in Spain, in the year 1680, Father James Serrano, a Spaniard, departed this life. Such was the opinion entertained of him, that, after his death, no one deemed it necessary to pray for him, every one judging that such exalted virtue needed not the assistance of the living to arrive at everlasting glory. Whilst he lay at the point of death, persons of undoubted sanctity, present in spirit only, beheld the Infant Jesus tenderly embracing him and covering him with affectionate caresses.

5. At Verdun, in France, in the year 1656, Father Peter le Brun, a Frenchman. His parents enjoyed such a reputation for virtue that he was called "the child of the Saints." On reading the life of St. Ignatius in the Novitiate he was intimately convinced that the shortest way to arrive at sanctity was that of the cross and humiliation. From that moment he conjured our Lord to conduct him by the road of tribulation. Heaven seems to have heard his prayer, for during the time of his Novitiate he lived in a perpetual alternation of joy and grief, and during all the rest of his life he experienced no consolation or devotion. A prey to continual sufferings, which at times reduced him to a sort of agony, he never allowed himself the slightest negligence in the observance of the smallest rule. It was the will of God that he should also be tried with calumny, when his patience shone with a fresh brilliancy. "I am," he said, "the anvil of the Lord: the anvil sustains every blow, and never changes its shape." What may appear admirable is, that whilst in preaching he felt all dry and desolate himself, his hearers on the contrary were penetrated with a compunction and sweetness altogether heavenly. He was confessor to Charles of Lorraine, Bishop of Verdun, and contributed to the resolution which this virtuous Prelate formed of renouncing the ecclesiastical dignities which he held, and entering the Society.

February 20.

1. At London, in England, in the year 1647, died Cuthbert Stephen Prescott, a Temporal Coadjutor. Having for a long time escaped the pursuit of the Priest-hunters, he at length fell into their hands; but not being a Priest, it was not deemed advisable to put him to death. He was therefore in hatred of the Catholic Faith thrust into prison, where after years of great suffering he closed his earthly career.

2. At Valladolid, in Spain, in the year 1595, Father Francis de Morales met a precious death, after having suffered pains so intolerable that they were equalled only by the heavenly consolation with which God inundated his soul. In his last illness, when the intensity of his sufferings forced from his lips an exclamation of complaint, he saw and heard our Divine Lord gently reproaching him in these words: "You complain, and I smile." Francis incredibly comforted replied: "What is there, Lord, that I desire more than to delight You: if my pains make You smile, let them come in abundance; I shall be ever ready to receive them." After having uttered these words, fortified with patience from on high, he went to receive an eternal reward. He was a man of unwearied zeal, and possessed singular tact in preparing people for death; particularly those who were to die by the hand of the public executioner.

3. In America, in the year 1693, Father Vincent Liverza merited the palm of martyrdom, being slain by the Caribees through hatred of the faith.

February 21.

1. At Cadillac in France, in the year 1573, Father Martin Guttierez, a Spaniard. Whilst journeying through France to Rome, as deputy of the Province of Castile to the third General Congregation, he was waylaid by the heretics, and so cruelly handled, that in a few days he died of his wounds. St. Teresa, in a letter sent to Rome to the Father Assistant of Spain, declared that Father Martin "had been shown to her by God amongst the Choir of Martyrs." Distinguished in an excellent degree for every religious virtue, he was pre-eminent in the worship and filial love of the Virgin Mother of God, whom in turn he found to be a most loving mother.

Once he saw in a vision the whole Society, like little birds under their mother's wing, gathered beneath the protecting mantle of the Mother of God. When Father Martin died in prison, a beautiful lady came, and having laid out the corpse reverently was seen no more.

2. At Seville, in Spain, in the year 1616, Father Alphonsus Rodriguez died full of days and of merits, for he had reached his ninetieth year, having passed seventy in the Society. He discharged the office of Master of Novices for forty years with the highest distinction, and acquired that knowledge of religious perfection which he displayed as well in his own life as in that excellent work, the *Practice of Perfection*, which has been adopted by all orders of Religious, and published again and again in every language.

3. At Clerac, in France, in the year 1622, Father Nervé Malvése, a Frenchman, having laboured in the missions of the camp and others, was slain by the heretics whilst engaged in the charitable work of hearing confessions, after the city had been seized upon by treachery. His priestly dignity only earned for him more cruel treatment, and he received ten wounds before he went to his reward.

FEBRUARY 22.

1. In Japan, in the year 1644, Father Diego Carvalho, a Portuguese, after numberless journeys undertaken and toils endured, first in Cochin China and afterwards in Japan, received the crown of martyrdom. Having been arrested in the latter country along with nine Christian companions, he was in a time of severe frost plunged into icy water and there tortured for a space of three hours. After he had been drawn out, and had been urged to set the example to his companions and forsake the faith, he on the contrary with all his power exhorted them to remain firm and faithful. In consequence they were again immersed in the frozen pond, and after having been bound to stakes continued firm and resolute from dinner-time to the middle of the night, which was made more bitterly cold by a cutting wind and falls of snow. At last their souls, released from their bodies by the intensity of cold, took their flight to Heaven, Father Diego being the last of this glorious band.

2. At Gratz, in Styria, in the 1612, died Father Martin Ertmer,

a German, a religious according to the heart of the Society. When in his youth he was admitted into the Sodality of our Blessed Lady, he espoused the Virgin Mother of God with a ring which his mother had given him, and which the young men of his family used to wear at their betrothal. Once, when his eyes were fixed more intently than usual upon the crucifix he felt himself warned of his approaching death. In consequence, although there did not appear to be any symptoms of his health declining, he gave notice to the Rector and disposed himself by the reception of the Sacraments for death. Soon after he became insensible, and in a few days died.

3. At Hildesheim, in Germany, in the year 1656, died Henry Werden, a Temporal Coadjutor. He was conspicuous for every religious virtue, but especially for a wonderful readiness and eagerness in any offices of charity, even when his life was in jeopardy. In an heretical city he was welcomed with sticks and stones, and was so badly wounded by the heretics that they left him for dead. However, far from showing any sign of indignation, he imposed upon himself certain daily prayers in their behalf, and these he faithfully performed. He had consecrated all his life, but especially his declining years, to a zealous worship of the Most Blessed Sacrament, and his repeated long and humble prayers upon his knees before It bore witness to the fervour of his devotion.

February 23.

1. At Glatz, in Germany, in the year 1657, died Father Andrew Metsch, a German, gifted with wonderful eloquence and charity, and of great skill in the direction of souls. In consequence more than ten thousand heretics are computed to have been brought over by him from heresy to the Church of Christ, including nine sectarian ministers, and one hundred and nine apostates from the faith. He established eight Sodalities of the Blessed Virgin; nor did he fail to propagate on every occasion the practice of piety and the love of our holy religion.

2. In France, in the year 1620, Louis Fréredoux, a native of Burgundy, a Scholastic, gave up his happy soul into the hands of his Creator, not only unstained with the guilt of mortal sin, but adorned with the highest excellence of virtue. His extraordinary charity and humility prompted him to kiss the footsteps of his companions, and to esteem it a privilege

February 23, 24.

to clean their shoes. He had great devotion to his Angel Guardian, and on one occasion was directly assisted by him at an examination in philosophy, for upon being asked whence he obtained such an unusual facility in answering, he candidly replied, that the answer to each question was whispered distinctly in his ear by a secret voice.

3. At Posen, in Poland, in the year 1667, Father Martin Hincza, a Prussian, a man of wonderful art in governing according to the spirit he had imbibed in the Roman Noviceship. He governed the Colleges of Thorn, Dantzig, and Jaroslaw, the House of Probation, and the Professed House at Wilna and Cracow. He also held the office of Provincial twice, and deserved great praise for his prudence, zeal, charity, and courage.

FEBRUARY 24.

1. At Naples, in Italy, in the year 1637, died Father Francis Pavone. He was no sooner born than, as those who were present bear witness, he fell upon his knees, and as though in prayer raised his hands towards Heaven. When in the Society, he understood by divine inspiration that he would render a more pleasing service to God by forming secular youth to virtue in a Sodality than by entering upon the Indian mission. Sixty of his class of philosophy, and all his scholars of the class of poetry, embraced the Religious State, so great was the efficacy of his discourses upon eternity and heavenly things. He was seen sometimes radiant with celestial light.

2. At Saragossa, in Spain, in the year 1579, John Ximenes, a Spaniard, a Temporal Coadjutor, went to eternal happiness, having travelled by the secure road of blind obedience under the guidance of the Virgin Mother of God. For when before an image of our Blessed Lady he was one day earnestly asking whether he was in the right way to salvation and perfection, the Blessed Virgin clearly answered, "Be of good heart, Ximenes, advance prosperously on the road of blind obedience which you have taken; you are marching by a straight and royal road." At another time he was admonished by our Lady to remember the souls in Purgatory. Father Bartholomew Alvarez, Visitor of the Province of Aragon, has left us in his writings an account of the virtues by which the soul of this holy Brother was adorned.

3. At Manilla, in the Philippines, in the year 1615, died Mathias

Sanga, a Japanese, a Scholastic. After great and very fruitful labours in instructing his countrymen by catechising and preaching, during a persecution raised against the Christians by the Emperor Daifusama, he was banished, and after a dangerous passage to Manilla, there closed his days in exile in the most fervent sentiments of piety.

FEBRUARY 25.

1. In Paraguay, a district of America, in the year 1651, Father Adrian Kundde Crispian, a Belgian, died after twenty-three years of Apostolic labour, bestowed in the instruction of an uncivilised people. He prepared his discourses with the utmost care, frequently repeating that sentence, "Cursed be he who does the work of God negligently." He obtained the good will of the barbarians by ingeniously wrought presents, which they esteemed miraculous. As often as he went out of or returned to his room, he saluted with reverence the Virgin Mother of God, and allowed no Saturday to pass without fasting.

2. At Marseilles, in France, in the year 1655, Philip le Fort, a Frenchman, a Temporal Coadjutor, after twice serving the plague stricken, went to his reward, leaving such a reputation of sanctity, that during his funeral the people could not be prevented from carrying off his rosary, shreds of his dress, and the like, for the purpose of veneration. Being intent upon any opportunity of mortifying himself, during forty years he never made use of a bed.

3. At Catania, in Sicily, Basil Lazzari, a Sicilian, a Temporal Coadjutor. For the space of eighteen years, during which he held the office of Porter, he never broke the rule of silence; weighing so carefully the replies which necessity drew from him that they contained no superfluous words. He was constantly occupied with God, enjoying both in the house and elsewhere the reputation of a Saint. It is said that he foretold some future events, and wrought miracles with the cap of Father Lætavalli, and that he was observed before the Blessed Sacrament raised from the ground. He saw the soul of Father Lætavalli carried in triumph by Angels to Heaven.

4. In England, in the year 1679, Father Francis Neville died at the age of eighty-four, having passed forty-eight years in the missions of that country during times of persecution. From the moment of his entry

into the Society he resolved to perform all his actions in the manner that should be most perfect and most pleasing to God, and he ever after observed this resolution with the most heroic fidelity. The sweetness of his character made him loved and respected by every one, and to himself only he was austere. In order to observe the Rules more perfectly, and to yield nothing to human respect, he had engraven on his heart those words of our Lord—*Euge, serve bone et fidelis ; quia in pauca fuisti fidelis*—" Well done, good and faithful servant ; because thou hast been faithful over few things." And as the occasion to do great things for God rarely presents itself, he supplied the want by doing the smallest with the most exact fidelity. The exercise of the presence of God was, as it were, the soul of all his actions. Although serious infirmities subjected him to the most acute pain, the serenity of his countenance was never known to change; he endured all his sufferings as a preparation for that martyrdom which was the sole object of his desires. But God did not grant it to him, unless indeed we may regard as a martyrdom a long life passed in continual labour amid trials and sufferings of every sort.

February 26.

1. At Loretto in Italy, in the year 1594, died Father John Leleszy, a Hungarian. Being driven from Transylvania by the false believers, a certain illustrious but heretical woman had given him a cup of poison out of hatred to the faith, from the effects of which he gradually pined away. The *Annual Letters* mention him as a man born for everything great. He laboured with no less diligence in teaching Sigismund Bater, the son of the Prince of Transylvania, than in combating heresy throughout that country.

2. At Ferrara in Italy, in the year 1611, Father Anthony Posevianus, an Italian, rested in our Lord from his toilsome missions, embassies, and works. He was a man of great talents, eminent prudence, and surpassing piety. He did and suffered much in Savoy and France from the heretics, whom he strenuously opposed. He was employed by Gregory XIII. on very important embassies to King John III. of Sweden, to John the Grand Duke of Muscovy, to Stephen the King of Poland, and to the German Emperor, with whom he accomplished his mission with equal good fortune and dispatch. The Society obtained a footing through him at Cracow, and through him and by the liberality of the Pope seminaries were founded at Olmutz, Prague,

Brunsberg, and Vilna. Broken down in body, he still applied himself to writing, especially in defence of the Catholic Faith. Southwell in his *Bibliotheca Societatis* enumerates twenty-four of his works on different subjects.

FEBRUARY 27.

1. At London, in the year 1601, Father Roger Filcox, an Englishman. After many and great toils for the faith he was at last caught, and hanged, drawn, and quartered.

2. At Lincoln, in the year 1645, Father John Gross, an Englishman. He laboured for twenty-seven years before he was thrown into a loathsome prison, where he was confined and cruelly treated for the space of seven months. At the expiration of this time, he was bought out by his friends, but his health was so shattered, that he scarcely survived his imprisonment a month. He had just said Mass when he gave up his blessed spirit to God.

3. At Lisbon, in the year 1580, Alexander Cortho, a Portuguese Lay-brother. He was saved from death by a special providence whilst yet an infant. When he grew to be a man, he became a soldier, and fought against the Turks. But aiming at higher ends, he resolves to serve his Heavenly King, and he makes himself a Lay-brother in the Society of Jesus. He was a model of humility, patience, charity and obedience. He at last died a martyr of charity, in the service of the plague stricken.

FEBRUARY 28.

1. At Coimbra in Portugal, in the year 1598, died Father Ignatius Martin. He was at first a florid speaker, but after a while he changed the manner of his oratory to a more simple and apostolic style. During the last seventeen years of his life, in order that he might atone for his error in striving after an affected eloquence, he devoted himself to the labours of a catechist. He never celebrated Mass without wearing a hairshirt. It was his custom to give five hours a night to meditation.

2. At Manilla, in the Philippines, in the year 1615, died Andrew Saito, a Japanese Lay-brother. Not only by word of mouth but by the more eloquent language of actions, such as a constant self-contempt, zeal for the faith and love of poverty, he preached Christ to his fellow

citizens and brought salvation to many. Being seized, and remaining firm in his adherence to Christ, and prepared even to endure torture, he was driven into banishment. During the voyage, being broken down by his sufferings, he changed his exile for the country of the blessed.

3. At Wilna in Poland, in the year 1670, Father Benedict Boym; He told a friend that he had been admonished by the Virgin Mother of God, whom he especially honoured, to enter the Society. That his elder brother might not hinder him, he gave him 10,000 florins out of his own inheritance, and at that price purchased religious poverty. In the Society he was ever inflamed with a most ardent zeal for souls; and, when he could not obtain permission to go to the Indian Mission, he directed all his efforts to bring back the Schismatic Russians to the bosom of the Church, both by preaching and the publication of pious books. When near his last end he addressed the Priest who stood by. "Father do you see? Here are the Holy Fathers present. Behold they stand in front of my bed. Here is St. Nilus: St. Nilus, pray for me!" And so praying he expired

MARCH.

March 1.

1. In America amongst the Papigochs, in the year 1652, Father James Anthony Basile, an Italian, was put to death for his faith, at the very time that he was engaged hearing the confessions of his converts. During the Sacrifice of the Mass, on the day of his martyrdom, the Sacred Host at the elevation was seen to have a crimson circle round It, and when placed on the corporal stained it with blood. From his tender years he had prepared himself for the glory of such a happy death by the purity and innocence of his life. No one in his presence presumed to utter an indelicate word.

2. In the East Indies, in the year 1645, Peter Bastus, a Portuguese Lay-brother, was received into Heaven by the Blessed Virgin. Devotion to her and to his Angel Guardian he had always cultivated with the tenderest and most persevering affection. Once on a time when making a pilgrimage of devotion with some novices of the Society, it is said that he and his party were joined by a venerable looking man with a lady and her comely little boy. Anxious to know the name and quality of their companions, the pilgrims asked them who they were. "We founded your Society," was the reply, and they immediately disappeared. At midnight he would often rise from his bed and spend the rest of the night in prayer.

3. In Portugal, in the year 1561, Gaspar Fonseca, a Novice. Though he had only been a few months in the novitiate he gave such proofs of heroic virtue and courage when his wounds were lanced, that his medical attendants wondered how such fortitude and greatness of mind could exist in so delicate a frame. They did not know that the Novice derived his courage from the wounds of Christ our Lord, which were the objects of his constant contemplation. He sought no other solace, assistance or remedy. When they asked him how he was, "Well, praise be to God!" was his only reply. When told that his life was despaired of, he was filled with joy that he was so speedily to be dissolved and to be with Christ.

March 2.

1. At Wilna, in the year 1591, Father Antony Arias, a most learned Spanish Professor of theology. He died with feelings of penitential joy; at one time exclaiming with the Psalmist, "I will sing to the Lord as long as I live, I will sing praise to my God while I have my being," at another repeating portions of the Penitential Psalms, and then saying with St. Austin, that, "No one, however holy he may be, ought to depart this life without sentiments of penance." Being troubled in mind for not having, as he thought, submitted his judgment to that of his medical attendant, though in reality he was blameless in this respect, he entreated the Father Rector to allow his faults to be told for him in the refectory, and reverted to the subject again three hours before his death. He was a model of delicacy of conscience, which all ought to aim at if they would be true religious men.

2. At Naples, in the year 1590, Father Austin Justinian departed this life to receive the crown of eternal glory. He was a son of Paul Justinian Duke of Genoa, and was endowed with such powers of intellect, and such a prodigious memory, that when teaching philosophy and theology at Milan, Padua, and Rome, he gave his lectures *viva voce*, without once referring to his notes. He had made a digest of the works of St. Austin in the form of *loci communes*, according to the method of St. Thomas, so that he could quote from memory any apt passage from the Father with as much facility as if he was reading from a book. A higher tribute of praise however is due to him for he lived the life of a strictly religious man. Genius the most sublime in a Jesuit, unaccompanied by virtue, is but a ring without its diamond.

3. In Spain soon after his return from Rome in the year 1649, Father Antony Perez closed his meritorious career. He was an acute and solid theologian. Cardinal Pallavicini, who was Professor of theology with him at Rome, gives him this encomium in the *Vindication of the Society*; "Antony Perez my colleague, as a Professor of theology, was a man of transcendent talents, second to none that I have ever known or read of in the Society." He was distinguished too for his religious spirit and fervent piety. The Franciscan Father who attended him on his death bed averred that Father Antony never lost his baptismal innocence.

March 3.

1. The glorious triumph of Father Robert Southwell at Tyburn in the year 1595. He had been zealously employed on the toilsome and dangerous mission of England for eight years, when he was betrayed near London into the hands of the priest-hunters. He was cast into a dungeon of the Tower of London, so noisome and filthy that when brought out at the end of a month to undergo a judicial examination his clothes were covered with vermin. For three years he was kept in prison, and ten times during these three years put to the torture and most cruelly racked. Some days before his martyrdom they removed him from the Tower to Newgate, and there confined him in the hole called Limbo. Care was taken not to let the public know beforehand the day on which he was to suffer, in order to prevent the presence of a large concourse of people; and a notorious highwayman who had been condemned to death was ordered to be hanged on the same morning, but at another place, to divert the crowd from Tyburn. These precautions availed little: great numbers and amongst them many persons of distinction flocked to Tyburn, the streets through which he was drawn on a sledge were thickly lined with people, and as he passed by they were all struck with the exulting overflow of joy in his heart, so clearly manifested in his eyes and whole countenance. Being come to the scaffold, he made the sign of the cross as best he could with pinioned arms. He then rose up and spoke to the crowds, fearlessly making his profession of Faith, disclaiming any thought or intention of treason against the Queen, praying for her welfare and the conversion of his country. He then raised his eyes to Heaven, and blessed himself once more, and while repeating the words of the Psalmist, "Into Thy hands, O Lord, I commend my spirit," the cart was drawn from under him, and so from the scaffold this happy soul ascended into Heaven, open to receive him amongst the white-robed army of Martyrs. (*Memoirs of Missionary Priests.*)

2. In Corsica, in the year 1564, Father Silvester Landini, an Italian. For some irritability of temper, and want of edification, St. Ignatius, without dismissing him, sent him back to his own home. This penance stimulated him to do and to suffer much in order to prove himself worthy of being again received into favour by St. Ignatius. He was a man of superior talents,

was active and industrious; his fasts were almost continual; his days were days of toil, his nights were nights of almost sleepless prayer. The harvest of souls he gathered together corresponded with the extraordinary efforts he made to gain them. Men honoured him by their praise, and God honoured him by ecstacies, by interior illuminations, and by the gift of prophecy.

3. In Vienna, in the year 1679, Father John Nadasi, a Hungarian. He was a man of singular piety and erudition, and he wrote many books of devotion. He was Latin secretary for the German assistancy to two Generals of the Society, Father Nickel and Father Oliva. He was also confessor of the Empress Eleanor.

March 4.

1. At Messana in Sicily, (year unknown,) Father Jerome Otelli. Though devoid of eminent natural gifts, whether of personal appearance, agreeable voice, or polished diction, he nevertheless acquired such influence by his preaching at Rome, Florence and Messana, that he was called the ruler of hearts, and a very lion in the pulpit. And yet, though it was said of him, "Never did man so speak," he was gentle as a lamb. He was a man of a most profound humility and continual prayer.

2. At Yaroslave in Poland, in the year 1593, Father Benedict Herbest. He was found dead in the middle of his room on his knees, and to all appearances like one engaged in prayer. He had renounced a canonry at Posen, to devote himself to unwearied and truly apostolical missionary labours in the Society. Powerful in word and work, he gained many victories over heretics, the chief of which was the conversion of the Princess Elizabeth, who was first a Calvinist, then an Arian, then a Jewess, and lastly a Catholic.

3. At Posen in Poland, in the year 1613, Father Stanislaus Grodzicki, a Pole. Having been present in Rome at the funeral of St. Stanislaus, he conceived the desire of entering the Society. His application was met with a request that he would first take his degree as Doctor of Theology. Returning to his own country after his noviceship, he laboured so strenuously and so efficaciously for the salvation of the Lithuanians, that he was called their Apostle. As he was passing through one of the public streets of their chief city, a Protestant boy went up to him and spat in his face. A Catholic woman happening to see this insult offered to the Father shouted loudly for

help. A crowd was quickly gathering round; but Father Stanislaus would not allow that he had received any insult, adding that he considered nothing more honourable than to suffer something for Christ's sake.

March 5.

1. At Malabar, in the year 1596, Father Peter Aloysius, a son of one of the leading families of the Malabar Brahmins. While fervently engaged in preaching the Faith of Christ, and in reproving the inhuman practices of the infidels, some pagans ran him through with their lances, and left him for dead. But it pleased God for the further good of the Church to preserve the life of His servant, and crown the faithful minister of His word with the laurel wreath of Confessors.

2. In Peru, in the year 1630, Father John Villalobos, a Peruvian. He made great account of the very smallest things connected with a religious house; frequently saying that there was nothing unimportant or abject in it. Whenever he heard confessions he wore his hairshirt. He never knew any of his female penitents by sight. One day, while plunged in grief he was praying fervently, a large cross flamed before him, as if in the heavens, and a voice was distinctly heard saying, "Be of good courage, son; a greater and far more severe cross awaits thee." The heroes of Christ are rewarded with a heavier cross when they patiently bear a lighter one.

3. In the same Country, in the year 1654, at the College of the Assumption, Father John Ignatius Beizama, who from his noviceship to the time of his death was esteemed as a Saint. No one could ever detect in him any violation of a rule. When in his third probation, being told to water a young tree at a stated hour, he did so even when it was raining. And when his companions expressed their surprise at his conduct, he simply said, "I have been ordered to water the tree, but nothing was added about the weather being wet or dry."

4. At Belmont near Winchester, in the year 1615, Thomas Pond. He was descended from an ancient family, and was distinguished for his apostolic labours and sufferings. He was among the foremost in introducing Missioners of the Society into England. Though a member of the Society he was never promoted to Holy Orders, but contributed much to the preservation and advancement of religion by the valuable assistance he gave to

the Priests. On this account he was an object of hatred to the heretics. Writing to Father Persons in the year 1609 he says, "I have, during the last thirty years, been confined in ten different prisons." He had a good estate, but it was so pillaged by fines and exactions, that even his enemies were ashamed of their cruelty. Released from prison he retired to Belmont, and there died in the very same apartment in which he had been born seventy-six years before. (Dr. Oliver.)

March 6.

1. At Perugia in Italy, in the year 1557, Father Andrew Galvanelli, an Italian. Appointed by St. Ignatius to be Rector of the College at Venice, he fulfilled the duties of his office with such satisfaction, that he was chosen to preside over several other Colleges. Being sent by the Pope to Valtellin, he was most honourably received, and so fully satisfied the wishes of the people as to leave nothing to be desired. All that a Missioner Apostolic could do for them, he did. His government of the College at Perugia, was such as to merit for him the title of the "Light and strength" of that College. So assiduously did he devote himself to procure the greater glory of God and the salvation of souls, that he was called and honoured as a Saint.

2. In Spain, in the year 1565, Father Peter Tablares. While making a retreat, as a secular, under the direction of Father Villanova, he could not reconcile himself at all to the poverty of the followers of Christ, and was tempted to give up the retreat and make off, but not before giving a blow with his fist to Father Villanova. Suddenly however, horror-struck at his conduct, and manifesting his repugnance to all poverty, he was at length so convinced by Father Villanova, that he determined to enter the Society, and embrace that very Evangelical Poverty which he had so dreaded. A man, of acute penetration, and of great powers of eloquence, he had a special influence over the nobility, and in moving sinners to tears of repentance.

March 7.

1. At Caravaga in Spain, in the year 1579, Father Ferdinand Garcia, a man of such an extraordinary austerity towards himself that he wished for nothing else but to suffer and be despised. He was not disappointed; for

he was confined to a bed of sickness four years. He bore this cross with such heroic patience that he refused every alleviation in the shape of extra indulgence. When given up by the physician, and urgently requested to ask without hesitation for whatever he thought might be agreeable to him, he replied with some emotion, and not without an appearance of dread. "Shall I, O my good Lord, be asking for what is pleasing to myself?" And so speaking the good man died.

2. In Peru, in the year 1626, Father James de Samaniego, remarkable for his innocence of life and dread of sin. He had a special devotion to the Queen of Angels and to St. Michael the Archangel, who sometimes appeared to him surrounded with a heavenly glory. Through their holy prayers he led many unbelievers to the faith, and many hardened sinners to repentance. He loved poverty so dearly that for thirty-three years he wore but one habit.

3. At Messina in Sicily, in the year 1625, Father Francis Torres. For the three days before Ash Wednesday he retired to the villa house and passed the time in fasting and earnest prayer, to appease the anger of Almighty God for the sinful practices of a senseless people. His death, which he had foreseen and foretold a year before, was welcomed by him when it did come with the hymn *Te Deum*, which he fervently recited.

MARCH 8.

1. At Brussels, in the year 1625, Father Thomas Saile. He was particularly devout to our Blessed Lady, and he never went out of his room without falling on his knees before her statue. During his preparation for Holy Mass he begged of her to obtain for him the favour that he might not be wanting in respectful reverence towards her Divine Son. When Military Chaplain he prevailed upon the Duke of Parma to have the *Angelus* announced to the troops every morning by sound of trumpet, and to have the image of our Lady painted on the regimental banners. As soon as the signal for battle was given he would throw his beads round his shoulder like a belt, and always escaped without a wound, though oftentimes obliged by duty to be where danger was most imminent. He died full of days and merits.

2. At Antwerp, in the year 1670, Father Henry Engelgrave. He was the author of some celebrated instructions to preachers, and was a successful Rector of the Colleges of Oudenarde, Cassel and Bruges. Although he was

assiduously engaged as confessor in the church, director of a confraternity, and giver of exhortations to various religious communities, he found time to study so deeply that he was called the "Repository of knowledge."

MARCH 9.

1. At Valentia in Spain, in the year 1595, Father John Fernandez, a Spaniard. He was military chaplain to the Spanish troops in Belgium, a duty which he discharged with much zeal and fidelity. He spent the day in instructing the soldiers and in attending the sick, while a great part of the night was devoted to prayer. St. Ignatius appeared to him repeatedly, so too did our Blessed Lady with St. Maurice and a numerous band of Martyrs and holy Virgins, to strengthen and console this holy and devout army chaplain.

2. At Hesdin in France, in the year 1655, Father Robert Planterose. He spent his whole life in teaching; and this was his method. He would begin with a class of elements and take it up to the end of rhetoric. And so did he persevere even until death.

3. In England, in the year 1666, Father James Mumford. He had served the English Mission twenty-six years, when he was apprehended at Norwich, and led round the City in his priestly vestments, amidst the scoffs of the rabble. He was sent off to Yarmouth, but in consequence of some dispute between the two towns respecting their chartered rights, he was remanded to Norwich. After some months imprisonment he was let out on bail. Though of delicate health, his labours were incessant. He was distinguished for his charitable compassion for the suffering souls in Purgatory. His name will ever be remembered by his controversial work entitled the *Question of Questions*. (Dr. Oliver's *Collectanea*).

MARCH 10.

1. At Glasgow, in the year 1615, Father John Ogilvie, the first of our Society who suffered death for the faith in Scotland. Scarcely had he been a year on the mission, when he was betrayed by one who had been admitted to hear his Mass. He was apprehended with a number of Catholics who had assisted at it, and committed to gaol. Removed to **Edinburgh** to be

examined before the High Court, by which the realm of Scotland was governed in the King's absence, he was accused before the so-called Bishops, but replied to their accusations with so much learning, acuteness and courage, that he reduced his adversaries to silence. Nothing less than the torture and blood of their innocent victim could satisfy the vindictive spirit of his assailants. Incredible were the wanton barbarities the holy man had to endure; they are scarcely paralleled by the refined cruelty of the persecutors during the three first centuries. And it is difficult to say which is the more astonishing, the implacable cruelty of the tormentors, or the meekness, patience and alacrity of the sufferer. In a letter written by him in his prison at Glasgow to the Father General, he says, "Your Reverence will easily judge of my present condition from the bearer of this letter. It is a capital offence to be caught writing, so that before the return of the turnkey I must needs hurry . . . . I lie under the load of two hundred weight of irons; looking for death, unless I accept the proffered favour of the King, that is, a rich preferment and another religion. Once I have sustained the torture of being kept without sleep for nine nights and eight days, now I expect two other tortures and then death." Condemned as guilty of death, he affectionately embraced the messenger who first gave him the news, and when the day came, went joyfully to the gallows as to a feast, proving himself a true disciple of the great Apostle St. Andrew. He was not quartered, but after hanging until he was dead, the body was laid in a coffin, and interred in the common ground allotted to executed malefactors. "*Primus ille est ex nostra Societate qui in Scotia tali honore dignatus est,*" are the words of his friend and superior Father Gordon. (Dr. Oliver's *Collectanea*).

2. At Piacenza in Italy, in the year 1651, John Baptist Mocchio, a Lay-brother, of extraordinary virtue. The room he used to live in was adorned with the triple ornament of smallness, darkness, and poverty. When he had anything more than usual to suffer, he would say, "This is short: O holy Patience!" So remarkable was his respect through life for the Fathers to whom he was assigned as a companion, that he seemed rather to follow than to accompany them. After his death he was interred in the plot of ground set apart as the burial place of the Fathers.

3. At Alcala in Spain, in the year 1570, Father Consalez. He was low of stature, and was a very diminutive looking little man, but possessed high intellectual powers, which were cultivated by every branch of learning, both

sacred and profane. In him there shone conspicuously the heavenly and profound wisdom of the Saints. His Rector and his Provincial were wont to say that his room was like an oracle, to which when they had recourse they received answers that guided and assisted them in the difficulties of their government. His conversation was with God: with men he seldom spoke, and then but in few words. When Master of Novices he strenuously exhorted them never to tarnish the good name of another, even by the least word. For five years he suffered acute pains of body, but rejoiced in all his sufferings because it was the will of God.

March 11.

1. At Naples, in the year 1610, Father Peter Albizi. He was in great repute for his exalted sanctity. The Bishop of Acerno used to say, that if he survived Father Peter he would relate wonderful things concerning him, but the Bishop died first, and the good father's humility and abnegation did not disclose what appertained to himself. When saying Mass he was not unfrequently favoured with the sweetest consolations, and with ecstacies from Heaven. He was singularly skilful in the treatment of souls, and more than three hundred were counted who were indebted to him under God for their vocation to religious life.

2. Also at Naples, in the year 1622, Father William Levesque. He died on the exact day which had been foretold to him four years previously; namely the day before that on which the Bull of the Canonization of St. Ignatius and St. Francis Xavier was prepared by the Pope. He had the power of healing diseases, and reading the secret thoughts of others, but a higher commendation than all this was his sterling, solid virtue.

3. At Vienna, in the year 1662, Father John Gans, gifted as a preacher and a controversialist. Selected by the Emperor Ferdinand III. to be his preacher and director, he was deservedly praised for the manner in which he fulfilled both these duties. Devotion to the Immaculate Conception of our Blessed Lady was assiduously promoted by him; her statue was placed in the great square in Vienna, and the Universities of the hereditary States bound their graduates by oath to defend the truth, which was then a pious belief, and now is a dogma of our faith.

MARCH 12.

1. At Rome, in the year 1652, the Very Reverend Father Alexander Gottifried, the ninth General of our Society. Two months had not elapsed after his election when he was taken off by death, and the Society which just saw him as its General was deprived of the advantage of his services. He was honoured by having at his baptism Pope Paul V. for his god-father. If any one spoke against his family, which was distinguished for its services both in time of peace and war, he would answer, "True nobility, is true humility." He was of a staid character, and seriously intent upon accomplishing with accuracy whatever he undertook. He did nothing superficially, and disliked anything being done so by others. For personal conveniences he had an utter contempt, his thoughts tended to what was great and eternal. He cherished the feelings of a father towards his brethren of all nations, and to any one who asked his assistance he was prompt to give it more by deeds than words.

2. At St. Omers, in the year 1604, Ralph Emerson, an English Laybrother. This faithful and prudent brother left Rome for England with Father Persons and Father Campion. After invaluable services to them and to other Fathers who followed them soon after to the English mission, he was captured and cast into prison, where he remained twenty years, *i.e.*, until the death of Queen Elizabeth. Upon the accession of her successor, James I., he was banished from the kingdom. He is mentioned in the Narrative of Father John Gerard, who says of him, "My next door neighbour (in the Clink prison) was our brother, Ralph Emerson, of whom Father Campion in a letter to Father General made mention in these terms, 'My little man and I.' He was indeed small in body, but in steadfastness and endurance he was great. He had been already many long years in bonds, ever keeping godly and devout, like a man of the Society; and after my coming to the Clink he remained six or seven yeare more. At last he was sent off with other confessors of Christ, to the Castle of Wisbeach, where he was attacked with palsy. One half of his body was powerless, so that he could not move about or do the least thing for himself. He lived notwithstanding, to add by his patience fresh jewels to the crown that awaited him. Being driven into banishment, he went to St. Omer's, and died a holy death there, to the great edification of all the by-standers."

MARCH 13.

1. At the Scoth College of Douay, in the year 1633, Father John Robe. He was appointed to the Scotch Mission after the glorious death of Father Ogilvie, and, on arriving there, was one of the four Jesuit Fathers for the whole of Scotland, two in the Highlands, and two in the Lowlands. After labouring some years in that country, where the Priests were fiercely hunted down by the pursuivants, he was recalled by his Superior, and chosen to preside over the Scotch College at Douay. When ill of fever, a certain pious virgin prayed that he might be restored to health, and that his fever might be transferred to her. Her prayer was heard, Father John recovered, and she was taken ill; the fever was obstinate; after being a sufferer from it for four months, she began to condemn herself of rashness, in asking for a sickness she knew so little about. Forthwith, the fever left her, and again seized upon the Father, who soon died of it.

2. At Morica in Sicily, in the year 1648, Father Fabius Justinian, a Greek. After many years hard toil on the laborious mission of the Cyclades, death called him to a life of endless happiness. It was his custom on the mission to chastise his own body severely, "Lest whilst preaching to others, he himself might become a castaway." For three whole years he never took off a hairshirt interwoven with small iron chains. With difficulty could he be prevailed upon in his last illness to lay aside his armour. After his death, the people were so eager to secure small portions of his religious habit, that to prevent them from stripping him entirely his corpse had to be carried away from the Church to the sacristy.

3. At Pekin in China, in the year 1630, Father John Terentius, a German. When he entered the Society, he was celebrated through the whole of Germany as a Doctor, a Philosopher, and Mathematician. Matured in virtue for apostolic duties, he sailed for China, and there laboured with great fruit, giving help to the souls of many by the opportunity of curing their bodies Called to Pekin at the request of the Emperor, to whom he had been proposed as the fittest person to correct the Chinese Calendar, he died whilst preparing himself for the task. He was the author of a large work in two volumes called the *Indian Pliny*, materials for which he prepared on his journey through India, Bengal, Sumatra, Cochin-China and China-proper

where he made accurate observations on the nature of the plants, minerals, animals and inhabitants in each of these countries.

4. At Mayence in Germany, in the year 1665, Father Melchior Cornœus, a German. He was the hero of many victories over heretics. Father Southwell mentions twenty-six volumes published by Father Melchior.

March 14.

1. At Dole in Burgundy, in the year 1623, Father Valerian Reginald, a native of Burgundy, at the advanced age of eighty, celebrated for his learning, he was an eminently humble man. He thought so little of his famous work on Moral Theology, that he had an idea of suppressing his own name, for fear of bringing discredit on the Society. No one ever knew him to utter a word that could give offence, and if he imagined at any time that a severe remark had escaped him, he would studiously endeavour to make amends for it by a humble apology. If called to the gate to speak to visitors, he would not return to his room again without making a passing visit of adoration to the Blessed Sacrament. His funeral was attended by a large concourse of people; and many of the leading men in the town, as well secular as religious, were so moved by the thought of his virtues that instead of recommending him to God they seemed rather to recommend themselves to his prayers.

2. At Rome, in the year 1631, Father Virgil Ceparius, an Italian. He was eloquent in the pulpit, and had the gift in a high degree of leading souls to a state of perfection. When Rector at Florence, he was confessor of St. Mary Magdalen de Pazzis, who related of him, that when he was giving an exhortation to the Community the Holy Ghost dictated to him every word he uttered. He wrote the Life of this Saint, as also the Lives of St. Francis of Rome, of St. Aloysius, and of Blessed John Berchmans.

3. At Worcester, in the year 1834, Father Nicholas Sewall. Born in Maryland, many years before the independence of America, he was sent to St. Omers for his education, and being blessed with a call to religious life, entered our Novitiate at Ghent. The year after the suppression of the Society he came to England, and served successively the missions of Preston, Eccleston Hall, Scholes near Prescot, and Portico. At this last place he built

the Chapel and House. His name occurs in the list of those who in 1803 presented themselves at Stonyhurst to renew their vows (the first renewal in England after the suppression) in the hands of the recently appointed Provincial, Father Stone. Five years later, he was called from the mission to preside over the College of Stonyhurst. He was subsequently Master of Novices at Hodder, and Provincial of the English Province. His government was mild, but firm. His unaffected piety, his exactness in the observance of rules, his paternal considerateness towards his religious brethren, particularly in their difficulties and wants, gained for him their lasting esteem and affection. It was said of him that from the time he left college to come to England in 1774 up to the last days of his life, a period of sixty years, he kept up the practice of rising every morning at four o'clock: and never omitted a daily lecture in his favourite spiritual book, Rodriguez. He was a man of prayer and mortification, always cheerful and obliging. His death was like his life, most edifying to men, honourable to religion, and precious in the sight of God. He calmly surrendered his soul to his Creator in the eighty-ninth year of his age. (Dr. Oliver's *Collectanea*).

MARCH 15.

1. At Monomotapa in Africa in the year 1561, Father Gonsales Sylveria, a Portuguese, who added to the distinction of his illustrious birth the honour of a Martyr's death. He preached the Gospel to the barbarous Caffres, and converted to the faith the King of Monomotapa, his mother, and many of the princes. The King however soon after was prevailed upon by the Mahometan Priests and certain men of rank to abjure his faith, and gave orders for Father Sylveria to be strangled. But Almighty God so favoured his servant as to illumine with celestial light the spot where his body was thrown into the water, and, when it floated to the bank of the river, it was protected by five eagles from the attacks of other birds of prey. Father Gonsales had prepared himself for this glorious death by a singular innocence of life, and by aiming so intensely at the perfection of his religious state that, had he not been honoured with the glory of martyrdom, he would have deserved to be ranked in the number of saintly Confessors.

2. At Lisbon, in the year 1575, Father Louis Gonsalvo. He was taken

by the Kings John and Sebastian of Portugal for their confessor; and was indefatigable as a missioner in Africa. Complying with the wish of John III. he went to Rome for the purpose of quietly and attentively observing the manner of life, the virtues, and whole conduct of St. Ignatius. He became intimate with the Saint, whom he not unfrequently saw shining in the midst of celestial light.

3. At Seville, in the year 1632, Father Diego Ruiz, distinguished for his erudition and for his constant study of religious perfection. His published works on theology consisted of five volumes. On days not devoted to class work he relaxed his mind by extra prayer. He gave proof of his humility by asking to do the menial works of the house, to sweep the rooms, and to be employed in the kitchen. He set apart one full day in each month for the special examination of his own interior, and to prepare himself well for eternity, which he frequently and ardently longed for, saying, "O eternity, when shall I see thee?" He studied on bended knees, the better to dispose himself by this humble posture to receive light from Heaven.

MARCH 16.

1. In Canada, in the year 1649, Father John Brebœuf. Whilst labouring amongst the Hurons, a tribe subject to the French, he was captured by the Iraquois Indians, who put him to death after a series of tortures, the very recital of which makes the heart shudder. They tore away his finger nails, beat him with sticks, cut off his hands, bruised his mouth with stones, and burnt out his tongue; they applied burning hot irons to his armpits and loins, placed a burning collar round his neck, and girded him with a belt of pitch and resinous bark, which they set fire to. The Father all this time was still and motionless, whilst his heart was fixed on God alone. When at last he began to speak of heavenly things, his tormentors gagged him, tore off his lips, and cut away his nose. With a scornful mockery of baptism, they poured boiling water on his forehead; then tying him fast to a post, which he affectionately kissed, they tore the skin from his head, cut off his feet, ripped away the flesh from his thighs to the very bone, broke his jawbones with an axe, burnt the extremities of his legs, cut open his breast, and in the end tore out his heart and ate it. He was in truth a worthy disciple of the early Martyrs. In him too was verified the truth—*Sanguis martyrum*

est semen Christianorum—"The blood of martyrs is the seed of Christians." Where he found not one believer, he left seven thousand worshippers in spirit and truth.

2. At Rome, in the year 1626, John Tibald, a Lay-brother. He was once a soldier, and, on becoming a Religious, bewailed the disorder of his past life with such deep contrition that his Master of Novices had to moderate his sorrow, and bid him entertain himself with the more joyful thoughts of the love of God and of Heaven. He so abounded in spiritual consolations, that he exclaimed, "No more, O Lord, no more, or I shall die." But he had his hours of temptation, for it is written that, when he had been working in the kitchen, there came over him such a violent temptation, that he thought of quitting, not the kitchen only, but the Society itself. In this distress of soul he said with many deep sighs, "JESUS, O good JESUS, do not abandon me!" Our Lord answered, "Have confidence in Me your Saviour, acknowledge your own pride, and know that without Me you can do nothing." The good man was ashamed of his little faith; but the temptation vanished, never to return.

MARCH 17.

1. In Canada, in the year 1649, Father Gabriel Lallemant, a Frenchman. He was Father Brebœuf's companion on the mission and also in the tortures inflicted by the Indians. Besides the cruelties which were mentioned yesterday, Father Lallemant had also to endure the torment of having spikes thrust into his body, of having his eyes torn out, and burning coals put into their sockets. Nor were the barbarous tormentors satisfied with this; they took and roasted his body, then tore him to pieces and devoured him. On his mission, and on other occasions, Father Lallemant was accustomed to animate and excite himself with these words, "Courage, my soul! Let us go on in holiness of life, thus to give all the joy we can to the most loving Heart of JESUS; for He is worthy of being served by us, even though the service brings with it sufferings of every kind."

2. In Mexico, in the year 1610, Father Ferdinand Gomez, who from a Mexican magistrate became an indefatigable missioner of the Society. The day after his death, a religious of the Order of St. Dominic saw a white cloud ascending from the roof of the Jesuit College towards Heaven in the

shape of a ladder; and, whilst he was yet gazing on the strange sight, he was informed of the death of Father Ferdinand, and concluded at once from the well known sanctity of the holy man that this representation indicated his entrance into Heaven.

3. At Paris, in the year 1667, Father Philip Labbé, remarkable for the number and importance of the works he published. He edited the most complete collection of all the Councils in seventeen volumes, fourteen of which were published by himself, the other three by Father Gabriel Cossart. Besides these voluminous works, Father Labbé also wrote many others upon various subjects. Southwell in his *Bibliotheca Societatis* mentions sixty-three.

MARCH 18.

1. At Cahors in France, in the year 1633, Father James Roche. Most affectionately devout to the Blessed Sacrament, he earnestly requested once in his early life, when in danger of death from sickness, to receive it rather as a remedy than as Viaticum. He had no sooner communicated than he recovered, to the astonishment of his medical attendants. He was so inflamed with the fire of divine love, that, when he spoke of heavenly subjects, it seemed as if sparks came issuing from his mouth, and enkindled in the breasts of his hearers a burning love of God.

2. In Mexico, in the year 1640, Father Alphonsus Guerer. He was so given to meditation and prayer, that the caller in the morning would sometimes find him in the middle of his room raised up in the air in a kneeling posture. Such was his tenderness towards the sick, that the only exception he ever made to his resolution of never asking for a general leave, was his request for permission to visit the sick as often as he liked. When ill himself, he gave thanks to God, and often repeated the words, "We belong to the Lord, we belong to the Lord;" then he would often say, "I thirst; but thanks to God that we are at so short a distance from the fountain of living waters." One night he composed himself in his bed like one going to sleep, and bade his companions to be at ease about him and go and take their rest. In the morning it was found that he had peacefully expired.

March 19.

1. At Paris, in the year 1626, Father Peter Coton, confessor and preacher to Henry IV., who confided to him the inmost secrets of his soul, and would sometimes take him to the church in his own carriage, and lead him with his own hand to the steps of the pulpit. Besides this, he appointed him tutor to the Dauphin, and wished to procure for him the Archbishopric of Arles, and a Cardinal's hat. But Father Coton deprecated these honours with such earnestness that the King conceived a still greater esteem of him. His learning, his eminent piety, his singular skill and efficiency in everything he undertook to do, fitted him for any duty of his state of life. So far was he from being affected by the empty allurements of the Court that he was commonly called its Angel.

2. At Presburg, in the year 1637, a great luminary of the Church and of our Society ceased to shine in the person of Cardinal Pazman. Pope Urban VIII. and the Emperor had honoured his virtue and learning with a Cardinal's hat and the Archbishopric of Gran. They hoped by this to strengthen and support the tottering fabric of Catholicity in Hungary; nor were they deceived in their expectations. He was most assiduous in reforming the manners of the clergy, and in bringing back to the Church many persons of distinction who had left it. His success lay in his mild and persuasive words, as well as in his publications in the Hungarian tongue, which were written with all the eloquence of a ripe scholar. He munificently founded at Presburg a college of the Society, an academy at Tirnaw, and an ecclesiastical seminary at Vienna, as also a convent of Franciscans at Neusazt, and a convent of the Poor Clares at Presburg. Wherever he went he gave proofs of his zeal, of his generosity, and still more of his humility.

3. At Goa, in the year 1634, Father Antony de Andrade, a Portuguese, an indefatigable missioner in the kingdom of Tibet. He was poisoned for his faith and preaching. God honoured his tomb by the cure of many sick persons who went thither to invoke his holy intercession.

March 20.

1. At Rome, in the year 1597, Father James Terry (Tyrie), a native of Scotland. While he was yet a child, bright rays were seen around his head, the harbingers of his future sanctity. When studying logic at the Roman College, he had a vision of St. Ignatius, who gravely rebuked him for stealthily and unbecomingly curtailing his prayer, in order to give more time to study. "More virtue, James, and less learning," were the concluding words of the Saint. Aroused by this rebuke, he gave himself thenceforth unreservedly to God, and became one of the most distinguished ornaments of the Society. After filling the chairs of philosophy and divinity at Paris, he returned to Rome. He was the first Father of the Society born in these islands who was chosen as Assistant. In the fifth General Congregation, holden in the year 1593, the Fathers elected him Assistant for the French Province, to which our missions of England, Ireland and Scotland were then united by the first decree of the same Congregation. He held this office nearly four years, during which a fierce persecution raged against the Jesuits in these islands. His life was meritorious, and his death was happy.

2. At Genoa, in the year 1662, Father Antony Brignole. Before his entrance into the Society he was a senator of the Genoese republic. He was possessed of great wealth, and remarkable for his liberal charities to the poor, who honoured him with the title of God's treasurer.

March 21.

1. At Antwerp, in the year 1616, Father Florens, an active and indefatigable missioner in Holland, where on one occasion he converted nearly an entire village. Prompt at every call of obedience, ready to assist and serve others, he made it his study to become all to all. While attending a sick man, he foretold (though then in perfect health) that he was to die before the patient. Sometime later he said, "I have but three days to live." The event proved the truth of his words.

2. In the island of Majorca, in the year 1621, Joseph Cladera, a Lay-brother. Anxious to enter the Society and yet not daring to make the request, he was advised by a pious lady to take courage; "Go," said she,

"ask to be admitted, and your request will be granted." He complied, and succeeded. It was his custom to rise in the morning an hour or two before the rest of the Community, and to spend the time in taking disciplines, pious reading, and prayer.

3. In Mexico, in the year 1622, Father Nicholas Arnaya, a Spaniard. He was one of the brightest ornaments of the Society in America, and deservedly called the Father of the North American missions. He was eminently a man of prayer and true humility; his long hours of meditation during the nights (not unfrequently prolonged until daybreak) were proofs of the first, while the latter was manifested by a fact that happened when he was Rector of the College of Guadiana. He was accused by a magistrate of a serious crime before the Viceroy; the report spread far and wide, and he was cast into prison. Yet he took no steps to refute the calumny, but prayed for his calumniator, and remained quiet in the consciousness of his innocence. God in his own good time gave glory to his servant, for remorse so worked upon the wicked man as to compel him in presence of many witnesses to confess the falsehood of his accusation. Thus his innocence received an increase of honour when all had been done to defame it.

March 22.

1. At Nangasachi in Japan, in the year 1643, Father Antony Rubini, an Italian. Scarcely had he set foot in Japan to preach the Gospel, when he was captured together with his companions, and commanded to abjure Christ our Lord. He spurned the command, and in consequence was thrown into a loathsome prison, where on fixed days for seven whole months he was tormented by "the torture of water." He was afterwards taken up and down the country with these words written in large characters on his back, "This man and his companions have come hither to preach the faith of Christ contrary to the Emperor's edict." Lastly he was hanged by the feet in a deep trench with his head downwards. Under this torture he expired.

2. In Paraguay, in the year 1645, Father Peter Romero and Father Matthew Fernandez were beaten to death with clubs by the Indians whom they had been endeavouring to civilize. Their hearts were torn out, their throats cut, and their tongues, which had preached the law of Christ, were plucked from their mouths.

3. At Antwerp, in the year 1655, Father Francis Perez. He was born on Christmas Day, and died on Good Friday. Before he entered the Society, he was remarkably charitable to the poor, and was favoured by having an Angel, or rather Christ himself, as his guest in the garb of a poor man. He had two sons who both entered the Society, and then he followed their example. As he was ordained Priest before them, he had the happiness of having them to serve his first Mass.

4. In France, in the year 1628, Peter Colet, a Lay-brother, surrendered his most obedient soul to God. When approaching his last end, he requested the Rector of the house to give him an order to die, that thus he might bear some resemblance to his Divine Saviour Who was obedient unto death. Father Rector declined the request; still, not to deprive the Brother of the wished for merit, he recommended him to aim at a most perfect comformity with that universal decree of Heaven, by which "it is appointed for all men once to die."

March 23.

1. At Nangasachi in Japan, in the year 1643, Father Albert Meczynski, a Pole, not less distinguished for his religious virtues than for his high birth. He suffered the same tortures as Father Rubini, of whom mention was made yesterday. When a Novice at Rome he took St. Stanislaus as his model; spoke of the Blessed Virgin to his fellow Novices with wonderful expression of language and feeling, and suggested new ways of honouring her. When entering his room, or going out of it, he would turn towards the Church of St. Mary Major, and do reverence to our Lady his Mother. After he had made over to the Society in Poland his large fortune, he repeated these words, "Now I have nothing but my blood to give to God." And that he might shed this for Christ's sake, he asked to be sent to Japan; his request was granted, and a glorious death crowned the novice-like innocence of his life.

2. At Oporto, in the year 1547, a Portuguese Scholastic named Vas Terras. From being a distinguished and rich Canon, he became a humble and poor Religious. He gave proof of his love for poverty and humility, when, being sent by the advice of the physician to his native air for the benefit of his health, he declined to go to his father's house, and betook himself to the public hospital. On the day of his death, which he had

foretold, it is said that he was favoured and consoled by a visit from the Blessed Virgin, St. John, and St. Austin.

3. At Placencia in Spain, in the year 1564, Father John Paul Alvarez, remarkable for the wonderful cures which the mercy of God wrought through his intercession. He healed the sick of their infirmities, and expelled demons from possessed persons by reading the Gospel over them. When Rector of the Colleges at Medina and Placencia, he introduced so perfect an exactness of religious discipline, that they were called "Colleges of Angels."

MARCH 24.

1. At Munster in Bavaria, in the year 1630, Father Adam Saller, a celebrated preacher. It is recorded that he received from Heaven two wonderful visions; the first from a departed member of the Society who appeared to him and said, If you do not become a member of the Society you will be lost; the second from the Blessed Virgin Mary, who consoled him with the assurance that he was to be numbered with the Blessed in eternal happiness. He was a man endowed with a profound humility and an ardent zeal for souls, of holy conversation and deep meditation on the truths of eternity. He wrote his sermons kneeling, for he looked on himself as an amanuensis of God, and as a messenger to convey to the people the orders of Heaven.

At Kilkenny, in the year 1650, Father Patrick Lee. He was the first Novice admitted into the House of Probation at Kilkenny, and there imbibed the blessed spirit of zeal and charity. He was distinguished not only for his proficiency in philosophy and theology, but also for his skill in medicine. A very angel of consolation, he went about assisting and relieving his poor suffering countrymen, ministering alike to their souls and bodies. He died a victim of charity, in the most edifying sentiments of piety and joy. His death was justly regarded as a public calamity.

3. At Terregles, near Dumfries, in the year 1810, Father John Pepper, a native of Scotland. He was one of the last members of the old Society in his country. Before the suppression of the Company he had taken his degree of Professed, had served the Scotch mission, and was Procurator and Rector of the Colleges at Douay and Dinant. When Clement XIV. issued the Bull

of suppression, he was compelled to seek refuge in his own country, where he laboured on the mission with exemplary zeal until his pious death. The religious spirit which he was taught to follow in his novitiate, and which he retained all his life, prompted him to avail himself of the first opportunity that was presented of re-entering the Order and renewing his vows. He was one of the seven who, having been professed of four vows in the old Society, gladly accepted the offer to renew them at Stonyhurst in 1803, when the English mission, again formed into a province, was aggregated to the Society existing in White Russia. It is no small tribute to the self-denying courage and devotedness of a missioner in those days to say of him, that "he laboured with zeal for many years on the Scotch mission;" for the spirit of Puritanism had not worn itself out in the life time of Father Pepper. Indeed a venerable Ecclesiastic still living in the year 1867 says from his own experience, "Such was the unrelenting hatred in Scotland to everything Catholic at the early part of the nineteenth century, that a Priest could hardly appear in that country."

March 25.

1. At Nangasachi in Japan, in the year 1643, the three companions of Father Antony Rubini (of whom mention was made on the twenty-second of March) and of Father Meczynski (commemorated on the twenty-third) won the palm of martyrdom. They were Father Antony Capeti, an Italian, Father Diego de Moralés, a Spaniard, and Father Francis Marquez, son of a Portuguese, but born in Japan. They are said to have endured the Japanese water-torture a hundred and five times; they then were hung for nine whole days head downwards in a pit, and at last beheaded.

2. At Messina in Sicily, in the year 1619, Bartholomew Valditaro, an Italian Novice. While yet a boy he had inspired his schoolmates with such a reverence for him, that, if he chanced to come upon them when conducting themselves with levity they would say, "Bartholomew is coming," and at once put on a modest behaviour. After a novitiate of scarcely six month's duration he was found ripe for Heaven. In his last sickness he would have the conversation turn on the Blessed Virgin Mary, and if those who discoursed with him wandered from the subject, he recalled them to it. He died upon the feast of the Annunciation as he had himself predicted.

March 26.

1. At Lima in Peru, in the year 1613, died Father Stephen Paez, esteemed for his great gift of government. At his funeral a person of great reputation for virtue saw him as in a vision going up to the altar, and there met by our holy Father St. Ignatius, who gave him a loving reception, and welcomed him with special marks of honour.

2. At Catania in Sicily, in the year 1604, Father Ferdinand Paterno, confessor to St. Aloysius Gonzaga at the time when he was deliberating on his state of life. It is well known that the most Blessed Virgin enjoined the young Saint to enter the Society of Jesus, and bade him declare her command to his confessor.

3. At Brun in Germany, in the year 1627, Balthasar Mayr, a German Lay-brother. As often as he passed a picture or statue of the Virgin Mother of God, he made her a most humble and reverent salutation. He loved to accompany the preacher to the pulpit, that like Magdalen he might sit at his feet, and hear with greater reverence the word of God.

4. At Dôle in France, in the year 1634, Father John Lorin, a Frenchman, born at Avignon. He was a man of universal learning, but he was especially known as an interpreter of Holy Scripture, on which he wrote eight volumes of Commentaries. He was long employed as a censor of books and theologian to the Father General at Rome, and was a professor both at Paris and Milan. He consecrated his pen to our Lady the Seat of Wisdom, and always had recourse to her for aid in explaining the obscurities of Holy Scripture. He promoted the devotion to her Immaculate Conception in Italy, France, and Spain, and obtained a decree at Dôle that no one should receive a Doctor's cap at that University unless he bound himself by oath to defend this first great privilege of our Blessed Mother. He introduced at Dôle, Avignon, and elsewhere, the pious custom of praying for the souls in Purgatory at the sound of an evening bell. He was a great lover of mortification, poverty, and common life, and would never accept of the most trifling gift for his own private use. Father Lorin died when he was seventy-five years old, fifty-nine of which he had spent in the Society of Jesus.

March 27.

1. At Sassari in Sardinia, in the year 1624, died Father Salvator Pisquedda a Sardinian. He was a most zealous labourer in missions, which he gave with unwearied patience, and not without signs of God working with him. For, though his voice and chest were both so weak, owing to his delicate constitution, that at times he could scarcely be heard when preaching in the Church, yet, when he spoke to the country people in the fields and hamlets, his voice seemed loud and strong, and something almost more than natural. He had great devotion to the Mystery of the Most Holy Trinity, and to our Lord in the Blessed Sacrament. He made many signal prophecies, and was honoured after death by undoubted miracles. Nor is it to be wondered at, for the historian of his life relates that Father Pisquedda never committed a mortal sin in his life, nor ever wilfully violated a rule in Religion.

2. At Glatz in Germany, in 1653, Father John Warlich, a German of singular candour and confidence in God. He discharged the duties of Procurator in the College of Glatz for twenty-five years, religiously, wisely, and exactly. Shortly before his death he told his confessor that he had begged of our Blessed Lady the favour to die in the place where he had so long laboured, and that she had distinctly promised to grant the request.

3. At Vienna in Austria, in the year 1657, Father Jodoc Kedd, a German. He was a zealous preacher and writer in defence of the Catholic Faith. He used even as a child to mount a stool or the trunk of a tree, and inveigh against the preachers of heresy. He chose a new plan of warfare against them by writing and printing little cheap publications. Thirty such books of his are reckoned by Southwell.

4. At Cracow in Poland, in the year 1669, Father Nicolas Chicoff, a Pole. He asked to be admitted into the Society as a Lay-brother, and lived three years most contentedly in that condition. But his talents and industry being discovered, he was put to his studies. He made such progress in them that he afterwards taught theology with eminent success. He attacked the Socinians with such zeal, that he obtained from the State a proclamation, by which they were banished from the kingdom under penalty of death.

MARCH 28.

1. At Cambray in France, in the year 1606, Father Alexander Huntley, a Scotchman. He was such an exact observer of the rules, that he might be called the living picture of a Jesuit. His knowledge of Greek and Latin literature was very profound, owing to the wonderful retentiveness of his memory. He so won the hearts of the soldiers as Army Chaplain, that, when they saw him coming, they awaited his approach upon their knees. In the space of a few months he is said to have reconciled to the Church two thousand heretics.

2. In Peru, Father Andrew Ortiz Orunnius, a native of Biscay, finished his glorious and apostolical career. He entered on the mission at the house of Santa Cruz della Sierra, and for thirty-nine years preached Christianity to the idolatrous savages with indefatigable labour and burning zeal. He was often exposed to the danger of death with his companions, but was preserved by the special protection of God. The savages looked upon him as a superior being; and he humanized the ferocious Caribbee tribes, who before were cannibals. He cured the sick both living and after death; and gained numbers of souls both among Christians and Infidels. He died at San Francisco d' Alfaro of very grief, when he saw the many obstacles put in the way of the conversion of the Indians for whom he had laboured so much and suffered so long : he was then in the sixty-sixth year of his age, and his forty-third in the Society. When laid out with the crucifix in his hands, Father Orunnius is said to have put it to his mouth to kiss it. His body was found after a considerable lapse of time not only incorrupt, but emitting a fragrant odour.

3. At Majorca, in the year 1583, Father Julius Cussola, a Spaniard. Continually intent upon the mortification of his body, he undertook especially to curb and afflict his appetite. At dinner he deprived himself of the choicer meats, and at supper scarce took anything. He went many days without drinking even so much as a drop of water. He loved poverty dearly, and, with a singular constancy, would never receive new clothes or new shoes.

March 29.

1. At Genoa in Italy, in the year 1620, Father Bernardine Zanoni, so careful of his words both in number and weight, that for the space of twenty years it is said he allowed no idle word to escape his lips. If the conversation turned on things of this world, he slept; if on heavenly or spiritual matters, he awoke. He introduced into Genoa the nuns of the blue habit, otherwise called Religious of the Annunciation; and he gave them rules which were commended and approved of by the Archbishop and the Pope.

2. In Peru, in the year 1654, Father John de Villalobos, a man remarkable for his innocence, and for an invincible patience during twenty-four years, in which he was a constant sufferer from rheumatism and paralysis. He never tasted wine, and made an offering to our Lord of all that was pleasing to the palate. He was gifted with powers of foreseeing future things and knowing distant occurrences, as was proved on more than one occasion. He was so exact in his observance of the rules, that he was called the "Pillar of Discipline." His confessor declared that he had preserved his baptismal innocence unto death.

3. At Ripoll in Spain, Gabriel Vayle, a Spanish Scholastic, endowed with many virtues, but especially devout to the Blessed Virgin. He received a great reward for his affectionate piety towards her; for when on a journey he had fallen ill, and was at the point of death, the Queen of Angels came to visit him attended by a bright company of the citizens of Heaven, and summoned her devout servant to his home of eternal happiness.

March 30.

1. In Germany on the Rhine, in the year 1622, died Father John Sands, a Belgian, shot by heretics out of hatred for the true faith and the Society of Jesus. He was remarkable for his love of prayer, zeal for souls, and desire of suffering.

2. At Valenciennes, in the year 1619, Father Henry Sommal, a Belgian, beloved by St. Ignatius himself, who received him into the Society, for his candour, affability, and desire of perfection. He was sent to Loretto to teach Greek, then to Germany to complete his studies, and afterwards into Belguim

to preach. His sermons there worked many conversions. He was the first Superior of the residence of Dinant; afterwards he was appointed Rector of the College of Douay. He filled this post according to the model given him by St. Ignatius with whom he had lived at Rome. He came to recreation prepared with three points of matter for religious conversation. In extreme old age he followed every detail of common life; he loved poverty as his mother, and at his death nothing was found in his room but his beads reliquary, and breviary. We are indebted to him for the compilation of the works of à Kempis, the *Soliliquies* and *Manuel* of St. Augustine, the *Garden of the Soul* of Albertus Magnus, and other works. Rich in merit and full of days Father Sommal died at the age of eighty-five.

3. At Cown in Lithuania, in the year 1652, the Venerable Father Nicholas Lancisius, born of honourable Polish parentage. Abjuring the errors of Calvin, he entered the Society at the age of seventeen, and converted to the faith his father, who was at that time more than sixty years old. As a Novice he made such progress in the perfection which the Institute requires, and as a student and master displayed such profound erudition, and the gift of guiding souls in so eminent a degree, that shortly after his studies, although so young, he was appointed by Father Claudius Acquaviva, Spiritual Father of the Roman College. He was afterwards Provincial and Rector in Bohemia and Poland, and was regarded everywhere with the highest esteem and veneration. He was never known to fail in any point of religious observance, nor had he ever a thought against the orders of Superiors. His union with God was continual, his prayer lasted twelve hours each day. He gave himself but four hours sleep upon a narrow board, and five times each day took the discipline. God made known his sanctity by extraordinary graces both before and after his death by miraculous cures, by knowledge of the future and of the secrets of hearts, by visions, and by ecstasies, in one of which during Mass he is said to have seen his name written in the Book of Life. After a painful malady of six months borne with invincible patience, Fr. Lancisius passed to a better life amid the songs of Angels, which were heard by the bystanders. When he died he was seventy-eight years old.

MARCH 31.

1. In a Chinese prison at Canton, in the year 1606, died Brother

March 31.

Francis Minore Martinez, a Chinese Scholastic. He was preparing with the neophytes of that city for the offices of Holy Week, when he was betrayed by an apostate to the mandarins, and dragged by torchlight to the tribunal by a company of armed soldiers. He was first subjected to the frightful torture of having his feet crushed by blows from hammers; next he was scourged several times with such barbarity that his flesh fell away in pieces; and lastly he was left to die of thirst in prison, his jailors refusing him the least drop of water during the heat of his burning fever. Enfeebled by his sufferings, Brother Martinez continued to exhort his neophytes to perseverance, till at last he gave up his soul to God at the age of thirty-three years, fifteen of which he had spent in the Society of Jesus.

2. At Valencia in Spain, in the year 1621, Brother Francis Rodes, a Scholastic, a youth of great patience and tender piety. Once, as he was on a journey, he was overtaken by the darkness of night and so dreadful a storm that he lost all knowledge of the way. In his distress he called upon our holy Father St. Ignatius, who appeared to him resplendent with light, and guided him into the right road.

3. At the Professed House in Paris, in the year 1663, Father Julian Hayneuve, a native of Laval. He was always regarded as one of the most able masters of spiritual life. We may form this judgment from his writings which are filled with a holy unction, and from the testimony of all who had him for their superior in the different houses that he governed during more than thirty years. His example was no less efficacious than his words in kindling the fire of divine love in the hearts of men. He waged a continual war against his body, which he afflicted by fasting, vigils, and all kinds of macerations, in spite of a disease which caused him violent and almost constant pains, and which he kept concealed for nearly half his life. Father Hayneuve died as holily as he had lived, in the seventy-fourth year of his age and the fifty-fifth of his life in the Society of Jesus.

4. At Padua in Italy, in the year 1538, in March, but on what day of the month is uncertain, Father Diego Hozez, one of the first Fathers of the Society, was summoned to his reward in Heaven. He was creating much excitement in the city by his sermons, and was put in prison by the Vicar General under suspicion of heresy, but he was soon honourably released. Father Hozez was the first Father of the Society of Jesus that was called away to Heaven. St. Ignatius saw his soul, radiant with light, carried by Angels into Paradise.

APRIL.

April 1.

1. In the year 1639, Father Gaspar Ozonio and Father Anthony Ripari were cruelly put to death by the Chacese in Paraguay. They appeared after death, according to the testimony of the barbarians themselves, clothed in white vestments, surrounded with light, and exhorting the natives to embrace the faith of Christ.

2. At Antwerp, in the year 1598, Father Francis Vandenbergen. The hope of martyrdom amongst the Indians led him into the Society, but when he found himself disappointed in this hope, he laboured the more earnestly and frequently to conquer himself, and all the weaknesses of his nature, and he called these victories "Small martyrdoms." He was particularly devout to the Blessed Virgin and St. Joseph, and was frequently heard to say that he had never asked anything from St. Joseph which was not granted to him. Within the College he was styled an Angel, out of it, an Apostle. They are names worthy of our highest ambition. When at home he was remarkable amongst his Religious Brethren for modesty, silence, composedness of manner, and strict observance of rules: when on missionary work his boundless zeal for souls and the glory of God was everywhere manifested both by his words and his example.

3. At Cracow, in the year 1612, Father Justin Raby. Born of Protestant parents he was sent by them in his early years to several heretical schools, with the hope that he might eventually become a pillar of their Church. But God designed otherwise, and whilst the youth was attending one of Father Maldonatus' lectures at Paris on controverted points of faith, he was so moved by divine grace, that he not only became a Catholic, but sought and obtained admittance into the Society. He excelled as a linguist, and preached with great fruit in various languages. He was selected by Sigismond III. as his preacher and confessor. At the close of his life his infirmities did not allow him to say Mass, but daily Communion prepared him for the eternal banquet of the Lord.

April 2.

1. At Lima, in the year 1626, Father Diego Martinez, a celebrated missioner. Our Blessed Lord himself from the Crucifix had commended to him, in clearly uttered words, the Indian mission, and he distinguished himself by promoting and extending it in the midst of many and severe toils. He learned the various languages of the tribes, traversed many districts, destroyed their idols, converted and baptized many. His gift of prayer was wonderful, he devoted whole nights to it with the exception of three hours given to sleep. The Blessed Virgin, the Angels and Saints often appeared to him, and he was several times found in an ecstacy, raised above the earth and surrounded by light. He restored an idolatrous Indian to life, and then baptizing him, prepared him for Heaven which death opened to him four hours afterwards.

2. At the village of St. Mary near Oleron in Bearn, in the year 1620, Father John Bordese, a native of Bourdeaux. He successfully taught rhetoric and philosophy for many years; but he was still more remarkable for his virtues than for his distinguished talents. It was at his instigation that the mission of Canada was begun in the time of Henry IV. King of France. He ardently desired to devote his labours and life to the conversion of that country, but God destined him to battle with heresy in his own. For ten years he endured the severest hardships in Charente and the lower Pyrenees. He was so formidable an enemy to all heretics, that they avoided all communication with him. But his zeal was not to be foiled thus. He changed the dress usually worn by members of the Society for another, that he might the more easily obtain access to them. He succeeded in this manner in bringing back many to the faith of Christ. He spared not himself night or day, and was indefatigable in attending on the sick, he was often to be seen carrying them himself to the hospital, and while carefully healing the wounds of their souls, did not neglect the maladies of their bodies. He died full of merit, aged sixty-one years, of which he spent forty-two in the Society.

3. At Posna in Poland, in the year 1662, Father Gaspar Druzbicki. He was ranked amongst the first men of the Polish Province, for his Apostolic spirit in active life, for his wisdom as a writer, and for his

wonderful prudence as a Superior. By cultivating the tenderest devotion to our Blessed Lady he was endowed with the gift of prophecy, and with the spirit of highest prayer, and he was justly venerated by the public as a man of exalted sanctity.

APRIL 3.

1. In the Novitiate at Rome, in the year 1580, Father Jerome Nadal. He was a student at the University of Paris when St. Ignatius arrived there, and though the Saint as well as Fathers Laynez and Father Le Févre were anxious to have him as an associate with them in their pious designs, he resisted all their overtures. The moment of grace had not yet come. Years after this he was so touched by the perusal of the letters which St. Francis Xavier sent from India, and the wonderful harvest of souls to be reaped in the East, that he resolved to become a member of the Society. He was received at Rome, and on the very day of his admission was sent by Saint Ignatius to assist the cook and gardener. In these occupations he received abundant consolations from Heaven; his health was manifestly benefited, and the symptoms of weakness and ill health to which he was previously subject entirely disappeared. Sent by the Saint to Messina, he there established a College, the first of the Society in Sicily, and after gaining for himself by his labours and charities the title of "Father of the Poor," he sailed for Africa, where he devoted himself to the care of the Christians. St. Ignatius had such confidence in his prudence and piety, that he commissioned him to publish in Sicily and Portugal the Constitutions he had just completed. Sending him to Spain with the title of Commissary, he empowered him to make any regulations or reforms he might deem advisable. He travelled and laboured much for the interests of the Church and of the Society, and he was appointed Assistant of France and Germany by the first General Congregation of the Order. The Sovereign Pontiff employed him on many important embassies, and Father Laynez nominated him Visitor General of the whole Society. After the third General Congregation, of which, as well as of the first two, he was a member, his enfeebled constitution required rest and repose. Retiring to the Noviceship at St. Andrea, he set the Novices an example of all religious virtues, and died there at the age of seventy-two, having spent thirty-five years in the Society.

2. At Antwerp, in the year 1643, Father John Tollenaire. He was

remarkable for his charity to the poor. The words, *Ad majorem Dei gloriam*, and *In nomine Domini*, were mottoes which his lofty mind and undaunted spirit always aimed at reducing to practice. On his death-bed he asked his soul, "Where shall we be to-day?" and answering, "In the bosom of JESUS and Mary," he expired. He was the author of the *Imago Primi Sæculi*.

3. At Vienna, in the year 1654, Brother John Baptist Lechner, a Laybrother. He died a martyr of charity during a plague that raged in the city. He was much admired for his spirit of religious poverty and obedience. Before his entrance into the Society he was a soldier, but when once enlisted under the banner of Christ he vowed perpetual service to the Mother of God.

APRIL 4.

1. In the year 1626, Father Charles Regi, a native of Amiens. His early years were marked by innocence and piety. Entering the ecclesiastical state, his virtues procured his promotion to the dignity of Archdeacon of his Diocese. He filled the duties of this office with so great an industry that he was consoled by the revival of many public devotions. His Bishop, appreciating his virtue and zeal, appointed him Superior of the Seminary at Amiens, where, with a view of perpetuating the good already begun, Father Charles exercised his influence in introducing the Society into Amiens. Soon after this he himself was called to join the Order; and, though somewhat advanced in years, was admitted, because of his virtues. He was a model of humility, obedience, and poverty. In his missionary labours he treated himself with such extreme severity, that the Superior, out of regard to his health, assigned him a companion whom he was implicitly to obey in everything regarding it. His charity preferred the poor and ill instructed as his portion in the confessional, and his patience with them was most edifyingly unalterable. He was never heard to utter an unkind word of any one; on the contrary, whenever he spoke of others he always found something to praise. As he lived, so he died, in the odour of sanctity, having spent thirteen years as a Religious of the Society of Jesus.

2. At Alcala, in the year 1586, Father John Ramirez, one of the

most eminent preachers of his time. By one of his apostolical discourses he induced twenty-two out of thirty "sinners in the city" to reform their lives and make a vow of chastity. During a Lenten course of sermons which he gave at Salamanca, two hundred young men of learning and talent (Francis Suarez was one of the number) left the world to enter Religion. On one occasion when he was in doubt and perplexity he knelt before a statue of our Lady and asked her advice; the statue inclined its head as if giving an affirmative answer; but as the Father still had some doubt, he heard a voice saying to him distinctly, "Yes, Father John, you must do it." When he was once praying earnestly for the soul of a noble lady who had just died, she appeared to him all in flames, and said that she was condemned to eternal torments for confessions that were sacrilegious through shame.

3. At Lisbon, in the year 1552, Father Gonsalez de Medeiros. Hearing a sermon in which the preacher gave the words, "Bring not to the King's table live birds, but such as are dead and plucked of their feathers," he resolved to leave all he had, and, dying to himself and the world, to prepare for the heavenly banquet. He spent much time in prayer, generally three hours in the morning and three in the evening. When he was once in an anguish of doubt with regard to his salvation, an Angel appeared to him and said, "Have confidence, you will be saved."

APRIL 5.

1. At Bourges in France, in the year 1635, Father Louis Lallemant. After filling the chairs of philosophy, mathematics, and moral and scholastic theology, he was made Rector, Master of Novices, and then Instructor of the Fathers in their third year's probation. He possessed a special talent for the government and direction of others, and the Religious whom he formed were always remarkable for their interior spirit and love of recollection. His grand lesson was purity of heart, as the shortest and safest way to union with God; he called it the test of our advancement in perfection. He acknowledged that Almighty God had conferred upon him a special talent for the direction of members of the Society, and had revealed to him His designs about them, as also the ways by which they were to secure the virtues to which they were called. The degree

he said, destined for each of us, was so exalted, and the graces in reserve so abundant, that if we only knew them, we should imagine the sanctity of St. Ignatius and St. Francis Xavier was going to be renewed in each individual member of the Society. For three years he asked for the mission of Canada, but his zeal had to content itself with preparing others for that apostolic field of labour. He had a tender love for the sacred person of our Blessed Lord, and for those who were the most intimately connected with His first appearance on earth, the Blessed Virgin, St. Joseph, and the Angels. The Blessed Virgin once appeared to him in a vision, called him her son, assured him of her love for him, and bade him always be devoted to the Sacred Humanity of her Divine Son, which was so much forgotten by mankind. The holy man asked her for two favours: first, that he might always remember her; and second, that he might never be separated from the adorable Humanity of our Blessed Lord. He died at the age of forty-seven; and, for the last eight years of his life, faithfully observed a vow he had been allowed to make, always to do what was most perfect.

2. At Coimbra, in the year 1599, Father George Tavora. So great was his compassion for the afflicted, and so active his charity, that to relieve the distress of others might have been thought the one sole object of his life. He carried the sick to the hospitals himself, washed them, clothed them, dressed their wounds, prepared their beds, brought and cut the wood for their fires; in a word, omitted no service he could render them, so that he might more easily and effectually heal the wounds of their souls. He fell a victim of charity whilst attending those stricken with the plague; and the multitudes who attended him to the grave manifested by their tears the esteem in which he was held, and the loss the city had sustained.

April 6.

1. At Pont-a-Mousson, in the year 1604, Father Thomas Darbyshire. He was nephew of the celebrated Bishop Bonner, and was Archdeacon of Essex, but for conscience' sake made a sacrifice of all his preferments and expectations in the beginning of the reign of Queen Elizabeth. Whilst deliberating whether he should join the Carthusians or enter the Society,

a venerable figure appeared to him in his room, the door of which was shut, and said, "If you become a Carthusian you will certainly consult the welfare of your own soul, but where will your neighbour be?" Upon this his choice was at once made in favour of the Society, and he entered the Novitiate of St. Andrea at Rome in the forty-fifth year of his age. Through his zealous representations the Fathers of the Council of Trent passed their decree, "De non adeundis Hæreticorum Ecclesiis."—Dr. Oliver's *Collectanea*.

2. At Wilna, in the year 1668, Brother Michael Judkiewicz, a Laybrother. He was cook in the large College of his province twenty-six years, and performed the duties of his laborious office with so much care and regularity, that he was a living expression of that sentiment of St. Ignatius, "When I am serving those who are the servants of my Lord, I consider that I am serving the Lord of all." Hence it was, that when his Superiors, two years before his death, wished to relieve him of his toilsome office, he entreated with tears in his eyes to be permitted to continue his work for the "holy ones of God" to the last day of life. His petition was granted.

3. In the Isle of St. John, in the year 1672, Father Diego San Vitorez was martyred. Born of a distinguished family at Burgos, he entered the Society at Madrid; and, to the innocence of a life adorned with every virtue, he added an ardent zeal for the salvation of souls, and a longing desire of martyrdom. He was sent to the foreign missions, and chose for his field of toil the Marian Islands, which were then in a state of spiritual barrenness and desolation. After four years of unwearied labour, his zeal was rewarded with a harvest of thirty thousand souls, whom he converted to the faith. One of his nine companions and two lay Christians were put to death for their faith, and Father Diego was honoured soon after with a similar crown of martyrdom. Whilst explaining the catechism to the assembled crowd, with a Crucifix in his hand, he was attacked by an apostate, who cut him down with his sword, and then pierced his heart with a spear.

April 7.

1. At Redhill, near Worcester, in the year 1606, Father Edward

Oldcorne suffered death for the faith. He was endowed with extraordinary gifts both of nature and grace. As a student he excelled in philosophy and theology: his chief care however was to advance in the science of the Saints. Ordered by his Superiors to go and share the dangers of the English mission, he immediately set out, succeeded in landing safely, and forthwith placed himself at the disposal of Father Garnett, the Superior of the mission. His tact in management was so admirable, his manners so amiable, and his success both as a preacher and confessor so great, that he was sought for everywhere, and was employed in the most difficult enterprises. Father Gerard said of him, "He was so highly esteemed in all places, that he could scarcely ever stay three days together at home without being summoned away." Whilst at Henlip House, near Worcester, his usual place of residence, where diligent search had been made for him twice before, he was at last caught with Father Garnett, and committed to the Tower of London. Here he was tortured during a space of five hours every day for four or five days together, which, as Father Gerard, who could speak from experience, remarks, "is a greater extremity than one would easily believe, that had not tried it." Remanded to Worcester gaol, he was led forth for execution to Redhill, and there gave his life for the faith of his Divine Master. His head and the four quarters of his body were placed on poles in the city of Worcester; his heart and bowels were cast into the fire.

2. At Rome, in the year 1760, Father Alexander Lesley, a native of Scotland, and a member of the noble family of Pitcaple. After teaching humanities for four years, and philosophy for the same period, he was sent to labour for souls in his own country, and share in the hardships of that persecuted mission. It is recorded of our Fathers in Scotland at this time, especially of those in the Highlands, that "they lived a very hard life; straw or heath served them for bedding; their drink was milk and water; wine or beer seldom passed their lips; their bread was made of barley." After the battle of Culloden the penal laws were carried out with increased fierceness, and one of the few Fathers of the Society then in Scotland was taken prisoner whilst saying Mass, and conveyed to Edinburgh in his sacerdotal vestments. Father Lesley, with others, being driven from his country by the force of persecution, repaired to Rome, and there devoted himself for the rest of his life to prayer and study. Besides the learned

works which he edited, he had a principal hand in compiling those treatises which gave so much celebrity to the name of Father Azevedo.—Dr. Oliver.

APRIL 8.

1. In Ireland, in the year 1643, Father Henry Cavell, a learned scholar, and a zealous labourer for the salvation of souls. He was a missioner in his native country at a time when it presented a scene of general disorder and bloodshed between the Catholics and the Puritans— the Catholics fighting for freedom of conscience, for their legitimate King, and for their country. It was not as to a place of quiet that the missioner had to go when sent to Ireland in those days. The zeal indeed of one Father when speaking of it, made him say in the fulness of his heart, and from his thirst after sufferings, that he thought himself honoured, though unworthy of the honour, in being named amongst the labourers in the holy and happy mission of Ireland. The wisdom of the prudent Superior when speaking of men destined for that mission, prescribed that none should be sent over to it but "men that were ripe and sedate, conversant with the Institute of the Society, interior, solid, and mortified, for such are truly required." Father Cavell was apprehended in Dublin by the pursuivants, dragged from his bed, whereon he was lying sick of the palsy, severely scourged, and then put on board a vessel with nineteen other Priests and Religious, and shipped off to Rochelle. The Rector of our College there honoured him as a sufferer for the faith, paid him every charitable attention, and gradually restored him to better health. As soon as he was able, the zealous Father hastened back to the scene of his previous labours in Ireland; but, within a few days after his return, he resigned his soul into the hands of God, a victim of charity for the salvation of his neighbour.—Dr. Oliver's *Collect.*

2. At Lisbon, in the year 1589, Father Leo Henriquez. He was small of stature, but great of soul. His obedience, his humility, and other eminent virtues, made him terrible to the devils, but most acceptable in the sight of God and man. What has been recorded of St. Francis Xavier and some other Saints, is said of him, that he was endowed with the gift of being in two places at one and the same time, assisting and consoling those in distress at a distance, without being absent from his own room.

Once at a time whilst he was engaged in prayer before the Blessed Sacrament, to avert some public calamity, a voice was heard from the Tabernacle, saying, "No, no! by no means. Leave me, leave me; for I will chastise, I will chastise."

APRIL 9.

1. At Valladolid, in the year 1615, Father William Weston. He entered the Society at Rome, and in due time his prudence, piety, engaging manners, and generous zeal, induced his Superiors to send him to the English mission. He arrived in 1584, and succeeded, as Superior, Father Jasper Heywood, who had been committed prisoner to the Tower of London. He was a true lover of holy poverty, and disliked to wear anything new, asserting that God would be more easily moved to recognize him as His own when dressed in poor, worn-out clothes. He always gave an hour to thanksgiving and prayer after Mass, and then it was that he more particularly presented his petitions. As he was once so engaged in prison, a ray of light, slender as a thread, seemed to descend from above, and along with it were the words, "You depend upon My providence by a thread such as this; I am with you, and will not desert you." The fruits of his indefatigable labours were most abundant, but he had much to suffer from the ingratitude and malice of false friends. For seventeen years he was prisoner for Christ, and, through the rigour of his confinement, almost lost his sight. He was denied the crown of martyrdom, which he so eagerly desired, and at one time daily expected; but being discharged from prison on the accession of James I. proceeded to Rome, and thence to Spain, where he died. His last words were from the Royal Psalmist, "I rejoiced at the things that were said to me; we shall go into the house of the Lord." The skull of Father Weston was for many years respectfully kept at Watten: it is now at the Noviceship in England.

2. At Tsian-tsi, in China, in the year 1640, Father Alphonus Vagnoni, a Piedmontese, one of the first missioners in that Empire. Having long had a desire for foreign missions, and petitioned for them nineteen years, he was sent in the year 1603 to India, where he exercised his zeal for two years, and then proceeded to China. The work of his apostolate began at Nankin, in the study of the language, which he so effectually

mastered that he wrote many books of religious instruction for the benefit of the natives. The practice of exposing children to die in the public thoroughfares moved his tenderest compassion. He had "Refuges" erected to which they were taken, baptized, and so secured to JESUS CHRIST. He had the consolation and the glory of suffering persecution for his faith. Being cast into prison, and subjected to every species of hard treatment, his health gave way. When liberated, as he was soon after, his solicitude for the recovery of his health arose only from his anxious wish to resume his labours on the misssion. When he did resume them, he was blessed with an abundant harvest. At the time of his death he left eight thousand Christians in Tsian-tsi, where he had found only twenty-five; and a hundred and two separate congregations scattered over the country where there was not one before. He died at the age of seventy-four, surrounded by his sorrowing Christians, who wept for him as for a father.

APRIL 10.

1. At Naples, in the year 1595, Father Emeric de Bonis. He was admitted by St. Ignatius, and by him formed to the virtues of an Apostle. When requested by the Saint to go and admonish a certain lady of her too great freedom of manner when speaking to Fathers of the Society, he felt great repugnance to deliver such a message to a lady, and begged one of the Community to go and do it for him. The Saint got to hear of this afterwards, and, though admiring him for his modest reserve, which deterred him from giving the message himself, he would not allow such an evasion of his Superior's request to pass without reproof or penance. The penance was, that Father de Bonis had to stand in the Refectory once a day for the term of six months, and say aloud before the assembled Community, "*I will*, or *I will not*, are words that are not to be heard in this house." He taught humanities for seven years, and afterwards for more than thirty years devoted his time and talents to the ministry of preaching. One Lent he was ordered to preach to the inhabitants of La Pouille, but they, being quite satisfied with their ordinary preacher, ventured to tell him candidly that he had better have remained at home, as they did not require his services. Father Emeric was not disturbed

at this, nor did he utter a word of complaint. Shortly afterwards he was saying Mass in a church in the town, and the people who assisted at it were so moved by his devout, recollected manner, and his angelic appearance, that they at once looked upon him not merely as a Father sent to them from Rome, but as a messenger sent from Heaven. They eagerly accepted his services; the mission was given, and resulted in a harvest of souls. As Rector of several Colleges he zealously maintained that vigour of religious discipline, which under St. Ignatius he had learned to be so essential to the purposes of the Society.

2. In Peru, the year unknown, Father Diego Strunica. He renounced his family estates and honours to embrace the humility and poverty of the Society, and the arduous labours of the foreign missions. He was for a considerable time engaged in civilizing and instructing the poor slaves of Peru; and then his Superiors, edified by his virtue, and admiring his great prudence, entrusted to him the care of the Novices in Lima. He came to Europe again in quest of fresh recruits for his adopted country, and was returning with a numerous supply when his ship was chased by the English pirates. There was no help for it but to have recourse to God. Father Diego and his companions prayed earnestly that they might not fall into the hands of the heretics. Their prayer was heard. A thick heavy cloud suddenly intervened between the two ships, and remained long enough to enable the Fathers to escape from the corsair.

April 11.

1. At Lima, in the year 1632, Father Ruez de Montaya, a Portuguese. He was a true Apostle in Paraguay, where he converted numberless idolaters to the faith, and established many missions. He travelled thousands of miles on foot, undergoing excessive labour, fatigue, and violent persecutions. He spent four hours a day in prayer, and always slept upon the bare ground. He was rewarded with extraordinary graces. By prayer and mortification he obtained a request he had earnestly made to the seraphic Mother of God, that she would procure for him an ardent love of God and of herself. Our Blessed Lord once pressed him to the wound in His side, and his soul was inundated with a torrent of delights. After death he was carried to the grave by the Viceroy and his Court. A

Religious of the Order of Mercy for the redemption of Captives saw his glorious soul enter Heaven.

2. At Lima, in the year 1673, Father Francis de Castillo, a Portuguese. He was renowned for his virtue, and justly regarded as an Apostle in his native country. When first coming to the use of reason he left his home, in order to satisfy a desire of a closer union with God in the concealment and solitude of a neighbouring forest. He was soon brought home again; but the longing to devote himself to God increased as he grew up, and eventually he gained admission into the Society. From the first he was a model of regularity, and won the love and esteem of every one. His affection for holy poverty made him contrive to go without the convenience of a private room for many years of his Religious life. His fasts were frequent, and sometimes he passed four, and even five days together without food. He slept little, and macerated his flesh by the constant use of the discipline, hairshirts, and chains. In his zeal for God's glory he endured labours and hardships almost incredible, especially whilst in Peru. For twenty years he devoted himself to the instruction of the negroes, and was a victim to their rudeness and malice. Many were the conversions he wrought, many the poor sinners he reclaimed, and many the candidates for perfection, whom he guided into Religious life. He founded and endowed a "Refuge" for penitent females. Father de Castillo was favoured by a share of those astonishing gifts with which God loves to distinguish eminent sanctity. He was often found in ecstasies, raised above the ground, and enveloped in light. He foretold future events, cured diseases that baffled all human skill, and more than once was present in different places at the same time. His Angel Guardian, St. Joseph, the Blessed Virgin, and our Lord, often comforted him by their visible presence. The process of his Beatification is filled with the accounts of similar wonders. He died on the day he had foretold, and his tomb was long famous for miracles. Seven months after death his body was found incorrupt, and a nail being removed from a finger, blood flowed freely from it.

APRIL 12.

1. In Abyssinia, in the year 1640, Fathers Louis Caldeira and Bruno de Santa Croce suffered martyrdom. The former a Portuguese, the latter

an Italian. During the reign of the perfidious Facilada, they continued their energetic efforts to console and preserve from eternal ruin the natives of their adopted country. So violent and unrelenting was the storm of persecution raised against them, that they were obliged to conceal themselves in caves, and wander amongst the mountains. Being betrayed at last, they were captured, loaded with chains, and led amidst the jeers and insults of the populace to Magoga. They were cast into prison, kept there five days, and then strangled. To their last hour they continued to announce and defend the faith, for which they were sacrificing their lives. Some years before his death, Father Bruno was once praying to our Blessed Lady to obtain for him a share of her fortitude and constancy in sufferings, and before he ended his prayer she appeared to him, and put a ring on his finger as a pledge of her help and protection.

2. In Peru, in the year 1605, Father Peter D'Agnasco, a Spaniard. In his youth the Blessed Virgin with her Divine Infant appeared to him during a severe illness, and bade him enter the Society of her Son. He attained a high degree of perfection in profiting by the example of others, taking for his own practice the particular virtues in which they excelled. He catechized, heard confessions, and preached in nine different languages, composed various works, vocabularies, grammars, catechisms, and prayer-books, for the use of the Indians; and thus was instrumental in saving many tribes of them, who otherwise might have been lost in infidelity. His death was preceded by a long and painful sickness, which he endured with invincible patience.

April 13.

1. In Ireland, in the year 1647, Father James Everard. For the long period of forty years he laboured with apostolic zeal in his native country, and chiefly at Cashel. As a preacher, he ranked in the first class; and, though of a delicate constitution, and generally unwell, was ever prompt and eager to fulfil the duties of his ministry. Severe to himself, he was all condescension and charity to his neighbours. It was during his missionary career that a petition came to him and his fellow-labourers, signed by twenty-five thousand of his countrymen, who by the persecution and injustice of the times had been forced to quit their own country,

and settle, some of them in the Isle of St. Kitts, others in the neighbouring isles. The prayer of the petition was, that two Jesuit Fathers might be sent to them, to administer the consolations of religion in their banishment, their destitution, and affliction. It was also during Father Everard's time that the violence of Cromwellian persecution was so severely felt by our Priests in Ireland, that one of them, Father Christopher Netterville, was obliged for more than a year to conceal himself in his own father's sepulchre, *instar primi Athanasii, anno integro et amplius in sepulchro paterno delituit.*—Dr. Oliver.

2. In Spain, in the year 1657, Father Francis de Saredo. For his eloquence and zeal he was considered one of the first preachers of his day. At his funeral obsequies the sermon was preached by a learned Religious of St. Augustine, one of his intimate friends during life. A few days later, as this Religious was sitting in his cell, Father Francis appeared to him dressed in the usual habit of the Society, with an extraordinary amenity of countenance, and beaming with celestial joy and majesty. Requesting the good Religious not to be disturbed at his presence, and taking a chair and sitting near him, like one friend with another, he said, "I have come, by the holy will of God, to thank you for the panegyric you delivered at my funeral, which was honoured by the presence of my Angel Guardian." Then he went on to say that the Society of Jesus was beloved of God, and that the duties which it undertakes are most pleasing to Him. Go to the Father Rector of the College, and tell him in my name to beware of allowing his preachers to spend their time in culling, and then scattering, flowers and ornaments of speech; rather let them try to move the minds and hearts of men by solid arguments and persuasive appeals. I have been detained in Purgatory several days to expiate the vanity of attending too much to elegance of diction in my sermons. So saying, he disappeared.

April 14.

1. At Seville, in the year 1587, Father Roderic Alvarez, an African. On the night of his death his soul was seen by more than one taken up into Heaven by Angels and the Fathers of the Society. Amongst his high virtues there was one that was more conspicuous than the rest,

his love of God and of the Blessed Virgin. Before he entered the Society, and when he was still in doubt as to his state of life, he heard our Lord saying, "Follow Me"; and being at a loss to know how and in what way he was to follow Him, the Blessed Virgin came to his relief, saying, he would be right if he entered the Society of her Divine Son.

2. At Coimbra, in the year 1615, Father Sebastian Barradas. In his youth the Blessed Virgin directed him to the Society. He was a powerful preacher, and spoke so forcibly of the inestimable value of the immortal soul, and the folly of risking its eternal happiness upon things of this world, which, whether we will or not, must so soon pass away, that in the course of one year more than sixty of his hearers left the world to embrace a Religious life. His love for holy poverty was remarkably edyfying. On his death-bed his Superior enjoined him to say a few words of edification to his Religious Brethren, who had assembled to receive his blessing. Turning towards them he said, "Be ye humbled under the almighty hand of God, that He may exalt you in the day of visitation"; adding, that he could do no better than advise them to practise humility, the virtue of our Lord.

3. At Lima, in the year 1601, Father Stephen Avila. He held a high position in the Holy Office, and was appointed by his Bishop, Inquisitor in Ordinary. Endowed with natural qualities of the highest order, he was no less distinguished by the supernatural gifts of grace. During his last illness his humility was overwhelmed with confusion by the honours and marked attentions which he received from the Archbishop, the Bishops, and Viceroy. With his eyes intently fixed on the Crucifix, he gave up his soul to God his Creator, in the fifty-second year of his age, and the thirtieth in the Society.

April 15.

1. At Rome, in the year 1610, Father Robert Persons. Of him it has been said, that he was the most active and indefatigable of all the leaders of the English Catholics during the reign of Queen Elizabeth; that he was honoured by the deepest hatred of the enemies of his religion, and looked upon by them as their most dangerous adversary. In the Holy City, in Spain, in France and in Belgium, he was considered by those

in authority, as the man of the greatest zeal, the greatest reach of mind, and the highest capacity for serving the cause of religion. After a brief but active missionary career in his own country, he retired to the Continent to confer with Dr. Allen (afterwards Cardinal) and others as to the best means of securing a continuous supply of Missionary Priests for England. The more effectually to carry out the plan approved of by them, he made long and frequent journies in his negotiations to found and organize establishments for English students at Valladolid, St. Lucar, Seville, Lisbon, and St. Omers; exerted his disinterested zeal and powerful support in favour of the College for the Secular Clergy at Douay and Rome; wrote many works for the instruction, reformation, and conversion of souls; governed the English College at Rome, and fulfilled the duties of Prefect of the English Mission, with moderation, sound discretion, condescension, and charity. Well might Cardinal Allen say of him, "The industry, prudence, and zeal, as exhibited in the writings and actions of that good man, are altogether incredible." He had not the happiness, like his companion on the mission, Father Campion, of shedding his blood for the faith; but he had the honour of carrying a two-fold cross to the end of his life; for besides the weight of odium from his heretical countrymen, he had to sustain censure and abuse from many of the English Catholics themselves. From his dying bed he dictated letters to his Brethren of the Society in England, and to the Archpriest, breathing seraphic peace and charity; and crowned a life of usefulness by a death precious in the sight of God.—Dr. Oliver's *Collectanea*.

2. At Granada, in the year 1567, Father Martin Gomez. During his last illness he was asked by his Superior when he expected to die; "To-morrow," he answered, "after receiving Holy Viaticum, if Father Rector will give me leave." "God's will be done," answered the Rector, "I consent." And so it happened; for Father Martin calmly expired next morning about half an hour after receiving the Most Holy Viaticum.

APRIL 16.

1. At Paris, in the year 1620, in the seventy-seventh year of his age, and fiftieth of his Religious Profession, Father James Gordon, of the noble family of Huntly in Scotland. After filling the highest offices in

various colleges of the Society in France he was appointed Apostolic Nuncio for Ireland, and Prefect of the Scotch Mission. He had not the happiness he so much longed for, of shedding his blood for the faith; but his glowing zeal secured for him the honour of being the *Vinctus Christi* both in his native country and in England. Upon the death of his four elder brothers, the right to the title and estates of his father, the Earl of Huntly, devolved upon him, and though the wily statesmen then in power requested him to avail himself of his rights, they were determined that if he did so, it should be with the sacrifice of his faith. The terrible engine of excommunication was then in full force throughout Scotland. When once that cruel sentence was pronounced by the Kirk against a Catholic victim, he could neither inherit property, nor enter into a legal contract, nor claim a debt; and at the end of a year's absence from the parish conventicle, he was liable to be cited by the "preacher of the word," who alone was to decide upon the sufficiency of his reasons for such absence. Should the Catholic continue firm, the frightful sentence was fulminated; his property at once became confiscated to the Crown; his body cast into prison; and if released therefrom, (such was the envenomed hatred of the Scotch Puritans to the professors of the ancient faith,) they would neither break bread with him nor speak to him, but would shun him as if infected with pestilence. Father Gordon peremptorily refusing the proffered titles and honours, chose rather, as his biographer narrates, "to be an abject in the house of God, and in the most holy Society of Jesus, in which he lived and died, and under the yoke of Obedience to pass a long and voluntary martyrdom in banishment, than to have that contentment and estate of temporal greatness and felicity." His death was precious in the sight of God. His interment was conducted with unusual pomp and solemnity.—Dr. Oliver's *Collectanea*.

2. At Naples, in the year 1548, William Elphinston, a native of Scotland, and of royal descent. Quitting the world and all its prospects, he devoted himself to God, and entered the Novitiate at Naples. He had not been long there before he was seized with an illness which baffled all medical skill. During his sickness he was consoled by the visible presence of Angels, and after death was seen conducted into Heaven by the Blessed Virgin, for whom he had always entertained a most tender and filial devotion.

April 17.

1. The glorious triumph of Father Henry Walpole, who was martyred at York in the year 1595. He became a member of the Society in 1584, and entered the Novitiate at Rome. After finishing his studies, and being promoted to the Priesthood, he was obliged to leave Rome for the sake of his health. His Superiors directed him to France, then to Spain, where at Seville and Valladolid he was employed in offices of authority; they next deputed him to Flanders to solicit aid for the new Seminary at St. Omers. This commission being satisfactorily fulfilled, he at length obtained the favour he had often asked for, to be allowed to join the Fathers on the English mission. He landed at Flamborough Head, but had not been twenty-four hours on English ground before he was apprehended and carried prisoner to York, and thence transferred to the Tower of London, where he remained for a year. In this imprisonment he met with the greatest misery and poverty; was without bed, or sufficient clothing, though the cold in winter was most sharp and piercing; and besides all this, he suffered various tortures fourteen times during the year. "It is very well known," writes Father Garnett, "how cruel is any one of these tortures which are now in use; for it is a common thing to hang up people by the hands for six or seven consecutive hours, and by the means of certain irons, which bind and lacerate them, they shed much blood." So far from complaining, or asking for a remission of his hardships, the good Father was full of joy and thanksgiving, adding to his mortifications by sleeping on the ground and praying on his knees a great part of the night. "I know not yet," he said, "what they will do with me, but whatever shall happen, by the grace of God, it shall be welcome. I am much astonished that so vile a creature as I am should be so near as they tell me to the crown of martyrdom; but this I know for certain, that the Blood of my Most Blessed Saviour and Redeemer, and His most sweet love, is able to make me worthy of it. I beg your Reverence to join your holy prayers to my poor ones, that I may walk worthy of that holy name and profession to which I am called." Remanded to York, there to take his trial, he was sentenced to die as in cases of high treason. He was drawn to the place of execution, a short distance

from the city, on the same hurdle with a Secular Priest, Alexander Rawlins, who, being placed on the hurdle first, took the left side for himself, yielding the right side, or, as he said, the place of honour to his betters. To prevent as much as possible the two martyrs from having any pious communication with each other on their last short journey, the persecutors ordered them to lie down on the hurdle in opposite directions, the feet of one touching the head of the other. Having reached the gallows, Mr. Rawlins was commanded to mount the ladder first, and, as a refinement of cruelty, Father Walpole was compelled to stand by, and see his companion cut down from the gallows, dismembered, embowelled, and quartered. They hoped to terrify him by the sight of such butchery. Life, honours, preferments, were even then offered him, if he would only conform and acknowledge the Queen's supremacy; but the heroic martyr scorned the tempter's offer, and began aloud from the ladder, as from his pulpit, to repeat the Lord's Prayer and the Angelical Salutation, which so exasperated his executioners that they turned the ladder, quickly cut him down, and inflicting upon him the same cruel treatment which he had just witnessed in his reverend companion, secured for him the everlasting crown of martyrs.

April 18.

1. At Nangasachi, in Japan, in the year 1609, Father Soldi. While making a pilgrimage to Loretto he was so touched by the kindness of our Fathers there that he resolved to become a member of the Society. Having completed his studies at the Roman College, he was sent to establish a residence at Frascati; later, he was Minister in the Roman College, and afterwards Rector at Loretto; but his longing desire was to go on the Indian missions. He had this desire from his early years; had made it known to Father Laynez and to St. Francis Borgia, the latter of whom sent him to Japan to share in the labours of the Apostolic members of the Society, who were then reaping such a rich harvest of souls in that country. For a long time he had easy access to the Court of the Emperor; but a terrible persecution ensuing, the good of the faithful required him to withdraw for a time into comparative concealment. He had not the honour of martyrdom to which he aspired,

but he had the consolation of witnessing the heroism of his three Sainted Brethren, John Goto, Paul Miki, and James Kisai. The extremities of their ears were cut off by order of their tyrant persecutor, and the Christians collecting together these valued relics, took them with great respect to Father Soldi, who accepted them with tears of greatful joy. In the fulness of his heart he said, "The sufferings and life-blood of these martyrs are the first fruits of the Society in Japan, the first offerings of the faith, and the earnest of a future abundant harvest of souls." He continued his unremitting labours for his dear Japanese twelve years more; was beloved by all who knew him, and so esteemed by the Emperor, that he was specially exempted from a decree which banished the Missioners from Japan. He died at the age of seventy-nine, and had spent forty-two years on the Japanese mission.

2. In Germany, in the year 1630, Daniel Rosner, a Lay-brother. Born and brought up in heresy, he pertinaciously resisted all the arguments of his Catholic friends, who wished to bring him into the true fold. He had no difficulty in going with them to hear Mass, and he did so repeatedly, but without any faith in the Real Presence. On one occasion however he distinctly beheld our Blessed Lord in the Sacred Host as if suffering on the Cross. Forthwith he abandoned his heresy, entered the Society, and was remarkable ever after for a tender devotion to the Blessed Sacrament.

3. At Cadiz, in the year 1601, Father Peter Bernel. He was a lawyer of considerable celebrity; but resolving to quit the world and enter our Society, he begged his way to the Novitiate. His subsequent life in Religion tallied with such a beginning; it was marked by self-denial and austerities, and distinguished by frequent miracles.

APRIL 19.

1. At Pont-à-Mousson, in the year 1657, Father Louis Maignet. He was distinguished amongst his Brethren by an extraordinary spirit of humility and self-abnegation. He took the discipline every morning on rising, and continued this practice until at a very advanced age he was ordered by his Superiors to desist. He generally abounded with consolations in prayer, and was wont to prostrate himself on the floor,

and there remain till the goodness of God gave him what he called a spiritual alms. Whilst he was Provincial, he thought himself destitute of the qualities requisite to fulfil the duties of that important post, and attributed whatever success he had in it to the prudence and wisdom of his Consultors. For the last eight years of his life he joined the Laybrothers every night when they received the points of meditation from the Spiritual Father. In his last illness he bore his severe pains in silent patience, and with ready obedience took whatever the medical attendant prescribed. The night after his funeral he appeared with a sweet majestic countenance to the Father who had assisted him in his last moments, filling the room with a heavenly light, and inspiring him with a spiritual joy that lasted several days.

April 20.

1. At Luxemburg, in Germany, in the year 1636, died Father Nicholas Cusan, a German, a holy and zealous labourer on the missions at home and abroad. He prepared himself for his apostolic career by telling his fault in the refectory, serving in the kitchen, and taking severe disciplines. He journeyed on foot, occupied in prayer. Wherever he went he recommended the evening recital of the Rosary and the Litany of the Blessed Virgin Mary. He was very devout to the Holy Name of JESUS. When attacked by scruples he banished them by constant laborious occupation, and he recommended the same remedy to all similarly afflicted.

2. At Innspruck, in the Tyrol, in the year 1650, Father Andrew Bruner, a German. He was led to take up the cross and enter the Society by St. Andrew the Apostle, who appeared to him while he was yet hesitating what to do. He was greatly given to prayer for the suffering souls in Purgatory, and received from them many favours in return. He was cured by St. Ignatius of hernia, and by St. Aloysius of a long and painful head-ache.

3. At Messina, in Sicily, in the year 1601, Francis Cajetano, an Italian, a young man of noble condition and holy life while yet in the world, and called to the Society in an extraordinary manner. He was very humble and mortified, and attained to a great and continual

union with God. Flames were seen issuing from his mouth when he received Holy Communion. He died on Good Friday, as he had desired, and thus was united in death with Christ crucified, Whom he had carried in his heart during life. He was visited by the Blessed Virgin and by Angels on his death-bed. From these and other extraordinary circumstances, the Provincial of Sicily, in a letter to Father Claudius Acquaviva was led to express a hope that he would one day be numbered among the Beatified.

4. At Hermanstadt, in Transylvania, in the year 1690, Father Luke Kölick, a Moravian, chaplain of the army in the war against the Turks. He was zealous and indefatigable in the performance of his duties; and at the taking of Bude was among the first to enter the city to assist the dying, and to baptize the Turkish infants slaughtered by the infuriated assailants, some of whom he saved and brought alive to the camp. He was accounted a holy man even by the heretics; was buried with military honours, and was followed to the grave by the greater portion of the townspeople.

APRIL 21.

1. At Messina, in Sicily, in the year 1634, on the day he had foretold, died Father Benedict Moleto, an Italian. He kept a constant union with God during his continual occupations, and spent a great part of the night in prayer. He not only forgave, but induced his mother and whole family to forgive, the shedder of the blood of his brother. Once, when Superior, having nothing in the house to set on the table in the refectory, he ordered the signal to be given as usual for dinner, and an abundant supply was brought to the door.

2. In America, in the year 1624, John Baptist Spinosa, a Spanish Lay-brother, aged ninety. His pure soul was never sullied with the stain of mortal sin. He endured a long captivity amongst the Turks in his early life, but providentially escaped and regained his liberty. Sailing to Mexico, he there became a member of the Society.

3. At Brunsberg, in Prussia, in the year 1669, Father Andrew Stibigk, a Prussian. He spent the greatest part of his life in preaching as missioner in Livonia, Courland, and Prussia. The people flocked in

numbers to hear his long and fervent discourses, and he gained many souls to God He expired peacefully on Easter Day.

4. In the College of Bordeaux, in the year 1665, Father John Joseph Surin, a Frenchman. From his early infancy God inspired him with a hatred of sin, especially of impurity, and excited him to mortification of the senses, and a renunciation of all that is agreeable to nature. Called to the Society, he asked his father's permission to enter it, but as he was an only child it was at first refused. One day the child said, "Father, I am quite willing to obey you, but if I do, will you assure me of my salvation?" The father then consented, and the youth entered the Noviceship at the age of fifteen. At thirty he was made Socius to the Master of Novices, and by his vigilance and mortification attained to high sanctity. At the age of thirty-five he was sent by his Superiors to the Convent of Loudun to help some Nuns who were possessed by the devil. The arms he used, and by which he finally triumphed, were prayer, recollection, and mortification; but the trials which he had to endure were incredible. Out of compassion for the state of the Superioress he offered himself to suffer in her place. It was granted; and on the Feast of the Finding of the Holy Cross, his mind being full of the Passion of our Lord, and his heart burning with a desire of sharing in His sufferings, an invisible power stretched out his arms, removed him from his chair, and laid him on the ground. He then felt the abandonment of JESUS on the Cross, and a voice asked him if he were willing to share so terrible a privation for the good of that soul, as God desired. "Yes, my God; yes," was his reply. He then for years was persecuted in every manner by the devil. He was long unable to read, and for twenty years to write; he had scarcely the use of his hands, and for fifteen years was partially blind. He was forced to commit such external extravagancies that he was universally reputed insane. For twenty years he was tormented with temptations of impurity, and for seven or eight with thoughts of self-destruction. Sufferings poured upon him from all sides, from heaven, earth, and hell, from good and bad, from his Brethren and Superiors; nay, he seemed abandoned by God Himself; so that for many years he considered himself damned. Yet he afterwards declared that, notwithstanding all this, nothing in the world was so sweet as the service of God; and that he had not suffered anything that with the grace of God he was

not able to support. His heart had always burned with the desire of doing something for the glory of God. He dictated for the service of others his *Spiritual Catechism* during the time he could not write, and it was revealed to him that it should be published and do much good. He afterwards wrote his dialogues and other works. After his death he was the object of universal veneration, and whatever had belonged to him was sought for as a relic.

APRIL 22.

1. At Catania, in Sicily, in the year 1611, died Father Bernard Colnago, a Sicilian, a man of high and heroic virtue. He was called to the Society from his earliest years, but met with much opposition from his parents. Appealing to the command of JESUS CHRIST, he obtained their consent, and at the age of fifteen entered the Novitiate. He made great progress in virtue and learning; and having completed his studies, taught philosophy for ten years and theology for twelve with great distinction, and gained the reputation of rare genius and profound learning. In order that he might completely annihilate self-love and vainglory he obtained the consent of his superiors to conduct himself as a fool in the public places of Naples. God rewarded this heroic action with an abundance of heavenly graces and consolations. His zeal for souls was immense, and he was urged to it by an apparition of the Blessed Virgin, who placed her hand upon his heart and said, "Labour without ceasing for the salvation of sinners, and bring me souls. This is the service which is the dearest to me of all that can be paid me." He was also very devout to St. Agatha and St. Antony of Padua. He traversed Italy as an Apostle, working wonderful conversions by his preaching and penitential exterior. He was assisted by divine communications, revealing to him the secrets of hearts and future events, and had in a remarkable degree the gift of tears. His love of prayer was intense, and the Altar was his paradise; and when it sometimes seemed physically impossible for him to say Mass, by prayer to the Blessed Virgin he obtained his desire. Paul V. would have raised him to the Purple, but he succeeded in avoiding that honour. He worked many miracles, and brought back a dead child to life. Together with these gifts and graces, he suffered

much persecution even from the servants of God. He was accused of false doctrine, of being possessed by the devil; his sanctity was suspected and misunderstood by Superiors, and his austerity reproved. He had a tender love and confidence in the Blessed Virgin Mary, and was one of the first in the Society who defended her Immaculate Conception. The day of his death was revealed to him by her ten years before it occurred—it was on a Friday, as he desired, from his love of our Lord's Passion. After death he was seen by the side of St. Ignatius, who said of him, "This is truly a son of mine." He was universally reputed to have kept his baptismal innocence, and was usually styled the Angel of Catania.

2. At Xeres, in Spain, in the year 1615, Father Antony de Cardenas, a Spaniard, peacefully ended his life in the Society, which he had entered by divine command. In preaching he seemed to know the secrets of hearts, and to bend them at will. He often went down to the door with his cloak and companion, saying that he should be wanted for a sick call, and presently a messenger would come for him. He sometimes took with him his young Sodalists, and by means of them worked wonderful conversions.

3. At Reggio, in Italy, in the year 1651, Father Albert Ruffino, an Italian. He was the first Rector of the College of Reggio, which he and his two brothers founded, and which he governed with exemplary exactness. He passed many years in the Court of the Dukes of Este; but, as Cardinal d'Este affirmed, he was not in the least affected by the Courtly atmosphere. The evening before he died a holy death he made a visit to the miraculous picture of our Lady of Reggio, to make a farewell salutation and invoke her aid.

April 23.

1. At Burgos in Spain, in the year 1565, died Father Gaspar de Azevedo, a Spaniard. He entered the Society somewhat advanced in life, having taken degrees in many branches of learning. He was remarkable for his charity, love of mortification, and prayer. To this last he gave six hours a day upon his knees on the ground without support. He wore a hairshirt which covered his whole body, night and day, and slept upon the bare boards. He took daily a severe discipline,

fasted often upon bread and water, and always upon Fridays and Saturdays. The plague having broken out at Burgos, he devoted himself to the service of the sick, and was soon taken with it. His sickness did not prevent his holy practice of kneeling in prayer, and in this position, as he had often wish, he expired.

2. In Peru, in South America, in the year 1620, Father Gonsalvo Barnuevo, a Spaniard. He breathed his last in sentiments of lively joy and exultation, exclaiming to the Fathers who stood around his bed, "Oh, who would not dearly love our holy Institute! Oh, what a happiness to be in the Society; how great is the hundredfold, how certain the reward of eternal life to those who die in it!"

. 3At Seville, in Spain, in the year 1677, Father Ignatius de Fonseca, a Spaniard, of singular humility, self-abnegation, and knowledge and practice of spiritual things. He was endowed also by God with the gifts of healing and of prophecy.

April 24.

1. At Mantua, in Italy, in the year 1607, died Brother James Magni, a Scholastic Novice, remarkable for his ardent desire to serve and please God in the most perfect manner. To profound humility and exact obedience he added a great spirit of prayer. His union with God was so intimate and perpetual, that it was found necessary for his health's sake to employ him in many external occupations; but, like St. Aloysius, the greater the efforts he made to distract his mind, the more he found his heart carried towards its only treasure. His love for his brethren gave him a sensible joy when he met one of them, and he made it the occasion of saying a "Hail Mary" for the person whom he met. He was soon ripe for Heaven; and after eighteen months in the Noviceship he began to spit blood, and then slowly sinking, died at the age of seventeen, on the very day on which two years before he had entered the Society.

2. At Nancy, in Lorraine, in the year 1630, Father John Gueret, a Frenchman. His soul was purified like gold in the fire by extraordinary suffering; for one of his scholars having committed a horrible parricide, Father John was seized under the suspicion of being cognizant of

the crime, and condemned to to be put to the torture. He asked for a quarter of an hour to pray, and then endured the rack with such courage, and answered with so much prudence, that the judges themselves were in admiration at his fortitude, and declared his innocence. He afterwards confessed that he had been strengthened by the invocation and aid of the Blessed Virgin, so as to feel no pain, and the following day he walked twenty-four miles.

3. At Naples, in the year 1580, Father Gonzalez Melendios, a Spaniard. Though a good and holy religious man, he could not escape the charges of malicious calumny. Sent by the King and the Apostolic Nuncio into Andalusia, to examine into the conduct of some Priests and Religious, he so incurred their anger, that he was accused before the Inquisition. He was summoned to Rome to free himself from these imputations, but he died on his road at Naples an edifying death. Christ appeared to console him, in his great pains of soul and body, bleeding and covered with wounds, and said, "See how little your sufferings are compared with Mine."

4. At Lima, in Peru, in the year 1654, Emmanuel de Arteaga, a Spanish Lay-brother, remarkable for his great devotion to his Guardian Angel, from whom he received timely notice of a dangerous occasion of sin, which he avoided by flight.

April 25.

1. In Paraguay, in the year 1635, died Father Christopher de Mendora, a Spaniard, a glorious martyr, shot with arrows by the savages in hatred of the faith, then beaten with a club about the head; and when, notwithstanding, he continued to preach the Christian faith, his mouth was pounded with a mallet, and his teeth broken; his nose, ears, lips, and tongue were cut off, his breast opened, and his heart torn out. To gain this crown he fled secretly from a noble parental home to Paraguay, there to enter the Society, and share these honours of martyrdom so frequently granted to its children.

2. In Abyssinia, in the year 1635, Father Gaspar Paez and Father John Pereira, Portuguese, martyred for the faith by the schismatical and heretical Abyssinians, to whom they preached obedience to the Roman Catholic Church. Father Gaspar died pierced with their spears; and,

as those who slew him afterwards confessed, his blood, to their astonishment, did not run down upon the ground, but flowed upwards and vanished in the air. Father Pereira was stripped, and left for dead, but survived for six days in acute sufferings, with no consolation but his invincible patience. On the seventh day he went to join his companion in glory.

3. At Naples, in the year 1603, Father Gregory de Valentia, a Spaniard, a renowned theologian. He was honoured by his former scholar, Pope Clement VIII., with the title of "Doctor of Doctors," and strenuously defended before him the doctrine of the Society on the "Efficacy of Divine Grace." He is the author of four volumes on scholastic theology, and of many works against the heretics, whom he opposed to the utmost during twenty-three years of professorship at Dillengen and Ingoldstadt.

4. At Osnaburg, in Germany, in the year 1619, Father Simon Wippermann, a German. He was very full of devotion to the Blessed Virgin Mother of God, and was noted for his singular suavity and graciousness of manner.

5. At Jaroslaw, in Poland, in the year 1651, Father John Slostowski, a Pole. In his youth he was turned out of doors by his parents for renouncing the Arian heresy, but welcomed by the Mother of God, who bid him join the Society, and more than once saved his life. On his death-bed he told his Confessor that he had always obtained from her his requests.

APRIL 26.

1. At Noto, in Sicily, in the year 1635, died Father Alfius Manfiti, an Italian. He was remarkable for love of recollection, and devotion to the tribunal of penance. His life was spent between his room and his confessional. He usually said little, but when called upon to speak on divine things he was full of sweet eloquence. His penitents were distinguished by their exemplary exact life; and it became a proverb to say of notably good persons, "A penitent of Father Manfiti." He was a great lover of punctuality, and observer of the smallest details of duty. He was giving an instruction to an assembly of pious persons when he was seized with an attack of gout; he concluded his discourse, and

as he retired said to his companion, "God summons me," and shortly after he died. Cures were obtained through him after death.

2. At Munich, in Bavaria, in the year 1615, Christian Schacher, a German Lay-brother. He was a great lover of holy poverty, and never asked for or received anything new. His habit, though quite threadbare, was always neat and clean.

3. At Madrid, in Spain, in the year 1648, Father John Martinez de Ripalda, a Spaniard, an acute, solid, and subtle theologian. His constant study of the Fathers, especially of St. Augustine and St. Thomas, and his retentive memory, enabled him to cite them readily on any question proposed. He filled with the greatest honour to the Society the chair of Salamanca. His works are in three folios.

4. The memory of Father Stephen Gelosse, an Irishman, the date of whose death is not known. During the cruel persecutions of Cromwell, when every Priest was captured as a wolf, and proclamation was made that in whatever house one was found, the owner of it should be hung up before his own door, no dangers could deter him from his duty. He visited the sick and dying, and daily said Mass. He adopted every kind of disguise, and personated various characters, such as porter, fagot dealer, gardener, tailor, and pedlar; was four times apprehended, but contrived to escape. His labours were chiefly in the neighbourhood of Ross, where he taught a school after the Restoration. He was living in 1675.

April 27.

1. At Pekin, in China, in the year 1638, died Father James Rho, an Italian, distinguished as a mathematician, but still more as a laborious preacher of the Gospel. He was held in high esteem by the Emperor of China, and the honours which he avoided during life were bestowed on him when dead. His body was carried with great pomp through the principal street of the city, and by order of the Mandarins his likeness was taken and preserved in painting to be handed down to posterity.

2. At Seville, in Spain, in the year 1598, Father Peter Monterey, a Spaniard. He left prospects of high preferment to become a Lay-brother, in which condition he remained ten years. Raised to the Priesthood through

obedience, and made Superior, he remained humble as before, seeking every opportunity of self-contempt and humiliation. His habit was old and threadbare, and his bed a board. His fervent prayers seemed always to obtain whatever he asked.

3. At Granada, in Spain, in the year 1725, Father Emmanuel Padial, of great repute for sanctity. His union with God was great, and he was often rapt in ecstasy. His austerities were extraordinary. To his hairshirt and severe disciplines he joined scanty sleep and so little food, that he was reduced almost to a skeleton. The fruit produced by his preaching and labours was wonderful. The marks of esteem which he received sensibly afflicted him, and the more highly he was honoured, the more vile and abject he seemed in his own eyes. His virtue was perfected in infirmity, God permitting that he should suffer long and acute pains of sickness and ulcerated wounds, from which the devil was allowed to tear off the bandages, and otherwise afflict him. His patience was unalterable, and his heart continually burned with intense love and devotion, his breast remaining warm even after death. His funeral was attended by an immense concourse of people. The Archbishop and Clergy, the Religious Orders, and the chief magistrate were present at it; and the body was carried by the Canons of the Cathedral.

4. At Brunsberg, in Prussia, in the year 1613, Father Robert Abercrombie, a Scotchman. He left his country to join the Society, and after twenty-three years spent at Brunsberg as missioner and Novice Master, he returned to Scotland, and remained nineteen years on that arduous mission, enduring countless hardships, and converting many noble persons to the faith. A very large reward was offered for his apprehension. Protected by Providence, he courageously continued his labours, and escaped the pursuivants. When once on a time the house in which he resided was surrounded, he hastily threw himself into an empty open chest, was covered with some old clothes, and so escaped. In his old age he returned to Brunsberg, and died in his eightieth year.

April 28.

1. At Toulouse, in France, in the year 1631, died Father Charles de Lorraine. He was a member of the royal family and Prince-Bishop of

Verdun, but left all to enter the Society. When he asked the consent of Pope Gregory XV., who was about to make him Cardinal, to leave his Bishopric (which he had governed for five years with admirable prudence and zeal), and enter the Noviceship, the Pontiff replied, "Yes; join that sacred militia, so renowned for its defence of the Catholic cause, and for its victories over heresy." He was received at Rome, and never remitted his first fervour. He afterwards declared that to enter the Society he would have gone on foot to Japan. In his intercourse with God he received the sweetest consolations, the hundredfold, as he often avowed, promised to those who forsake all for Christ. He was Superior of the Professed House at Toulouse, where he died in his fortieth year, a rare example of virtue, and especially of generous detachment from self; for in the opinion of his physicians he could have prolonged his life by change of air, but he preferred to remain at the post where obedience had placed him. To the four vows he added a fifth: to seek the greater glory of God in things of moment, and to defend the Immaculate Conception of the Blessed Virgin.

2. At Rome, in the year 1575, Father James Ceruto, an Italian, so great a lover of the Religious Vows, that he gradually increased his daily renewal of them until the number of times reached three thousand. Thrice every night he rose to recite the Litany of the Blessed Virgin. For poverty's sake he gave up even his beads, saying his Rosary on his fingers.

3. In Brazil, in the year 1607, Father Diego Fernandez. By his labours on the mission he converted twelve thousand savages.

4. At Warsaw, in Poland, in the year 1670, Father John Mambrecht, a Scotchman. He was for a time confessor to the French Embassy in London during the last years of James I. and the beginning of the reign of Charles. In 1626 he returned to Scotland to his mission, and the same year was apprehended at Dundee and committed to Edinburgh gaol. He was more than six months in this loathsome prison; no friend was admitted to visit him, and no writing materials were allowed him. His only comfort was his cross round his neck, and his Breviary when the light of his gloomy cell would permit him to use it. The warrant of his death had received the Royal signature, but at the earnest entreaty of the Queen was cancelled. Thus to his grief he lost martyrdom, but

was banished the kingdom with his health greatly impaired by his imprisonment. He retired to Poland, where he was employed in hearing confessions, not only of his own countrymen, but of Italians, Germans, French, Spaniards, and Flemings, with all whose languages he was well acquainted. His devotion to the Passion was very great, and he perpetually regretted his having been disappointed of suffering martyrdom for his Lord, Whom he called his "Love Crucified." When he passed a Crucifix he kissed the wounds of the feet, and if they were too high to be reached with his lips, he touched them, and then kissed his fingers.

April 29.

1. In London, at Tyburn, in the year 1602, Father Francis Page died for the faith. He was reconciled to the Church by Father John Gerard, then a prisoner in the Clink. Renouncing worldly prospects he went abroad, made his studies, and returned a Priest to England, and for some years laboured on the mission. He was admitted at his earnest solicitation into the Society by Father Henry Garnett, but before he could be sent to Belgium to make his Novitiate he was taken prisoner and condemned to death. He suffered solely for his priestly character, being full of joy and alacrity; and his last words as the cart was driven away were, "I confess before all that I am a Catholic Priest, and, although altogether unworthy, a member of the holy Society of Jesus."

2. At Poitiers, in France, in the year 1626, Father John Gualbert, a Frenchman. As he was deliberating on the choice of a state of life, he opened a book and his eye fell upon the words, "He who does not leave father and mother cannot be My disciple." He opened it a second time, and the same again occurred. This confirmed his mind already disposed to obey God's will, and he entered the Society, which he enriched by his benefactions, but still more by his virtues. His disposition was sweet, gentle, and full of compassion, so that he could hardly tear himself away from the care and service of the sick, for in serving them he considered that he was serving Christ.

April 30.

1. At Paris, in the year 1657, died Father John Baptist St. Jure. He was born at Metz, and entered the Society at the age of sixteen. At Amiens, Alençon, Orleans, and Paris he was Master of Novices, and acquitted himself of this office so successfully, that the Fathers and Brothers whom he trained were always easily known. He was endowed with a rare talent of directing souls in the way of the love of God, of penetrating the secrets of hearts, and applying suitable remedies to every spiritual disease. Burning with the most ardent love of our Lord JESUS CHRIST, his only desire was to make Him known and loved by all men, and to this he greatly contributed both by his example and by his writings, which reveal a man perfected in the science of the Saints. He lived fifty-three years in the Society, of which his virtues and his works made him so illustrious a member, and his holy life was crowned with a death precious in the sight of God.

2. At Arima, in Japan, in the year 1595, Father Joseph Furlanetto, an Italian, poisoned in hatred of the faith by the Japanese. He laboured much and successfully for the conversion of Japan. Besides others, elsewhere gathered into the fold of Christ, he baptized in one town two thousand and sixty adults.

3. At Le Puy, in France, in the year 1609, Father Claude Ponceot, a Frenchman. As he lay grievously sick he saw two Angels at the foot of his bed, preparing for him a nauseous-looking mixture, when a third arrived and bade them desist, saying that he came with a message from the Queen of Heaven—that the sick Father had suffered enough—and that she herself would soon be present there. Accordingly she came accompanied by St. Ignatius and other Fathers of the Society to carry the soul of the good Religious to the joys of Heaven.

4. At a town on the coast of the Red Sea, in the year 1595, Father George Abraham, a Maronite, who on his way to Abyssinia was put to death by Mahometans for the faith. The Governor kept him in prison twenty-six days, in hopes that he might be induced to renounce Christianity. He himself was born of Christian parents and was a renegade. For this the Father when brought out of prison boldly reproved him,

and was ordered instantly to be beheaded. The first sword broke upon his neck, the second inflicted a slight wound and broke, the third struck off his head and gave him a martyr's crown. The Saracens themselves declared that for forty days lights were seen over his tomb. He had a vision when praying before the Miraculous Host at Santarem in Portugal, of JESUS CHRIST laden with a heavy cross, and received an assurance that after many hardships he would suffer death for His sake. In the privations of missionary life, when in want of all things, he would exclaim, "Oh, the happiness, the hidden treasure of this holy poverty!"

MAY.

1. At Luxembourg, in Germany, in the year 1636, died Father William Weltheim, a native of that city. He was of a sweet and amiable character, and of great literary attainments. His room contained what was barely necessary, and he wrote his comments on history upon the backs of his scholars' themes. When it was remarked that this was carrying the virtue of poverty too far, he replied that Bellarmine and other great writers of the Society had done the same. He studied solely to the greater glory of God, never lost time, and only interrupted his labour to renew his intention by prayer. From his childhood he had the gift of chastity, seldom conversed with the other sex, and then always with his eyes cast down, and was never heard to utter an uncharitable or impatient word. Before his Priesthood he had asked for and obtained the appointment to the foreign missions, but God was content that his good will and zeal should be exercised in preaching, visiting the sick, assisting the dying, and consoling the distressed. Attending a case of malignant fever, he took it, and died a martyr of charity at the age of thirty-six.

2. At Compostella, in Spain, in the year 1593, Father Martin de San Domingo, a Spaniard, celebrated as a giver of missions, and for the conversion of multitudes of sinners. He prepared for giving a Retreat by weeks or days of prolonged prayer, fasts, disciplines to blood, and Masses, which he begged also of others. Taking care to arrive at the place of his destination before some Sunday or Feast-day, he gave such a moving discourse, that the people flocked to hear him during the following week, filled the confessionals, and came in great numbers to the General Communion at the close of the Retreat.

3. At Nimeguen, in Belgium, in the 1636, Father Antony de Greef, a martyr of charity, dying in service of the sick. His life was often

in peril on the mission from the hands of heretics; and once he was delivered by the appearance of a young stranger, who claimed his acquaintance, and bid the soldiers about to seize him to let him pass free.

MAY 2.

At Goa, in the East Indies, in the year 1583, died Father Dominic Fernandez, a Portuguese, an indefatigable missioner, especially in the Isle of Coran, in which at his arrival he found only seven Christians, and at his death left five thousand.

2. At Rouen, in Normandy, in the 1610, Father Antony du Four, a Frenchman. The holiness of his life was attested by the fact that his body was found incorrupt twelve years after his death, and exhaling a sweet odour, although it had been buried in quicklime. The linen cloth in which it had been wrapped applied to a Lay-brother infected with a pestilential disease, caught in attending the sick, freed him from it.

2. At Mexico, in America, Father Jerome de Mercado, a Spaniard. From his entrance into the Noviceship an over delicate conscience kept him in continual fears, but shortly before death he enjoyed great peace and tranquillity. He wore a hairshirt, slept upon bare boards three times a week, and took the discipline twice daily, to add efficacy to his prayers. Three days before he died a bright company of Angels was seen by a Religious man entering his room in long procession, to protect him in his agony, and accompany him on his departure to receive his heavenly crown.

3. In Japan, at the beginning of this month, in the year 1564, Brother Edward da Silva, a Portuguese, sent as a Novice to Goa, and from thence by St. Francis Xavier, who appreciated his virtues and capacities, to Japan. He was made infirmarian in the hospital erected by Father Cosmo di Torres; it was also his duty to bury the dead. This he performed with so much zeal and charity, rendering the last duties with the same respect to rich and poor, that many infidels attending out of curiosity conceived a high idea of the Christian religion, and were converted to the faith. His strength gave way under his great labours and mortifications, and he died at the age of thirty-seven.

4. In the year 1711, the time unknown, Father John Gérard, a

Frenchman. He entered the Noviceship at sixteen, and was remarkable for his devotion to the Blessed Virgin and St. Francis Xavier. He was permitted to add to his three Vows two others—never voluntarily to transgress a rule, and always to aim at what was most perfect. Later he offered himself by vow to St. Francis Xavier to undergo toil, suffering, torments and death for the good of souls in any part of the world. He was employed for many years in teaching, and as Minister in various Colleges, and as missioner in Lower Brittany. At last he was sent to the Islands of Martinique, St. Christopher and St. Domingo to preach the Gospel to the African slaves. He laboured and suffered much, and converted many. A wound in the thigh induced his Superiors to recal him to France that his health might be restored, but he gained only the merit of obedience, the malady was too inveterate, and he died aged sixty-three, having spent forty-six years in the Society.

May 3.

1. At St. Paul's Churchyard, London, in the year 1606, died Father Henry Garnett, hanged, drawn, and quartered for the faith. He was born at Nottingham and educated at Winchester school, where his talents gave promise of a successful career at Oxford. Being convinced of the errors of Protestantism, he became a Catholic, went to Rome, and joined the Society in 1571. After his noviceship and studies he was Professor of Hebrew and Mathematics at the Roman College, and in 1586 was sent with Father Robert Southwell on the English mission. He succeeded Father William Weston as Superior, and for seventeen years fulfilled his difficult duty with consummate prudence, and the love and esteem of all. On the discovery of the Powder Plot a warrant was issued for his apprehension, and he was seized with Father Oldcorne at Henlip House, near Worcester, and sent to the Tower. He was examined twenty-three times without the discovery of anything sufficient for his condemnation, but libellous accounts were published and transmitted to Catholic Sovereigns, that he had confessed himself guilty. Designedly apprised by the gaoler of means of communicating with Father Oldcorne, he was treacherously overheard, and it was discovered that under seal of confession he had received some communication with regard to the Plot, though he had

done all in his power to prevent it. On this he was condemned to die. As he passed through the streets drawn on a sledge, his hands and eyes were lifted up to Heaven. At the scaffold he saluted the immense multitude of spectators with a smiling countenance. They had been loud in their reproaches, but were silenced by his venerable appearance. Avowing his innocence, and, in answer to the ministers, making profession of the Catholic faith, and declaring that he was ready to give for it not one but many lives, he repeated the words of the Office of the day, "We adore Thee, O Christ, and we bless Thee, because by Thy holy Cross Thou hast redeemed the world. This sign of the Cross shall be seen in heaven when the Lord shall come to judgment." Then crossing his hands on his breast he was flung off the ladder. The executioner three times attempted to cut the rope, that he might be butchered yet alive, but the people would not allow it; and when his head was shown, instead of huzzas, as was usual, they went away in silence. It was placed on London Bridge, and his countenance retained for twenty days the freshness of life. A straw found at the place of his execution, bore, in a drop of blood which had fallen on it as he was quartered, a most accurate and miraculous portrait of him, such as could not have been delineated by the hand of man.

2. At Murcia, in Spain, in the year 1560, Father John Baptist Barma, a Spaniard. He was theologian to St. Francis Borgia, and a man of great prayer. During a drought he obtained by his petitions rain from God; and by his earnest supplication to the Blessed Virgin he kept off the Turkish fleet from the coast of Spain. He fasted on bread and water, though he preached through the whole of Lent; and he slept but little, and that on the bare ground.

3. At Vienna, in Austria, in the year 1571, Father Adalbert Bausech, a Bohemian. He was ordered to enter the Society by our Lord, Who appeared to him in the Sacred Host. He was conspicuous for zeal in gaining souls, the conversion of heretics, and for theological learning.

MAY 4.

1. At Rome, in the year 1755, died Father Ignatius Visconti, sixteenth General of the Society. An enemy to all singularity, his conduct was ever uniform, exemplary, and a perfect model of community life. The

serenity of his countenance and the peace of his soul were unalterable in the most unforeseen and disagreeable events of life. Besides the ordinary times of prayer and examen, to which the most important occupations could not make him unfaithful, he noted down with the exactness of a novice his particular examen, his lights in meditation, and the acts of virtue he proposed to practise. He taught the higher studies at Milan with a success that showed the greatness of his genius and acquirements; but as he was endowed with a particular talent for government, he was suddenly removed from teaching and made Provincial, and shortly afterwards chosen Assistant for Italy, then Vicar-General, and finally charged with the government of the whole Society. During his exercise of this high office, his uprightness, moderation, and charity, won for him the admiration even of the enemies of the Society, and he was commonly called "the Angel of Peace." He died at the age of seventy-three, in the fourth year of his Generalship. A few days before his death, though in perfect health, he made an exact general confession, "to be ready," he said, "to die."

2. At Cadiz, in Spain, in the year 1571, in the service of the sick, Father James de Sotomayor. At Granada, when he was seeking a lodging to pursue his philosophy, a voice from Heaven bid him seek for it in the Society; while he yet hesitated, the voice again and again repeated, in a manner compelled him to obey. As a Religious, he lived in the continual presence of God, as though in all his actions he was saying to himself, "The Lord lives before Whom I stand." He used to declare that when he was unwell, the recital of the Rosary cured him.

3. At Valladolid, in Spain, in the year 1599, Father John de Castillo, a Spaniard. He had from his infancy a most tender love and devotion to the Blessed Virgin. The devils by their molestations and corporal chastisement endeavoured to divert him from it, but in vain. On the Feast of Pentecost he saw the Holy Ghost descend on our Brothers who were receiving Communion from Father Louis da Ponte.

4. At Parma, in Italy, in the year 1630, Father Venusto Roberti, an Italian, died of the pestilence, caught while attending the sick. This year was disastrous to Italy, but glorious to the Society, for at Parma eighteen others also died in the same manner; ten at Mantua, two at Cremona, nine at Bologna, three at Pinarolo, eleven at Milan, Ticino,

and Castiglione; five at Placentia and Valtelino, three at Modena, two at Florence, four at Como, Montereale, and Cunio: altogether sixty-eight.

MAY 5.

1. At Alcala, in Spain, in the year 1557, died Father Francis de Villanova, a Spaniard. He was admitted by St. Ignatius, who said of him, when some Fathers requested that he might be restrained in his spirit of penance, "No; he has strength enough for anything; let him alone." He was of humble birth, of repulsive exterior, and without knowledge of letters, but became by the disposition of Divine Providence the principal support of the College of Alcala. Of admirable humility, piety, prudence, and confidence in God, he had a particular gift of easing troubled souls, skill in giving the Spiritual Exercises, and a force and address which triumphed over all obstacles. To encourge himself to mortification and charity he would often ask, "Villanova, why have you come hither? To crucify yourself. Do so then. At least bear in others, what you fear to cure in yourself." When Rector he often served in the kitchen, and performed most humiliating services. His clothes and food were the poorest of the Community. He used to say that a Rector ought not to dread poverty so much as the fear of it, which arises from want of confidence in God. His studies had been brief, but he was a very learned divine, and consulted by persons from every quarter. " I make more account of the theology of Villanova," said a learned Doctor of the University, " than of all the theology of Alcala." He died at the age of forty-eight, in the odour of sanctity, having passed sixteen years in the Society. God revealed to Father Martin Guttierez the glory he enjoyed in Heaven.

2. In Poland, in the year 1642, Father Stanislaus Brunow, Father Gaspar Woynicz, Father Christopher Carnostaw, and Brother John Domagalski, Poles, martyred by the Russian schismatics in a forest, in hatred of the Catholic faith. As they were labouring to reconcile schismatics to the Catholic Church, a decree was issued to kill them wherever they could be found. The assassins fell upon them as they were on the road, crying out, "We do not want your money but your lives." It is declared

that a light was seen over the place where they were martyred, as well as in the church where they were buried.

3. At Ikizuki, in Japan, in the year 1592, Father George Carvahal, a Portuguese. He laboured much and with fruit in the island of Scimo, in Firando, and the kingdom of Bungo, and died by poison.

MAY 6.

1. At Manilla, in the Philippine Islands, in the year 1639, died Father Valerius de Ledesma, a Spaniard, remarkable for his love of prayer and the heroic mortification of his passions. Although from his natural temperament he was extremely irascible, yet he acquired such self-command that no excitement was ever seen in him. He slept but three hours, giving the rest of the night to prayer. He once received commendation from JESUS CHRIST Himself for having done under most difficult circumstances what he thought most pleasing to the Divine will. The Blessed Virgin assured him of his salvation saying, "My son, you will be saved." He had great devotion to that Divine Name, "I am Who am," and once he was inspired with great confidence in God by hearing these words, "I am Who am: I am with you."

2. In the same Philippine Islands, in the year 1660, Father Francis Colin, a man of prayer, silence, and the gift of tears. He denied himself the use of chocolate, for which he received praise from the Blessed Virgin herself, and an admonition from her never to partake of it. Once when seized with a great and sudden fear about his eternal salvation, he had recourse to earnest prayer, and begged God to give him as a pledge of it two pagans of high rank but great obstinacy, whose conversion he thought would influence others. His prayer was heard, and the following day to his great joy they voluntarily presented themselves and asked to be baptized.

3. At Madrid, in Spain, in the year 1643, Father John Louis de la Cerda, for fifty years together Professor of humanities. The renown of his literature was so great, that Cardinal Barberini, Legate a Latere, paid him a visit of honour, by desire, as he said, of Pope Urban VIII. He published three volumes of learned annotations for the use of classical Professors.

MAY 7.

1. At Nangasachi, in Japan, in the year 1626, died Father John Baptist de Baeza, a Spaniard. Sentence of banishment was pronounced against him by the Emperor, but he would not abandon his flock, and remained concealed in caverns, in forests, and in the mountains, deprived of all human aid, and a prey to disease. All this served the more to inflame his charity, and he had but one regret, that he had not been found worthy to give his life for JESUS CHRIST. Towards the close of his career he often asked the Christians to take him before the tyrant. The fruits of his labours were great, for in the space of three years he baptized seventy-five thousand adults in Macao, Goa, Mozambique, and Japan.

2. At Palermo, in Sicily, in the year 1586, died Father Paul Achilli. He was so gentle, and yet so firm, in maintaining discipline, that he was engaged for thirty days in disposing a subject to receive with equanimity a penance which he had deserved. He was of great modesty and abstinence, taking no collation in Lent. Once while in prayer, he suddenly ordered a Father who was taking ship to be recalled. The vessel fell into the hands of the Turks. He was seen while saying Mass to hold a beautiful infant in his hands. A sword struck at his breast bent like wax. At the hour of his death his soul was seen by many in glory.

3. At Mindanao, an island of Philippines, in the year 1642, Father Francis de Mendoza, put to death by the Mahometans, whom he endeavoured to win to CHRIST.

4. At Toulouse, in France, in the year 1627, Father John Francis Suarez, a Frenchman. He was a man of such eminent perfection and singular power in prayer that he obtained for many spiritual and temporal health. That he might attain to a high degree of virtue, he laid down for himself the rule, to live firstly, as a Novice, the last and least of all; secondly, as a dead body; thirdly, as one delivered from hell; fourthly, as crucified with CHRIST, and as the Infant JESUS in the manger. Such was his practice, and he arrived at such perfection that it may be said that no virtue was wanting in him, nor could his mind be drawn away by any occupation from union with God.

May 8.

1. At Seville, in Spain, in the year 1606, died Father James de Guzman, of the blood royal of Spain, a man of Apostolical spirit and virtue. Under the direction of John of Avila he received the Priesthood, and refusing all dignities, devoted himself together with Gaspar Loarte, Doctor of Salamanca, to teaching catechism and administering the Sacraments. After three years spent in this manner, he was admitted to the Society by St. Francis Borgia. At the wish of St. Ignatius, as soon as he finished his noviceship, he resumed the same labours, and continued in them until he was eighty-three years of age. He toiled at Rome and in its vicinity, in Tuscany, Naples, and the marches of Ancona, in the Isle of Corfu, and in many dioceses of Spain. He always travelled on foot and lodged in the hospitals. To relieve the fatigue of his journeys he sang the praises of the Blessed Virgin or meditated on her mysteries; and arriving at any town, he first paid a visit to the Blessed Sacrament to pray for many hours and ask a blessing on his labours. He spent the whole night of Thursdays before the Altar, in honour of the institution of the Blessed Sacrament. The fruit of his humble toilsome missions was very great. He was looked upon as a Saint, and a portrait was taken of him by desire of some great persons, without his knowledge. When it was shown to him, at first he was somewhat troubled, and then he said, "Our Lord Jesus be praised! I have seen before this Judas painted; well, you have now a genuine likeness of him." At the close of his life he suffered painful infirmities. At his death, which was full of joy, he cried, "I come, O Lord, I come!—I rejoice in the things that are said to me, we will go into the house of the Lord."

2. At Palermo, in Sicily, in the year 1576, Antony Oliveri, a Lay-brother, who died a martyr of charity attending on the sick of the plague. Two sons of his had entered the Society before him.

3. At Madrid, in Spain, in the year 1577, Dominic Fernandez, a Lay-brother. Attending the death-bed of Father Peter Mauriguez, who had been his master in the world, and seeing him die very holily at Alcala, he besought him that he would, when in the presence of God, remember Dominic, once his faithful servant, and now his poor assistant in Religion.

The Father promised that he would. Some months passed, and Dominic, healthy and strong, began to be sad that his exile was prolonged. The Father Procurator, whose Socius he was, asked him the reason, and he replied, "Because Father Peter Mauriquez, my master in the world and my Father in Religion, has not kept his promise." Shortly after he took a fever, and, fortified with the rites of the Church, obtained his wish, and the fulfilment of the promise.

MAY 9.

1. At Auxerre, in France, in the year 1613, died Father Adrian Chessoy, a Frenchman, a man of holy simplicity, exact poverty, and so special a devotion to the holy Angels, that he was given the name of "Father Adrian of the Angels." Whatever he could find in praise of the holy Angels he read, noted down, and spoke of in conversation, never letting a recreation pass without something on this subject. From his infancy he was tenderly devout to his Guardian Angel, by whom he was guided to enter the Society; and, as a faithful imitator of the invisible ministers of the will of God, he was remarkable for his obedience. He received many favours from them in return, and was frequently sensible of their presence, especially of two who accompanied him from his room to the Altar, and remained with him during Mass. He possessed nothing but his Breviary, Beads, and a picture of his Guardian Angel.

2. At Caen, in Normandy, in the 1655, Father Gabriel Potier, remarkable for his religious regularity, modesty, and abandonment of self in the hands of Superiors. Of this he gave a great example, when by mistake he received notice to take the three Vows instead of the four. The error was occasioned by the similarity of his name to some other, and this he perceived, but he said nothing, and took his Vows as a Spiritual Coadjutor. Afterwards the mistake was discovered, and he was admitted with so much the more honour to the profession of the four Vows.

MAY 10.

1. At Quito, in South America, in the year 1649, Father Bartholomew

Polo, a Spaniard, died in the midst of his Apostolical labours. All his life was a succession of sorrows, dangers, sufferings, and Evangelical toils. These accompanied him from his early years to his grave. But nothing could diminish his indefatigable zeal for the salvation of souls.

2. In Canada, in the year 1652, Father James Buteux, a Frenchman. He was shot by the Iroquois savages, among whom he had fearlessly laboured and preached with Apostolic zeal for eighteen years.

3. At Hang-tcheou-fou, in China, in the 1657, Father Stephen le Fevre, a Frenchman, justly reckoned one of the greatest missioners of the East. He long prepared himself for the Apostolic life by great austerities and constant prayer, frequently spending whole nights in that holy exercise. On the mission he soon gained by his admirable virtues the title of a "Second Xavier." Finding it impossible to enter Japan, he made his way into China. There he was listened to so eagerly, that men mounted into trees to see and hear him. He was assisted by Angels in his long journeys, and once, when carried away by the current of a river, he was transported by them to the bank. He delivered the possessed and worked miracles. His fervent recollection in prayer was so striking, that the sight of him thus engaged effected the conversion of a Tartar Prince, the near relative of the Emperor, whom no arguments could before induce to embrace the faith. When asked to diminish somewhat his austerities, he replied that, "each one was the best judge of what his beast of burden could carry." The day of his death was revealed to him, and assembling the Christians in the church, and exhorting them to perseverance in the faith, full of hope and joy, with the holy names of JESUS and Mary on his lips, he passed from this life on the day of the Ascension.

4. At Lisbon, in Portugal, in the year 1644, Dominic da Cuñha, a Portuguese Lay-brother. He was renowned as a painter, but more as representing in his soul the portrait of a good religious man. He was permitted to suffer much from the persecutions of the devils, and the torments they inflicted on him, until God at last rewarded his patient endurance by heavenly consolations, almost too much for his physical strength. Obedience was most dear to him, and sometimes the face of his Superior appeared to him to change and assume the form of the face of CHRIST, a grace which wonderfully confirmed him in his love of that virtue.

May 11.

1. In the Professed House at Naples, in the year 1716, St. Francis Jerome. Appointed by Superiors to labour in the Kingdom of Naples instead of the Indian mission, for which he applied. He continued for forty-one years toiling in this field, amidst incredible trials, contradictions, and sufferings, which he surmounted with invincible fortitude, gathering a copious harvest of souls, and no less abundant merit for himself and glory to God. His heroic virtues, and especially his contempt of self and of the world, and his charity, were crowned with the choicest gifts of discretion of spirits, prophecy, knowledge of the interior of souls, and frequent miracles, by which even the dead were recalled to life. He was universally esteemed an Apostolic man and a true Saint. At length, worn out by his labours and the austerities with which he preserved his virginity unimpaired, he died at the time he had predicted, at the age of seventy-four years, forty-six of which he had spent in the Society. The lame, the dumb, and those otherwise afflicted, by invocation of his name, or touching his body, obtained their health; and this not only in Naples, but in Germany, where a portion of his relics was sent; and in the year 1839 Pope Gregory XVI. solemnly enrolled him in the number of the Saints.

2. At Salerno, in Italy, in the year 1607, died Father Michael Ruggieri, an Italian. He was the first preacher of the Gospel to penetrate into China and obtain a settled residence there. This he accomplished at the cost of great pains and trouble, gaining the favour of the Mandarins by his address, prudence, and patience. He returned to Europe to obtain the authority and assistance of the Holy See in promoting and establishing the mission of China. He arrived safe after suffering and danger on his voyage, but was not destined to return; his place was supplied by his great successor, Father Ricci.

3. At Pekin, in China, in the year 1610, Father Matthew Ricci, an Italian, born at Macerata in the March of Ancona, about the very time that St. Francis Xavier dying on the confines of the great Empire of the East, was asking our Lord to send labourers into His vineyard. Father Ricci entered the Society at the age of nineteen, made his noviceship under

Father Valignani, the Apostle of the East, and when his studies were finished followed him to India. He was chosen with two others for the Chinese mission. For a time they were successful, but after a time were banished. Father Ricci contrived to return a second time, and after many labours reached Pekin. He concluded from the character of the people that science was the only means by which Christianity could be introduced amongst them, and he began to make use of his great knowledge of mathematics for that end. He soon became famous; his house was frequented by the great, and his society was courted by the most powerful mandarins. The attention of the Emperor was attracted to him, and he wished to see so extraordinary a man. From the Emperor he received permission to establish himself in Pekin and Nankin, thus verifying a revelation received from our Lord, Who appeared to him to console him in his labours, by telling him that He would be his protector in both these royal cities. He made converts first among the mandarins, and gradually among the people, augmenting the numbers of his fellow-labourers, and dispersing them in the provinces. His renown increasing, he became the most celebrated man in China. He was ever in correspondence with the most learned men and the mandarins, who consulted him on matters of science and religion. Every one who came to the Court to Pekin visited him, and he took every occasion to speak of the doctrines of Christianity. His unremitted bodily and mental labours undermined his health, and having received warning of his death, he prepared for it with joy, kneeling in the middle of his room for the Holy Viaticum. He died at the age of fifty-seven, having spent twenty-five years in China and thirty-eight in the Society. Father Ricci was a man of lofty mind and indomitable courage, patient, and circumspect, prudently slow at first that he might afterwards be more successful. He was not cast down by failure, and was endowed with that learning and address that fitted him to be the Apostle of a people full of self-esteem, isolated from the rest of the world, and believing that they had nothing to learn from others. His funeral was celebrated with the greatest pomp and honour.

4. In Peru, in the year 1609, Father Ildephonsus de Miranda, a Spaniard, for forty years a missioner of indefatigable zeal and love of the poor. His body was found incorrupt after the lapse of sixteen months, though buried in quicklime.

MAY 12.

1. At the residence of St. Joseph, in Canada, in the year 1643, died Father Edmund Massé, a native of Lyons in France. He was sometime companion of Father Coton, Confessor to Henry IV., but preferred Canada to the Court. Arriving in that country in 1611 he was taken by English pirates, and was on the point of being put to death, but was ransomed and sent back to France. His heart yearned for the Indian mission, and with prayers and mortifications he entreated the favour from God. For fourteen years, like Jacob for Rachel, he served God for Canada, and to obtain it resolved to practise the following penances:—To sleep on the ground; to wear no linen; to wear a hairshirt during Mass; to take the discipline daily; to allow nothing to his senses merely for their gratification; to fast three times a week; and to mortify his sense of taste whenever he said anything the least uncharitable. Thus he prepared himself for the cross he desired while Minister of the College of La Flèche, and in 1625 he found it, for in that year he was again in Canada. He laboured and suffered much, but was again taken by the English and sent back to Europe. He vowed to use every effort to return, and once more succeeded arriving there in 1633; toiled on the mission for ten years, and died at the age of seventy-two, having spent fifty years in the Society.

2. At Mayence, in Germany, in the year 1607, Father Conrad Onneking, a German, remarkable for his zeal for the salvation of souls and his devotion to the Blessed Virgin. He wrote his sermons on his knees. When asked why he laboured so perpetually, and gave his body no rest, he replied, "Why have I entered the Society?" He would also exclaim, "O good God, what a thing it is to save but one single soul and deliver it from hell!"

3. At Pont-a-Mousson, in Lorraine, in the year 1631, Matthias le Coussi, a Lay-brother, a native of that country. He was called to the Society in a singular manner. When a servant at the College of Treves, he was ordered to accompany a Postulant to the Noviceship with letters of recommendation from the Rector to the French Provincial. In the letters no name was mentioned. On the way the Postulant changed his

mind, and giving to Matthias the letters for the Provincial, went elsewhere. Thus "the lot fell upon Matthias," for the Provincial reading the letters, and thinking he was the person spoken of in them, received him kindly, and asked him if he wished for God's glory to live in the Society. Matthias assented, though he wondered much and could scarce believe that such an unexpected happiness could be destined for him. Received as a Laybrother, he made good use of his fortune, and showed himself worthy of the grace. After his death he was seen surrounded by a heavenly light, and heard to say, "All is well with me."

May 13.

1. At the Professed House in Paris, in the year 1704, died Father Louis Bourdaloue. He entered the Society at the age of fifteen, and for eighteen years was occupied either in his own studies or in teaching philosophy and theology. His rare talent for preaching induced his Superiors to devote him exclusively to that ministry, and his reputation was soon established and continued to increase. In the midst of the applause of the Court and the Capital, he remained indifferent and detached, a model of the virtues which constitute the true Religious. He had a profound contempt for the world, deep devotion to the service of the Church, and love for his vocation. He regarded prayer as the most important of duties, and at the foot of the Altar he derived strength to announce the Gospel to the Kings and the great ones of the earth. He had a particular talent for assisting the dying, and devoted five or six hours a day to the confessional. In a touching letter written to the General, he expressed a desire to spend the latter years of his life in retirement, and repass his life in the bitterness of his heart. This being refused, he devoted himself with renewed zeal to the duties of his ministry, and died at the age of seventy-two, after a few days' illness.

2. At Berlanga, in Spain, in the year 1578, Father Rodriguez Hurtado, a Spaniard. He was remarkable for his heroic patience and love of prayer. There seemed to be no limits to his power of obtaining what he asked of God. Once he was seen by a Bishop raised in the air, absorbed in prayer, lying as in repose upon a bed. At Mass he was often rapt in ecstasy and unconscious of what passed around him.

3. At Louvain, in Belgium, in the year 1610, John Thenens, a Belgian Lay-brother. For thirty years he filled the office of caller, always awaking in time, though a sound sleeper, without the warning of an alarum, which he attributed to his Angel Guardian, to whom he recommended himself before sleep. He showed great fortitude of mind in a long and severe malady, during which he had to endure many painful surgical operations. God gave him much consolation; and once while the knife was piercing his flesh he was heard to say, "Now I know how sweet it is to suffer."

4. At Seville, in Spain, in the year 1649, Gregory de Arrogo, a Lay-brother, employed for forty-four years in begging alms for the Professed House in that city. He died of a pestilential fever caught in attending upon the sick a victim to his charity.

MAY 14.

1. At Liege, in Belgium, in the year 1649, died Father Thomas Cornforth, an Englishman. He was a native of Durham, and admitted into the Society by Father Henry Garnett in 1600. He died at the age of eighty.

2. At Lisbon, in Portugal, in the year 1563, Father Gonzalvez Vas de Mello, a Portuguese, a man of great eloquence as a preacher, and very persuasive in leading his hearers to embrace a Religious life. In one month, besides those whom he led to enter other Religious Orders, he brought thirty-two into the Society. Going to give a mission, and recommending it in prayer to the Blessed Virgin, he was seen to be ccompanied by her, walking in the air beside him, as was attested by his companion.

3. At Seville, in Spain, in the year 1578, Father John Altobodos, born of a Moorish family in Granada. He devoted himself with Apostolic zeal to the conversion of his own race, despising all danger, and using every means in his power with great success. The magistrates confided to his instructions criminals about to die; and the Parish Priests, the children and the ignorant. The most obstinate heretics, apostates, and infidels were put into his hands by the Inquisition. God protected his life in dangers. He was called out at midnight by the Moors, who had

conspired to kill him, as if to attend a dying person, but when he came to the spot where they intended to assassinate him, they were seized with a sudden panic, and fled away, leaving him alone. As he returned to the College he heard groans, and found a dying Moor, whom he brought to confession and prepared for death. Another Moor, reprehended by him for bad conversation, threatened to cut off his nose unless he went away. The next day that mutilation was inflicted on the Moor himself in a quarrel.

4. At Toulouse, in France, in the year 1636, Father John Arnoux, a Frenchman, Confessor to Louis XIII. Cardinal Ubaldino declared, speaking of him in the presence of Father Aloysius Albriet, that when Apostolic Nuncio in France, he knew of no one who had rendered greater service to the Church at Paris, Grenoble and Toulouse, than Father Arnoux. He laboured much for the good of the Society both as Rector and Provincial.

May 15.

1. At Watten, in Belgium, in the year 1699, died Father Edward Petre. Entering the Society at the age of twenty-one, he was sent at the conclusion of his studies upon the English mission, having the repute of much learning and virtue. At the time of the popular fury occasioned by Oates' pretended Plot he was thrown into Newgate, where he was an angel of comfort to his fellow-prisoners, two of whom, Mr. Gerard and Father Richard Lacy, died in his arms. After a year's imprisonment in Newgate he was removed to easier confinement through the influence of James, Duke of York. At James' accession to the throne he was called to Court, and was after a time made a Privy Councillor. This occasioned much illwill against him, and he often besought the King on his knees to be allowed to retire from Court; and afterwards, when dethroned, James was heard to say, that had he listened to Father Petre's advice his affairs would have been in a different state. At the Revolution he escaped to the Continent, and in 1693 was appointed Rector of St. Omers. The affability of his manners and his charitable care of the Community made him beloved by all. He retired to Watten, and died at the age of sixty-eight.

2. Also at Watten, in the year 1697, Father John Keynes. He

May 15.

made his studies of humanity at St. Omers, and of philosophy at Valladolid, where he entered the Society. He taught philosophy at Compostella, and theology at Salamanca. Sent to Liege to direct the studies, he obtained leave to devote himself to the service of the English soldiers, amongst whom the plague was raging. He was seized with it, and for the recovery of his health was sent to England. He was Superior at the time of Oates' Plot, and search was everywhere made for him, but in vain. He wrote several controversial works, and filled the offices of Rector of the College of Liege and Provincial, and died at the age of seventy-three.

3. In Abyssinia, in the year 1597, Father Francis Lopez, a Portuguese, companion of Father Andrew Oviedo, Patriarch of Abyssinia, and partaker of his labours for twenty-nine years. His life was a practice of heroic virtues. All that he had he gave to the poor, even to his clothes as far as he could. His bed was the bare ground. He gave to the sick his own poor mat. God recompensed his austerities with many favours. He was seen at Mass shining like the sun; and he foretold his death two years before it happened.

4. At Augsburg in Germany, in the year 1628, Father Gregory Roseff, a German. He was successor of Father Canisius in the pulpit of Vienna, and by his preaching saved Augsburg from heresy. The infant establishments of the Society in Germany owed much to him. He suffered much from the pains of sickness at the close of his labours, but sought for consolation in prayer, and was often heard to say, " Give me patience, O Lord, and increase my pain."

5. At the College of Paz, in Peru, in the year 1614, Father Gabriel de Baeza, a Spaniard, for forty-two years a laborious and successful missioner. In prayer his breast was so inflamed that he was forced to cool it with wetted cloths. To guard his virginal purity he wore perpetually a hairshirt. He frequently read the secrets of hearts. His funeral was celebrated throughout the city.

6. At Horodlo, in Poland, in the year 1657, Father Simon Maffon, cruelly martyred by the Cossacks. He had joined the Society to which he gave a considerable patrimony, and was engaged in reconciling the schismatics to the Catholic Church. He was seized, fastened to a plank by irons driven through his thighs, had the sinews of his neck torn out, and then having been scourged cruelly, he was beheaded.

MAY 16.

1. At Janow, in Poland, in the year 1657, Blessed Andrew Bobola, a Pole of noble family, called the Apostle of Pinsk from his labours in that province for twenty years, died an illustrious martyr by the hands of the Cossacks. Falling into their power as they ravaged those parts in search of Priests, he was regarded with savage joy as the principal promoter of the Catholic faith, and they tried every threat in vain to force him to abjure it. They then stripped him, tied him to a stake, beat him cruelly, tore away his nails, struck out his teeth, and flayed off his skin. Seeing that he remained unshaken, they dragged him between two horsemen to the town of Janow, inflicting on him several deep wounds with a hatchet. There his cruel butchers plucked out his eyes, cut off his ears and nose, and, as he still repeated the holy names of JESUS and Mary, they tore out his tongue from his throat, and then with two blows cleft his head asunder, and gave him a martyr's crown. One hundred and six miracles, most of them juridically proved before the Bishop of the province, Alexander Wyhowski, declare how precious in the sight of God was his life and death.

2. At the College of Klatau, in Bohemia, in the year 1643, died Father Albert Klatauski, of a distinguished Bohemian family. He was employed for thirty years in laborious missions, and it was his consolation to restore to the Church that part of Bohemia which, bordering on Bavaria, had fallen into the heresy of Huss. In all seasons, and on foot, notwithstanding the pains of the gout, he went through towns and villages, dragging himself painfully along on his swollen feet. To these sufferings he added great austerities and prolonged fasts. His labours were very pleasing to God, as was shown by the ministry of Angels who accompanied him with torches by night, or conveyed him long distances, and by a light which shone around him at prayer or during the Holy Sacrifice.

3. At Seville, in Spain, in the year 1601, Father Antony Cordés, a Spaniard. He was appointed Rector of the College of Gandia by St. Ignatius, and Provincial of Aragon by Father Laynez, and continued Superior for forty years. He was always the first to give example in every humble and painful employment. He died at the age of eighty-three, of the plague,

caught in hearing the confessions of the sick at the time of the great mortality in Seville, when thirty thousand died in a few months. On a former occasion when the plague was raging at Gandia, he assigned districts of the city to the other Fathers, but he himself traversed the whole. Passing by a closed house he heard the cries of an infant, and entering by a window saw a little girl lying sick of the plague, with her father and mother dead beside her. He took the little girl in his arms, and meeting with a woman with a baby at her breast gave the child to her, requesting her to bring her up also. She asked in horror how she could venture to do so, and bring the plague home to her husband and family. The Father reassured her, promising that if she did so, the child would soon recover, and she and all the family would be preserved. She obeyed, and the promise was verified. When he was Rector of the College of Seville the whole of the city was thrown into distress by the loss of the fleet, and the house for want of alms reduced to penury, yet he ordered alms to be given to every one that asked, and part of the supper of the Community to be given to a lady of rank and her children. Returning to his room, he found three hundred pieces of gold on his table.

4. At Brunsberg, in Prussia, in the 1650, Father Simon Berens, a Prussian, an excellent missioner, and skilled in directing troubled consciences. He suffered with exemplary patience the fracture of six ribs by the upsetting of a car.

MAY 17.

1. At London, in the year 1633, died Father Thomas Everard, a native of Suffolk. Having made with fervour the Spiritual Exercises under Father John Gerard, he went to Rheims, and afterwards entered the Society. His amiable manners, meekness, humility and piety, endeared him to all. Being at the point of death of a slow fever, he recovered by a singular favour of God, and was for some years Minister at Oudenarde and Watten; then, though advanced in life, he was allowed to devote himself to the English mission in Norfolk. He effected numerous conversions, was sought for, and captured twice, and imprisoned for many years. He died at at the age of seventy-three, scarce able to see or walk, consoling himself by saying his Beads, the Litanies, and the

Jesus Psalter, to which from early years he had great devotion, and other prayers he knew by heart.

2. At Courtrai, in Belgium, in the year 1636, Father Valentine Bischoff, a native of Bourges. He was an able theologian, but his great love for visiting the sick and dying, and for the Apostolic ministry, induced Superiors to send him on the mission of Holland. In this service, exposed to danger of losing liberty or life, his labours were consoled by numerous conversions. He was recalled to Belgium to assist the sick of the plague, he was seized by it, and died a martyr of charity, eight days after his arrival.

3. At Jaroslow, in Poland, in the year 1647, Father Albert Wiglocki, a Pole. He was noted for his devotion to the Blessed Virgin, and never gave a sermon without some praise of her. He always carried with his crucifix an image of our Lady of Dolours, and with this he arrested a mass of flames rolling from the blazing city, and which threatened to consume the College.

4. At Rome, in the year 1658, James Goffetti, an Italian Lay-brother, whom Father Mutius Vitelleschi, General of the Society, used to call the Angel Guardian of the Professed House at Rome. No one ever noticed in him anything worthing of blame, but on the contrary everything deserving the highest praise. His hands hardened with constant work as a mason, his rigorous poverty in his room and clothes, his continual prayer joined with his industry, his humble and prompt obedience, and his tender piety towards the Blessed Sacrament, gained for him universal esteem as a man of admirable virtues, and a model of Lay-brothers.

5. Also at Rome, in the year 1606, Father Nicolas Orlandini, an Italian, the first writer of the history of the Society, remarkable for his candour, sweetness of disposition, and piety. He had been Master of Novices for seven years, when he was summoned to Rome by Father Acquaviva, and employed to write the first Annual Letters of the Society, and then its history. He had scarce completed the half of the first part when his health, always delicate, began to decline. There was little hope of his concluding the work, but he confided in St. Ignatius, with whose history he was then engaged. His strength returned and he resumed his labours, which, when he had brought to a happy close, his strength again sank and he died.

MAY 18.

1. At Rome, in the year 1597, died Father John Paul Navarola, an Italian, a man of great gifts and consummate virtue. In all his multiferious occupations he was so self-possessed and mindful of the presence of God, that he seemed by his daily actions to be ever repeating, "The Lord lives, in Whose sight I stand." Hence his uniform tranquillity and composure was so great, that no one ever remarked in him any sign of disturbance of mind.

2. At Saragossa, in Spain, in the year 1617, John Martini, a Spanish Lay-brother. He is represented in the letter which announces his death as a perfect model of a Lay-brother. He united to solid virtue all the capabilities requisite for the duties of his state, and his Superiors could be always satisfied that whatever they charged him with would be exactly and promptly executed. He loved poverty with a scupulous care, allowing nothing to be wasted through neglect, and attending to the furniture of the house, benches, chairs, and tables, and the rest, which he kept in careful repair. His vigilance kept him in constant fatigue and self-sacrifice, and he everywhere displayed that generous spirit and courage which mark true children of the Society. He was most obedient, exact in keeping the Rule, and full of fraternal charity. A precious death was the reward of his unwearied charity; for, assisting day and night Ours who were sick, he was taken ill and died.

3. At Monterey, in Spain, in the 1575, Father Peter Cuevas, a Spaniard. He devoted himself to the care of the sick during the plague, and in this task of charity he gave his life. Father Thomas Orduna died together with him in the same service, a martyr of charity.

MAY 19.

1. In London, at Tyburn, in the year 1651, died Father Peter Wright, suffering martyrdom for the faith. He was born in Northamptonshire, and in his early years lost his religion, but, being reclaimed, went abroad and was fully reconciled by the Fathers of the Society at Liege, and at the age of twenty-six entered the Novitiate at Watten. Being naturally

passionate he became remarkably sedate and calm; and when after his studies he was appointed Prefect at St. Omers, an office little suited to his inclinations, he offered to continue in it all his life if Superiors thought fit. He was first appointed to the care of the English soldiers, whose affections he gained, and very many of whom he reclaimed. He was then sent on the English mission, residing chiefly with the Marquis of Westminster. On the Feast of the Purification, as he was about to say Mass, he was seized and committed to Newgate. On his trial, being accused on the evidence of an apostate of being a Priest and a Jesuit, he gave God thanks that he was arraigned, "not," he said, "for any crime, but only for the Catholic religion, which is, and ever will be, illustrious over all the earth"; upon which the jury brought him in guilty, and to his own great joy but to his friends' sorrow he was condemned to die. The concourse of Catholics to the prison to see him, confess to him, and obtain his blessing or some memorial of him, was very great. The last two nights he slept very soundly, so that the morning of his execution it was not easy to awake him at five o'clock to celebrate the Holy Mysteries. He declared to the Father sent him by the Provincial that he never experienced so great joy in his life as at the approach of death. He heard the knocking at the iron grate as a summons from Heaven, and said, "I come, sweet JESUS," and went to the hurdle with such alacrity that the officers could scarce keep pace with him. He passed through the streets with a cheerful smiling countenance and an air of majesty which astonished the beholders. Near twenty thousand people were assembled at Tyburn, and he addressed them from the scaffold, glorying that he laid down his life as a Catholic Priest and a Jesuit. Being told that his life would be spared if he would retract, he replied that if he had a thousand lives he would lay them down for the faith. The rope was put round his neck, he recollected himself in prayer, and the cart was drawn away. He was allowed to hang till he expired, then cut down, beheaded, disembowelled and quartered. He was forty-eight years of age.

2. At Granada, in Spain, in the year 1610, Father Thomas Sanchez, a great theologian. He was prevented from entering the Society by an impediment in his speech, until prostrate before the image of the Blessed Virgin he besought its removal, declaring that he would not move without obtaining his request. His holy obstinacy prevailed, and he entered the Society.

It soon became doubtful whether he would excel most in learning or in sanctity. Though naturally delicate, he gave ten or twelve hours a day to study, taking but one meal and that at night. He aimed at the highest perfection, each morning noting down what he would do that day to advance in it, and devoting a day each month to recollection, and to examine his progress, which holy practice he never interrupted during the forty-three years he lived in the Society. He took a vow never to wear new clothes. He had recourse to prayer in all his theological difficulties, and visited the Blessed Sacrament five times daily. He went to his reward at the age of sixty. His funeral was attended by the Archbishop, the council and nobility, and a great concourse of people.

3. At Madrid, in Spain, in the year 1578, Diego Mendoza, a Lay-brother. He had learned blind obedience under Father Araoz. In his last agony he saw the Blessed Virgin coming to visit him, and exclaiming, "What a happiness that you have come to me, dear Lady, Mother of God and Mother of Mercy! Oh, how is this? What goodness to come to me!" he expired.

4. At Perigueux, in France, in the year 1596, Father Francis Bordese, a Frenchman. When his brother, who with three of his sons had entered the Society, after an edifying religious life died a happy death, Father Francis begged at his grave that he might soon join him in Heaven. On the following day at Mass he heard a voice "Your prayer is heard." He prepared for death, and after a few days joined his brother. He had never let a day pass without thoughts on death.

MAY 20.

1. At Mayence, in Germany, in the year 1609, died Father Nicholas Serrarier, a native of Lorraine. He taught theology at Würtzburg with great success, but his especial study was Holy Scripture, to which he applied himself with diligence and prayer. He explained it for twenty years at Würtzburg and Mayence, and thus prevented heresy from extending its ravages in Germany. He used to say, that for the conversion of heretics it was necessary to pray much as well as to study much, and not only to have arms, but to know how to use them in such a manner as to enable the vanquished easily to bear the shame of defeat. Naturally hasty, he

gained such command over himself as to become remarkable for gentleness and sweetness, so that even the enemies of the Society confessed that he was at the same time "a learned Jesuit and a man of admirable goodness." He died at the age of fifty-four, worn out with study. He is praised by Baronius as a light of the Church in Germany. He had extraordinary devotion to the *Gloria Patri*, and never heard it recited without great emotion.

2. At Gorgona, in Abyssinia, in the year 1622, Father Peter Paez, a Spaniard. It is incredible what sufferings and ill treatment he endured on that mission, being imprisoned, put in chains, and condemned to labour as a galley slave. At last being sent for in order to reconcile the Emperor Segued to the Catholic Church, he undertook on foot a journey, of ten days in the heats of summer and almost without food. He accomplished his object, but his strength was broken by the journey and he died, to the Emperor's great grief, who mourned for him as for his master and father, weeping at his sepulchre with outstretched arms, and refusing for a long time food or consolation.

3. At Granada, in Spain, in the year 1607, John Sevilla, a Laybrother, memorable for his persevering application for admission into the Society, and for his long concealment of his knowledge of the Latin language. He remained for three nights in winter time at the door of the house, determined not to move until he was admitted. Being received, although he knew Latin well, and had studied Canon Law two years, and was in Minor Orders, he could never be induced to prosecute his studies, and for the fifty-two years he spent in the Society he never gave any indication that he knew Latin at all.

May 21.

1. At Lima, in Peru, in the year 1612, died Father John Sebastian Parricios, a Spaniard. For some years he taught philosophy and theology in the Province of Toledo, and was then sent to Peru, where, by his virtues, labours, and the wonders he worked, he merited the reputation of a Saint; and in the process of his canonization, which was commenced, he was styled the Apostle of Peru. He took the discipline daily, and spent seven hours in prayer; for thirty years he had no other bed than the

bare ground and a sheepskin. Before preaching he served an hour in the kitchen, and after it recited on his knees the Seven Penitential Psalms. He made the Spiritual Exercises three times in the year, and spent in them forty days before his death, which he foresaw and foretold. He was twice Provincial, and forty years Superior. He never let an hour pass without entering into himself and renewing his intention of doing all for the greater glory of God. Many wonders are related of his virtues and virginal purity. He was much assailed by the devil, and honoured by God, Who revealed to him future and secret things, bestowing on him miraculous favours. He was seen raised from the earth in prayer, and after his death in glory.

2. At Rome, in the year 1670, Father Nicholas Zucchi, an Italian, died with the reputation of a Saint. Great natural talents and gifts of grace, faithfully employed in the service of God and the good of his neighbour, rendered him a man such as our Constitutions require. The General, Father Mutius Vitelleschi, said that he did not know of any two others in the Society whose virtues could be said to equal his. He left his birth-place, Parma, to enter the Society at Padua, at the age of sixteen. He made quick progress in every virtue, sighed for martyrdom, and asked for the Indian mission. As it was not granted him, he resolved to devote himself to the good of Italy. He possessed in an eminent degree the talent for preaching, and this without preparation, so that the most learned audiences were astonished. As he knew that he had received this gift, he considered it his duty to be ready to preach on every occasion without more notice than was necessary to determine the subject. Thus he would preach five, six, or seven times in a day, to the amazement of his companion, varying the matter of his discourse. He was equally admirable in familiar exhortations, and was specially deputed to direct and renovate in the spirit of their institute Convents of Nuns, whose special wants he had particular light to discern. He was confessor and Apostolic preacher to the Sacred College. He withdrew from vice many abandoned souls. He obtained these heavenly graces by complete mortification, annihilation of self and nature, and profound humility, being a great imitator of St. Francis Borgia, to whom he had particular devotion, and to the Infant Jesus. During the latter years of his life he was confined to his bed, and with tranquillity and

joy endured the painful sufferings which completed his sanctification. Full of merits, he died at the age of eighty-four.

MAY 22.

1. At Nangasachi, in Japan, in the year 1617, died Father John Baptist Maccadio, a Portuguese, beheaded for the faith. He was an eminent preacher and holy Religious, and suffered imprisonment at Omura. There it was revealed to him that he should die the following day, upon which he sung the *Te Deum*, and declared to his companion, Father Peter of the Ascension, a Franciscan, who suffered with him, that the three happiest days of his life had been "that of his admission into the Society, that of his entrance into prison, and this of the news of such a happy death." They died together in sentiments of lively joy, and two bright stars were seen by the neophytes shining over the spot where they suffered. Léon, a young seminarist and catechist, who might if he pleased have escaped by flight, suffered martyrdom a few days after them.

2. In Abyssinia, in the year 1573, Father Gonzalez Cardoses, a Portuguese, slain while returning from a journey undertaken to reconcile to the Church some schismatical monks. To effect this he left nothing undone, and suffered much. It was generally supposed that he was killed in hatred of the faith. His death was revealed to him beforehand.

3. At Parma, in Italy, in the year 1630, Father Hyacinth Grillo died a martyr of charity while attending on the plague-sticken. The day before he was attacked with it, he met a venerable looking old man dressed as a Priest, in appearance more than human, who told him that his labours in behalf of the sick were very pleasing to God, and that he must prepare soon to receive his reward; he then disappeared, and Father Hyacinth prepared for death.

4. At Würtzburg, in Germany, in the year 1666, Father Gaspar Scott, a German. He was remarkable for his piety, sincerity, and patient labour. He was a great mathematician and experimental philosopher, on which subjects he wrote many volumes, comprising works on curiosities of physical science, and a lucid compendious course of mathematics, much and generally esteemed.

5. At Rome, in the year 1608, Father John Baptist Villalpandos,

a Spaniard, renowned for his science of architecture and mathematics. His Commentary on the Prophet Ezechiel and laborious description of the Temple of Solomon is a work of great name, in which he had as a fellow labourer Father Jerome Prado.

MAY 23.

1. At Dijon, in France, in the year 1669, died Father Anne Francis de Beauvais. He was of noble family, allied to the royal house of France. At the age of forty-four, with the consent of the Marchioness his wife, he left a beloved family and large possessions to consecrate himself to God in the Society. His son had already entered it before him. He had a very tender devotion to the Blessed Virgin, almost continual union with God, and so ardent a love for the Blessed Sacrament that he spent all his spare time before it, sometimes nine hours a day. From his humility he desired to be a Lay-brother, while in his zeal he longed for the foreign missions. He endured with heroic patience a long and painful illness, and died in sentiments of great confidence in God, and gratitude for the grace of dying in the Society.

2. At Cracow, in Poland, in the year 1615, Father Martin Laski, a Pole. By his persuasion, example, and powerful influence, he was most successful in the conversion of heretics. He brought the whole House of Assembly of Cracow to embrace the Catholic faith, and pass a decree that no one should be admitted as a member except a Catholic. He was the first to introduce into Poland the devotion of the Forty Hours; and he established sodalities to collect subscriptions to provide dowries for poor girls. He showed no sign of fear when some heretics presented muskets at his breast; and when the plague was raging, sending his companions away he devoted himself to the service of the sick.

3. At Posen, in Poland, in the year 1625, Father Nicholas Czyzowski, a Pole. He three times recovered when at the point of death, by the intercession of St. Ignatius, St. Francis Xavier, and SS. Barbara and Bibiana. At length he died a sweet and pious death, singing hymns which he had composed expressive of contrition and love. He used to say, " that for the Society one should have a ploughman's palate in indif-

ference as to food, a camel's knees for constant prayer, and an ass's back for bearing labour. It was his opinion that, as the sanctity of Brothers consists in continual labour and taking reproof, they should not be treated softly; and he declared that a Lay-brother had appeared to him a few days after his death, to thank him for having kept him assiduously employed and frequently penanced.

4. In Silesia, in the year 1634, Father Jerome Fischer, a Bohemian, shot in a wood by heretical soldiers, who stripped and plundered other passengers, sparing their lives; but seeing Father Jerome they exclaimed, "A Jesuit! a Jesuit!" and shot him dead. It was evident from this that they slew him out of hatred to the faith. He had foreseen and foretold his death.

MAY 24.

1. At Rome, in the year 1596, died Father Antony de Mendoza, a Spaniard, Assistant for Spain to Father General Acquaviva. Humility was ever in his heart, and conspicuous in his words and actions. Even when he was Superior he would perform the lowest services of the kitchen, or office of porter, without any human respect or regard to his nobility of origin and rank. Before speaking he always raised his mind to God. The heavenly light shed around him in prayer manifested a soul not of this world; and his body, found unchanged in colour, fresh and flexible, after a year and a half had elapsed, attested the opinion entertained of his sanctity. In his last sickness when told by the physician to bid the window be opened, and to look out upon the heaven to which his soul was about to take its flight, he pointed to his Crucifix and replied, "Here is my heaven; here is all my joy."

2. At Tournon, in France, in the year 1596, died Father Charles Sager, born at Beauvais, distinguished both for virtue and learning. He taught philosophy at Paris, Sacred Scripture at Bordeaux, and theology at Tournon. He defended the Catholic faith against the Calvinists, to whom he rendered himself formidable, while his meekness made him amiable even in the eyes of his adversaries. He passed forty years in the Society, to which his learning and zeal gave lustre, and his example added to its ranks his father and his three brothers.

3. In the North of England, in the year 1640, Father Richard Holtby, a native of Yorkshire. He studied both at Cambridge and Oxford, but convinced of the truth of the Catholic faith, he went abroad to Douay and then to Rheims, whence he returned, being ordained Priest, to the North of England. Hearing of the death of Father Edmund Campion, with whom he had been acquainted, he fell on his knees and took the three Vows of the Society, adding another, to ask admission into it after the coming Easter. He rode to London to find the Superior, but as he was absent, selling his horse he proceeded with the money he thus obtained to France, and was admitted by Father Darbyshire at Paris. He made his noviceship at Verdun, studied theology four years at Pont-a-Mousson, and was appointed Superior of the Scotch College. The town being attacked by pestilence, he and twelve companions devoted themselves to the service of the sick. Ten of these died. He and two others alone survived. He was then sent by Father Acquaviva into England, where he laboured for more than fifty years with uninterrupted health, escaping all the snares laid to entrap him. He was a skilful carpenter, and the hiding-places he constructed in various houses baffled the search of Priest-hunters. He died at the age of eighty-seven, after having been fifty-eight years in the Society.

MAY 25.

1. At Seville, in the year 1649, died Father Nicholas de Salasar. He entered the Society at a mature age. When he was in the noviceship the enemy of souls endeavoured to inspire him with a disgust for his vocation, under the plea that he would not have strength to lead a life so perfect as the rules require, and that he had better return to the world and aim at a less elevated sanctity. He discovered his temptation to the Master of Novices, who, knowing that he had led an easy life in the world, resorted to the same means that St. Ignatius employed in a similar case. He charged a fervent Novice, who had also been delicately brought up, to sweep his room and wait upon him. This at first was pleasing to Father Salasar, but reflecting that the Novice who waited on him had been as delicately nurtured as himself, and was born of a higher family than his own, covered with confusion he went to the Master of

Novices and begged him not to require him to receive this affront, and promised for the future to submit to every trial. For the rest of his life he never lost his fervour. He was afterwards made Master of Novices, and died a martyr of charity serving the sick of the plague.

2. At Canzuca, in Japan, in the year 1590, Father Gaspar Coelho, a Portuguese, renowned for his missionary labours, and the multitudes of souls rescued from hell by his ministry. In the kingdom of Omura alone he added, with the aid of his companion, thirty-five thousand to the Church, and sixty houses of Bonzes. He was the first Vice-Provincial of Japan, and greatly honoured by the King.

3. In the Tyrol, in the year 1632, Father Adam Tanner, a Tyrolese. He was a man of few words, of great soul, and profound humility. It was his delight to converse with the simplest Brothers. His reputation for learning being extensive, the Emperor Matthias sent for him to Vienna to take the Chair of Theology in place of Martin Becan. He was made Chancellor of the University of Prague by Ferdinand II. He employed his talents and learning and knowledge of Greek and Hebrew to confute the heretics of the time. He published many works. Southwell enumerates twenty-eight, and among these are included four volumes in folio on theology, and disputations on all parts of St. Thomas.

4. At Guinea, on the Coast of Africa, in the year 1610, Father John Delgado, a Portuguese. He was both a learned theologian and a laborious missioner. When he found all his efforts in vain to convert the King of Bicongo, he burst into tears in his presence. The King asked why he wept, and he answered, "I bewail your obstinacy, which will consign you to everlasting fires." "Well," said the King, "you weep because you are so good, and perhaps you think that I shall die soon." He was much beloved, as was proved by the crowds who flocked to his grave after his death.

May 26.

1. At Cologne, in the year 1627, died John Corneille, a Lay-brother. He was born of good family, and entered the army, in which he had attained high rank when he joined the Society. He was ambitious of the humblest offices, and for twenty years was Porter. Although he

May 26.

suffered from many infirmities, he practised great austerities, wearing a hairshirt and chains, and taking a discipline every day. He was forewarned of his death on Corpus Christi Day. In his agony he implored with great fervour the aid and protection of St. Ignatius and the Blessed Virgin, and when his prayer was over he burst out into songs of joy, and with "Alleluia" on his lips expired.

2. At St. Omers, in Belgium, in the year 1597, Father Nicholas Buri, a Belgian, a martyr of charity in service of the sick. As he was taking the Blessed Sacrament to the dying, he found a sick woman lying in the street in the rain. Having put the sacred pyx in a convenient place, with the help of the Lay-brother his companion, he was carrying the poor creature into a house, when the master of it, a soldier, with oaths bid him take her out again, that if he did not he would kill him. The Father offered his throat to the drawn sword, which only provoked greater fury and blasphemy. Upon which recollecting the story of St. Bernard and the Duke of Aquitain, the Father taking the Blessed Sacrament in his hands said in a tone of authority, "You see here your Creator, your Saviour, and your Judge. Go down upon your knees and ask pardon for your offence against Him and your cruelty to this poor woman." The people around all falling on their knees, the soldier followed their example, and humbly begged pardon of God and those present, and changed his whole conduct into the greatest respect for the Father and the Blessed Sacrament.

3. At Naples, in the year 1619, Antony Loffredo, an Italian Scholastic. While he was thinking of entering Religious life he was challenged to a duel by a man of high rank, and, to save his honour, accepted it. Being superior in fence he had his adversary at his mercy, and, when he petitioned it for Christ's sake, spared his life. For this act of mercy, he used to say that God had given him in recompense the grace of a vocation to the Society. He lived in it like another St. Aloysius; and it is said that when dying he saw a lovely road leading to Heaven, and St. Ignatius at the summit praying to the Blessed Virgin, and asking for innocence of life for the members of the Society.

4. At Munich, in the year 1697, Father Tobias Löhner, a German, a learned and laborious Religious man, a great lover of his room, in which

he was ever employed writing pious books for the use and instruction of Preachers and the Clergy, especially those who have the cure of souls.

MAY 27.

1. At Evora, in Portugal, in the year 1567, died Francis Coetho, a Portuguese Scholastic. In the world he had been remarkable for innocence, and in the Society he added the practice of very perfect virtue in obedience, generosity of soul, and love of suffering, which he manifested especially in his last illness, to the admiration of those who went to visit him. Nothing reprehensible could be ever remarked in his conduct, and in his papers were found written resolutions for which heroic virtue would be requisite. Some days before his death, awaking as from a sleep he said, in the presence of the Rector and some others, "Who told me just now that on the twenth-seventh of May I should go to enjoy the happiness of being with God in Heaven?" His death on the day predicted proved the promise to be true.

2. At Coimbra, in the year 1630, Father Diego Montera, also a Portuguese, a Religious of great prayer and mortification. He rose two or three hours before the usual time to make meditation, and gave daily half an hour to the visit he paid in the evening to the Blessed Sacrament, and half an hour to dwell on the prerogatives of the Blessed Virgin, from whom he is said to have received familiar visits. He was sometimes seen raised from the earth in prayer. His mortifications were great, and he went daily to confession, and each month made a general one at its close.

3. At Cagliari, in Sardinia, in the year 1656, Father Simon Marica with two companions gained their heavenly crown, dying in service of the sick. He is thought to have had the favour from his Angel Guardian of being waked at what hour he pleased duing the night to rise for prayer. Prepared for death, he said that he should not die until ordered by obedience. His confessor, unwilling to give the command, bid him die so soon as it was God's will. Immediately Father Simon without any sign of pain breathed his last.

MAY 28.

1. At Rome, in the year 1654, Leonetto Gagliardi, an Italian Scholastic of great talent and virtue. When his three brothers, all in the Society, were lamenting his early death, he rejoiced that he died young and in the bosom of the Society, and said to his brother Achilles, "Cheer up, and give our Lord JESUS CHRIST thanks for His great love to me."

2. At Paris, in the year 1582, Peter Monier, a French Scholastic. When the devil troubled him grievously in his last sickness, he was ordered by his confessor to ask the tempter if he had anything against him. Shortly afterwards turning to his confessor with a smiling countenance he said, "He has nothing;" and, having exhorted all present to the practice of solid virtue, he gave up his innocent soul to God.

3. At Iglau, in Bohemia, in the year 1648, died Father Frederic Huncken, a Saxon, an indefatigable missioner. He reconciled to the Church many thousands of heretics. In his expeditions he usually carried with him a little smoked meat and dried herring, that he might be burdensome to no one. On his return he served almost daily in the kitchen. Fot the last fifteen years of his decrepid old age he never slept in a bed, but in his clothes upon a wooden chair. He wept while dying, that there still remained one heretic in the town of which he had the charge, in which, when he undertook the care of it, there was not a single Catholic. This remaining one was converted by his death, for hearing of the anxiety of the Father about him in his last moments, he renounced his errors.

MAY 29.

1. At St. Omers, in the year 1617, died Father Thomas Stanney, a native of Wiltshire. He was recommended by Cardinal Allen to the Rector of the English College at Rome, as a youth of good birth and great modesty. He entered the Society at Rome and returned to England, where he was received and held in much esteem by Father Henry Garnett. He suffered much on the mission, preparing others for martyrdom, and was himself obliged to wander in the woods in cold and hunger to avoid being

taken. At last he fell into the hands of the officers, and was thrown into the Gatehouse prison. Here he suffered from gout, cramps, hernia, and the stone; and finally, when banished for life, returned to Flanders with his health much broken. He devoted his remaining years with great charity to the care of the sick, whom he amused with edifying and entertaining stories, and died at the age of sixty-two.

2. At Cracow, in Poland, in the year 1638, died John Parnese, a Lay-brother. He gave three hours daily, and five or seven on Festivals, to prayer. This time he took almost entirely from his sleep. He was allowed to communicate three times a week, took the discipline daily, and wore a double chain. Working as a stone-mason in the heats of summer, he never took additional refreshment, not even a drink of water. For the last five years of his life he obtained permission to abstain entirely from meat and fish, and live on bread and vegetables. He died holily on a Saturday as he had desired and foretold.

3. At Toledo, in Spain, died Father Peter Rodrigo, a Spaniard. He foretold his death three months before the time. On the day itself being in perfect health he offered the Holy Sacrifice with more than usual fervour, and prolonged his usual discipline which he took daily for half an hour. He was Procurator, and he drew the attention of the Lay-brother, his assistant, to some business which he gave him an order to have done by a certain hour. At the hour he had fixed, standing at the door of a house in the country, he expired.

May 30.

1. In London, at Tyburn, in the year 1582, Father Thomas Cottam suffered for the faith. He was born in Lancashire, and having studied at Brazenose College, Oxford, took his degree of Bachelor of Arts. Afterwards meeting with Thomas Pond in London, he became a Catholic and went to Douay. From thence he went to Rome with a desire of entering the Society. He was admitted at the age of thirty to the Novice-ship of St. Andrea, and his health being weak was ordered to France, where he was ordained though still a Novice, and sent on the English mission. A description was sent of his person and designs by Sledd, the Priest-hunter, who made his acquaintance at Rheims, and he was

captured. A person named Havard, a Catholic in secret, had him in charge to conduct to London, and allowed him to escape, by which his own life was in danger. Lest he should suffer on his account, the Father gave himself up, and was confined in the Marshalsea. From thence he was sent to the Tower, put to the torture, and with Father Campion and some others condemned to die. He was taken to Tyburn in company with the Reverend Lawrence Richardson, who was first executed, and whilst he was being quartered Father Cottam was bid look and avoid a like fate. But he replied, "My heart is far from that; O good Lawrence, pray for me. O Lord, have mercy on them, and give me grace to endure to the end." When the head was held up with the usual exclamation of "God save the Queen," he also prayed for her as Queen. When the sheriff would have him add, "and as his chief in Ecclesiastical matters," he replied, "No; if I would have put in those words, I had been discharged almost two years since." Then adding that if he had ten thousand lives he would rather lose them all than swerve in any point from the Catholic faith. He looked up to heaven in prayer saying, "*In Te Domine speravi—Domine Tu plura pro me passus es,*" repeating the word *plura* three times; then asking forgiveness of all, praying for all his enemies, and begging all Catholics present to join with him, he recited the *Pater* and then the *Ave*, during which the cart was drawn away, and he was left hanging till he was dead. When stripped, a shirt of very coarse canvass reaching down beneath his middle, and rough as a hairshirt, was found upon him.

2. At Brunn, in Germany, in the year 1649, died Michael Martz, a Silesian Scholastic. He was of singular openness in giving an account of his conscience to his Superior, and his face, as he was rendering it, often shone like an Angel's. He experienced in Holy Communion a foretaste of the joys of Heaven. He said that he owed much to our Blessed Lady; that he had been born on her Nativity; that as a child he had seen her visibly in a glorious apparition; that by her he had been called to the Society, and through her had many tokens of predestination to eternal life. He died on the day and hour he had foretold.

3. At Mayence, in Germany, in the year 1611, Father John Busæus, a Belgian. For many years he taught Dogmatic and Moral Theology; was Prefect and promoter of the Sodality of the Blessed Virgin, and published a variety of pious and learned works.

May 31.

1. At Manilla, in the Philippine Islands, in the year 1621, died Father Angelo Armano, an Italian, a laborious and devoted missioner. No journey was too difficult, nor want nor danger too great, for his zeal in the conversion of the natives. He calmed a storm at sea with a medal of St. Ignatius, and miraculously escaped from attempts upon his life and fire set to his house. He was buried with great honour by his neophytes.

2. In Bohemia, in the year 1739, Father John Meagh, an Irishman, with two companions, Wenceslaus Trnoska and Martin Ignatius, Lay-brothers, slain by the heretics in hatred of the faith. They were staying in the neighbourhood of Ruttenberg, and were shot and cut down by the boors of the country. Father John in a retreat which he had lately made was fervently impelled to desire martyrdom, and felt a strong assurance that in some manner, he knew not how, he should obtain it. Brother Martin had been also similarly impressed while receiving Holy Communion. His devotion to the Blessed Sacrament was very great, and he often shed abundance of tears. His love and service to the Holy Mother of God was equally remarkable, and our Lady is said to have appeared to him.

3. In Spain, in the year 1598, John Junceda died a martyr of charity in service of the sick of the plague. Eight others died in Spain that same year. And in the year 1617, at Lisle in Belgium, John Tendenier, a Lay-brother, a model of piety, modesty, and industry, with two others, died also in the service of the sick. In Italy, Theodore Varesino, in the year 1631, in the same office of charity. Ten others died the same year in Italy.

JUNE.

June 1.

1. At Murcia, in Spain, in the year 1566, died Father James Suarez, a Spaniard, memorable for his constancy in his Religious vocation. When he could not be induced by any threats or entreaties to leave the Society, his father drew his sword upon him in the church, but James having led him aside into the house succeeded in calming him. He was so given to prayer, that he may be said to have fulfilled to the letter the injunction of our Lord, "Pray always." The nuns of St. Clare sent more than once to the College to say, that there appeared a bright fire at night over the roof of the dwelling. On diligent inquiry made by the Father Minister and the Porter nothing was discovered except that Father James was found praying with great fervour, raised from the ground, and unconscious that any one had entered his room to observe him. The Father Rector was called and witnessed it, so that the fire which had been seen was believed to have originated from no other source than the heart of Father James.

2. In the Island of Majorca, in the 1601, James Ruiz, a Spanish Lay-brother. During the thirty years he was employed as Cook he never asked for a change of duty, or for permission to walk out and breathe the fresh air. His only relaxation was prayer, visiting the Blessed Sacrament, and practices of devotion in honour of the Blessed Virgin. In order to have more time for his spiritual exercises he retrenched from his sleep. After his death a gentleman asked for the little book from which he daily used to recite the Office of the Blessed Virgin, and preserved it as a precious relic. The Blessed Alphonsus Rodriguez while saying his beads for the repose of the soul of Brother Ruiz, saw him in Heaven with a bright face by the side of the Queen of Angels.

3. In Abyssinia, about the beginning of June, in the year 1658,

Father Apollinaris Almeida, a Portuguese, Bishop of Nice, was martyred with two companions, Father Hyacinth Francisci, an Italian, and Father Francis Rodriguez, a Portuguese. While they were labouring to recover Abyssinia from its errors, and to restore it to Catholic communion, they were seized, and hanged like dogs upon trees, and stoned to death as they hung. Their bodies were thrown to brute beasts, but were uninjured by them. The Bishop had for his seal the holy name of JESUS with the inscription, "Thou hast given him to be meat for the people of the Æthiopians" (Ps. lxxiii.).

JUNE 2.

1. At Rome, in the year 1591, died Father Louis Corbinelli, an Italian. He was a great benefactor to the Roman College, and an ornament to it by his virtues. When at the point of death, he appeared three several times the same night to St. Aloysius, who was also sick, and implored his aid that he might pass happily through his last agony, for he said, "I am sore afraid." Father Louis died that night, and in the morning St. Aloysius said to Father Bellarmine that he had gone to Heaven without being detained in Purgatory, being purified by the pains of his bitter agony.

2. Also at Rome, in the year 1593, Michael Herréra, a Spanish Lay-brother. When in the world he was employed as an envoy by the Emperor Charles V., first to England, and then to Constantinople to the Sultan, by whom, when war broke out between him and the Emperor, he was cast into prison. Liberated from captivity, he gave himself to the service of the Eternal King. He entered the Society when he was nearly sixty years of age. St. Francis Borgia, General of the Society, sent for him to Rome and wished him to receive Holy Orders, but he begged to be allowed to remain a Lay-brother. He lived for twenty-four years in that state, a great example of contempt of the world, full of charity and zeal in the fulfilment of his humble duties, and equally dear to all, both at home and abroad.

3. At Seville, in Spain, in the year 1649, Father Andrew de Cazorla, a Spaniard, a martyr in the service of the plague stricken. He was reckoned one of the most learned men in the Province of Andalusia.

Wherever he went his great object was to inspire a horror of sin into all with whom he had to do. He was eager for every opportunity of promoting the glory of God and saving souls. He gave missions, taught catechism to children in the streets, preached, heard confessions, and performed other works of zeal. He was a man of great sweetness of manner and influence over others.

June 3.

1. At Zagrabe, in Croatia, in the year 1617, died Father Peter Vragonitz, a Croat, and one of the two who introduced the Society into Croatia. Soon after his entrance into the Company he was waylaid and wounded so grievously as to be at the point of death. In this condition he was favoured with an apparition of Christ our Lord and His Blessed Mother. He heard our Lady say, "What shall we do for him—shall we grant his request?" and our Lord replied, "Let him live, My Mother, that he may labour for a little while longer." The vision disappeared, and Father Peter regained at once his health, and was an active missioner for thirty years in Hungary and Croatia.

2. On his way to India, in the year 1618, died Father Quintin Cousin, a Belgian, distinguished for his zeal in the salvation of souls. Although he had led a life of more than ordinary virtue, when near to death he broke forth with much vehemence into these expressions—"Narrow is the way which leads to Heaven—very narrow—most narrow!" Shortly afterwards lifting up his eyes to Heaven, and joining his hands upon his breast, he calmly expired.

3. At Lyons, in France, in the year 1626, Father Francis de Mendoza, a Portuguese of noble birth, a man of great and universal learning and singular innocence of life. He wrote Commentaries on the Books of Kings. Being sent to Rome as Procurator of the Province, he received this eulogy from the Father General, that he was a most excellent preacher, writer, Doctor, and Superior, and a perfect Religious man. He died on his return to France from Rome, and death found him watchful and well prepared. He had preserved his baptismal innocence, was most exact in observance of Rule, and always preached in a hairshirt. He joined to the highest talents, the greatest labour and zeal.

4. At Messina, in Sicily, in the year 1577, Father Angelo Sibilla, the elder, a martyr of charity. He entered the Society a Priest and already advanced in years, led thereto by the example of a younger brother who had entered before him. He had but very ordinary talents and a disagreeable exterior, but these defects were compensated for by the qualities of his soul, and especially by an admirable candour and simplicity, and an ardent desire of perfection. He was very soon employed in hearing confessions in our church, and acquitted himself with so much zeal and good of souls that he may be proposed as a model of an Evangelical labourer. Not content with his own share of work, he begged the Sacristan and Porter to call him when any one of the Fathers was prevented by business from attending the confessional that he might replace him. His mission was to gain souls to God by assiduity in the confessional, since he had not the talent of attracting them by preaching. He died of the plague, caught in hearing a poor man's confession.

June 4.

1. In America, among the savages of New Biscay, in the year 1650, Father Cornelius Beudin Godinez, a Belgian, suffered martyrdom for the faith. Full of zeal for the conversion and salvation of souls he had established a mission, when his catechumens and other savages having conspired to kill him, set fire to his cabin. The flames forcing him to leave it, they flung a rope round his neck, dragged him to the church, and there beat him so cruelly that the floor was covered with his blood. He was taken thence to the cemetery cross which he had planted, around which he threw his arms, and died strangled with the cord, his head beaten in with clubs, and his body pierced with wounds. He was thirty-seven years of age, fifteen of which he had spent in the Society. Two years afterwards his body was found incorrupt.

2. At Waterford, in Ireland, in the year 1650, Father James Walsh, an Irishman, a victim of charity attending persons infected with the plague. He was of great purity both in mind and body, and very zealous in the conversion of heretics.

3. At Alcala, in Spain, in the year 1669, Father John de Almarza, a Spaniard, a zealous preacher, especially against public shows and luxury

in dress. Though he was a man of learning and talent, he taught lower grammar for many years. When going upon the mission during the time of vacations, he would take with him the Scholastics to catechize and instruct the people in the neighbouring villages, and prepare them for confession. He was very devout to St. Joseph, St. Joachim and St. Anne, and received more than once special favours from St. Ignatius.

4. At Rome, in the year 1667, Father Sforza Pallavicini, a Cardinal, an illustrious member both of the Sacred College and of the Society. Although he was the eldest son of a noble family he embraced the Ecclesiastical state, and at the age of twenty-one publicly maintained theses on the whole of theology, disputing for three days to the wonder and with the applause of all. Pope Urban VIII. made him a Prelate of his Court, and appointed him head over Ecclesiastical Congregations and to other dignities. These honours he forsook to enter the Society, overcoming with great courage the difficulties made to his vocation. As a Novice he was seen not without admiration clothed in a poor habit, asking alms, and eating with beggars, after having exercised such high functions at the Pontifical Court. For eight years he taught philosophy and theology, and for four years was Prefect of Studies, during which time he composed his history of the Council of Trent. The Sovereign Pontiff often entrusted him with very important affairs; and Alexander VII. commanded him in virtue of holy obedience to accept the Purple. Raised to this dignity, which he had in vain sought to avoid, he lived for eight years in the service of the Church, retaining an inviolable attachment to the Society, thanking God at the point of death for his vocation to it, and declaring that had he to choose a manner of life he would adopt no other than that of the Society. He bequeathed his little property to the Noviceship of St. Andrew.

JUNE 5.

1. At Manilla, in the Philippines, in the year 1622, died Father John de Ribera, a Spaniard, illustrious for his chastity and for heroic patience. When a youth, solicited to sin, like the Patriarch Joseph, leaving part of his cloak behind him, he sought safety in flight, and after this glorious victory entered the Society. In his last sickness, struck with a grievous ulcer from head to foot, he consoled himself by the recital

of the history of the patient Job, until death put an end to his sufferings on the day he had foretold.

2. At Lima, in Peru, in the year 1610, Francis Lopez, a Spaniard, who from Visitor-General of the whole Kingdom of Peru, became an humble and laborious Lay-brother of the Society. He could not be induced to receive Holy Orders by his Superiors or by the Archbishop; but God rewarded him for the loss of the prerogative of the Priesthood by a great gift of prayer and of tears.

3. At Manresa, in Spain, in the year 1627, Father James Tonéra, a Spaniard. For forty-two years he preached fervent discourses through the Lent, and by his eloquence and persevering toil, gained a multitude of souls. He was equally successful in giving missions. In one of these, arriving at a certain place over night, he was informed that there was in the locality a great want of rain. In the morning, which was without a cloud, he mounted the pulpit and spoke with such vehemence against sin, that shuts up heaven and closes it to us, that the audience was moved to abundance of tears; and before the people could leave the church a refreshing rain fell upon the gardens and fields from heaven.

JUNE 6.

1. At Yendi, in Japan, in the year 1634, Father Sebastian Vieyrea, a Portuguese, with five Japanese Novices, was put to death for the faith. He held the post of Vice-Provincial, and was exercising the duties of his office with great service to the Church of Japan. Portraits of him were dispersed everywhere that he might be seized, and a thousand pieces of gold were offered for his capture. At length he was taken and thrown into prison, and when he was urged to apostatize he replied, "For sixty-three years of life I have received the greatest and most abundant benefits from my God, but from the Emperor of Japan only fetters and imprisonment; how then shall I forsake my immortal Master for the sake of him?" Condemned to the pit, he was hung by the feet head downwards, and endured that torment together with his five companions, still surviving after three whole days, when the rest had died. He was then tortured to death by fire.

2. At Huete, in Spain, in the year 1583, Father John Gonzalez, a

victim to his heroic charity. Finding that he could not move a dying person to confession, in great grief for the eternal loss and misery of that soul he offered his life to God in the Sacrifice of the Mass for the salvation of the unhappy man. The Mass was scarcely finished when the dying sinner called for a confessor. Father John being summoned heard his earnest and contrite confession and absolved him, and he died almost within the hour with good hopes of his eternal salvation. But Father John himself also suddenly fell sick, and perceiving that his sacrifice was accepted, prepared himself immediately for death, which ensued, and was as happy as it was enviable.

3. At Seville, in Spain, in the year 1649, Michael Perez, a Lay-brother. He had served two hundred sick persons infected with the pestilence with great care and diligence, until he himself was seized, and died a martyr of charity.

4. At Hang-choo, in China, in the year 1661, Father Martin Martius, a German, a zealous and laborious missioner. In the year 1651 he was sent to Rome as Procurator of the Vice-Province of China. When he had transacted his business, he returned to the field of his labours with seventeen companions, of whom seven died on the journey. Besides books on the Christian religion published in the Chinese language, he printed in German an excellent work, the *Atlas Senensis*, or Description of the Chinese Empire, illustrated with geographical charts.

JUNE 7.

1. At Bubayeni, in the Philippines, in the year 1642, Father Bartholomew Sanchez, a Spaniard, died martyred by savages. He had great devotion to St. Francis Xavier, the Apostle of the Indies, relying on his aid with special confidence, and filled with a great desire of imitating his Apostolic virtues. He found in this Saint a sweet and powerful protection when any thought entered his mind contrary to angelic purity. He received as he thought, an inward warning from the Virgin Mother of God to take Xavier as his patron in this combat. While he was in prayer before the picture of his patron and protector, two days before his festival, he saw the whole of the portrait covered with the appearance of a great cross. This signified the death he died by the hands of the

savages, by one of whom he was stabbed in the throat and by another cut asunder. Afflicted by scruples whether he had been rightly ordained, he heard a voice telling him to leave himself in the hands of the Saint his protector, ready to suffer and follow his example.

2. At Prague, in Bohemia, in the year 1667, Father Rodriguez de Arriaga, a Spaniard, one of the greatest lights of the Society for the subtlety of his understanding, eminence of his learning, and merit of his religious virtues. Having spent his youth in innocence and piety, he entered the Society, and in his noviceship laid the foundations of a high perfection. He taught philosophy at Valladolid and theology at Salamanca, and from thence he went to Bohemia, at the invitation of Father Mutius Vitelleschi, the General, who wrote to Spain to ask for Professors for the above-mentioned Province. The Venerable Marina de Escobar, celebrated for her sanctity, signified that the departure of Father Arriaga for Bohemia was agreeable to the will of God. He was for more than forty years Professor of Theology, Chancellor of the University, and General Prefect of Studies. He wrote eight volumes, seven on theology and one on philosophy, and died preparing his last work, *De Jure et Justitia*. He assisted as Deputy from Bohemia at three General Congregations, the eighth, tenth, and eleventh. His piety was equal to his learning. He gave several hours a day to prayer, and even in his journeys found time and opportunity for converse with God. His life seemed usually divided between study and prayer. Although he was held in the highest esteem, not only by the learned, but by the Sovereign Pontiffs, Urban VIII. and Innocent X., and the Emperor Ferdinand III., he was little in his own eyes, and bore with undisturbed tranquillity severe attacks upon his writings.

JUNE 8.

1. At Rome, in the year 1649, died Father Vincent Carafa, General of the Society, an Italian of the princely house of Carafa. Prevented from his infancy by the grace of God, he ascended by the path of the great Saints to a sublime degree of sanctity. In youth for his piety and innocence he was called an Angel in the flesh; and Father Julius Mancinelli saw him with a bright angelic countenance, and surrounded with celestial light, as he approached to receive the Holy Eucharist. In his government,

whether of Colleges or of the Province, or the whole Society, he ever showed himself a Superior such as the Constitutions require, that is, most closely united to God, ruling by example rather than by command; mild, firm and sweet in his severity. In the year 1649 during a great scarcity he fed daily a thousand poor at the gate of the Professed House for two months together, having collected alms with much diligence for that purpose. They were arranged in order to receive the food, and he himself distributed it, adding words of spiritual advice. The poor being removed thence by command of the Pope to the Lateran Palace, he continued to serve them, until a fever brought on by the devotedness of his labour closed his life by a holy death. His pious works published by him breathe a spirit of seraphic love.

2. At St. Iago, in South America, in the year 1633, Father John Dario, an Italian, a man devoted to the service of all. He laboured chiefly in Peru and Paraguay. A board or chair was his bed for a short sleep of three hours during the space of forty years. Going out of his room or returning to it he threw himself at the foot of the Crucifix. Offences against JESUS Crucified were so continually deprecated and denounced by him that he was called the enemy of sin.

3. At Gräin, in Styria, in the year 1664, Father Paul Rosmer, a Belgian. He taught scholastic theology at Gräin and Vienna for sixteen years with great esteem for talent and learning. He was very devout to St. Dysmas, the good thief, Christ's companion on the Cross, to whom he prayed for a happy death. He left his room as poor as he had received it, having removed nothing and added nothing for thirteen years.

JUNE 9.

1. At Reritiba, in Brazil, in the year 1597, died Father Joseph Anchieta, the Thaumaturgus and Apostle of that country, where he laboured for forty-four years with unwearied zeal. Born at Teneriffe, one of the Canary Isles, he was called for his admirable innocence "Adam before the fall." The birds and beasts paid him reverence, and he seemed to have dominion over them. He was still more admirable for his virtues, of charity towards God and his neighbour, love of prayer and mortification, humility, patience, and a most tender devotion to the Virgin Mother of

x

God, whose life he wrote whilst detained a hostage among the savages in Latin elegiac verse in two thousand and eighty-six elegant couplets, composed without pen or paper, and committed to his faithful memory. God honoured the panegyrist of Mary with the gift of prophecy. His zeal for souls led him to undertake many painful labours. The government of the Province was entrusted to him, and he founded many churches and maintained and multiplied Houses of the Society. His life, translated into various languages, contains much that is most wonderful and extraordinary.

2. At Krems, in Bohemia, in the year 1615, Father Dominic Valesi, an Italian, very devout to the Blessed Virgin and a great lover of poverty. Hearing the lives of St. Catherine of Sienna and St. Aloysius, he was inflamed with the desire of exalted virtue. On his knees he read daily a chapter of *The Following of Christ*. In his room he had neither bed nor chair; his table was a chest, his own left hand was his candlestick, and his bed a large wooden cross, on which he lay down to sleep. Having attended with indefatigable zeal the infected with the plague at Neisse, he died soon after of exhaustion at Krems.

3. At Klaussenburg, in Transylvania, in the year 1603, Emmanuel Neri, an Italian Lay-brother. He fulfilled with great edification the offices of Infirmarian and Sacristan. When the city was taken and the heretical soldiery broke into the churches and trampled on the Holy Eucharist, Brother Emmanuel unable to contain himself at the sight of their sacrilegious impiety boldly remonstrated with them, and suffered death at their hands, cut down with an axe and shot through with a bullet.

June 10.

1. At Naples, in the year 1588, died Father Andrew Spinola, an Italian, distinguished for his noble birth, but more for his religious humility and charity. Taking food in the Refectory in one of our Houses before entering the Society he felt a loathing and disgust at the poor furniture of the table, having been accustomed to the splendour of wealth and luxury. But after his reception into it everything seemed excellent, and the plates and dishes as if they were of wrought silver. Thinking this a concession to his weakness and delicacy on the part of Superiors, he went to the Rector

and begged that he might not be treated with such indulgence, and that he would be content with the ordinary service of the table. Being told that the usual things had been given him, he perceived that it was a divine favour, and he thanked the goodness of God for it. Filling afterwards the office of Rector of the College of Naples, while humbly serving the infected with the plague he received a precious death as a reward of his charity.

2. At Paraña, in Paraguay, in the year 1653, Father Joseph Cataldini, an Italian, entirely devoted to instructing and civilizing the savages. He founded six Reductions, and baptized many thousands. In life he was sometimes seen in the figure of an Angel Guardian defending the Indians against the devils, at other times surrounded with celestial brightness, and after death clothed in a resplendent robe. He was comforted with heavenly visions, especially during the Holy Sacrifice, and at the elevation of the Sacred Chalice often saw an arm, clothed like a Priest's when vested, stretched forth from it and blessing him. When he was troubled with fears about his predestination, the Blessed Virgin said to him, " Fear not, my son."

3. At Lyons, in France, in the year 1623, Father Michael Goyssard, a Frenchman. He was received into the Society at the age of fifteen by Father Paschal Broet, companion of St. Ignatius and first Provincial of France. He governed many Colleges, and in the violent storm which was raised against the Society in France about the year 1594 he behaved with admirable wisdom, winning love and respect by his sweetness, politeness, and sanctity of life. He was an indefatigable labourer, often remaining eight hours fasting in the confessional. He rose an hour before the Community to pray, even in the depths of winter; and when in his old age better food was set before him he would not touch it. Troubled with an abscess, which caused him suffering night and day, through modesty he could not persuade himself to receive the visit of a surgeon, but making a vow to the Blessed Virgin obtained a perfect cure. He published many little cantiques set to music, to abolish the custom of bad songs. He loved to think of death, and as it drew near he said that he preferred to hear speak of the mercy rather than of the justice of God, Whom in simplicity of heart he had served from his childhood. He died at the age of seventy-six, sixty-two of which he had spent in

the Society in repute of sanctity. It is said that many who recommended themselves through his prayers to God obtained deliverance from long and inveterate temptations.

June 11.

1. At Gerona, in Spain, in the year 1607, died Father Gabriel Vasia, a Spaniard, versed in human and divine literature and learned in languages. He was most devout to the Virgin Mother of God, whom he frequently invoked in the words of the verse, *Monstra te esse Matrem*. When in sickness both of body and mind he had omitted this practice, this most holy Mother appeared to him and tenderly reproved him for being so forgetful of her.

2. At Quito, in Peru, in the year 1612, Mark Antonio, an Italian Lay-brother, known by no other name both within and without the house than that of "the Saint." To the age of eighty years he macerated his body with fasts, disciplines, and hairshirts. In prayer his attention was so great that he seemed a statue; no wonder therefore that he obtained whatever he asked. Once in the church during the Holy Sacrifice he was seen elevated in the air and his face shining like a live coal.

3. At Bilboa, in Spain, in the year 1623, Simon de Espalza, a Spanish Lay-brother. Seeing one of his Brothers lying sick, and anointed in preparation for death, he had recourse to the Blessed Virgin, to whom he was very devout, and begged that he might be substituted in his place and the dying brother restored to health, because he was very useful to the College, while he himself was of little service. He was heard, for the sick man revived and gradually recovered. Simon sickened within three days of the same disease and died.

4. At Vienna, in Austria, in the year 1655, Father Ignatius Josiski, a Pole, a martyr to heroic charity. He thrice asked for and twice obtained the service of the plague-stricken. He was a man in whose countenance and whole deportment there appeared the very picture of goodness and candour of soul. As he went by, men would say, "There goes the saintly Jesuit." At his death the poor and the sick lamented over his loss, weeping, as they said, "for their Father."

JUNE 12.

1. At Valladolid, in Spain, in the year 1575, died Father John Castañeda, a Spaniard. He had governed for some years the Colleges of Seville and Placentia, when he was summoned to Toledo by his Provincial, Father Bustamante, and employed in the kitchen, to subdue a certain outburst of temper which at times obscured his other eminent qualities. He obeyed with alacrity and constancy for some months, doing the meanest services with signal humility, until from the kitchen of Toledo he was removed to the government of the College of Valladolid, which he adorned with his virtues.

2. At Madrid, in Spain, in the year 1580, Father Rodrigo Gonzalez, a man of great zeal and industry in rescuing souls from the service of the devil. He brought to confession a sorceress who had done much harm at the Court of Madrid, and flung the implements of her magic art, which she had given up to him, into the sewer. The devil enraged, prepared revenge, which was permitted by the hidden judgment of God. He greatly tormented Father Rodrigo, and crushed his body with a heavy plank. But the power of the devil was thereby much broken, for afterwards he confessed that "for fifty years and more his power had been much restricted against the Fathers of the College of Madrid on account of one of the Fathers who had died there." These words seemed applicable to no other than Father Rodrigo.

3. At Cracow, in Poland, in the year 1622, Father Simon Wisoski, a Russian, who, in company with Father Peter Skarga, came to Rome to beg to enter the Society, and was admitted by St. Francis Borgia. Returning to his country after his noviceship, he became a zealous labourer in the vineyard, devoting himself especially to the poor, for whom he founded hospitals at Posna, Wilna, and Lublin, whence he acquired the title of the "Father of the Poor." Ordered to follow into Sweden Her Serene Highness Catherine, espoused to King John, he introduced into the Court great piety, and was the chief cause of Prince Sigismund receiving a Catholic education, who was afterwards the glorious King of Poland. He zealously employed his spare time in translating pious works into the Polish language, of which Southwell gives a long catalogue.

June 13.

1. At Prague, in Bohemia, in the year 1661, died Father John Hubat, a Bohemian. He took as addressed to himself the words: *Tibi derelictus est pauper*—"The poor is left to thee." To render assistance to the poor in their temporal as well as spiritual wants, he sought them out in the most miserable hovels, and only approached the houses of the rich to beg alms for the needy. As he was thus actively engaged in promoting the good of souls, he was seized by some heretical soldiers and put in prison, where he had much to suffer. Four times he exposed his life in the charitable service of those who were infected with the plague, but by the protection of Divine Providence he escaped from contagion.

2. At the College of La Paz, in Peru, in the year 1661, Father Christopher Viverez, a Peruvian, remarkable for his singular modesty, virginal purity, and exact observance of the Rules. When a child he fell into a rapid mill-stream, and was on the point of being drawn under the wheel, when, invoking the aid of the Mother of God, he escaped death. Shortly before he died, Father Gabriel Vasquez, not the celebrated theologian, but another of the same name, his Spiritual Father, some time deceased, whom he held in veneration, appeared to him, and giving Father Christopher a paternal embrace, said to him—"Come, my child," and disappeared. The Father shortly after went to join him, leaving much regret for his loss.

3. At Granada, in Spain, in the year 1610, Brother Baptista, a Spanish Lay-brother. When he was in his first probation, and was wavering in his vocation, the Blessed Virgin, with St. Peter and St. Barbara, appeared to him and admonished him to persevere in the state to which he was called, and that so he would obtain eternal life. He remained, and lived in close union with God, melting into tears whenever mention was made of heavenly things. While Brother Baptista was earnestly engaged in prayer for the Rector of the College of Granada, unjustly accused and summoned to plead his cause, he heard a voice from Heaven, "that the Rector would soon return with unblemished character and acquitted of all imputation." And it happened accordingly.

June 14.

1. In Sweden, in the year 1601, died Father Christopher Spotech, a Pole. Taken prisoner in Livonia with John Eston, a Lay-brother, by the Swedish troops, he suffered many cruelties from them, being scourged, starved, and imprisoned. Finally, with his companion, he was carried into banishment to Finland, where they both died in prison.

2. At Louvain, in Belgium, in the year 1610, Father Florence Burckhurst, a Belgian, a man of great name and authority both in the Society and out of it. He was President of the theological body in the University, and his words were regarded as oracles by the most distinguished of its members. Lipsius declared that he was never voluntarily absent from the lecture of Father Florence, and that he was moved to devotion by the very sight of him. The chief magistrate of the town, saluting him with courtesy, said—"I am your good friend." "But I," replied the Father, "am not yours, unless you amend your life." This rebuke at first made him angry, but afterwards entering into himself, he changed his life, and held his admonitor in higher esteem than ever. This liberty of speech and manner was derived from a close union with God, for he often spent seven hours a day in prayer.

3. At Poitiers, in France, in the year 1631, Father Francis Garasse, a Frenchman. He was a learned and talented writer, but he preferred charity to all other things, and obtained permission to serve the sick in the time of the plague. Being seized with it in the midst of his zealous labours, he would be put in no other place than the common hospital in which to die. Thirty-six of the Society died the same glorious death of charity in different parts of France the same year.

4. At Paris, in the year 1670, Father Francis Annat, a Frenchman. He was a great defender and support of the Catholic faith in France, and a bold vindicator of the true doctrine of St. Augustine against the Jansenists, whom he attacked and confounded by his learned writings, He was Confessor to Louis XIV. during sixteen years, and was so much esteemed by him that he could with difficulty obtain leave to retire from the Court and give a few months to a careful preparation for his passage to eternity. Charged with the disposal of benefices, he used his influence

only for the good of religion, and, while he sought to recompense merit, he asked no favour for any member of his family, which the King observing, asked—"Has then Father Annat no relations?" He died at the age of eighty, having lived sixty-three years in the Society.

June 15.

1. At Rome, in the year 1555, died Father James Eguia, a Spaniard, Confessor to our holy Father St. Ignatius. Before entering the Society he was so liberal to him, that opening a money-chest, he asked him to take from it as much as he pleased. Father Peter Faber used to entitle him "St. James," but he accounted himself like a piece of cracked coin that passes for good in a heap, and would often say, "That he who thinks himself something, is but little worth, but he who thinks much of himself is nothing." He had the highest opinion of the sanctity of our holy Father, and used to say that if he survived him but an hour he would relate such things of him as would fill men's minds with astonishment at the sanctity of Ignatius. This coming to the knowledge of our holy Father, he severely rebuked him, and would no more go to confession to him. Indeed, it is thought to be owing to the prayers of St. Ignatius that Father Eguia died six weeks before him.

2. At Ingolstadt, in Germany, in the year 1600, Father John Rastell, an Englishman. Seeing the Provincial of Germany, Father Paul Hoffe, at the point of death, and desirous to save a man so useful to the Society, he undertook a pilgrimage to the Church of St. Saviour, eight miles distant, and there offered his life instead. The sacrifice was accepted. Immediately on his return he took to his bed and died. And Father Paul was restored to health.

3. At Drogheda, in Ireland, in the year 1649, Father Robert Netterville, an Irishman. Dragged from his bed by the Puritan soldiers as a Priest and a Jesuit, and beaten unmercifully with clubs, so that his arms and collar-bones were broken, and being left half dead, he expired after four days, venerable for his age as well as for his sufferings and for his labours for the Church in Ireland.

4. At Naples, in the year 1656, Father Francis Macedonio, a Religious of consummate virtue. He had acquired a profound self-contempt and continual union with God, with Whose love he was so inflamed, and so full

of zeal for the salvation of souls, that he was commonly called the seraph. He was most devout to the Blessed Sacrament; and in offering the Holy Sacrifice was often raised from the ground in ecstacy, and seen resplendent with light. He preached missions going always on foot, inviting to the Sacraments and to a general Communion, of which practice he was a zealous promoter. He died a martyr of charity on the feast of Corpus Christi, in the service of the sick of the plague. Some days before he foretold his death, while he promised a long life to one of the sick whom he cured by the sign of the cross on the forehead.

5. In Tonquin, Father Baptist Massari went to receive the crown for his zeal and labours. Admitted into the Society in Austria, he was sent as a Missioner to the East, and preached the faith in Cochin China and Tonquin for the space of eight years, enduring hardships without number. At last being taken by command of the King, he confessed the faith before his judges, and after six month's imprisonment died of sufferings and privations.

JUNE 16.

1. At Palermo, in Sicily, in the year 1619, died Father John Baptist Carminata, celebrated for his preaching, prudence in government, and angelic purity. As Provincial he continued to preach with immense fruit, and was called both Apostle and Angel. More than once he exposed his life to win souls. He was Provincial of Sicily, Visitor of Venice and Poland, and Assistant of Italy. At Rome he was admired during twenty-six years as an extraordinary preacher, and enjoyed the esteem of the greatest persons and of the Sovereign Pontiffs. In the midst of these honours his humility was so great that he thought himself unworthy of the bread he ate. He was cured of sickness at Bologna by the visit and blessing of the Infant JESUS. During his life he wrought many cures; and at his death his soul was seen received into Heaven by St. Ignatius, St. Francis Xavier, and St. Aloysius, the day on which, sixty-four years before, he had been received into the Society.

2. At Pultowa, in Poland, in the year 1650, Father Bartholomew Oleskiewicz, a Lithuanian, a great preacher, and Professor of Theology. He daily read attentively the Passion on his knees. He gave an hour to

spiritual reading when he was giving Schools; at other times much more. He visited the Blessed Sacrament before and after Lecture, and before going out; and he made before It his meditation and examen on his knees. Before his own Mass he heard one, and after his own another. For love of Poverty, he not only deprived himself of superfluities in his room, but even of necessaries, and used the common washing-place for his ablutions. In his comportment, he was ever recollected and in union with God.

3. At Palermo, in the year 1617, at the Novitiate, Simon Buceri, a Sicilian Lay-brother, of great prayer and mortification. In the world he macerated his body and preserved his innocence, and for fifty-one years in the Society continued his austerities. Fasting, disciplines, iron girdles, hairshirts, which he never quitted and which covered his body, had made him almost lose the sense of pain. He lived under the stairs, sleeping a few hours on the ground, or seated on a stool. His soul was inundated with heavenly delights. He was visited by his Guardian Angel, and the Guardian Angels of many others, by St. Stanislaus, the Blessed Virgin, and our Lord. He had the gift of prophecy, and worked many miraculous cures during his life and after his death. A sweet odour filled the room in which he died.

JUNE 17.

1. At Rome, in the year 1651, died Father Francis Piccolomini, an Italian, the eighth General of the Society. He governed the Provinces of Venice, Naples, Milan, and Rome, was Visitor of Sicily, and seven years Secretary of the Society. In all these offices he deserved and won the highest commendations for prudence, charity, and zeal. He succeeded Father Vincent Carafa, and governed the Society for a year and a half, dying at the age of sixty-nine. He was eminent for prudence in government, and was a man of singular innocence and virtue. In his last sickness he poured out the whole of a draught of water that had been brought to refresh him, and said—"Let us offer it to God. It would be seeking pleasure on the Cross on which God has placed me, to drink it. O my crucified JESUS! keep for me some little corner on Thy Cross! Behold me ready to suffer more and yet more, even for all eternity, if it be Thy pleasure, O my God."

2. At Goa, in the East Indies, in the year 1617, Father Jerome Xavier, a Spaniard, a relative of the Apostle of the Indies and akin to him in virtue. After he had been Rector of the Colleges of Bazain and Cochin, Master of Novices, and Superior of the Professed House at Goa, emulous of the glories of his kinsman, he made an Apostolical expedition into the Empire of the Great Mogul, where he fearlessly preached the Gospel amid many dangers, and baptized four of the Emperor's nephews; but his success among the people did not correspond to his labours, for the Emperor himself became the founder of a new religion. Returning to Goa, he peacefully expired; and after his death, the vision of a beautiful room in Heaven was beheld by a certain person, who heard the words, "Here Jerome Xavier rests from his labours."

3. At Palermo, in Sicily, in the year 1611, Thomas Cannoni, a Sicilian Lay-brother of great merit and virtue. Once when he approached Holy Communion, bathed in sweat after labours imposed upon him by obedience, two Angels were seen wiping his face and holding the linen cloth before him as he received. Angels were also seen going round the bier and incensing his body when laid out for burial.

JUNE 18.

1. At Jaroslau, in Poland, in the year 1586, Father John Hart, an Englishman, was called to the reward of his labours. At London he was thrown into prison, starved and racked. His mother was sent to him to shake his constancy, but when she entered the prison and saw her son in chains, wasted, and with his limbs dislocated, she embraced him and said, "Courage, my child, now I know you for my own. Look up to Heaven. You will not lose your life, but change it for a better." Leaving him much comforted, she returned to the judges, and said that she found her son well disposed. Interpreting the words in their own sense, they hastened to the prison, where they found to their disappointment that they had been foiled by a woman. After this he was thrown into a dungeon twenty feet deep, full of mud and filth, where he lay for fifty days. Meanwhile Elizabeth, either desirous of repute for clemency or fearful of ill-will at so much cruel bloodshed, gave orders that seventy-three Priests of the number who were in prison should be chosen out and banished the

kingdom. Father Hart was one of them. In his prison he had made a vow to enter the Society, and this being told the General by Father Gaspar Haywood, he was admitted to it on the 18th of March, 1583, and sent for his noviceship to Verdun. Summoned afterwards to Rome, and sent to Jaroslau, he there died. Seven years later, his body was found incorrupt, and placed in the new church of the College of Jaroslau.

2. At Martinique, in the year 1675, Father Joseph Poncet, a Frenchman. From his early years he was surnamed the Saint, and in religion he continued to advance daily in perfection. Gifted with rare talents, he asked and obtained the mission of Canada, and devoted himself to the salvation of the Indians with apostolic zeal for eighteen years. His life may be said to have been during all this time a continual martyrdom. Falling into the hands of the Iroquois, he suffered frightful torments; they covered him with wounds, and bit off a finger with their teeth. On his return to Europe he was sent to Loretto as Penitentiary of the French. This employment was the more consoling to him as from his childhood he had a special devotion to the Holy Family; but thirsting still for the salvation of souls, he solicited anew the foreign missions, and was sent to the islands of South America. Exhausted by his labours, he died in the island of Martinique when he was sixty-five years of age, forty-five of which he spent in the Society. To the most ardent zeal he united the most profound humility and self-contempt, he took disciplines to blood daily, and wore a hairshirt furnished with sharp points, which obedience compelled him to remove a year before he died. He experienced great delights in prayer, to which he devoted daily five or six hours.

3. At Valencia, in Spain, in the year 1583, Father Peter Gascon, a Spaniard. While he lived in the world his house was so open to the poor that it was called the hospital of free bounty. He gave as a reason for not wearing gloves, that "Christ had not gloves but nails in His hands." Such was his zeal for souls after he had joined the Society, that the famous preacher in those parts, Father Ramirez, said of him, "Twelve such Gascons would convert the world." To a friend who asked him for an instruction how to spend life virtuously, he wrote on a slip of paper, "Silence, silence, silence."

June 19.

1. At Malacca, in the East Indies, in the year 1596, Father John de Caunas, held in high repute by all for sanctity. Alphonsus Turriano, an ecclesiastic remarkable for his piety, visited him on his death-bed, and expressed his earnest desire to follow him soon. Father John replied that if he wished it, he would obtain it of God. Alphonsus repeated that he truly desired it, and a few days after the death of the Father he was taken with fever and died. Among the papers of Father John was found his particular-examen, carefully kept for thirty years.

2. In Chili, in the year 1641, Father Melchoir de Venegas, an American Indian. For his greater progress in perfection he assigned to each day of the week a special virtue to be prayed for and practised. On the Sunday he exercised himself in the desire of seeing God, on Monday in acts of contrition, on Tuesday in thanksgiving, on Wednesday in acts of divine love, on Thursday in imitation of Christ, on Friday in compassion with His sufferings, on Saturday in resignation to the will of God. By this means he made wonderful progress in Religious perfection. Most devout to the Blessed Virgin, he fasted in her honour on Wednesdays and Saturdays. Being Rector, and receiving a new habit, he sent it to one in the House who had most need of it. He would never wear shoes or a hat which had not been already used, saying that a Superior should be a man of poverty from head to foot. To a contemplative life he joined the activity of a missioner. He was called the Apostle of the Tucumans, and was the first to preach the Gospel among the nation of the Chonese.

3. At Munich, in Germany, in the year 1635, Father Adam Contzen, a German, a pious and strenuous combatant of error. Southwell numbers twenty-one of his polemical writings. His great knowledge of the Greek, Hebrew, Syriac, and Chaldaic languages assisted him very much in the true explanation of Holy Scripture. He was highly eulogized by Cardinal Bellarmine, and was a man of a most pacific disposition and of virginal modesty. So great was his patience, that he never made known the most severe pains he suffered from the stone.

June 20.

1. At Nangasachi, in Japan, in the year 1626, Father Francis Pacecho, Provincial and Administrator of the diocese, suffered martyrdom with eight companions. Of these, two were Europeans, Father John Baptist Zola, native of Brescia in Italy, Father Balthazar de Torres, of Granada in Spain, and five Japanese Lay-brothers, Gaspar Sandamantaza, Peter Binxei, Paul Xingutke, John Kisaeu, Michael Toxo, and Brother Vincent Caun, of the Corea. These six were catechists. They were all seized during the persecution of the tyrant Xogunsama, and cast into prison, where they suffered much; then they were brought to Nangasachi, where so many martyrs had suffered, and were burned alive on the Mount of Martyrs. They kissed the ground embraced the stakes, sung Psalms, and with the holy names of Jesus and Mary on their lips they gave up their souls to God.

2. At Cordova, in Spain, in the year 1597, Father John Frias, a Spaniard. He entered the Society with a most ardent desire of pleasing God. By his sermons against sin and the occasions of it, he moved all hearts to penitence, so that more than once great storms and calumnies were raised against him. The Father's shield of protection was silence and patience. In the vehemence of his preaching he broke a bloodvessel and died.

3. At Madrid, in the year 1672, Father Alphonsus de Andrada. After having taught moral theology for some years and governed the College of Placentia, he spent the fifty remaining years of his life in preaching and giving Missions. He employed his spare time from these occupations in writing pious books, of which Southwell enumerates twenty-five. The composition of these works never interfered with his labours of charity.

June 21.

1. At Rome, in the year 1591, died St. Aloysius Gonzaga, in the words of the *Roman Martyrology*, "most illustrious for contempt of princely rank and for innocence of life." Commanded by a voice from Heaven, which distinctly bid him enter the Society, he obeyed, but had much to suffer before he could conquer the opposition made to his vocation by his

June 21.

Father. In the Society he has received the name of "the Angelical," which he had already merited in the world. Most men experience difficulty in keeping their mind fixed on God, but he found still greater in diverting his mind ever so little from Him, when commanded by his Superiors for the sake of God to do so, on account of his broken health. He had consecrated his virginity to God from his earliest years, and guarded it by a severe and continual mortification of his innocent and delicate body, although he never experienced any motion or thought against purity. His exceeding great glory in Heaven was revealed in an extacy to St. Mary Magdalen de Pazzi, who exclaimed — "What glory Aloysius the son of Ignatius enjoys! I could not have conceived so great a glory unless my JESUS had shown it me! I could traverse the world to tell all men that Aloysius the son of Ignatius is a great Saint! Aloysius was a hidden martyr. Oh, how much he loved whilst he was on earth."

2. At Trigueros, in Spain, in the year 1570, Father Bartholomew Bustamante, a Spaniard, so wise and perfect a master of Novices that St. Francis Borgia called his Noviciate the gem of the Society. Deliberating on the choice of a state of life when he was already a Priest and theologian of esteem and reputation, he felt a strong internal impulse to go to Guipuscoa and do what he should see Francis, late Duke of Gandia, doing. He went and saw, and followed the example of Borgia. Such was his love for the Society that, having given 500 gold crowns to the Roman College, he said that he would willingly sell himself to the Turks as a slave to procure the least advantage to the Society. He was Rector of many Colleges, and Provincial of Andalusia.

3. In Spain, near Bilboa, in the year 1625, John Marino, a Spanish Scholastic. He was called by the physicians, who admired his astonishing patience in the most severe sufferings, "the gentle patient brother." By others he was called "the Saint." Kept by the grace of God free from mortal sin, he made also a vow that he would never deliberately commit a venial sin.

4. At Cologne, in Germany, in the year 1656, Father Maximilian Sandée, a Belgian, celebrated for his direction of Sodalities of the Blessed Virgin and for his unwearied labours in writing. He is said to have composed as many books as he lived years, in number seventy-eight. The chief of these are enumerated by Southwell.

5. At Alençon, in the flower of his age, Father Claude Gedoyn, a Frenchman. Sent to Alençon after the third year of probation, he began to announce the word of God with touching and persuasive eloquence. His profound humility and rare modesty gave influence to his instructions. He told his Confessor that he was assured he should not die until he had finished a psalter which he was composing in honour of the Blessed Virgin. The day he completed it he fell sick and died, when he was thirty-two years of age, of which he had been sixteen in the Society. All the town was filled with grief at his premature death. His praise was in every mouth, and multitudes shed tears.

JUNE 22.

1. At Coimbra, in Portugal, in the year 1612, died Andrew Saa, a Portuguese Scholastic. Hearing of the death of Father Rodriguez, he told the Infirmarian to make ready all things for his funeral also, but first to call the Father Rector to him; from whom, when he had come, he asked leave to depart from this present life. The Rector having assented, on condition that such were the will of God, he took in his hand the blest taper and his crucifix, entered into a brief agony, and expired in most ardent sentiments of divine love.

2. At Cambrai, in the year 1610, Claude Veley, a Belgian Lay-brother. As he lay on his death-bed, a legion of frightful apparitions rushed on him, as on St. Anthony, in the form of lions, bulls and dragons, but he, calling on the Saints for protection, was comforted with the sight of JESUS dying upon the Cross, and promising to be with him in his last agony.

3. At Parma, in Italy, in the year 1578, Joseph Martini, an Italian Scholastic. During his Novitiate, his fellow Novices could find no fault in him. Sent to Parma for his studies, he was attacked with a fatal sickness, during which he relaxed none of his fervour imbibed in the Noviceship. Being asked at the commencement of his attack if he thought that his native air would contribute to his recovery, he replied, "All I wish is to live among my dear Brothers and Fathers." During his illness of thirteen months, his Confessor declared he could not find in his confessions matter for absolution. And another said that he admired in this angelical young man the model and perfection of the most eminent

virtues. To guard him against vanity, his Confessor said to him, "Your Brothers in their charity show some esteem for you; be careful to confirm yourself in true self-contempt." "My Father," he replied, "my only hope is in the precious blood and merits of Jesus Christ." In these sentiments, at the age of twenty-one, he rendered his soul to God.

JUNE 23.

1. At Tyburn, in London, in the year 1609, Father Thomas Garnett, hanged and quartered for the Faith. He was son of Richard Garnett, brother of Father Henry Garnett, and a Confessor of the Faith. At the age of sixteen he entered St. Omers, made his higher studies at Valladolid, and returned a Priest on the English mission. He was admitted into the Society by his uncle in 1604, and falling into the hands of the persecutors was banished. Having made his novitiate at Louvain, and taken his vows, he returned to England, where he was betrayed and arrested when leaving London for Coldham Hall. Being asked whether he would save his life by taking the oath, he replied that he would not take it to save five thousand lives. Having prayed for the King and Queen, and his enemies, and devoutly repeated the Our Father, Creed, and *Veni Creator*, he suffered a glorious martyrdom at the age of thirty-four.

2. In Paraguay, in the year 1628, Father John Vasée, a Fleming. He died at the age of thirty-nine, in the midst of his labours in the field of the Gospel, having spent seven years in Paraguay. In the world, being a Priest, and playing excellently on the violin, he heard that the savages of Paraguay were passionately fond of music, and thought that by means of his instrument he might contribute to their conversion. For this purpose he asked to be admitted into the Society, and having given proof of solid virtue, was sent at his request on the Paraguay mission. He was there employed in teaching the children catechism and singing, with the happiest results. Through his care the festivals celebrated with music drew together immense crowds, and increased the reverence of the savages for the mysteries of religion. His virtues were no less a charm to the people than his music. The very sight of him moved to piety. He was very devout to the Blessed Virgin and his Guardian Angel, and a man of great modesty. He was so guarded with his tongue that he could

not recollect ever having told a falsehood in his whole life. After his labours of the day he prayed for the whole town and people among whom he lived, making the sign of the cross towards the four quarters of the place, that it might be protected from evil.

June 24.

1. At Antwerp, in Belgium, in the year 1629, died Father Charles Scribani, a Belgian, born at Brussels of a noble family originally from Italy. For some years he filled the chairs of Rhetoric and Philosophy, and then for twenty-eight years without interruption held the office of a Superior. His rare prudence, generosity of mind, and admirable writings won the esteem of all his contemporaries. Pope Urban VIII., Philip IV. of Spain, and Ferdinand II. honoured him with letters, and Henry IV. made him a French citizen. His religious virtue and humility were not impaired by these honours. He slept little, to give time to prayer. Every day before ascending the altar he went to confession. During the Holy Sacrifice he often shed tears. His practice was, when he left his room, to kiss the feet of the statue of the Blessed Virgin and commend to her the business he had to transact. His charity was admirable. When Rector of the House at Antwerp, he begged that all the sick of the Province might be sent to him, and he treated them with the greatest tenderness and generosity. A few days before his death, he said to Father Philip Bultinck, who was going to Mechlin—"Father, we shall go to Heaven together." And it came to pass that both died about the same time. Father Scribani died at the age of sixty-nine; and a monument recording his life and virtues was raised to him at Antwerp.

2. At Orta, in Lombardy, where he was giving a Mission, in the year 1703, Father John Peter Pinamonti, an Italian. He was engaged upon the work of the Missions for thirty-eight years, and for twenty-six of them was the inseparable companion of Father Segneri, who loved and revered him as a saint. Prevented by headaches from study, he devoted twelve or fifteen hours a day to the confessional and to giving instructions, which were delivered with so much clearness and unction that they were listened to with avidity and fruit by all classes. He was conspicuous for his indefatigable charity in consoling and assisting the sick in their corporal

as well as spiritual wants, and ingeniously humble in concealing the supernatural gifts of grace and natural talents which he possessed. An evidence of this are the valuable and useful works that he left behind him. He died aged seventy-one, having been fifty-six years in the Society. The people of thirty surrounding parishes attended his funeral; his body was regarded as a sacred treasure, and graces were received through his intercession.

3. At Tivoli, in Italy, in the year 1602, Antonio de Henrici, an Italian Lay-brother. He supported in a great measure the College of Tivoli by his labour and industry, having been sent to it by St. Ignatius himself. When asked by the Father Rector, in a serious illness, how many years he thought he had to live, he replied—"One and a half." And it proved true.

4. At Rome, in the year 1650, Father Balthasar Corderius, a Belgian. A profound Greek scholar, he undertook to collate the writings of the Greek Fathers with Holy Scripture. For this purpose he visited and explored the principal libraries of Europe—in Germany, France, Spain, and Italy. He elaborated, chiefly from the Greek Fathers, a catena of exposition on the Psalms, and on the Gospels of St. John and St. Luke. On St. Luke alone he brought passages to elucidate the text out of sixty-five Greek Fathers.

JUNE 25.

1. At Ratisbon, in Germany, in the year 1609, died Father John Bredane, a Belgian; a pattern of a good Religious in life and death. He was eminent as a preacher and an able confessor, especially in assisting the dying. He is said to have thus assisted as many as nine hundred, so that the town council of Friburg sent an embassy of honourable persons to the Provincial to beg him to send back Father John to Friburg. His death at Ratisbon prevented it.

2. On his way to the Philippine Islands, in the year 1622, Father Francis Joanelli, an Italian. Having embarked for the missions of New Spain, full of ardour, his fervour cooled during the voyage, but having made the Exercises, he recovered the zeal with which he was first

animated. He prayed so long and so fervently that the sight of him inspired devotion. He took daily such severe disciplines that his body streamed with blood. He passed a great deal of the night before the Blessed Sacrament. His chief devotional practice was conformity to the will of God, and he loved to repeat, and carried written with him, the words—"I have found a man according to My own Heart to do all My wills." This disposition fortified him in his last moments, when he tasted so profound a peace that those who stood around his bed thought they saw a Saint die. When embarking, he foretold that he should die on the voyage.

3. At Bologna, in Italy, in the year 1671, Father John Baptist Riccioli, an Italian; deeply versed in every kind of science. He taught scholastic theology for ten years, partly at Bologna and partly at Parma; but excelling chiefly in mathematics he gave his mind to that study, and was the author of some highly esteemed volumes, not merely theoretical but practical, and illustrated by experimental proofs. He wrote *Astronomy Reformed*, two volumes; *Astronomy Old and New*, two volumes; *Chronology Reformed*, three volumes; twelve books on *Cosmography*; *A Defence of the Gregorian Calendar*, and other works.

JUNE 26.

1. At Würtsburg, in Germany, in the year 1625, Father John George Vogler, a German; who excelled in the gift of preaching and in prayer. His favourite authors were St. Augustine and St. John Chrysostom; the first he studied to nourish his own private devotion, and the second for his instructions to the people. He was as much hated by the heretics, as he was beloved by the Catholics, and when he for a time left Haguenau to go elsewhere, they impudently spread a report that he was seized by an evil spirit, had to be put in chains, and finally had been carried off. To their confusion Father Vogler soon returned sound and well, more vigorous than ever to combat and defeat them.

2. At Firando, in Japan, in the year 1587, John Fernandez, a Spanish Lay-brother, the companion of St. Francis Xavier in Japan. He was highly esteemed by the Saint, and was very serviceable and

active in spreading the faith among several nations. At Amangucci, a man of note came up to him while preaching to ridicule his doctrine; but seeing a fellow from the crowd spit deliberately in the face of Brother John, and that he quietly, without taking notice of it, wiped his face with his handkerchief and continued his discourse, he was so struck with the greatness of soul which it displayed, that casting himself at the feet of Brother John, he was the first to ask for Baptism. Such was the Brother's reverence for Priests, that he never spoke in their presence unless commanded.

3. At Cracow, in Poland, Father James Wiecz, born at Vangrovich, in Poland. In his youth he had imbibed heresy by reading heretical books, but providentially the book of Cardinal Ilosius, entitled *Confession*, fell into his hands, and this antidote expelled the poison. Admitted into the Society at Rome, and having finished his studies, he returned to Poland, and was usefully employed in teaching theology, writing books, preaching, and governing. He was the first Rector, and may be called the founder, of the College of Posna. At the request of King Stephen he went into Transylvania, and was the first Superior of the College of Clausenberg. He was the first of our Fathers to publish a book in the vernacular tongue, a refutation of the *Confession of Sendomir* put forth by the Calvinists. By order of Pope Gregory XIII. he was translating the Bible into Polish, and had retired to Cracow to perfect his work, when he died. While he had life and strength he used continually to meditate on the Penitential Psalms, shedding abundance of tears, and when he was sick and dying he would have them read to him, after the example of St. Augustine. He passed the last night in prayer, with his gaze steadfastly fixed on the crucifix.

JUNE 27.

1. In America, in the year 1610, Father Raphael Ferrer, a Spaniard, died a martyr. This zealous missioner civilized and made a large Reduction of Indians in a short time, and baptized four hundred. At Popayana, when a play was about to be represented of which he could not approve, and he was not able otherwise to prevent it, he rushed into

the theatre before it began, and spoke in such a manner as to move all to tears and stop the play. Some savages, infuriated because he had overthrown their idols, flung him into a river, and launched him into a happy eternity.

2. At Valencia, in Spain, in the year 1558, Diego Sarabias, a Lay-brother. When he lived in the world as a weaver, content with a small pittance of his earnings, he gave the rest to the poor. In the Society having received in public a blow from a passionate person, he fell at his feet and asked pardon, as if he had offered and not received the insult. Having fallen in with Moorish pirates, he held out his rosary as a defence against them without any fear, and they passed quietly by, either not observing him or prevented by the Blessed Virgin from harming him. He rejoiced on his death-bed that he died in the Society, and that he had sacrificed his life in the service of the sick.

3. In Carmona, in Andalusia, in the year 1719, Father John Francis Ramos, twenty-eight years of age. From his childhood he was noted for piety, virtue, devotion to the Blessed Virgin, and innocence. Admitted to the noviceship, he was a model of perfection, and was never known to transgress a rule. His obedience was that of the Institute both in will and in judgment, and his profound humility inspired him with a holy hatred and contempt of himself. Divine love beamed on his countenance when he spoke of God, or received Holy Communion, or as a Priest celebrated Mass, so that the sight of him moved the assistants to tender devotion. Burning for the salvation of souls, he endeavoured to procure it by preaching, conversation and assiduity in the confessional. His virtues, and above all his rare modesty, rendered him dear to all, and especially to the venerable Father Emmanuel Padial his confessor. His zeal gave hopes of a future Apostle, but being ripe for heaven, he was called away in the flower of his age, after a long and painful illness endured with invincible patience. He was seen by a Religious distant from Carmona enter heaven in triumph, and he appeared frequently afterwards to her, exhorting her to support her very great sufferings with courage, to perfect herself in the love of God and the practice of virtues. Miraculous favours were obtained by his intercession, and his memory was held in veneration.

JUNE 28.

1. At Wisbeach, in England, in the year 1592, Father Thomas Mettam, an Englishman, died after seventeen years' imprisonment. Four of these he spent in the Tower of London; then he was removed to other prisons, and finally, when more than sixty years of age, he expired at Wisbeach, assisted by Father William Weston. He was a learned and holy Priest and one of the first missionaries sent from Douay, and was admitted into the Society by Father Everard Mercurian in answer to his earnest petition in 1579.

2. In Africa, in the year 1575, Father Francis Govéa, a Portuguese. He laboured and suffered much in the kingdom of Angola, and was kept prisoner for fourteen years. The King of Angola ordered his singers to go round the house where he lay sick, night and day, to keep death from him, but death came to release him, and gave him rest from his labours.

3. In Naples, in the year 1656, Father Lucius Pignatelli, a Neapolitan, with sixty others in the same service of attending the sick of the plague. He was nephew to Pope Innocent XII, and his zeal had carried him to India and Portugal. Recalled to Italy, he governed the Roman College, and then the Province of Naples, where he died a holy death, which he had sought in India.

4. In the same year 1656, Father Joseph Gustapane, attending the sick. His mortifications were so great that his life was in danger, but Saint Joseph appearing to him restored him to health. After fifty years of Religious life in most difficult employments and important posts, he obtained leave to devote himself to the service of the sick. He was seized with the plague, and obliged to retire for some days, after which he returned to resume his labours, in the midst of which he expired, being found dead on his knees with his crucifix in his hand.

5. At Pekin, in China, in the year 1732, Father James Bouvet, a Frenchman. Being a great mathematician he was sent to China in 1685, and was honoured with the confidence of the Emperor Canghi, who gave him a large plot of ground in his palace grounds on which to raise a Church. He burned with most ardent zeal for the conversion of the Chinese. He was of a sweet and sociable character, never suffering a word to escape

him to the disadvantage of others of whom he might have reason to to complain. He was an exact observer of rules, lover of poverty and suffering, so far as to deprive himself even of necessaries. He died aged seventy-four, fifty-four of which he had spent in the Society.

6 At Antwerp, in 1714, Father Daniel Papebrock. After he had finished his studies and taught philosophy for a year, he was associated with Father Bollandus, and Father Henschenius, to work at the continuation of the *Acta Sanctorum*. His writings attest his vast erudition. He was not less distinguished for the practice of Religious virtues. His admirable humility, modesty, greatness of soul, obedience, mortification and poverty, were most exemplary. He had tender devotion to the Blessed Virgin and the Blessed Sacrament, to which he made long visits by night. His amiable, frank, and open character gained him every heart. Entering the Society at eighteen, he died at the age of eighty-seven, having passed fifty-five years in writing the *Acta Sanctorum* and sixty-nine in the Society.

7. At Stockholm, in Sweden, in the year 1610, Mathias and Nicholas, Polish Lay-brothers, died in prison, companions of Father Spotech, mentioned on the 14th of June.

June 29.

1. At Gusco, in Peru, in the year 1606, Father Ildephonsus à Poso a Spaniard. He was naturally of a passionate temper, but so overcame himself, that no one ever saw him angry in the Society. He was so modest, and kept such custody of eyes, that the Indians who confessed to him used to say they had been to confession to the "Blind Father."

2 At Goa, in the East Indies, in the year 1656, Father Alphonsus Mendez, a Portuguese, the Patriarch of Abyssinia. When he first landed there, the Emperor Seged embraced him, and said the *Nunc dimittis*, &c. In a brief time the false Alexandrian Creed was changed for the Catholic faith, thirteen Religious Houses were founded under the direction of nineteen Fathers of the Society; and in the year 1628, full 100,000 souls were brought into the communion of the Church by their labours, and by Father Alphonsus. But on the succession of the son of Seged, Facilladas, the good commenced was interrupted; and the Patriarch with his companions banished. This was not all. Perfidiously seized upon his journey, the

Patriarch was thrown into prison, loaded with chains, and detained for a year. At times, he and two other Fathers linked together with chains were led out to beg their bread. At last delivered from captivity by Christian contributions, he returned to Goa, but never laid aside his solicitude for Abyssinia, sending letters and instructions, books and missioners, until in his seventy-seventh year he died, no richer except by merits and sufferings for being Patriarch of Abyssinia.

3. On the same day, according to Southwell, in the year 1580—although Nadasi gives the fourteenth of September, 1577—another and an earlier Patriarch of Abyssinia, Andrew Oviedo, passed to a better life. He was greviously persecuted by Claudius and his successor Seged. Once in a fury of passion Claudius rushed on him with his drawn sword, and would have killed him unless the Queen by interposing her own body had prevented it. Such were the riches of his Patriarchate, that writing to Pope Pius V., for want of paper he cut of the margins of his Breviary and stitched them together. The holy Pope shed tears on the receipt of such a letter.

4. At Rome, a victim of charity in the year 1716, Father Peter Martin of the province of Lyons. Returning to France from the mission of Madura where he had spent many years, he was called to Rome, and sent thence to Civita Vecchia to attend on the troops destined by the Pope to succour Corfu against the Turks. To prepare them he gave them the Exercises, serving at the same time those in the hospital. A contagious disease broke out, his strength gave way, and he was attacked with the prevailing sickness. He died in the Professed House at Rome, full of consolation. He united the qualities requisite for the apostolic life—a robust constitution, grave and modest exterior, learning, and a happy memory, ardent zeal for souls, and intrepid courage.

JUNE 30.

1. At Tyburn in London, in the year 1679, five English Fathers died victims of Oates' perjuries, Father Thomas Harcourt, Provincial, whose real name was Whitbread, Father William Waring, or Barrow, Father John Fenwick, Father Anthony Turner, and Father John Gawen. Father Whitbread, was thirty years missioner, of great zeal and charity, and was author of some pious works. Father Fenwick suffered much

from the inhuman way in which he was chained in prison. Father Barrow was Rector of London, Father Turner eighteen years missioner, and Father Gawen remarkable for innocence of life. Their remains were buried in St. Giles' Churchyard under the north wall.

2. On the Western Ocean, in the year 1554, Father Leonard Nugñez a Portuguese. One of the first missioners sent to Brazil, he penetrated to its furthest parts. He undertook an expedition into the interior of the country, inhabited by the most ferocious savages, to bring back to the faith an apostate European. Having succeeded in his mission, he returned to his Station and laboured with unwearied zeal in instructing both Natives and Europeans: from thence he was sent as first Procurator of that Province to Rome, and died upon the voyage.

3. In Chili, South America, Diego Lopez de Salazar a native Scholastic. Hearing a sermon on the vanity of the world, he joined the Society without delay, despising his high and wealthy condition. In his noviceship he pressed forward with such eagerness towards perfection, that he soon surpassed in virtue and fervour many of those who were far advanced in years. Being at the point of death, he exclaimed, turning towards the crucifix, " O Lord Thou knowest how earnestly I have striven to seek Thee during these two years. Desert me not now, O Lord, at this hour I beseech Thee, by these Thy wounds which Thou receivedst for my sake." JESUS, ever most benign to His fervent followers, heard his prayer, and bid him be confident of his eternal salvation. Thus he departed happily, in the company and under the protection of JESUS.

4. At Moulins, in the year 1561, William Pierre, a Laybrother. He was forty years tailor to the College of Moulins. All his spare time he gave to prayer, by which he arrived at a high degree of union with God. He was never once seen during the whole time to speak to a secular, though often attending the Fathers as companion; and his fidelity to silence gained for him the title of the "Silent Brother." He eat very sparingly, of coarse food, taking no meat, sleeping little, on a mattrass of straw, and in his clothes, that he might give more time to prayer. When told that he should spare himself more, and allow his body a little better fare, he replied, " It is not right that I should be treated in Religion better than my position would have allowed in the world." His edifying life was crowned with a holy death. After a short illness, prostrate on the ground, he peacefully rendered his soul to God at the age of seventy-one.

JULY.

1. At Seville, in Spain, in the year 1605, died Father John Geronimo, a Spaniard, celebrated as a preacher and for his singular innocence. When Rector of the College of Granada he was slanderously accused of a shameful crime. The Father Provincial was entrusting the investigation of the matter to a grave and wise Father, who (seized with horror at the charge laid against Father John, and convinced of his complete innocence,) held his hand in the flame of a candle that was near, that he might thus witness to his belief, while the Provincial recounted the whole of the accusation. His hand was unhurt; but the accuser herself gave still more evident proof of his innocence, for being seized with great pains, and thus brought to repentance, she confessed in presence of the Provincial, a public notary, and other witnesses, that she had falsely accused him. He endured patiently another calumnious charge, laid against him before Pope Gregory XIII., of preaching heresy. He was honourably acquitted of the accusation; so that he might well apply to himself the words of our Lord, in the Gospel of St. John—"The prince of this world cometh, and in Me he hath nothing."

2. At Lima, in Peru, in the year 1655, Father Paul Æmiliani, an Italian, learned in the Indian languages, of great zeal for souls, and much enduring patience. Deprived of sight for twenty years, he lived in great peace and resignation to the Divine will, occupied in drilling holes in rosary beads to distribute to the poor. He took food only thrice in the week, and daily disciplines so severe, that those who heard them were moved to horror. He went to his eternal reward on the day which he had foretold.

3. At Leon, in Spain, in the year 1599, died Brother Gregory Flores, in service of the sick of the plague. Seven others died in the same service at Leon, and twenty-nine at Soria, Salamanca, and Villagarcia.

July 2.

1. At Lecce, in Apulia, in the year 1616, died the Venerable Father Bernardine Realino. For sixty-two years he laboured in the town of Lecce, which he was often on the point of leaving, but was always by the disposition of Providence prevented from doing so. Invited by the Blessed Virgin to enter the Society, he was often favoured with visits by her, and on one occasion the Divine Mother placed her Infant Son on the bed beside him, and consoled him with most familiar conversation. An ardent lover of religious perfection, and of great recollection of mind, he was once reprimanded by our Lord for entering upon some business, though enjoined by obedience, over hastily, without having first implored the help of Heaven. He was often seen during prayer with a countenance radiant with light, and sometimes bright rays were seen to shine from his whole body. Maximilian, Duke of Bavaria, besought him by letter to obtain for him a son from God by his prayers. Father Realino replied that he would have a son, which was fulfilled a long time after the Venerable Father's death.

2. At Neustadt, in Belgium, in the year 1600, Father Paul Bucclin, Father Laurence Everard, and Father Otho Campens, Belgians, taken by the Dutch soldiers and slain while hearing the confessions of the wounded. Father Paul, who was Superior, declared that he and his companions were following the army of the Archduke, not as soldiers but in the service of God, for the good of souls. This only infuriated their captors, who out of hatred to the faith shot them dead.

3. At Krems, in Germany, in the year 1658, Father Mathias Klinka, a Moravian, for more than thirty years a most zealous and laborious preacher. He preached a sermon every Sunday and Holiday, and always composed new ones each year, giving the old ones away. The soul of a good and honourable man, whom he had well known, having appeared to him and asked his prayers, the Father expressed surprise, as on the preceding day, the Assumption of the Blessed Virgin, he had seen him well, and knew that he had been to confession and Communion and gained a plenary indulgence. He received the reply that the indulgence had been gained, but that subsequent cause for the pains of Purgatory had been given by some sensuality in drinking.

4. At Paris, in the year 1651, Father Nicolas Caussin, a Frenchman, a man of great erudition, eloquence, and religious virtues. The great and wise Henry IV. predicted from his countenance when young, that he would be one day an honour to France and to the Society; and such he truly became on account of his extraordinary learning and eminent virtue, which gained for him the name of "the Angel of Peace." He was confessor to Louis XIII. and a man of consummate ability, so that he might be said to be ready at all times and on all circumstance. He wrote much and elegantly, as appears in his *Holy Court* and the *Parallels of Eloquence*.

5. At Pekin, in China, in the year 1741, Father Francis Xavier d'Entrecolles, a native of Lyons, distinguished on the missions of China for his pure and ardent zeal. He was loved and revered by all during the twenty-three years that he was Superior of the mission or the house of Pekin for his sweetness and gentleness. Great infirmities, the fruit of his constant labours, kept him confined to his room for the last four years of his life, and there he could bear no posture but that of sitting in an arm-chair. He profited by this to make preparation for death, but without ceasing to fulfil his duties as a missioner, receiving a crowd of neophytes who came to visit him, hearing their confessions and directing them by his salutary counsels. He died at the age of seventy-seven.

JULY 3.

1. At Dorchester, in England, in the year 1594, Father John Cornelius, died for the faith, being hanged and quartered. He was born of Irish parentage at Bodmin, and educated at Oxford, which he left for Rheims, and was sent from thence to the English College at Rome in 1580. He returned to England having received the Priesthood, and resided chiefly with the Arundell family. He was betrayed and taken at Chidiock, and sent to London, where he was confined in the Marshalsea prison, and tortured. He was there received into the Society and admitted to his vows by commission from Father Henry Garnett. Remanded to Dorchester, he suffered with great joy. He was hanged until he was dead, as no caldron could be obtained, nor any man found to quarter him alive for any money. His body was quartered after death, and his remains came into the possession of Catholics. His preparation for this holy death had been frequent fasts, disciplines, and hairshirts.

2. In Paraguay, in South America, in the year 1637, Father Peter de Espinosa, a Spaniard, suffered martyrdom, his head being cleft asunder by the savages. At the moment he thus died he appeared in glory to one of the Society two hundred leagues distant, and said—"Good bye, Brother Julius, I go happily to Heaven." He devoted himself in life entirely to the instruction of the savages with astounding patience.

3. At Palermo, in Sicily, in the year 1575, Father Paul Mantuano, an Italian, received by St. Ignatius as a Lay-brother, but by his command raised to the Priesthood when his talents and virtues were known. He offered to be sold as a slave to redeem a Father from the Moors, and not obtaining his request, he asked to serve the sick of the plague, in which service of charity he died.

4. At Ocaña, in Spain, in the year 1584, Father Ferdinand Marquez, a Spaniard, beloved by all for sweetness and amiable manners. A light shone over the room in which he died, and a sweet odour issued from his tomb when opened after a lapse of some years.

5. In Peru, in the College of Guamando, in the year 1609, Father Alphonsus de Miranda. Called by the Blessed Virgin to enter the Society at the age of twenty, he spent in it forty years. For eighteen of these he was uninterruptedly employed on the missions in Europe, preaching with wonderful success and effecting many conversions. After the age of fifty he went three times on foot from Toledo to Seville, to obtain leave from his Superiors to go to Peru. He was perfect master of his passions and dead to himself. He slept in his clothes, fasting on bread and water several days each week, and, by his constancy in prayer, he obtained ordinarily whatever he asked of God.

July 4.

1. In Canada, among the Hurons, in the year 1649, died Father Antony Daniel, a Frenchman, martyred by the Iroquois. After fifteen years of labour as a missioner, hearing that these enemies of the Hurons were coming, he gathered his people together, baptized the catechumens, heard the confessions of others, and prepared them for a Christian death, saying, "To-day, brethren, we shall be in Paradise." When the Iroquois rushed upon them, he went first to meet them, keeping the door-way until

he was shot down, to give time to his people to escape, like a good shepherd giving his life for the sheep. The savages having inflicted each one a wound upon his body, set fire to the church and cast him into the flames. After his death appearing to a holy man several times, he earnestly exhorted him to promote in all ways the conversion of the infidels.

2. At Neustadt, in Belgium, in the year 1624, Father Theodore Riswig, a Belgian, who died from the hardships of his imprisonment at the hands of heretics, after six months' patient endurance. He was condemned to it by judges who considered that to be a Jesuit was a capital crime.

3. At Valladolid, in Spain, in the year 1669, Father Antonio de Escobar e Mendoza, a Spaniard. He preached the Lent for fifty years, and often two sermons a day, rigorously keeping the fast, which he never relaxed until the last year of his life, when he was eighty years old and sickly. He guided to high perfection in piety two sodalities, one of ecclesiastics, the other of laymen. He published, besides other works, two volumes folio on the Old Testament, six *De vero Vitæ Ligno*, and seven on the more received opinions in Moral Theology.

4. At Lisbon, in the year 1618, in his ninetieth year, Father Peter Paul Ferrer, called the "Living Library," for his universal knowledge of sacred writings, ancient history, and chronology. He retained to the last the same simplicity, humility, and affability which he brought with him to the noviceship. The renowned John of Avila calling him and Fernando Perez, said to them, "After the example of St. John the Baptist, I send you to a better school. Father Francis Borgia has asked of me two Theologians, fully qualified to conduct the University of Evora, newly founded by the Cardinal Henry. I think you fit to apply for the post. It is the school of Christ; go, and I feel sure you will be worthy scholars of so great a Master." They were accepted, and Perez taught for forty years in the Universities of Evora and Coimbra.

5. At Paris, in the year 1639, the precious death of Father Stephen Binet, a native of Dijon. To a theologian who said, "You must know that I am the greatest enemy your Society can have," he replied—"If we both are happy enough to save our souls we shall be great friends in Heaven." His sweet manners brought many of high rank to piety of life, and his preaching won every heart. His book on the *Holy Family* shows his devotion to the Infant Jesus, the Blessed Virgin, and St. Joseph. He com-

posed other works of piety adapted to give consolation to the afflicted At his death he acknowledged, that during forty years as Superior he could not reproach himself with having been influenced in his conduct by any passion, or any other motive than the glory of God and the good of souls.

JULY 5.

1. At Naples, in the year 1586, died Father William Good, an Englishman. Resigning ecclesiastical preferment at the accession of Elizabeth, he entered the Society at Tournay. After his noviceship he was sent into Ireland where he laboured for four years. Returning to Belgium he was stationed at Louvain, where he gave the Exercises to Father Robert Parsons who not long after joined the Society. In 1577 he made his profession at Rome, and was sent with Father Antony Possevin to Poland and Sweden. On his return to Rome he was appointed Confessor to the English College, to the special satisfaction of Cardinal Allen. He published at Rome *Ecclesiæ Anglicanæ Trophæa*, and left in MSS. an abstract of the lives of the British Saints. He was a prudent and saintly man. He closed his laborious life by a saintly death at Naples.

2. At Oropesa, in Spain, in the year 1615, Peter Carillo, a Spanish Lay-brother. He preferred the lowly and laborious life of Martha, and passed at his own request from the scholasticate and the study of philosophy to the state of a Temporal Coadjutor. Instead of the science of this world, he received the gift of a knowledge of futurity. He prepared himself for a holy death by iron chains, a discipline twice a day, and one scanty meal. He died kneeling, with his arms extended, and his body, like that of St. Paul the hermit, was found in that posture.

3. At Alcala, in Spain, in the year 1599, Louis Ruiz, a Spanish Lay-brother. His disposition was so lively that it amounted to the jocose, and he with difficulty obtained admission to the Society. He was most severely tried in his noviceship within and without, but came off victorious. He was not only an excellent Lay-brother in domestic duties, but also a good and ready speaker, and promoted the glory of God by catechism and public and private instructions, being gifted with extraordinary powers of persuasion. He died a martyr of charity attending the plague-stricken.

4. At Tonquin, in the year 1695, Father Francis Paregard, of the

French Province, one of the fifteen missioners sent to Siam in 1637. Prevented by a revolution from entering that kingdom, he went to Tonquin where he was placed over a church, one of the most numerous in those parts, which he unfortunately governed but a short time. He caught a fever in a dangerous expedition, and being carried back to the church, and having received the Sacraments with great sentiments of joy and gratitude, passed to a better life. He was an indefatigable missioner, of great mortification, full of the desire to promote the glory of God, and had made a vow to do what he thought best calculated to advance it.

JULY 6.

1. At Modena, in Italy, in the year 1607, died Father Achilles Gagliardi, an Italian. Together with two brothers, of whom he was the eldest, he joined the Society; and such were the gifts and graces of the three, that Father Simon Rodriguez, the companion of St. Ignatius, said of them, that if a choice were made out of the whole of Italy, more fitting persons for the Society could not have been found. Father Achilles after teaching the higher studies with great success was made Superior. He was the model of a Rector. On festival days he held spiritual conferences with the Scholastics, and on appointed days in each week with all classes of men, Ecclesiastics, merchants, and artizans; visited convents and other places of piety, exhorting all to holiness of life both by word and example. In his extreme old age, deprived of the use of his limbs, eyesight, and memory, his body paralyzed and falling to decay, he gave an admirable example of patience during the space of eighteen months.

2. At Barcelona, in Spain, in the year 1621, Father Alphonsus Hernandez, a Spaniard. Although he was not conscious of having ever committed a mortal sin, he scourged himself with sharp disciplines, and sternly mortified his senses, especially the eyes. He called the little ornaments or conveniences to which some are so attached, the idols of half religious souls, and wished them to be banished from their rooms even though their health suffered from it.

3. At Saragossa, in Spain, in the year 1564, Father John Paul Moxica died a victim of charity in the service of the plague-stricken. He had

been Master of Novices, and had discharged that office with great success. Six others died before or after him in the same service of charity.

4. At the College of Naples, in the year 1695, Brother St. Apicella passed to a better life. He was celebrated for his indefatigable charity to the sick, of whom he had the care for forty years. In this employment, which he exercised till extreme old age, he only neglected the care of himself. He died of a contagious disease caught in attending the hospital of Naples. His mortification was equal to his charity. He had rendered himself perfect master of his passions, and amongst other austerities with which he macerated his body, he carried as a girdle an iron chain till his last breath. Obedience, the characteristic virtue of our Institute, was extremely dear to him. The submission of his will and judgment suggested to him a thousand motives to persuade himself and others that what was ordered was always the best. He was never known to show any repugnance at passing from one employment to another, or to complain with being burdened with work beyond his strength. He obeyed all alike who exercised authority over him. He fell asleep at the age of eighty-four, on the day of St. Trofimena, whose devotion he had propagated.

JULY 7.

1. At Yendi, in Japan, in the year 1639, Father Peter Cassui, a Japanese, died in prison. Banished as a Christian from Japan, he visited Jerusalem and afterwards Rome, where he was received into the Society. He entered Japan in the disguise of a sailor, or galley-slave, and served two years in that capacity to effect it. He was taken at Nangasachi encouraging Christians who were vacillating under the severity of the persecution, and bringing back those who had fallen away. He was put in prison, and died there of the hardships and torments he endured.

2. At Naples, in the year 1591, Father John Pescatore, an Italian, a friend in his early years of St. Charles Borromeo, and in the Society Novice Master of St. Aloysius. Out of humility he would not accept the offer of the profession of the four vows made to him by the General, Father Claudius Aquaviva. For six years he never put off his hairshirt, and took a daily discipline to blood, though a virgin in body and mind. More than once he was seen shining with celestial light or raised from the

ground, and his predictions of the future were found true. When Rector of the College of Naples, in a pressing necessity he was called to the gate by an Angel and presented with gold sufficient for his wants; the messenger then vanished. Nor was this the only time that his needs were thus providentially supplied. The Visitor, Provincial, and others declared that the presence of this Father, and the air of reverence which accompanied him, created in them more than usual composure and modesty. In his last sickness he foretold to one of the Society a severe trial that would come upon him, but that God and the Blessed Virgin, and himself, would come from Heaven to help him. Accordingly when this person was in great temptation, and in danger of losing his vocation, he appeared, and assured the tempted man that his troubles would soon end; and so it came to pass.

3. At Ghent, in Belgium, in the year 1634, Father Charles Christynen, with eight companions, died a martyr of charity in the service of the plague-stricken. He was remarkable for innocence, modesty, and love of holy poverty. Nine others died the same year in Belgium in different places in the same service of charity.

July 8.

1. At Annecy, in Savoy, in the year 1596, died Father Arnold Vicine, a Frenchman. The only request he made to Superiors was, that he might not be put to govern or be sent to his own country; but he governed both Colleges and the Province successfully by their orders. He introduced a custom at the cost of much labour, long held in grateful memory by the people of Annecy, of making at least once in their lives a very exact confession. He himself, to his great consolation and the benefit of his penitents, heard two thousand such confessions.

2. At Nangasachi, in Japan, in the year 1597, Father Lewis Fröes, a Portuguese. He embarked for the Indies with Father Gaspar Barzeo in 1548 and asked to pass into Japan, but as he was not yet a Priest, Father Nugñez, the Provincial, did not think fit to grant it. In 1563 he arrived there, and endured for thirty-three years privation, sickness, and accidents of all kinds. He journeyed much by sea and land, was often obliged to change his retreat, and to remain hid day and night, not to fall into the

hands of those who sought his life. A reward was offered by the Bonzes to whosoever should kill him, but Divine Providence protected him. By his zeal, love of prayer, sweetness, and knowledge of the language of Japan, he effected many signal conversions. He often tried to gain a footing in the principal city, Meaco, but was as often prevented by the Bonzes, until he received a written permission from Nobunanga, who then occupied the imperial throne, to have a fixed abode in that city, with freedom from imposts, and liberty to go whither he would. Shortly after, his life was again sought by a Bonze, but he was again protected by Providence, and after fifty years spent in the Society he passed to eternal repose. Augustine Sancri, a Japanese of known virtue, declared that Father Lewis appeared to him after death, gazing up to Heaven with an expression of intense piety, and saying—"Praise God; I praise Him now for ever."

JULY 9.

1. At Manilla, in the Philippine Islands, in the year 1631, died Father Bartholomew de Saura, a Spaniard, singularly devout to JESUS, Mary, and the Holy Angels. He received special favours from them, and once saw the Infant JESUS in the arms of Mary, and heard Him say, "Bartholomew my friend." Sometimes, however, he was reprehended by Him for not meditating sufficiently on the Passion. He renewed hourly his vows, and added the arduous one of doing always what he knew to be most pleasing to God. In his agony being asked what gave him most comfort, he replied, "the protection of the Blessed Virgin." Her help, he said, he had experienced even in the smallest things.

2. At Bordeaux, in France, in the year 1636, Father Claude Cluselle, a Frenchman. Humility, sincerity, and charity, together with a look of unaffected modesty, marked his sanctity. He was director of the Sodality of the Blessed Virgin, to whom he was tenderly devout; and Angels are said to have appeared to him to ask him for six Masses for a Sodalist dangerously sick; they were said, and the sick man recovered. Notwithstanding these graces and the innocence of his life, he feared greatly the judgments of God. He was spared the terrors of death by a sudden attack of gout. His reputation of sanctity drew crowds to his funeral.

3. At Pultowa, in Poland, in the year 1653, Father Thomas Porzecky,

a Lithuanian. Having successfully taught philosophy and theology, he was Rector of the College in the time of the plague in the city. Sending away his subjects, he remained to take the place of the Father who attended the sick. He caught the infection from a domestic servant whom he attended, and died a victim of charity.

4. In Abyssinia, in the year 1699, died Father Francis Xavier de Brevedent, of a noble family at Rouen. After scientific labours which gained for him a reputation among the learned, he obtained permission to devote himself to the missions. The isles of the Archipelago and Syria were the theatre of his zeal for ten years, and he made many conversions. He was regarded as a true apostle. His ordinary food was a little bran steeped in water, with a few herbs and roots. He lay upon boards or on the ground, and passed some hours of the night in prayer. He treated his body so pitilessly that his Superiors were obliged to moderate his penance. His union with God was almost continual. He devoted himself in the city of Cairo to the service of the sick of the plague. To his great joy he was allowed to undertake the mission to Abyssinia. He ardently desired martyrdom, but God was content with his good will. He consummated his sacrifice at Basko, a town half a day's journey from Gondar.

JULY 10.

1. At Roborosa, in South America, in the year 1594, died Father Gonsalvo de Tapia, a Spaniard, of the Province of Castile, a man of much labour in cultivating those new fields, which he finally watered with his blood. He was the first to penetrate to the Topians, a cannibal tribe. Then he preached to the Cinaloese, a people of a gentler disposition, among whom there were neither thieves nor mendicants. Thence proceeding to neighbouring tribes with Father Martin Paez, in a short time he baptized two thousand souls. His admonitions provoked an old chief, Nabaceda, whom he endeavoured to bring back to chastity; and assassins instigated by him killed Father Gonsalvo. The following day his body was found, the head and left arm cut off, and the right raised as if to make the sign of the cross in token of the faith for which he died.

2. In Paraguay, in the year 1619, Father Alphonsus de Aragona,

an indefatigable labourer in that vineyard, and a living portrait of St. Aloysius. The Father Provincial, after receiving his manifestation of conscience, said of him, "that a hidden treasure lay concealed in Alphonsus." He had to an extraordinary degree the gift of prayer, and was favoured with many supernatural graces.

3. At St. Omers, in Belgium, in the year 1612, Father Denis Sannois, a Belgian. He was vehemently incited to eminent virtue, especially to zeal in assisting the sick and dying, by the apparition of the soul of one of his Religious Brethren in Purgatory, who told him that Religious were grievously tormented there for neglect or tepidity in assisting souls and particularly the dying; that this charity was great and admirable in the sight of God, and that it was a great favour of God to the Society to make use of it as a means for the salvation of souls.

JULY 11.

1. At Carpentras, in France, in the year 1591, died Father Peter Pequet, a Frenchman, in the heroic discharge of the duty of attending the sick of the plague. He was remarkable for love of prayer and a singular gift of assisting his penitents. After death he was seen by several persons in priestly vestments and surrounded with light. The room in which his body was laid was filled with light and a sweet odour whilst it remained there, and a cross was seen over it in the air when it was laid in the grave. The body was removed from the town of Carpentras, where he died, to the College, in the year 1626, for the following reason:—For many days the appearance of a Religious in the dress of the Society was seen kneeling before the steps of the high-altar of the College with a countenance of dazzling brightness. Those who had seen Father Pequet recognized his face. His body was therefore translated and buried on that spot. When it was removed the beads of his rosary were found entire, and one of these applied to a lady cured her of a heart disease. During his life time, as is asserted on grave testimony, he restored to life a dead infant to receive Baptism.

2. At Haguenau, in France, in the year 1617, Father Bernard Aubas, a Frenchman. He was sweet to others, but to himself severe, with a complete mastery of his passions. He obtained by practice great and easy

recollection of the presence of God. In his sickness he slowly swallowed the bitterest draughts, and for fourteen days took with a smile a prescription which, by the carelessness or ignorance of the compounder, had been made intolerably nauseous. The medical man, on discovering the mistake, was amazed at the sick man's mastery over himself.

3. At Hang-choo-foo, in China, in the year 1638, Father John Fröes, a Portuguese, a zealous and holy missioner. Posthumous honours were given to him not only by the Christians but by the pagans. The Christians celebrated his obsequies for seven days, and bewailed with great grief the loss of their Father. Two hundred accompanied the funeral for five miles, to the place of burial, with respect and veneration; and as they passed through the gate of the city the guards, though pagans, bent their knees to the bier, saluting him aloud with the title of holy Father.

4. At Genoa, in Italy, in the year 1657, Father Julio Pallavicini, a Genoese. He was Rector of the Professed House at Genoa, and when a pestilence attacked the city, he devoted himself to hearing the confessions of the infected, and in this heroic work fell a victim of charity.

JULY 12.

1. At Wilna, in Lithuania, in the year 1653, died Father George Giedroycz, a Lithuanian. His descent from the Great Dukes of Lithuania was ennobled by his exalted virtue. He never lost the first fervour of his noviceship. Silence, temperance in food, and a constant devotion to the Wounds of our Blessed Redeemer aided him in the path of perfection. By these he preserved himself in such innocence, that in the Society he was never known to commit any deliberate venial sin, yet he treated his body with great rigour by constant and severe disciplines for the space of half an hour at a time. As a master at the College of Polock he brought back many schismatics to the true Church. When a Priest, he employed zealous persons to give him notice of the sick, to whom by night or day he took spiritual and temporal aid, often at the peril of his life. On the missions he would spend the entire day in the confessional without food. His name was enough to shut the mouths of the licentious. The plague having broken out in Wilna, on his knees he begged of the Rector permission to attend the sick, and

died after six months' service of them, at the age of forty-five. Fifty others died in the same work of charity.

2. At Brussels, in Belgium, in the year 1614, Father Joachim Arents, a Belgian. He came into the Society, into which he had sent four brothers before him, adorned with the honours of a degree of Doctor of Law, innocence of life, the Priesthood, zeal for the faith, and sufferings endured from heretics. In the Society he gave a bright example, striving after perfection, which he attained in a high degree by the use of the two wings of fervent prayer and continual exterior and interior mortification.

3. At Oviedo, in Spain, in the year 1599, when a terrible pestilence devastated the whole province of the Asturias, so that scarce a third part of the inhabitants survived, John de Villasante was the first of ten of the Society who laid down their lives for their friends and brethren. Besides those who died at Oviedo, twenty-five others the same year sacrificed their lives in the same heroic service of charity in other parts of Spain.

July 13.

1. At Syracuse, in Sicily, in the year 1605, died Father Sebastian Cabarasi, a Sicilian. To promote the worship of the Virgin Mother of God he established three sodalities, which he directed with extraordinary diligence and care. Once on a journey being ill-treated by robbers he reproved them with such zeal and success, for their unholy life, that he not only brought them to repentance and a general confession of their life, but some entered into the Religious state, Father Sebastian obtaining their pardon from the Government.

2. At Brünn, in Moravia, in the year 1659, Father Gasper Aicha, a Bohemian. He was led to enter the Society by the apparition of a friend whom he saw enveloped in flames. He is said to have been consoled by the sight of St. Aloysius appearing to him; his extreme modesty and observance of rules and customs, like that of St. Aloysius, gave further reason to credit it. He could not be induced to drink out of the house; and when an acquaintance pressed him with threats to take a cup of wine, he preferred to have it flung in his face rather than drink it. He held in his hand as he died the formula of a pious will which he had

drawn up three years before, whereby he first gave thanks to God by the tongues of all imaginable creatures for the benefits granted, and hereafter to be granted, to himself and all creatures, and especially for the graces and gifts with which the Society has been or will be endowed. He then offered his body to the Body of Christ, his soul to the Soul of Christ, and his heart to the Sacred Heart, that he might love God with the love of the Heart of Christ.

3. At St. Germain in Laye, in the year 1774, Father Charles Frey de Neuville, born of a noble family at Constance in Brittany. He entered the Society at the age of seventeen, and after eighteen years of teaching or study was employed in preaching, for which he had great talent. He was remarkable for mildness, charity, and compassion for the afflicted. To his great grief he saw the dissolution of the Society, and expressed his sorrow thereat in a touching letter. He died at the age of eighty-one, having just finished a retreat. Out of love for poverty and the poor he asked to be buried among them.

JULY 14.

1. At Utrecht, in Belgium, in the year 1638, died Philip Nottin, a Belgian Lay-brother, who suffered great torments at the hands of heretics for the Catholic Faith. He was made to sit down on an iron cross; his hands and feet squeezed in fetters and manacles armed with sharp points were tied back by the fingers and toes; his neck was enclosed in an iron collar set with three rows of spikes turned inwards, upwards, and downwards; he was then roasted at a slow fire. As the skin rose in blisters it was cut open, and vinegar, salt, and gunpowder rubbed in. After Brother Philip had been thus tortured for ten hours his head was struck off as that of a traitor.

2. At Manilla, in the Philippine Islands, in the year 1627, Father Thomas de Montoya, an Indian of Florida. After thirty years of indefatigable labour among those nations, he died by slow poison, given by the Basaians out of hated to the faith.

3. At Pont-a-Mousson, in Lorraine, in the year 1654, Gerard Dominique, a French Lay-brother, adorned with all the virtues of his state, but especially with a zeal for discoursing on pious subjects. He appeared after death to

a Professor of Theology, with whom he had been familiar, as he was praying by night, with his head surrounded by rays, and from his mouth there shone a splendid star as a symbol of the reward given him for his pious discourse. Being asked if he enjoyed the happiness of Heaven, he modestly gave token of assent, and earnestly commended to the Father conversation on spiritual subjects "as most displeasing to hell, but most pleasing to those in Heaven."

4. At Evora, in Portugal, in the year 1602, Father John Ribellio. From his novitiate he was remarkable for love of prayer, mortification, and charity. His life was spent in hearing confessions, preaching, and directing sodalities. He always recommended three things: devotion to the Passion, charity to the souls in Purgatory, and confidence in the Blessed Virgin Mary. His heart was ever full of tender love to her, his mouth ever full of her praises, and to her protection he attributed the freedom during thirty years of temptations of the flesh. These three devotions he wonderfully spread in Portugal. He was also remarkable for great contempt of self. He rose at midnight in the College of Evora, and, clothed in a penitential dress with a rope round his neck, ascended a flight of twenty-three steps, taking at each stair a severe discipline, saying, "Such is the punishment adjudged to John Rebellio for his sins." All the times of prayer, examen, and office he spent on his knees. Having endured a painful operation without a murmur of complaint, he tranquilly gave up his soul at the age of sixty.

July 15.

1. At Palma, one of the Canary Isles, in the year 1570, the Blessed Ignatius Azevedo, a Portuguese, with thirty-nine companions, thrown into the sea and drowned by heretical pirates out of hatred to the faith. Clasping to his heart the picture of the Blessed Virgin, trodden under foot, with a wound on the head, and run through with pikes, he continued to exhort his companions to courage until he was flung into the sea. The rest were slain with similar cruelties, the murderers exclaiming—"Death to the Jesuits, who go to spread their vile doctrines in Brazil." St. Teresa saw in spirit the martyrdom of these glorious champions, and their crowns given them in Heaven.

2. At Lisbon, in Portugal, in the year 1579, died Father Simon Rodriguez, a Portuguese, one of the first ten Fathers of the Society. Having happily passed through the difficulties of a tempted and troubled mind, he held on with constancy, and continued to the end the course of perfection under the Rule of St. Ignatius. Judged by the Holy Father fit for the apostolic office of the conversion of the Indies, he was sent to Portugal with St. Francis Xavier. There they displayed their zeal to such an extent in the reformation of morals and the instruction of youth, that they acquired the name of Apostles, and it was resolved unanimously by the King and nobles to keep them in Portugal. Xavier at last being allowed to depart, Father Simon was kept and destined by the King for the Bishopric of Coimbra, but he obtained a release from his appointment by many tears and arguments, declaring that the rewards of his vocation were labours, and not honours.

3. In the Salsette Isles, near Goa, in the year 1583, Father Rudolph Aquaviva, an Italian, with four companions, massacred for the faith by the savages. In his youth he defended his chastity by an act similar to that of St. Thomas of Aquin, and never after suffered from rebellion of the flesh. He prayed for his murderers, and after death was seen with a glorious jewelled crown, an emblem of the many rare virtues with which he adorned the nobility of his descent.

4. At Pont-a-Mousson, in Lorraine, in the year 1685, during a plague and famine, ten of ours fell victims assisting the sufferers in their temporal and spiritual need. Among them Brother Bertrand, a zealous labourer in that service of charity.

5. At the College of Gandia, in the year 1636, having preserved his baptismal innocence, Father Joseph Calatayud, at the age of seventy-eight. God would have him in the Society, for the Father Provincial having written that he could not be received, the contrary was found in the letter. He was an apostolic missioner, sleeping on boards, passing much of the night in prayer, most severe in mortification and austerities, and favoured with many gifts and graces.

July 16.

1. At Mexico, in the year 1609, died Father Peter Sanchez, a Spaniard. He had in the world a high reputation as a preacher and theologian, but reading an account of the foreign missions he felt impelled to join the Society. In the noviceship he sought in a special manner to acquire the virtue of self-contempt, and made a vow to serve in the kitchen or refectory as often as his occupations would allow. He was the first of the Society who taught theology publicly at Valladolid. He was afterwards appointed Rector of Salamanca, and gave a great example of humility in carrying the materials for the construction of the College on his shoulders. He was sent by St. Francis Borgia with thirteen others to establish a new Province in Mexico, and founded there three Seminaries and many Colleges. For twenty-three years he preached every Sunday and Holiday. He took a discipline daily, and abstained from wine. His union with God was great, and his confidence was so unshaken that he obtained all his petitions. The cure of two sick persons given up by the physician was granted to his prayers. Being told to prepare for death, he ordered his room to be stripped of its poor furniture, that he might die like our Lord in complete poverty. The Viceroy came to visit him in his last sickness and spoke of public affairs, upon which he begged to be allowed to employ with God the little time of life that remained. He died at the age of eighty-three, having spent fifty-one years in the Society. He was bewailed by all the city as a Father and Apostle. The Viceroy esteemed himself happy to obtain his biretta and a picture of St. Bernard, his favourite Saint. Father Sanchez is said to have been visited familiarly by the Saints, and to have known them by their countenances.

2. At Seville, in Spain, in the year 1648, Father Ferdinand de Mendoza, a Spaniard. He was most devout to the Blessed Virgin, and daily from his childhood said the rosary in her honour. It happened on one occasion that he went to bed having forgotten it, but awaking he remembered that he had omitted it, and immediately rose to recite it. As he was thus engaged the Blessed Virgin appeared to him surrounded with bright light, and sweetly bidding him be constant in this holy practice, promised him her help in all his necessities. This promise was afterwards abundantly fulfilled.

JULY 17.

1. At Logrono, in Spain, in the year 1564, died Father Antonio Martinez, a Spaniard, of singular charity, sweetness, and dexterity in gaining souls. These excellent gifts brought about the conversion of many obstinate sinners. As he spoke to the people on the rosary, a large wax light was seen burning above the statue of the Blessed Virgin. Hence the name was given him of "Our Lady's Torchlight." This light was at last quenched in the service of the plague-stricken, or, to speak more correctly, began to burn more brightly in Heaven, with three other companions who died in the same work of charity.

3. At Alcala, in Spain, in the year 1637, Father Alphonsus Esquéra, a Spaniard, of eminent gifts and virtues. He took the discipline twice a day, eat his food without salt or condiment, and drank no wine except when ordered to do so during the last few months of his life. Meditating upon Christ compelled by the Disciples to remain with them at Emmaus, and thinking how he might also compel Him to remain, he heard a distinct interior voice, "Do violence to thyself, and thou wilt also do it to Me." Hence he derived a new and powerful motive to conquer himself. In the year 1621, on the Feast of the Guardian Angels, he saw his Angel Guardian arrayed in armour standing by his side in the form of a beautiful youth, and with a lance in his hand. Alphonsus walked with him about the room, and conversed with him familiarly, and begged pardon with tears for his defects in honouring him. The Angel accompanied him to Mass, and after the consecration remained kneeling. Alphonsus saw that after the Communion he was regarded with greater reverence by the Angel, who remained visible to him for two days.

4. In Sicily, in the 1577, Father Blasius Sanchez, a Spaniard. Attached to the Court of the Viceroy, he entered the Society. The success of his labours in the holy ministry raised the jealousy of the devil, who urged assassins to attempt his life; but these he made his friends. Having heard that a certain Priest had a special aversion to him, he went to him and asked to be allowed to give a mission with him. The Priest complied through civility, resolving to watch him closely, but soon found so much matter for edification, that he became his greatest friend and panegyrist.

He gave many hours daily to meditation, eat and slept little, and took severe disciplines; his modesty was so great, that the sight of him inspired this virtue. He died a victim of charity serving the plague-stricken, having predicted the time of his death. Thirteen of ours died with him in the same service.

5. At Mechlin, in Belgium, in the year 1613, Father Andrew Bottelberg, a Belgian, called the "Preacher of the Blessed Virgin," for his eloquence and zeal in praise of the Mother of God. Being asked in his sickness if he wanted anything. "Heaven," he replied, and expired.

July 18.

1. At Avignon, in France, in the year 1604, died Peter Doligier, a French Lay-brother. He had gone to confession over night in preparation for Holy Communion, and was found dead in the morning, having placidly expired. Though unassisted by human aid at the hour of death, he was not without divine; for one of ours was touched on the shoulder and awakened in the night, and heard a voice, "Awake, and commend to God one of the Brothers, whose soul is now departing."

2. In Prussian Brandenberg, near Resel, in the year 1693, Father Adalbert Graben, LL.D., born at Warsaw of Swedish parentage. Being inclined in his early life to enter the Capuchin Order, he was advised by a Capuchin to enter the Society. He was received at Rome, and had for his master and guide in piety Father John Paul Oliva, under whom he laid solid foundations of religious perfection. He was thrice sent from Poland to Rome on the business of the Province. At the sound of the bell he was most punctual, and being praised for it said—"Yes; write over me this epitaph: 'First to bed, first in the refectory, first at recreation.'" He had a great gift of directing youth, and sent many into Religious life. He sent fifty-three to the Cistercians; thirty to the Bernardine Franciscans; twelve to the Dominicans; five to the Basilians; twenty-eight to the Reformed Carmelites; twelve to the Brigittines; one hundred and seventeen to the Society; besides some to the Carthusians and Augustinians. Almost all of them persevered. He died on his return from the Provincial Congregation at Wilna, suddenly, but not unprepared.

3. At San Salvador, in Brazil, in the year 1697, nearly ninety years

of age, Father Antony Vieyra, famed for his extraordinary talents and holiness of life. He had bound himself by vow to renounce entirely the study of letters, to devote himself wholly to the conversion of the savages. Ordered by his Superiors to apply himself to the sciences, he made such progress that his prodigious learning was soon noised abroad. Though brought into intimate and frequent relations with the greatest princes, he refused the most lucrative offers and the highest dignities of the Church, and preferred to live retired in Martinique. His toils and sufferings for the salvation of infidels were astonishing. He twice crossed the sea to Portugal to meet, and triumph over by his patience, the calumnies of those who envied his extraordinary reputation. Trampling under foot human applause he returned to Brazil, and employed his last five years in the contemplation of divine things, and in retouching his sermons, which are esteemed among the first in the world as models of composition.

JULY 19.

1. At Jaroslaw, in Poland, in the year 1586, died Father John Hart, an Englishman, admitted into the Society whilst in prison in the Tower, where he suffered the rack and lay under sentence of death. After two years' confinement he was banished, and went to Rome, from whence he was sent to Poland, where he died. His body is said to have been found incorrupt after the lapse of seven years.

2. . At Manilla, in the Philippine Islands, in the year 1631, Father Laurence Massoni, an Italian, a great missioner in the Indies for thirty years. After administering the Sacraments to the Catholic army, and promising them victory, he advanced with the Crucifix before them. They gained a great victory, and won from the Dutch the island of Ternate. Though esteemed a perfect Religious, he was often seen to shed tears, because, he said, he knew not whether he had wiped away his sins.

3. At Cali, in America, in the year 1649, Father John Ribera, a Spaniard. He converted many hardened sinners, and foretold to others who were obstinate their death without the Sacraments, which briefly ensued. He silenced a devil in a preacher, who proclaimed himself Adam the first father. He was so much beloved by the people of Popayan and Cali, that in his sickness they declared they would gladly give their life for his.

4. At Turin, in Piedmont, in the year 1599, Christopher Mariani, a Lay-brother, with nine companions, a martyr of charity serving the plague-stricken. And at Constance, in Germany, in the year 1611, Father James Stitz, an apostolic man, in the same service of charity, with ten others.

5. At Brunsberg, in the year 1657, Father George Marchienicz, a Pole. Born in heresy, he abjured his errors, and asked for admission into the Society. His lively character and conversation, joined with great modesty and devotion to the Blessed Virgin, eminently fitted him to lead young persons to piety. He was a Professor of Rhetoric. Eulogies of the Blessed Virgin were the frequent theme of his scholars' compositions, and at the close of the year he conducted them with music to a sanctuary of hers at some distance from the city. A holy emulation was raised among them, and many entered the Society or other Religious Orders. He died at the early age of thirty-six, embracing the Crucifix, full of joy at dying in the Society, to which, after God, he acknowledged himself indebted for the happiness of the faith. "O Society of Jesus," he often exclaimed, "the glory which surrounds the throne of kings is nothing compared with thine!"

July 20.

1. At Utrecht, in Belgium, in the year 1638, died Father John Baptist Boddey and Father Gerard Paesman, put to a cruel death by heretics. Father John, who was Rector of the College, was horribly and shamefully tormented for twenty-six hours, and was finally beheaded with a hatchet. Father Gerard was placed upon a sharp iron cross, with spiked collar, and manacles and fetters armed with spikes, and then tortured before a slow fire for ten hours, with salt and vinegar rubbed into his blistered flesh. A wretched heretical minister vainly urged him to abjure the faith, for which he gloriously suffered and died.

2. At Naples, in the year 1656, Father Francis Corciono, an Italian, a martyr of charity. He directed with much fruit and zealous care for many years the Sodality of the Blessed Sacrament, called the "Silent Confraternity," because they performed their duties in holy silence. A man of interior hidden life he was all heart, all humility and charity. He foretold to one of his companions, who feared being carried off by the plague in discharge of his pious duties, that he would survive, which proved true.

3. At Cracow, in Poland, in the year 1624, John Laskowski, a Polish Scholastic. He was remarkable for his talents and great humility, which appeared in his dress, words, and every motion, whether he taught in schools, or accompanied the purveyor of provisions. He daily took a severe discipline; and though not conscious of mortal sin in his life, was so tormented with scruples, that he was accounted by his confessors a martyr of interior suffering. He prayed much, and offered up his penances for condemned criminals who had to suffer death.

4. At Madrid, in the year 1604, Father Michael de Reyno. This holy man for twenty years taught a class of grammar, though he was endowed with rare talents. Gratitude to God was his favourite virtue, and he carried round his neck a list of the benefits he had received from Him. He also taught publicly the catechism to the children and the ignorant. He insisted on our Fathers undertaking this duty, having learned by light from God that the College of Madrid, which for forty years had been without a Founder, would not receive a foundation until catechism was taught to the ignorant. In fact, no sooner was this done than Mary of Austria became Foundress of the College, and assigned revenues to it. He also established a confraternity for men, which contributed greatly to the benefit of all classes in the city. The magistrate declared that after its establishment it rarely happened that an inhabitant was condemned in fine or other punishment.

JULY 21.

1. On the Japanese sea, in the year 1573, died Father Gonsalvo Alvarez, a Portuguese, a man of prayer and exact punctuality at the sound of the bell. Once on a recreation day hearing the bell before dinner for examen he went into the Chapel, and when the quarter had elapsed, it happened either no signal was given or he did not hear it. The rest went to the Refectory and afterwards to recreation, while he remained unobserved and forgotten for eight hours in prayer until supper time. In after years sent as Visitor to Japan, he suffered and laboured much until he was shipwrecked. His body was found on shore in a kneeling posture, with the hands lifted up as in prayer to Heaven.

2. At Cuidad Real, in the year 1585, Father James a Costa, à Spaniard.

In the Professor's chair, in the pulpit, and in the government of the Province, he displayed talents that made him esteemed one of the first men of the age. The Viceroy of Castile, going to visit him, said to his attendants—"Let us go and see one of the old Doctors of Holy Church." After thirty years his body was found incorrupt.

3. At the College of Bari, in Apulia, in the year 1639, Father Christopher Corquera, a Spaniard. For forty-six years he lived in College with the repute of consummate virtue, and was regarded in the city as a second Father Realino. He sometimes spent the whole day in hearing confessions, and part of the night in assisting the sick. He practised great austerities, and was never known to take other food than bread and vegetables. He was sweet and indulgent to others, and wonderful success attended his labours.

July 22.

1. At Nangasachi, in Japan, in the year 1633, Thomas Nicofori, a Japanese Lay-brother, was burnt by a slow fire. Both before and after his entrance into the Society he actively promoted the spread of Christianity. On this account he was first banished, and afterwards returning secretly, was taken and condemned to be burned alive.

2. At Majorca, in the year 1587, Father Bartholomew Cochez, a Spaniard. By the holiness of his life and his fervent eloquence he worked great conversions, and on one occasion brought to penitence eight persons of abandoned life. Though suffering from intolerable thirst caused by dropsy, he would never take more to drink than was prescribed for him by the physician or by the infirmarian. The Blessed Alphonsus Rodriguez attended him on his death-bed, and saw Heaven open to receive among its citizens the soul of Father Bartholomew.

3. At Malabar, in the East Indies, in the year 1656, Father Emmanuel Martinez, a Portuguese. He wrote and suffered much for the faith. Besides a cruel imprisonment, he was twice cruelly scourged, and four times banished. His life was often sought for by the idolatrous priests, but he was protected even by the pagans themselves on account of the esteem they had of his sanctity. For thirty years he ate neither flesh nor fish; and the food he took was so scanty, that he might be said to keep

a perpetual fast. He treated with severity his virginal body, never sleeping in a bed nor taking off his clothes, even when burning with fever. He conducted his Christian converts to such high perfection that many of them seemed like novices of the Society.

4. At Lisbon, in Portugal, in the year 1569, at the time of what was called the "Great Plague," many Fathers eagerly offered themselves to assist the sick and dying. Father Leo Henrici, the Provincial, was among the first, but by order of his Superiors was restrained from exposing his life. The first to die in this work of charity was Father Alphonsus Ægidio, a Religious of great perfection. Thirteen others, true to their Apostolic calling, died in the same service. More than ten thousand sick were committed to their care.

5. At Cardiff, in South Wales, in the year 1679, Father Philip Evans, a Welshman, suffered for the faith, a victim of Oates' Plot. He was apprehended whilst on the mission in South Wales, and executed at the age of thirty-four, after fourteen years spent in the Society.

July 23.

1. In Peru, in the year 1596, died Father Antony Lopez, a Spaniard, renowned for his learning, zeal for souls, and contempt of self. He was held in great estimation for his sanctity; and his body, when laid out after death, gave a fragrant odour, as was testified by those who performed that office. He is believed to have been poisoned by the savages, whose vices and intemperance he endeavoured to correct by his reproofs.

2. At Avignon, in France, in the year 1598, Michael Suarez, a French Lay-brother. He made it a rule when any circumstance prevented his making meditation or examination of conscience at the appointed hours, of taking no food until he had fully complied with these duties.

3. At Evora, in Portugal, when the Plague raged in the year 1580, four of ours died martyrs of charity; and again, in 1585, on the return of the pestilence, five others, among whom Father Antony Sequeira was called on this day to a heavenly crown. And in the 1599, at Alcala, in Spain, Brothers Peter Lozan and Diego Garcez died in the same office of charity, with five companions who followed them.

4. At Salonica, in the year 1733, Father John Baptist Souciet, a native

of Bourges. He was the fifth of six brothers who consecrated themselves to God in the Society. He was gifted with great talents for literature, and was distinguished for his erudition and profound researches. His zeal for the salvation of souls led him to ask for the missions of the Levant, where he was occupied in the instruction of sailors. He assembled them in the house of the missions, and went on board the vessels to prepare them for a general confession and for Holy Communion. In this unremitted labour he took a fever and died a victim of his zeal and charity.

JULY 24.

1. At Alcala, in Spain, in the year 1572, died Father Peter de Savedra, a Spaniard. Released from the ties of matrimony by the death of his wife, he was deliberating on a state of life, and going to the shrine of St. Didacus for counsel, he heard first a movement of the sacred body, then a voice saying that it would be for God's greater glory if he entered the Society. In it he ever lived as one who had a continual and earnest desire of promoting God's greater glory. The soul of his deceased wife appeared to him resplendent after his first Mass to thank him for the fulfilment of his promise to offer it for her.

2. At Milan, in the year 1634, died Father Cosmo Alemanni, an Italian. His father was the first to give hospitality to the Society in Milan, and received as a reward that five of his sons entered the Society. By his obedience and prayer Father Cosmo obtained all his requests from God; so that, as he listened to the voice of his Superior, so God seemed to listen to him. His favourite devout ejaculations were, "Praised be God," "Blessed be God."

3. At Novellara, in Italy, in the year 1656, Gerard Angelini, an Italian Lay-brother. In time of prayer he often received heavenly consolations. Once when harassed with anxiety for his salvation he heard a voice bidding him be of good courage, for he was numbered among the Elect. A few days before his death he received the joyful message from an Angel, "to take comfort, that the Angels were longing to welcome him to Heaven."

4. In China, the precise day unknown, in the year 1627, Brother Sebastian Fernandez, rich in virtues and merits. Born of a distinguished

family, he served Father Matthew Ricci as companion and interpreter, and employed himself in the humblest offices, with the hope of being admitted to the Society, which was the object of his ardent desires. It would be long to narrate all that he suffered for the faith. He was imprisoned four times, exposed to the insults of the populace, banished the kingdom, reduced to slavery, and many times so cruelly beaten that he nearly died. He was an excellent catechist as he was perfectly acquainted with the Chinese language, and he went from one part of the country to another fortifying the Christians in the faith, and replacing as far as he could the missioners, who were obliged to remain concealed during the persecution. In an advanced age he took long journeys to obtain resources for the subsistence of the missioners, and though exhausted by labour and infirmity, through a spirit of mortification and poverty he would have no exemption from any thing of rule.

July 25.

1. At Belmonte, in Spain, in the year 1580, died the Venerable Father Balthasar Alvarez, Master of Novices, and Provincial of three different Provinces. Born of a high family, he entered the Society at twenty-two, and died at the age of forty-seven. From his infancy he was greatly given to prayer, and by this he gained more during his studies after one year's novitiate than others by long labour, so that he shortly became fitted for any occupation to which he might be appointed. When Superior he often spent the whole night in prayer, and for six years followed exactly the method prescribed by St. Ignatius without seeking anything higher. His manner of saying Mass was most edifying, and he accounted the power of keeping and visiting the Blessed Sacrament often, one of the highest privileges of Religious life. St. Teresa used to say that she owed to his direction much of the holiness she had attained. He was not remarkable as a preacher, but had a wonderful talent for spiritual exhortations. A year before his death he was named Provincial of Peru, but such opposition was made to the nomination that it was revoked. His life was made up of alternations of consolation and desolation, through which he preserved a perfect equanimity and acquiescence to the Divine will; and it was revealed to St. Teresa that he was one of the most perfect men upon

earth. He slept on a board, and his disciplines every day were so severe, that the number and force of the strokes had to be limited; but his interior mortification was more wonderful, by which he annihilated his passions and gained such empire over them, that nothing could disturb the serenity of his soul.

2. At Prague, in Bohemia, in the year 1649, Father Martin Benedict, a Moravian, a man of most signal obedience. He devoted himself to the plague-stricken, and died a martyr of charity.

3. At Czestokoff, in Poland, in the year 1657, Father William Rose, a Frenchman, confessor to the Queen of Poland. His bed was a board, two books his pillow, and a stool his chair and table. He fasted the whole year except Sundays. Forbidden to wear a chain round his waist in his last sickness, he hung it round his neck, in token, he said, of his servitude to the Blessed Virgin. In his sickness the holy Bishop Nicolas appeared to him holding various scrolls. On one was written, "Poland shall be destroyed, but we must pray;" and on the last, "Poland shall be wholly destroyed, but we must pray." This holy courtier, gentle to others but severe to himself, departed at the hour he had foreseen, and after his death signal favours were granted through his intercession.

JULY 26.

1. At Kalisch, in Poland, in the year 1618, died Father Martin Smigletz, a Pole. His tact in introducing and keeping up pious discourse was remarkable. He confuted heretics both by pen and word of mouth with success, and was aided by a miracle. For after a public disputation held at Wilna with a Calvinist, in which he came off clearly victorious, a young man of that sect, about the Court, publicly maintained with sectarian audacity that Father Martin had been completely worsted, and ventured to confirm the falsehood with an oath, imprecating curses on himself if he lied. The punishment of his falsehood fell upon him, for by the judgment of God his throat so contracted with a sudden spasm that he nearly died. Having recovered by the help of the bystanders, he repeated what he had said, but with more disastrous issue; for, seized with a convulsive contraction of throat and jaws, he choked and died miserably.

2. At Prague, in Bohemia, in the year 1646, Father Gaspar Tausch,

a Prussian, regarded by all as a Saint. His most pious little works on the Wounds of our Saviour, Our Lady of Dolours, and the Wisdom of Christ or Profound Humility, show his spirit of piety. He displayed the perfection of his obedience by the manner in which when sick he took some nauseous medicine. For having a naturally excessive aversion to all such medicine, so that even when in health he fainted at the sight of the draught prepared for another, he received the potion when sick himself, and said, "We must obey," and drank it off, not at once, but slowly sipping it, to gain a perfect victory over his repugnance.

3. At Palença, in Old Castile, about the year 1580, Father Andrew Ascensias. He had a special gift of adapting the Spiritual Exercises to different states and dispositions, by which means he converted many sinners, and led others to great virtue and perfection. Many distributed their possessions to the poor, renounced the world, gave themselves to penance, or, remaining in the world, were examples of solid piety and perfection. Among these were Ecclesiastics of high dignity and men of noble birth. Five years after his death his body was found incorrupt, which was regarded as a proof of the purity he had preserved during his life.

JULY 27.

1. At Rome, in the year 1637, died Father John Gerard, an Englishman. At the age of fifteen he was sent to Exeter College, Oxford, but soon quitted it to pursue his studies at home. He went afterwards to study at Rheims, where he met with a Novice of S. Andrea from Rome, who had quitted for a time on account of health. The example of the Novice inspired the young Englishman with a desire of entering the Society. Returning to England to settle his affairs, he was imprisoned for three years. Being set at liberty, he hastened to Rome, where he was ordained Priest, and entered the Society on the Feast of the Assumption, 1588. He was sent to England, and laboured for nearly eighteen years. His own *Narrative* shows his patient zeal, extraordinary tact and prudence, charity, love of suffering, and tender piety. He was apprehended and put to inhuman torture several times in the Tower. In 1606 he bade farewell to England after his escape; he remained several years an outlaw, and a price was set upon his head. After his profession he successfully

laboured to found the College of Liège, and was appointed its first Rector. The last ten years of his life he spent in the English College at Rome, where he died of fever at the age of seventy-three.

2. At Cracow, in Poland, in the year 1597, died Father James Wujeck, a Pole. Being a man learned in Latin, Greek, and Hebrew, at the desire of King Stephen he was appointed instructor in learning and piety to Sigismund, Prince of Transylvania. He was afterwards Rector of the Professed House at Cracow, and then Provincial. But he still continued to preach, and by word of mouth and writings to wage war with heresy. By command of Pope Gregory XIII., and with the approbation of Clement VIII., he translated the Vulgate into the Polish language. His talents were of the highest order, his learning extraordinary, his manners very engaging, and his zeal for the salvation of souls most active. His right hand, which had written so much in defence of the faith, was found incorrupt some years after his death, when the rest of the body had decayed.

3. At Utrecht, in Belgium, in the year 1612, Father William Leon, a Belgian. He laboured for twenty-two years in Holland amid toils and dangers, with much success in the salvation of souls, which was owing chiefly to his earnest prayer, during which he was seen surrounded with heavenly light, and was illumined to discover the secrets of hearts.

4. At Evora, in Portugal, in the year 1597, Michael Alvarez, a Portuguese Scholastic Novice. He entered the Society at the age of eighteen, and lived in it only eight months, but in that short space he fulfilled a long time. He was a model of virtue and exactness. Having obtained permission to serve a person attacked with contagious erysipelas, he was taken with it, and assured the Rector that he had but a short time to live. Seven days afterwards he fell into a stupor for six hours, and coming to himself said to the Rector—"Father, I go to see the face of our Lord; He awaits me, and the Blessed Virgin, and the Archangels St. Michael and St. Gabriel." He then asked leave to die. Reminded that the longer he lived, the greater would be his merit, he replied—"No pain is so great as that of one who longs to see God." The sight of the Crucifix would at once alleviate his pains. Shortly before expiring he asked pardon of the Community, and said, "Oh, if we knew what it was to die we should live very differently." The room in which he expired long retained the name of the room of the Angel.

JULY 28.

1. At Tournay, in Belgium, in the year 1556, died Father Quentin Charlart, a Belgian, and deemed a Saint before entering the Society. When Canon of Tournay he would sometimes return home without shoes, mantle, or coat, all of which he had given to the poor. After the example of St. Nicholas, he visited by night the houses of those who were ashamed to beg, and assisted them most liberally. He progressed still more rapidly in virtue after his entrance into the Society, and was appointed Rector of the Roman College by St. Ignatius. He died a martyr of charity in the service of the sick.

2. At Villagarcia, in Spain, in the year 1580, Father Francis de Cordova, son of the Duke of Cordova, called to the Society when Rector of the University of Salamanca. The first time that he made the Exercises of St. Ignatius his soul was inundated with heavenly consolations, and he declared to one of his friends who came to visit him, and who expected to find him buried in sadness, that he would not change his state for all the dignities in the world. He practised the most entire abnegation and self-contempt. Having charge of the Refectory, he swept it on his knees. He sought the company of those who seemed to slight him; and in his third year of probation, while driving some pigs from the farm to Villagarcia, perceiving that one of them was tired, he took it on his shoulders and carried it through the streets. In sentiments of great fervour and holy resignation he expired three days after Father Balthasar Alvarez, under whom he had made his noviceship and third year of probation.

3. At Salamanca, in Spain, John Ortunez, a Spanish Scholastic. Father Balthasar Alzarez, who had been his Master in the Noviceship, used to say of him, that he had never read of greater things in the lives of the Fathers of the Desert than what he had witnessed in Brother John. The following are two instances of his blind obedience. Having received an order to wait, he stood in the open air during severe weather while the snow was falling, and would have stopped the whole night there, had he not been found and called away. Ordered to give a certain plot of ground three cansful of water every day, he continued to do so perseveringly even on those days on which fell abundant showers.

July 29.

1. At Toledo, in Spain, in the year 1586, died Father John Manuel, a Spaniard, remarkable for charity to the sick and poor. When Rector of the Professed House at Toledo, and there were only three loaves in the house, he ordered one to be given to a beggar. Shortly after, before the Brothers went to prepare the Refectory, a young man, a stranger, brought some loaves and gave them without saying from whom they came. Father John used to ask for the sick and infirm to be sent to him, saying, that by this work of charity, and by their prayers, the blessing of Heaven would come down upon the house. After his death he is said to have been seen in glory.

2. At Lima, in Peru, in the year 1611, Father Balthasar de Piña, a Spaniard. He was much esteemed by St. Ignatius, during whose life-time he entered the Society, and he was sent by Father Laynez to found the Province of Sardinia. At the age of fifty he went to Peru, where his preaching was compared to that of St. Vincent Ferrer, St. Bernardine of Sienna, and even of St. Paul. He had an extraordinary gift of prayer, and was a man of singular innocence. He died at the age of eighty-four, and all the town crowded to his funeral as to that of a Saint and an Apostle.

3. At Bar-le-duc, in France, in the year 1632, Father Claude Viola, a Frenchman. He preferred the abjection of the house of God to the certain prospect of the Archbishopric of Paris. In his treatment of himself he was so severe that it amounted to cruelty. With a reed in his hand, and a crown of thorns on his head, he disciplined himself so terribly with cords, and then with rods, and after that with iron chains armed with spikes, that the walls were sprinkled with his blood. He would repay in some manner the blood shed for him by our Blessed Saviour. In a private little book he had these words often repeated, "Jesus, Mary—blood for blood."

July 30.

1. At Liège, in Belgium, in the year 1656, died Father Peter Halloix, a Belgian, a man of primitive simplicity but great learning. He slept on

the ground, and that usually but for a short time. He used to say that to watch was to imitate in the flesh the Angels and God Himself. Before study he always repeated the hymn *Veni Creator*, and persuaded others to do the same, saying that studies could never turn to good account unless they were begun by reference to God and ended in Him. Compelled by obedience to discontinue the use of a girdle armed with sharp points, he compensated for it by the use of the discipline. At the age of seventy he was obliged by Superiors to moderate his austerities. However acute were his pains from gout he never ceased to give to prayer and his daily examens the time prescribed by the rule, and to perform on his knees his exercises of piety.

2. At Rome, in the year 1541, Mark Laynez, a Spanish Lay-brother, the brother of Father James Laynez. He had heard that his brother James had entered a new Order of Clerks Regular, and fearing lest he might have fallen into some heretical society, he said daily for three years the Apostles' Creed for him. Entering the Society at Rome he became an excellent Religious. After his death, when the funeral had been performed, he appeared to Father Laynez, and desired him to inform his relatives to be at ease about him, for he was saved and happy.

JULY 31.

1. At Rome, the birth-day of St. Ignatius, Confessor, Founder of the Society of JESUS, illustrious for his sanctity, miracles, and zeal in spreading throughout the world the Catholic Faith, according to the words of the *Roman Martyrology*. He founded the Society at the cost of great labours and as great glory, with the manifest aid of the finger of God. This his work is the summary of all his praise. The greatest of his miracles (which have been innumerable, especially in the assistance of women in childbirth,) was his daily continued progress in perfection, a thing rare even in the greatest Saints. His zeal for the propagation of the faith is witnessed by Asia in a great measure converted, Africa brought to obedience, America civilized, and Europe made holier and more learned. He gloriously consummated a most laborious life, spent for the greater and yet greater glory of God, in the Professed House at Rome, upon a Friday, in the year 1556.

July 31.

2. At Rome, in the year 1664, died Father Goswin Nickel, the tenth General of the Society. He had been Rector several times, and governed for twelve years the Province of the Lower Rhine. He was chosen Assistant of Germany, in which office he showed such virtue, prudence, and talent, that Father Francis Piccolomini, General of the Society, on appointing him Vicar General, wrote—"I commit to him, whom I name Vicar General, the Society; and declare under oath that I consider him most fit for the post." His conduct as General is well described by Cardinal Pallavicini, who says of him—"That he won the highest opinions of all in the Society, of the greatest dignitaries without it, and of the Supreme Head of the Church; that he was beloved by his subjects, approved of by rulers, and successful in his undertakings." He reestablished the Society in Venice by the intervention of Pope Alexander VII. after it had been excluded from that city for fifty years. His love of prayer was so great that, for fear of being compelled to interrupt it, he rose to have it completed before the rising of the Community. After nine years of rule, worn down with age and infirmities, he asked for a Vicar. Father John Paul Oliva was appointed to the office, but the holy General lived five years after a model of invincible patience, and daily receiving Holy Communion. He died on the evening of the Feast of St. Ignatius, to whom he had a tender devotion.

3. At Nangasachi, in Japan, in the year 1633, Nicholas Kéyan Jucumanga, a Japanese Scholastic. He died a glorious martyr after three years spent in study and the practise of all virtue. He was the first to suffer the torment of the pit, so famous in Japan, being hung with his head downwards for four whole days. His guards found him each day with his bonds broken and suffering no pain. On being questioned, he replied that he had been visited by the Queen of Heaven, who had given him to drink from a spring of pure water, which so refreshed him that he felt no suffering, and only pity for the Daifusama who had invented that torment. By his preaching, which numbers flocked to hear, he caused many conversions to the faith.

4. At Castiglione, in Italy, in the year 1630, Father Peter Justinelli, an Italian. He was the gift of God to the prayers of his mother, who till then had no child. Entering the Society, he fulfilled the prophecies made about his Apostolic zeal by devoting himself to the service of the plague-stricken, and so died a martyr of charity.

AUGUST.

AUGUST 1.

1. At Rome, in the year 1546, died Father Peter Faber, a Savoyard, the eldest companion of St. Ignatius, and his eldest son in the Society, renowned for his Apostolical labours in Spain, Portugal, Italy, and Germany. When making his first retreat under St. Ignatius, and deliberating on a state of life, he passed many hours in the open air in deep snow, and for six days fasted without food or drink until forbidden to do so by St. Ignatius. By this heroic act he was freed from all inordinate appetite for food, and from scruples, with which he had been troubled. After a life spent in laborious missions and toilsome journeys for the propagation of the faith and the good of souls, he was summoned to Rome by St. Ignatius in the summer heats, a time often fatal to travellers entering the city. He started at the voice of obedience, but was seized with fever, and died after a short illness. He appeared after death to a holy person in great glory, saying that he had died through love of obedience, and spoke much and sweetly of the special happiness he enjoyed in Heaven on account of that manner of death.

2. At Rome, in the year 1580, Father Everard Mercurian, a Belgian, the fourth General of the Society. He knew so well the mind of St. Ignatius in the Institute of the Society, that the holy Father seemed to live again in him. He governed the Society with great wisdom for seven years. He was most remarkable for mature deliberation in speaking and writing, and for the art of forming good superiors and preachers. He was a great lover of poverty, and a man of indomitable endurance, even as Provincial visiting on foot the houses of his Province. As General he put into their present order the Summary of the Constitutions and the Common Rules. He established the missions to the Maronites and to

England, sending to our island Father Parsons and Father Campian. He replied to his brother, who asked him to relieve the poverty of his family, that he had no more power to do so than the humblest Lay-brother. He died at an advanced age in the house of the Novitiate of S. Andrea, having announced his death the day before to the Fathers present.

3. At Pont-a-Mousson, in France, in the year 1633, Father John Collignon, a Frenchman, remarkable for humility and charity. From a desire of remaining unknown, he taught grammar, nor would he accept any higher post though fully capable of filling it. Eleven times he devoted himself to the service of the plague-stricken, and in his last sickness lamented that he was dying at home idly in his bed, and not among the sick of the plague.

4. At Wilna, in Lithuania, in the year 1689, the Venerable Father Thomas de Rupniew Ujeysky, a Pole, who from being Bishop of Czenichoff became a Religious of the Society. He was chosen by God to give an example of holiness to the world in the various states of life which he filled, as a Christian Courtier, Counsellor of the State, Minister, whether of Kings or Pontiffs, then as Bishop, and lastly as a Perfect Religious. He had an extraordinary gift of pacifying enmities, and was commonly called by princes and people the holy Bishop; but he thought and spoke of himself as a miserable nothing, and sought with holy eagerness and desire to enter the Society, that, as he said, he might at last learn how to serve God. The General, Father John Paul Oliva, held him in high esteem, honouring his consummate virtue with the profession of the four Vows after scarce a year's noviceship. Father Charles Noyelle appointed him shortly afterwards Superior of the Professed House at Wilna. His life, written by Father John Brictius, contains many extrarodinary things which seem as miracles.

AUGUST 2.

1. At Ikizuki, in Japan, in the year 1590, died Father Francis Carrion, a Spaniard, an indefatigable labourer in the Japanese vineyard. He lived in continual expectation of death in the kingdom of Bungo, but found it at last in Firando, where, after many glorious victories over infidelity, and many conversions, he was poisoned out of hatred to the faith, and died a martyr after three days of suffering.

2. At Tournay, in Belgium, in the year 1644, Father Francis de la Croix, a Belgian. He was singularly devout to the Blessed Virgin, had the most exalted thoughts of her, and wrote most sweetly in her praise, as his *Garden of Mary* testifies, a book published in almost all known languages. Appointed Provincial, he placed the Province at her feet, to govern it and protect it as her own. When he woke from his first sleep he used to rise and salute her with the hymn of St. Casimir. Father Mutius Vitelleschi, the General of the Society, called him "the Angel," for his modesty and air of angelic innocence.

3. At Halle, in Germany, Father Earnest Mairhofer, a German, who died the oldest, so far as can be ascertained, of all the Fathers who have lived under the standard of St. Ignatius. He reached the age of ninety-eight, was eighty-one years in the Society, and a Priest sixty-eight. He did not make use of his great age as an excuse for any relaxation in Religious life, but rather as a reason for a more exact observance of the rule. He kept the fasts of Lent strictly, and fasted on Wednesdays, Fridays, and Saturdays throughout the year.

4. At Lima, in Peru, in the year 1642, Augustine Salumbrino, a Lay-brother. He entered the Society by command of the Blessed Virgin; and after his noviceship at S. Andrea in Rome, was sent to Peru, where for forty-two years he was Infirmarian. He daily took a discipline to blood, made three hours' prayer, and wore continually a hairshirt. He preserved his baptismal innocence until death. The Blessed Virgin often appeared to him, and by her aid he triumphed over the demons who visibly assailed him.

August 3.

1. At York, in England, in the year 1645, died Father Brian Cansfield, born in Lancashire. He was a laborous missioner, and was taken at the altar, and carried in his vestments amid insults to gaol. He suffered so much there that his health was shattered, and he died about a month after his release. He was sixty-five years of age, thirty-nine of which he had spent in the Society.

2. At Granada, in Spain, in the year 1600, Father Peter de Molina, a Spaniard. A most zealous missioner on the coast of Spain and in Africa, he converted to the faith many Moors and Jews and other infidels.

Returning to Granada, he went at once to the hospital, where, in tending assiduously the wounded and plague-stricken, he died a martyr of charity. Father Mark Antonio and Father Francis de Cuellar died in the same service, and all three were seen after death in the glory of the Saints.

3. At Louvain, in Belgium, in the year 1621, Martin Becchaert, a Belgian Scholastic. He was remarkable for his love and devotion of silence, for never speaking well of himself or ill of others, and for his tender devotion to the Blessed Virgin, whom he reverenced as a mother, and whose benediction he asked morning and night. He gave three hours a day and sometimes four to prayer, and was a young man of great modesty and recollection. He used to say that he prayed for five things: To die before he was entangled in the dangers of intercourse with others; in the Society; in full possession of his senses; in the morning before the Masses had begun; and within the Octave of St. Ignatius. All these things he obtained.

4. At Bourdeaux, in the year 1720, Father Francis Duvergier, a Frenchman. Ardently desiring the missions of Canada, he prepared himself by enduring the cold of winter without providing against it, an austerity which he practised to the end of his life. He made no use of a bed, and passed the greatest part of the night before the Blessed Sacrament. The serenity of his soul was depicted on his countenance, on which he never showed any emotion except when God's glory was in question. The prayers, labours, and austerities, which he employed for the conversion of sinners produced abundant fruit; and though he was regarded as a Saint, he looked upon himself as a useless servant and the last of men.

August 4.

1. In Mauritania, in the year 1578, died Father Gaspar Maurice Serpe, a Portuguese. He was Superior of the Professed House at Lisbon, and Rector of the College of Evora; admirable for his zeal, especially as a confessor of the poor. He daily took a severe discipline, and wore almost continually a hairshirt. He accompanied King Sebastian as confessor and missionary to the army in the unfortunate expedition into Africa, of which he both disapproved and foretold the fatal issue, saying to one of his Brethren as he left, "We shall meet next in Heaven."

In the route of the army he was cut down by a Moor while he was confessing a wounded soldier. The Moor who killed him seeing him thus holily engaged, said—"Dog of a Nazarene, what impiety art thou about!" and cleft his head in twain with his scimitar.

2. At Pernambuco, in Brazil, in the year 1638, Father Antonio Bellavia, an Italian, killed while hearing the confession of a wounded soldier in a battle between the Portuguese and the Dutch, though he himself had been struck with a bullet. He was of such angelic modesty that in his countenance he appeared what he was, a virgin in body and mind. When he was a child he was once observed by his father tapping the ground with his foot, and being asked why he did so, replied, that there was a world below us to which he would have to go. As he returned from school, mothers would say, "Let us go and see the little Angel, Bellavia's son." In Brazil he converted many souls.

3. At Alcala, in Spain, in the year 1565, Peter Gomez, a Spanish Lay-brother. He was bailiff of the farm; and was a man of such holiness, care, and diligence in his duty, that on his return to the house he was welcomed back by the Fathers with a joy and affection, as though he were one come from a long distance or after a long absence. The sight of this great charity between Fathers and Brothers moved a layman of great note to enter the Society.

4. At Wilna, in Lithuania, in the year 1663, Father Michael Ginkiewicz, a Pole. He was seven years Penitentiary at St. Peter's in Rome; was Rector of the Colleges of Neswish and Wilna, and of the Professed Houses of Warsaw and Wilna, all of which establishments he governed with a repute for much wisdom and charity. He broke a blood vessel while preaching. He died in such reputation of sanctity, that the Bishop of Wilna with his Canons performed his obsequies in the most solemn manner, and he prevailed upon the Vice-Rector to allow him to pass the night lying on the ground at the foot of the bed in the room where the body lay.

August 5.

1. At Palermo, in the year 1651, died Cæsar Cajetan, an Italian Novice. He entered the Society at Rome, renouncing the principality of

Cassaro and the Marquisate of Sortino, to the great sorrow of his vassals, whom he had governed with mildness and prudence for fourteen years. To gain his admission into the Society, to which he had bound himself by vow, he struggled through gigantic difficulties; and he quitted the world in the vigour of life and the height of his fortune. He arrived in a short time to a high degree in the love of God, Whom, he said, he could not understand how it was possible to offend. During his sickness of eight months he was a model of patience, and joy was ever beaming on his countenance. He asked of God and obtained three favours—To die in the Noviceship in his first fervour; of a slow fever, like St. Aloysius; on (Saturday) a day consecrated to the Blessed Virgin.

2. At Alcala, in Spain, in the year 1646, Father Gaspar Hurtado, a Spaniard. After filling the highest Professors' Chairs in the University, he entered the Society, and was remarkable for his simplicity, purity of soul, and religious perfection. He passed through the dangers of a Court without a tincture of the vanity of the world. He taught scholastic theology for more than thirty years at Murcia, Madrid, and Alcala. His learned works form eight volumes in folio.

3. At Klausenburg, in Transylvania, in the year 1586, Brother Adam Tensier, a victim of charity in the service of the plague-stricken. Nineteen others followed or preceded him in the same place, tending on the sick without or within the domestic walls.

4. In America, among the Iroquois, Brother Renée, a French Novice, was martyred for the faith. The date of his death is uncertain, but Father Isaac Jogues, his great fellow-sufferer in torments from the Indians, wrote on this day to announce it. He had been seen to make the sign of the Cross on the forehead of a boy, and for that cause he was murdered.

August 6.

1. At Vienna, in Austria, in the year 1552, died Father Claude le Jay, a Savoyard, one of the first companions of St. Ignatius, illustrious for his wisdom, modesty, humility, and zeal for the salvation of souls. Blessed Peter Canisius called him the Apostle of Germany, others an Angel of God, and others the father and defender of Catholics. His consummate virtue obtained for him the offer of the Bishoprics of Trieste and Vienna,

both of which he humbly but resolutely declined. He was of a gentle and mild disposition, ready and eloquent in speech, without pretence or pride, of a cheerful countenance and modest demeanour, and it was by these virtues that he obtained a hearing from the heretics and gained access to their hearts.

2. At Sassari, in Sardinia, in the year 1608, Father John Sebastian à Campo, a Sardinian. His devotion and love towards the Blessed Virgin were extraordinary. Every Saturday, from sunset to the dawn of the following day, he spent the night bareheaded on his knees in prayer, even in the depth of winter, before her statue in the hospital. He fasted on Fridays and Saturdays throughout the year, and in Lent on bread and water. Carried by the Moors captive into Africa, he was charged by the Blessed Virgin to devote himself to strengthening Christian captives in the faith, and he is believed to have received from her hand a great quantity of rosaries to distribute among them.

3. At Seville, in Spain, in the year 1627, Antonio de Leon, a Spanish Lay-Brother. When threatened with death he did not hesitate to imperil his life to preserve his chastity.

4. In the year 1628, Father Philip de Noyelle, native of Arras, a martyr of charity in the service of the plague-stricken. One hundred and fifty of Ours died in the same service with him.

August 7.

1. At Toulouse, in France, in the year 1598, died Father Sebastian Miller, a Belgian, a great director of souls. He never failed to soften the most obdurate by his combined prudence and prayers to Heaven. He performed great penances for his penitents, and once, to win an obstinate soul, took a severe discipline of a thousand strokes, and so gained it to God.

2. At Madrid, in Spain, in the year 1662, Father Diego de Castillo, a Spaniard, the model of a Procurator in the Society. He filled this office during thirty-five years. In the stress of the most urgent business he was ever most exact in all his religious duties, and he was so mortified that he was styled a self-tormentor. During the space of forty-four years which he lived in the Society, he used while in health neither bed nor pillow, nor drank any wine until he was ordered to do so in sickness by

the physician. He was never known to be wrong in his accounts so much as one penny, and his word was considered by men of business as equal to a bond. In the intervals of business he kept silence so exactly that he was surnamed the hermit.

3. At Bourdeaux, in France, in the year 1571, Father Charles Sanguinot, a Frenchman. He was of the Court of the Duke of Lorraine, and in possession of a splendid fortune. After the example of St. Alexius, he left his newly married wife on the wedding-day and entered the Society, where he soon made great progress in perfection. He predicted his death a year before, and died in raptures of heavenly consolations.

4. At Messina, in Sicily, in the year 1551, John Antonio, an Italian Novice. Obedience was his special virtue. Being asked by the Brothers round his death-bed what blessing they should ask of God to give him, he replied—"That His will may be done with me in all things." When asked if he wished anything to be done for him, his answer was—"Whatever Obedience orders." Again, to the questions, What now gave him the greatest comfort? he replied—"Obedience;" What virtue he now wished to have practised most? "Obedience." And, commanded to tell a certain Brother in what virtue he desired him to excel, he repeated —"In Obedience." When the Master of Novices, Father Cornelius Wishans, asked him when he would like to die, John answered— "When you give me permission, Father." He received the command to die on the first or second hour of the following day, and, like a true child of Obedience, expired at the second hour. Just before his death he suffered violent temptations, but he won the victory over the enemy, according to the words, "The obedient man shall speak victories."

5. At Madrid, in the year 1723, Father William d'Aubenton, native of Auxerre. He filled the several posts of Rector, Provincial, and Assistant, was Confessor to Philip V. of Spain, and honoured with the favour of Clement XI., who wrote to him with his own hand. By his zeal and energy he obtained the decree of the Beatification of St. John Francis Regis. In all his distracting employments he was most exact in religious duties, frequent in visits to the Blessed Sacrament, took daily discipline, made use of other penances, and though delicate in health, fasted very rigorously. He kept most strict watch over his senses. His learning was profound, but he loved, through humility, to converse on the simplest

topics. He expired in sentiments of deep contrition, after a general confession, at the age of seventy-six, sixty of which were spent in the Society. His obsequies were attended by the Archbishop of Toledo and many distinguished persons of every rank and order.

August 8.

1. At Burgos, in Spain, in the year 1643, died Father Sebastian Sarmiento, a Spaniard, a preacher of great powers, and a laborious Missioner. He was of noble birth, but nobler far for his virtues. Devils were subject to him, though he suffered much from their molestation. At his death he was comforted by the sight of the Blessed Virgin and the songs of Angels, by whose sweet music his soul, delivered from profound sadness arising from scruples, was thrown into ecstacy. A little bird came also to console him, which one day he chanced to find in the hands of some boys, who held it by a string, and were pulling out its feathers and tormenting it to death; he begged them to let it go, to sing the praise of God; they did so, and it came daily to sing at the Father's room, as if to give thanks for its life.

2. At Marchenas, in Spain, in the year 1662, Father Ximenes Bertenda, a Spaniard. He was remarkable for his charity both to the sick and the sound in health, and for his ingenuity in finding means to humble himself. He tasted heavenly delights in prayer, especially at the foot of the Crucifix. As he lay sick of the plague, he saw our Lord standing near his bed with an amiable majestic countenance, and heard him say, "I have come that they may have life, and have it more abundantly." By which words the violence of the sickness was checked, and he was restored to health.

3. At Cracow, in Poland, in the year 1636, Laurence Gorczyn, a Polish Lay-brother. He was offered the priesthood by the Provincial, but preferred to live in humility in the house of God. One day after Holy Communion, being more than usually recollected, he received warning of his death in a year's time, and prepared himself for it by daily reciting the Office of the Blessed Virgin. The year passed, and the good man died. In the last night of his life he was violently assailed by the devil, but

being commanded to implore the aid of the Blessed Virgin, he seemed to behold her, and address her as present, saying, "Dear Lady, where were you when the enemy would have taken me in his snares? To you I owe the victory." Having thus spoken, he calmly expired.

4. In China, in the year 1730, Father Stephen Lecouteux, a Frenchman. He laboured for eighteen years in the province of Honkoang, where he established a fervent congregation. Driven from his mission by an imperial edict, he returned secretly, living in a boat, and visiting the different Christian congregations, He thus contrived for three years to avoid detection until he was compelled to fly. As soon however as the danger ceased, he returned with another Father; but being exhausted on the journey, was obliged to stop, and for fear of compromising the Christians, to reembark for Canton. He died on the third day after his embarcation.

August 9.

1. In Bohemia, in the year 1629, died Father Matthew Burnat, a German. A zealous and fervent Missioner throughout Bohemia, gaining by his labours a great harvest of souls. His life was sought for on account of the numbers that he drew from heresy, and he was at last put to death by his enemies and the enemies of the faith.

2. At Antwerp, in Belgium, in the year 1613, Father John David, a Belgian. Before entering the Society, he was the zealous and eloquent Parish Priest of Courtray, and defended the Catholic faith with such ardour, that he was thrice driven from the city by the persecution of sectarians. He lived a mortified life, not suffering even his mother to reside with him, having a poor and hard pallet bed, and a coffin beside it to remind him of death. He entered the Society at the age of thirty-two, at which his fellow-citizens were so edified, that they petitioned for a College of the Society, and Father David was charged with the government of it before finishing his novitiate, and he filled that post for eight years. He was afterwards Rector of the Colleges of Brussels and Ghent. He restored the statues of the Saints at Ghent, which had been broken down by the heretics; and was everywhere indefatigable in preaching, hearing confessions, and composing books of piety and controversy. He died at

the age of sixty-four. Southwell reckons more than twenty works composed by him.

3. In the East Indies, in the year 1684, the precise day is not known, Father Augustine Shobach, a Moravian, of the Province of Bohemia. From his early years he ardently desired the Indian mission, for which he prepared himself by fervent prayer, frequent acts of humiliation and disciplines, and entire abnegation of self, seeking on all occasions affronts and humiliations. He thus arrived at a close union with God, Who discovered to him the future and secrets of hearts. Sailing from Cadiz to the Indian islands, and miraculously protected from shipwreck by the Blessed Virgin and his special patron, St. Francis Xavier, he laboured in them for the conversion of souls until he was slain by one of the natives in an outbreak of hostility to the faith in one of these isles.

August 10.

1. In Canada, in the year 1661, died Father Renée Menard, a Frenchman. He was Missionary among the Algonquins, Hurons, and savage Iroquois; and he laboured with such great fruit, that he was called among our Fathers, "the successful Missioner." He gave three hours of the night to prayer, slept on the bare ground, and for many years neither tasted bread nor drank wine. He saw with joy a pile which the savages had raised to burn him alive. After long fastings, shipwrecks, and hardships, he fell a victim either to the privations he had to suffer in a toilsome journey to the Hurons, or to the cruelty of the savages, of which latter mode of death there were some indications.

2. At Goa, in the East Indies, in the year 1752, Father Melchior Nugnez, a Portuguese. In the noviceship he gained a great victory over himself, for he carried a sheep upon his back through the crowded streets, although he had been in the world a member of a family of nobles. He laboured and suffered much, with Apostolic zeal, in India, Japan, and China; and hearing in a Chinese port, that there was a man who had in his possession the reliquary which St. Francis Xavier had worn round his neck, and which had been taken from the Saint after his death, he strenuously sought to procure it. It was a poor case of brass, containing a very small particle of the relics of St. Thomas the Apostle, the name of

St. Ignatius from one of his letters, and his Vows of profession written in his own handwriting.

3. At Ikinosima, in Japan, in the year 1622, Augustine Ota, a Japanese Lay-brother and Catechist, beheaded for the faith. He was a holy Religious, having been baptized in his youth by Father Camillus Constance on the eve of his martyrdom by fire, while he was his companion in prison. Having entered the Society, he devoted himself to the labours of a Catechist until he obtained the palm of martyrdom.

4. At the College of Palermo, in the year 1704, Father Albert Schafili, a Religious of consummate virtue and perfection. He observed the Rules with a scrupulous exactitude; adding to the Religious vows three others very difficult to observe—(1.) in his words, as well as actions, to seek always the glory of God; (2.) never to excuse himself; (3.) to do good to all who should oppose or calumniate him. And these vows he kept with great fidelity. His application to prayer raised him to so high a degree of contemplation, that he was often seen in ecstacies, during which he received special light for the guidance of souls confided to his care. He kept himself spotlessly pure throughout all his life, and to guard it he practised many extraordinary penances. He was full of charity and gentleness to others, and of an admirable patience, which he showed in the great sufferings of his last sickness, undergone with an admirable silence and resignation.

August 11.

1. In England, in the year 1650, died Father Matthew Grimes Bazier, a Frenchman. Active, shrewd, and endowd with a mind well adapted to his holy duties, he long baffled the search and cunning of his persecutors At length being taken, he died from the hardships of his imprisonment, rejoicing that he died a captive in so glorious a cause, but grieved that his death was a bloodless one.

2. At Lyons, in France, in the year 1617, Francis Caguin, a French Lay-brother. He was a man of spotless innocence and of a singularly tender conscience; but anxious about the sins of his former life, he asked of God some suffering to expiate them, and he was suddenly seized with a severe toothache. It is said that nothing that he asked for in

prayer was refused him. Amongst other things, he asked and obtained that he should live as many years in the Society as he had lived in the world.

3. At Mindanao, in the Philippines, in the year 1596, Father John à Campo, a Spaniard, of extraordinary fervour, piety, and engaging manners; renowned for victories over himself, obedience, and missionary labours. His great virtues while he yet lived in Spain were recompensed with many divine favours and heavenly visions; and being warned by the great master in ascetic life, Father Louis da Ponte, not to rely too much on these, whilst occupied in examination of them, he heard the words—"If you are hungry, and a branch laden with fruit is offered you, what do you do?" Father John replied—"I pull the fruit and eat it, and throw away the bough." "Then do so," said our Lord, "with these visions; gather the fruit—humility, patience, and other virtues—and put away all other thoughts about them." Ever intent on missionary toil, and ready at every call of obedience, he rose two hours before the rest on days of obligation to go out of the city to hear confessions. At last having obtained the mission of the Philippine Islands, he died there a holy death.

4. At Wurtenberg, in Silesia, in the 1651, Father Jules César Coture, a Belgian, of great devotion to the Infant JESUS, Whom he adored during Christmas time lying prostrate for half an hour each day upon the floor. When Rector of Neuhaus the College was in great want; he prayed to his Guardian Angel, and found a sum of money in a drawer, where he had neither seen nor put any. At Glatz he served the sick of the plague without taking it; and when he was Rector of Wratislaw, he defeated the heretics after continuing in prayer the whole night.

AUGUST 12.

1. At Lille, in Belgium, in the year 1659, died Father Florence Montmorency, a Belgian. He filled all the chief posts in the Society except that of Father General, being Professor, Rector, Master of Tertians, Provincial, Visitor, Assistant, and Vicar General; and when received by Father Claudius Acquaviva at Rome, was judged by him a fit person to whom some day the government of the Society might be entrusted, as he wrote to Father Manaréo. Though so great a man, in his government he paid

the greatest deference to the opinions of others, saying, "One man alone is not a man." He never deferred to another day what he could do upon the present; and that nothing might be forgotten, he kept at his desk a list hung up before his eyes of things to be done. To the aged, to the sick, to strangers, and to the afflicted, he was of a most tender and liberal charity. From time to time he would take a crucifix from his bosom, and devoutly kissing it would say—"In Thy hands Thou hast written me; look upon thy handwriting and save me." His devotion to the Blessed Virgin was great from his early years, and he often saluted her with fervent ejaculations, and recommended to her and his Guardian Angel all business of importance. He practised some penance each day, and usually wore an iron chain as a girdle. When from loss of sight he could not ascend the altar, he daily received Holy Communion. He died at the of seventy-nine, having lived sixty years in the Society. His memory is in benediction.

2. At Paderborn, in Germany, in the year 1629, John Bitter, a German Scholastic and Master, of great obedience, humility, and love for the poor, whom he served every other day at the College gate. He was found dead on his knees, having been previously seized with a sudden fit of coughing. Shortly afterwards two other Scholastics, Peter Hauzer and Peter Khor also died; one of whom, Peter Hauzer, appeared to the Sacristan in the Church, and said that Brother John Bitter had been freed from Purgatory at the second Mass said for him, and Brother Peter Khor more quickly still. The soul which then appeared, changing the colour of its vesture from dark to white, and suddenly resplendent, was seen to go up to Heaven.

3. At Warsaw, in Poland, in the year 1646, Father John Gruzewski, a Lithuanian. He was a man of great perfection, full of charity to those under him, zealous, candid, severe to himself, and of close union with God, on which subject he wrote three volumes. He was twice Rector of the College and University of Wilna, and of the Professed Houses of Wilna and Warsaw, and then Provincial, in all of which offices he was most highly esteemed. A Father, who narrowly observed him, declared that he never could detect in him the appearance of a venial sin. In appearance he he wore linen like others, but, except the collar and wristbands, it was a shirt of hair.

August 13.

1. At Rome, in the year 1621, died the Blessed John Charles Berchmans, a Belgian Scholastic, admirable for his innocence and most exact observance of every letter of the rule. He followed the example of St. Aloysius so closely, that he seemed either a second Aloysius or the Saint himself restored to life. It was said of him when he defended his theses in philosophy at Rome, that if an Angel in the flesh were to have undertaken the same task, he could not have done it with greater modesty. His guard over his senses, watchfulness, command over his mind and actions, unstained purity, and tender devotion to the Blessed Virgin, made him the model of students. He held in his embrace his Crucifix, his Rule Book, and his Rosary as he died, saying—"These three things are most dear to me; with these I willingly die." The night after his death, a Religious of tried virtue saw the Blessed Virgin join the Community of the Roman College, carried in a chair of state, borne upon the shoulders of St. Aloysius and Blessed John Berchmans. The vision typified the pious custom they introduced of speaking of her in time of recreation.

2. At Antwerp, in Belgium, in the year 1619, Father Adrian Crutz, a Fleming. He filled the offices of Rector and Professor, was a man of eminent virtue, and devoted to attending on the sick. He died in the service of the plague-stricken. During life he daily took a severe discipline, saying to himself—"Adrian, blood for blood!" Every year he made it a practice to abstain from some particular pleasant fruit in honour of the Blessed Virgin.

3. At Parma, in Italy, in the year 1657, Father Francis Raulino, an Italian, beloved by all for his amiable and angelic manners. Though highly esteemed as a learned Professor of Theology, which he taught for many years, he devoted himself to explaining the catechism in public and directing three sodalities: one of boys of the poorest class, and another of children of the middle classes, and a third of a select body of the scholars, whom he formed to perfection by meditations and the practice of solid virtues. Many of these youths entered Religious life. After his death a person worthy of credit beheld our Lord coming to meet his soul on the way to Heaven; and then welcoming it with a loving

embrace, Christ was heard to say, speaking to St. Ignatius—"Come and reap the fruit of your labours and of mine—the fruit, that is to say, of the perfection achieved in that soul.

AUGUST 14.

1. At Rome, in the year 1591, died Father Jerome Platus, a Milanese, of exalted virtue and sanctity. He is the author of the famous work, On the Happiness of a Religious State, a book which has led numbers to embrace a Religious life and to a closer following of Christ. He was composing another excellent work, On the Love of Poverty, but, as he had written it on loose papers, a Lay-brother in adjusting his room threw them all as waste paper into the fire. The Father, without showing any emotion, offered them as a holocaust to God. He was employed by Father Acquaviva as Secretary to the Assistancies of France and Germany, and had the care of the Novices at the Professed House, amongst whom was St. Aloysius Gonzaga.

2. At Naples, in the year 1618, Father Julius Mancinelli, an Italian. He was a man of apostolic zeal and labours both in Europe and Africa for the salvation of souls. He visited and evangelized many dioceses of Italy, receiving extensive powers from the Bishops. He spent three years in Constantinople and Dalmatia, and many more years in Poland, Wallachia, Moldavia, Hungary, and Bohemia, as well as parts of Germany, hearing confessions in the languages of these and other countries, which he received the grace of understanding in the confessional, though out of it he did not know a word of some of them. Even the deaf and dumb could make themselves intelligible to him, and understand him. He passed several times from Naples to Algiers to redeem and to console the captives; and in Italy he visited the prisons and hospitals and those condemned to galleys; spending whole days and sometimes whole nights in the confessional, saying his Office by snatches, or composing sermons in the intervals. He received great graces and consolations from God, and Angels were seen weaving his crown. He died at a great age, having spent sixty-two years in the Society.

3. At Cracow, in Poland, in the year 1625, Father George Tyszkiewicz, son of a Count Palatine of Poland. He was a student at Rome where,

falling sick, he made a vow if he recovered, to join that Religious Order of which he should first meet a member on going forth from his house. He did recover, and the Very Rev. Father Mutius Vitelleschi was the first man he fell in with. In compliance with his vow he entered the Noviceship of the Society, of which he became a distinguished member. After a brilliant course of theology he was made Rector of several Colleges, and died Provincial of Poland.

AUGUST 15.

1. At Rome, in the year 1568, died St. Stanislaus Kostka, a Pole, leaving this world to join the heavenly citizens on the very day of the Feast of the Assumption of the Virgin Mother of God, according to his own petition, made through the intercession of the Martyr St. Lawrence. The most Holy Name inscribed in purple characters on his mother's breast foretold, while he was yet unborn, his future state of life. His acts, and the sufferings which he passed through to obtain admission into the Society, are worthy of all admiration. Before he entered it he was innocent and a Saint; after he had entered it he was an Angel and a model of all sanctity. It is enough to say that the Angels brought him the Heavenly Banquet, and that the Queen of Angels placed in his arms her Infant Son. The fever of which he died was rather the ardour of divine love than the heat of sickness. His bosom had often burned with so ardent a charity, that to cool it he had been forced to apply cloths dipped in water. He was the first of the Society to be placed on the list of the Beatified, and almost the youngest Confessor who has obtained that honour. Clement X. allowed his feast to be kept on the first Sunday after St. Martin's, as one of the principal Patrons of Poland.

2. At Alcala, in Spain, in the year 1602, Father Ignatius Mendoza, a Spaniard. Upon his reception into the Society Philip III. said, "Ignatius has chosen the better part." He was a noble of Spain of the highest rank, profoundly learned in Civil and Canon Law, and had admirably discharged the duties of Ambassador at the Court of France and at Venice for Philip II. and Philip III. He held the Fathers in such reverence, that he said he did not dare so much as open his lips in their presence. He took great delight in serving in the kitchen, and in all that tended

to his humiliation. He died after a few months' noviceship, ripe for Heaven, saying that, having left all for Christ, he had great hopes of an eternal reward.

3. At Valladolid, in Spain, in the year 1647, Father Diego de Baëza, a Spaniard. After the time allotted for philosophy and theology, he was appointed to the duty of preaching, and he became one of the most eminent preachers in Spain, and continued to be so to the end of his life. He perpetuated his instructive labours by publishing eleven volumes on the History of the Old and New Testament.

August 16.

1. At Drogheda, in Ireland, in the year 1649, died Father John Bath, an Irishman. At the storming of Drogheda by the soldiers of Cromwell, the house in which he was taken was given up to plunder, and he and his brother, a Secular Priest, were led to the market-place, tied to a post, and there shot.

2. At Huete, in Spain, in the year 1622, Father Francis de Otazo, a Spaniard. Although he was a man of great innocence, he was in anxiety about his salvation, and earnestly implored the assistance of the Blessed Virgin. She appeared to him accompanied with a bright concourse of Saints. She bore in her hand a large and beautiful book, into which she bid him look, saying that it was the Book of Life. He read his own name at the beginning of a page in characters of gold. She then showed him a number of other names, adding, that by his means God would lead all these to a happy eternity. Comforted by this vision, he went on the mission to the Philippine Islands, where he converted very many to the faith and to a holy life.

3. At Nangasachi, in Japan, in the year 1633, Father Emmanuel Borgés, a Portuguese, martyred by the death of the pit, with two Novices, Joseph Resmul and Ignatius Kindo, Japanese. He had laboured secretly for twelve years in that Empire, after having been banished, but was at length taken and condemned with his two companions. They were hung in the fosse with their head downwards for four days, when they passed from that cruel torment to the joys of Heaven.

4. - At Gonsano, in Sicily, in the year 1624, Father Charles Romano,

remarkable for his innocence and purity, unstained by any mortal sin. Pure of heart, he received the gift of penetrating the secrets of hearts. At the holy house of Loretto he was favoured with a vision of St. Joseph, the Blessed Virgin, and the Infant JESUS. Going to the altar to say Mass for the soul of a young man addicted to impurity, whom he had disposed for death, he saw that soul in a pool of fire, and heard it say that it was condemned to eternal flames for consenting to a sin of thought after absolution.

AUGUST 17.

1. At Rome, in the year 1556, died Father Martin Olave, a Spaniard. It was from him that St. Ignatius received an alms when going to Barcelona as a mendicant. He was afterwards Doctor of Philosophy and Theology at Paris, and honoured at the Court of Charles V. as a most able theologian. He had naturally a great repugnance to the Society; but feeling himself called to Religion, he begged direction in the choice of a state of life from our Lord, as he held Him in his hands during Mass, and he received for answer—"In this Society it is My will that thou shouldst live and die—it is hard for thee to kick against the goad." He humbly acquiesced, and made his noviceship under St. Ignatius, by whom he was appointed to teach Theology in the Roman College, and to be its Rector. He was often heard to say, looking on the members of the Society, whom he revered as Angels—"O holy Society, how little did I know it when I fled from it and spoke ill of it." He died seventeen days after our holy Father; and it was for him that St. Ignatius asked the Pope's blessing when he begged it for himself and another. The joy upon his countenance before his death showed that he had received some extraordinary favour from our Lord before he died.

2. At Saragossa, in Spain, in the year 1594, Father Antony Ibannez, a Spaniard. As Provincial and Visitor he manifested great prudence in promoting both spiritual advancement and progress in studies. He exerted himself to carry out the full observance of all the holy Rules of the Institute: no human respect ever could deter him from his duty. He was wonderfully enlightened in the discernment of spirits, and in directing souls to the highest perfection. He kept his purity unstained to his death.

3. At Novellara, in Italy, in the year 1583, Lælius Nichesoli, an Italian Novice. He used to say that no load was heavier, nor wild beast more savage than one's own self-will, and therefore that he wholly flung himself into the hands of his Superiors. He died after ten months' novitiate; and for more than two hours as he lay in his agony, Angels and the Blessed Virgin, and Christ our Lord, shining bright as the sun, appeared visible both to him and to another of those who stood beside him.

August 18.

1. At Seville, in Spain, in the year 1575, died Father Gonzalez Esquiel, a Spaniard. He entered the Society with his servant, under whom he was shortly placed, the servant being appointed cook, and Gonzalez to serve in the kitchen under him.

2. At Aurillac, in France, in the year 1628, Father John Francis Martincourt, a Frenchman. The plague raging for three years in France, forty of our Society died in the service of the sick. The first of these was Father John, a man of great soul. Twenty-five plague spots broke out upon him, and brought him to the death which he had ardently desired in expiation for his sins.

3. At Kalisch, in Poland, in the year 1639, Ladislaus Czaplinski, a Pole. He was exceedingly devout to the Blessed Sacrament, and rigorously severe to himself. Among other pious practices he made use of the letters of the alphabet to aid him in making ejaculations, adding to each a psalm or a verse beginning with that letter, which he found a great help to him in his last sickness. He was often heard to repeat—"O that from all the powers of my body and soul put together I could distil one drop of satisfaction to the Divine will!"

4. On the coast of Cayenne, Father Thomas de Crevilly, of an ancient family in Normandy. He earnestly begged for the foreign missions, and was sent to Cayenne, where for thirty-three years he followed in the steps of a Xavier, embracing in his zeal French, Negroes, and Indians. He traversed forests under excessive heat, or drenched with rain. His food was a little dried fish, or bread from roots, and usually he slept on the ground. To these fatigues he added other austerities, and spent many hours night and day in prayer. The purity and innocence of his

life were eminent, yet when he had opportunity he had recourse daily to the Sacrament of Penance. When offered the office of Superior he humbly begged to decline it. He was loved by all and regarded as a Saint, and after death his countenance beamed with extraordinary beauty. It is said that he extinguished a fire with his crucifix, cured the sick, and raised to life a young man who had been some hours buried. He died at the age of sixty-seven, having spent forty years in the Society.

AUGUST 19.

1. At the island of Macao, on the coast of China, in the year 1583, died Father Melchior Carnero, Bishop of Nice. Appointed as companion of Father Barreti, Patriarch of Abyssinia, and finding it impossible to penetrate into that country, he exercised his Apostolate at Macao and in its vicinity. He vigorously opposed the Nestorian Bishop of the Armenian Rite at the risk of his life. When he was made Bishop he not only promised to listen to the advice of the Society, but vowed to return to it whenever he should have the leave of the Pope.

2. At Bivona, in Italy, in the year 1614, Father Barnabas la Vecchia, an Italian. He took his food without salt, ate no fruit for many years, disciplined himself to blood, wore continually a hairshirt, and slept his brief sleep on the ground, and yet with others he was gentle as a lamb. He gained signal victories over plots laid against his chastity. After death he appeared to a Procurator who was anxious about a paper which was missing, and showed him where it was put. He moved to extraordinary fervour a friend in Religion, who was growing lukewarm, by the words— "Oh, that they were wise and understood, and would provide for their last end."

3. At Seville, in Spain, in the year 1584, Rodriguez de Flores, a Spanish Lay-brother. At his entrance into the Noviceship he experienced painful aridity in the Spiritual Exercises, but having supported it with courage and perseverance, it was exchanged for great lights and consolation, so that he spoke of the things of God like a learned theologian. He prolonged his prayer into the night and sometimes through the whole of it; in which state he remained on Holy Thursday from sun-set to the next morning, his arms crossed on his breast. His love of prayer never interfered

with his labour, but as soon as his work was over he went to the church to pray. His habit was very short, discoloured, and patched all over; but he would not consent to wear a new one, saying he ought to be treated as the last of the Community. He was very silent, but when he spoke he inflamed his hearers with divine love. He was insatiable in penancing his body with hairshirts, disciplines, and fasts, refusing it everything that could please nature. He asked for suffering from God, and was heard, enduring a painful sickness for six months before his death.

AUGUST 20.

1. At Liege, in the year 1637, died William Brown, an English Lay-brother, of noble family, related to the Montagues. Received into the Church at Louvain, he entered the Society, and for twenty-three years was daily occupied in the humblest offices, washing pots in the kitchen or in other domestic labours. He would dig the garden or carry earth while he read the *Imitation of Christ*, or joined constant prayer with his work. When thoughts of Heaven or the reward of his toil occurred to him he would say—"As to Heaven, let God do what seems good to Him; I desire only to please God, and to do His holy will." He died with the *Office of the Blessed Virgin* in his hand, his beads round his neck, and the holy name of JESUS on his lips.

2. In Spain, in the year 1600, Father Thomas de Soto, a Spaniard. He was often consoled with the sight of CHRIST our Lord and His Blessed Mother. Our Saviour appeared to him sometimes as a beautiful infant; sometimes grown to manhood, with a crown of thorns, or—when he ardently petitioned for a more perfect knowledge of God upon the Cross—crucified.

3. At Innspruck, in the Tyrol, in the year 1650, Father Wolfgang Graveney, a German. The strength and vigour, as well as the sweetness, with which he governed as Provincial, were obtained chiefly by prayer. Composing himself to sleep, he signed each sense with that of the Cross, saying, in the words of Extreme Unction—"By this holy Cross and His great mercy, may God forgive me whatever I have sinned this day by memory, intellect, will, sight, or hearing." For the last two years of his life, like holy Job, he was afflicted with various and grievous sufferings, and he bore them all with invincible patience.

AUGUST 21.

1. At Rome, in the year 1660, Cardinal John de Lugo, a Spaniard. From his noviceship he was remarkable for his love of humble employments and for his fervour. He left a large inheritance to be distributed for pious purposes; and being appointed Professor of Theology in the Roman College by Father Vitelleschi, he occupied that chair for twenty years with great applause. Pope Urban VIII. conversing with him was struck with his prudence, learning, and wisdom, and without giving him any notice, created him Cardinal in the year 1643. Nor could he in any way escape from the dignity, it being imposed upon him by the most express order of Obedience. His elevation made no change in his habits; he always had near his person one of our Society to be witness of his actions. He arose and retired to rest without assistance, made daily meditation and examen as prescribed by the Rules, and withdrew to one of our houses for his yearly retreat. For his charity he was surnamed the Father of the Poor; and at his death he left the money he had as alms to the Professed House, and, as he desired, was buried at the feet of St. Ignatius.

2. At Sienna, in Italy, in the year 1571, died Father Jerome Rubiola, a Spaniard. St. Francis Borgia had so high an idea of his virtue, that he called him to Italy to take charge of the Colleges of Sienna and of Florence. The times, on account of the preceding wars, were so disastrous that our Fathers had resolved upon closing the College for want of resources; but Father Rubiola, relying on the aid of Divine Providence, was of a contrary opinion, and by his active solicitude provided for its necessities for many years. One day when there was no bread in the house, he went to a rich man who was hostile to the Society, and asked him for fifty crowns for the love of God. The man was surprised, and asked him—"Do you not know my sentiments with regard to the Society?" Father Rubiola replied—"Yes, I do; and that is the reason why I have come, hoping that for the sake of God you will do good even to your enemies." This frankness pleased the man so much, that he gave the Father the sum he asked, and told him to come to him with confidence whenever he was in want. He showed great humility in his last sickness, considering always that he was treated

far better than he deserved. Appearing, contrary to his wont, somewhat sad, he was asked the reason, and he replied, "I fear that God has a wish to recompense me in this life for the little good I have done, for my heart is filled with inexpressible joy." In these holy sentiments he died.

3. At Pont-a-Mousson, in France, in the year 1616, Father William Murdoch, a Scotchman. When Minister in the College at Paris, he was surrounded by some insubordinate members of the University, in a retired part of the house, and bid to bare his shoulders for a beating. He replied he was quite willing to do so for Christ's sake, and proceeded to lay bare his shoulders, but when they saw that he wore a hairshirt under his linen, anger was changed to veneration, and they knelt down and asked his pardon. He did and suffered much in Scotland for the Catholic faith.

August 22.

1. At Amboyna, in the East Indies, in the year 1549, died Father Nugnez Ribera, a Portuguese. He preached the faith amid perils from shipwreck and from fire. He died at last poisoned by Mahometans, preaching even up to the last day of his life. When he was too weak to walk to visit his sick, he would be carried to them.

2. At Tournay, in Belgium, in the year 1556, Father Bernard Olivarez, a Belgian. He showed great constancy in his vocation, for when he was Minister of the Roman College, and the holy Father Ignatius had ordered a certain draught to be given to a sick person, Father Bernard gave the order to the Infirmarian, and he forgot. At night St. Ignatius visiting the sick man according to his custom, and finding that the medicine had not been given, ordered Father Bernard out of the house that night, as guilty of disobedience. He went out, but remained between the door and the outer gates, until he was readmitted by the holy Father, who praised his constancy. He was a man of such exemplary virtue, that he was shortly after appointed Rector of the Roman College.

3. At Bracciano, in Italy, in the year 1626, Alexander Orsini, Cardinal of the Holy Roman Church and Duke of Bracciano. He loved and earnestly desired to enter the Society; but being prevented from resigning his Dukedom and the Purple, he found an expedient by which to satisfy his ardent wishes. He wrote to Father Mutius Vitelleschi, the General, giving

himself wholly to the Society so far as the state of a Cardinal permitted, and upon this understanding was received. He took the usual Vows of the Society and lived in a most religious manner, and was put upon the Catalogue of the Roman Province. From that time he increased the holiness of his hitherto upright and irreproachable life, and would have his heart buried in the Church of the Gesù, near the tomb of Cardinal Bellarmine, whom he had endeavoured to imitate as a model of sanctity.

4. At Trichinopoly, on the Madura Mission, in the year 1656, Father Emmanuel Martez, a Portuguese. When his beloved and loving neophytes wished to express attachment to any one, they would say of him, "He is as good and gentle as Father Martez." To be equal to the Brahmins in austerity he ate neither flesh nor fish. A dish of rice was his dinner, and a cake of rice his supper, and he slept in his clothes upon a tiger's skin. He was four times imprisoned, twice cruelly beaten, and four times publicly expelled from cities amid the insults of the populace, for preaching the faith. At last he closed his laborious life by a death in extreme want. So great was the poverty of the Residence wherein he dwelt that, as he lay in a poor cabin, no pillow could be found to put under his head. In the dress he had worn nearly thirty years, holding tender colloquies with his Crucifix, he expired tranquilly without a sign of any agony.

August 23.

1. In Holland, in the year 1651, died Father James Sluyskens, a Fleming, an intrepid and indefatigable missioner. Even the heretics admired the power of his faith, through which he extinguished, by the sprinkling of a little holy water, the conflagration of the tower of Amorfort, set on fire by lightning.

2. At Pont-a-Mousson, in France, in the year 1622, John Domyne, a French Scholastic. In his manners, and especially in his words, he kept such exact conformity with the Rules, that he bore the general reputation of a youth of extraordinary virtue. This opinion was increased by the following incident which occurred after his death. A Scholastic Divine about to be dismissed from the Society, felt himself interiorly

impelled to approach the body of John, and embracing it, exclaimed—"Good young man draw me after thee." On the same day he was taken with a mortal sickness, and died a pious and religious death in the Society.

3. At Wilna, in Lithuania, in the year 1631, Father Constantine Syrwid, a Lithuanian. Adorned with a singular innocence and purity, he was remarkable for his zeal for religious perfection and for his love of work. Amidst the labours of Professor of Scripture, he preached every Holiday, first to the people in Lithuanian, then to the chapter of the cathedral in Polish, and in the afternoon in the church of the Professed House gave a lecture on Holy Scripture to a crowded audience. Being advised not to ruin his health by his too great zeal and excessive labour, he gave the noble answer—"For what is my health given me if not for labour?"

4. In Canada, in the year 1724, Father Sebastian Rasles, a Frenchman. He was missioner of the Abnaki Indians, and living among them when they were attacked by the English. To procure the safety of his neophytes, he exposed himself in front of his flock, and was shot dead, falling at the foot of the cross that he had planted in the midst of the village. He was sixty-seven years of age, and had passed thirty-seven on the mission. He acquitted himself daily of the holy observances of religious life, making at prescribed times his meditations and annual retreat in the midst of all his labours. He observed great poverty in furniture, food, and dress; mending his own clothes, which he kept as long as possible; cultivating his garden, and cutting his fire-wood. He was beloved both by the French and by the Indians, and greatly regretted by all when he died.

August 24.

1. In the Mission of Peru, in the year 1609, died Father John Perez, a Spaniard. He served Christ in the poor and sick in the hospital with such care and charity, that a stream of light shone on him from the wound in the side of the crucifix.

2. In Brazil, among the Caribee Indians, in the year 1554, Peter Correa, a Portuguese Lay-brother. Before entering the Society he was captain of a band of soldiers, hunting, capturing, and selling into slavery the cannibal savages of Brazil. Having entered the Society, he exercised

the same industry to make them captives of Christ. At their own desire he baptized secretly the victims of the cannibals as they were about to be eaten, dexterously squeezing some water from a wet cloth. Being sent with John Sosa among the savage tribes, he promoted Christianity among them with much skill and at the cost of great labours. Finally, obliging a convert to give up a plurality of wives, he and his companion were shot to death by the savages.

3. At Lisbon, in Portugal, in the year 1614, Bartholomew Alvaro, a Portuguese Lay-brother. He was a most diligent and devout Sacristan, increasing always in devotion to the Blessed Sacrament, keeping the church in a most perfect state of cleanliness, and having the greatest care of the altar furniture. His delight was to serve as many Masses as possible. He waited also on the sick with the greatest charity as Infirmarian for forty years. When a sick person of the city after receiving the Holy Viaticum had been unable to retain it upon his stomach, Brother John had the courage to conquer his natural repugnance, and consumed the sacred species. The Bishop of Japan, Sebastian Moralez, wished to have him ordained Priest, and to take him to Japan; but he preferred to remain in his humble condition, and edified the city of Lisbon by his conduct there until his death.

August 25.

1. At Loretto, in Italy, in the year 1559, died Father Cornelius Wishaw, a Fleming, a man of great obedience, mortification, and prayer. He is said to have obtained from our Lord by his prayers a fever to detain Father Peter Faber at Louvain. Being ordered to pray for the Father's recovery he did so, and Father Faber was restored to health. Both in Belgium and Sicily his exhortations had wonderful effect in filling the cloisters with Nuns. Miracles were not wanting to assist his pious work in attracting spouses to Christ.

2. At Rome, in the year 1590, Father James Miro, a Spaniard, remarkable for his constant prayer and severe mortification. His position in prayer was to hide in some corner, or fling himself beneath a table, as unworthy to appear before the Majesty of God. With a perpetual hairshirt, he wore a chain as a girdle so tight that it could not be taken

off without danger of serious injury. Father Everard Mercurian committed to his care the drawing up of the Summary and of the Rules.

3. At Omura, in Japan, in the year 1624, Blessed Michael Carvalho, a Portuguese, burned alive for the faith after thirteen months' imprisonment. His life was that of an Angel rather than of a man. Led forth to die, he carried the stake to which he was to be bound, and sang psalms of joy with those who accompanied him.

4. At Mayence, in Germany, in the year 1595, Father Peter Brilmacher, a German, a man of great mind, learned and eloquent, dear to Catholics and hated by heretics, whom he combated, and by whom he was poisoned.

5. At Pekin, in China, in the year 1666, Father John Adam Schall, a German of Cologne. By his profound knowledge of mathematics and astronomy he attained such fame, that the Emperor entrusted to him the reformation of the Chinese calendar. For this work, held in the highest esteem, Father Adam was honoured with a diploma as Master of the Secrets of the Heavens, and made first mandarin of the department of mathematics, and taken as adviser in the good government of the kingdom. The Father made use of these favours for the propagation of the faith and the protection of the faithful. So that in fourteen years a hundred thousand were brought into the Church. But upon the death of the Emperor the government fell into the hands of four mandarins, under whom the hatred long restrained was let loose against Father Schall and his companions. He and nine others were falsely accused and put in chains. After a grievous imprisonment of six months, the heavens themselves contending for their innocence, they were liberated; but Father Adam was now seventy years old, and the hardships of his imprisonment, added to previous paralysis, caused his death, and he sank under his labours.

AUGUST 26.

1. At Brünn, in Moravia, in the year 1649, died Father Martin Stredonitz, a Silesian, renowned for his sanctity and the prophecy of success which he made to the Emperor Leopold I. When he was seven years old, and was preparing for his first Communion, he remained for

three days almost without food. In the Society, during his studies at Graïn, he was called the Angel of the Society. His every action was so modest, chaste, and religious, that he was named at Nissa, "the Father by whose mouth the Angels speak." The Emperor himself, Ferdinand III., attributed to his prayers the successful defence of Brünn against the Swedes. During the last five years of his life he rose every night, and flinging himself at the feet of a statue of the Blessed Virgin, made acts of preparation for his last agony. While praying near the church he was sometimes seen raised up in the air, his body following the spirit absorbed in the contemplation of God. He was Rector of several Colleges, and twice Provincial of Bohemia. By his prayers he obtained miraculous cures for the sick.

2. At Bivona, in Italy, in the 1611, Father Francis Miroldi, an Italian. The sweetness with which he governed both young and old, caused him to be regarded as a Rector filled with a maternal tenderness. By humble and constant begging he collected alms to give marriage portions to young persons without dowry, and to rebuild an hospital. Moreover, he established a confraternity for the assistance of the souls in Purgatory. Desirous of dying at the same hour on which Christ died, he expired on a Friday about three o'clock.

3. At Barcelona, in Spain, in the year 1589, Brother James Manriquez, with five companions, fell a victim of charity in attendance upon the plague-stricken; and on the same day, but in the year 1626, at Heilgenstadt in Germany, Father John Kempis, with five others, died in the same duty of charity.

AUGUST 27.

1. At Usk, in Monmouthshire, in the year 1616, Father Charles Baker, whose true name was David Lewis, a Welshman, suffered death in the popular fury occasioned by Oates' pretended Plot. He laboured for thirty years in Wales, and was apprehended while preparing for Mass. Conducted in mock triumph to Monmouth, and from thence to Usk, where he exercised his zeal in assisting many Catholics in prison, he showed forth in his defence the absurdity of the accusation against him; but it was enough that he was a Catholic Priest: the jury appalled by the epidemic terror condemned him to die.

2. At Ferrara, in Italy, in the year 1575, died Father Fulvius Androti, an Italian, a man of eminent and uncompromising virtue. Being greatly esteemed by the Duke of Ferrara, he would make no use of his favour for the benefit of the College of which he was Rector, but turned all to the good of that prince's soul. Like a wise physician, he treated with no false leniency the souls committed to his care; so that it was said of him that he might, if he had been a little more condescending to infirmity, have made his College a house of gold. He preferred the salvation of souls to an increase of wealth.

3. In the Philippine islands, in the year 1603, Father Melchior Hurtado, a Spaniard, whom the Bishop of Zebu praised for his learning, Apostolic virtue and thirst for suffering and toil. He found abundance to satisfy his longing among the Tattoed Indians, in whose instruction he spent ten years, and afterwards in a year's hard slavery in the Isle of Mindanao. He endured it all with a great and courageous equanimity of soul. Returning to Manilla, after his liberation, he begged to be sent again upon his old mission. God recompensed his zeal by granting him the conversion of many nations. Exhausted by his labours, he caught a fever from which he died. He had predicted the time of his death.

4. At Gerona, in Spain, in the year 1605, John Naves, a Spanish Lay-brother. He was amazingly clever and accomplished in every duty and office proper to his grade. As carpenter, carriage driver, gardener, sacristan, infirmarian, or cook, he was in all an example of virtue and excellence. He assisted with every attention both day and night two of Ours who had been seized by the plague. He caught the malady himself and died a victim of fraternal charity, giving his life for his neighbour.

August 28.

1. In Peru, in the year 1597, by martyrdom, died Father Michael de Urrea, a Spaniard. He begged with tears to be released from the post of Rector and to be sent on the mission. He prepared himself for his by a year's austerities, feeding on roots, sleeping on some vine branches, taking disciplines to blood, and studying the language of the savages, in which he composed a catechism and dictionary. By his zeal he made a number

of conversions. Whilst occupied in prayer he was slain by the wooden swords of Chunchee savages, for having overthrown an idol, and for having as they said killed the son of a Cacique, whom he had attended in his sickness with great charity. He died invoking the Holy Name. His murderers while feasting were fallen on by the panthers and pumas, and those who were not torn in pieces perished by a leprosy. His body was afterwards carried to the College of la Paz, and visited with veneration by crowds as that of a Saint.

2. At Ximabara, in Japan, in the year 1633, Father James Antony Gianni, born in the Kingdom of Naples. For twenty-four years he laboured amid many hardships in Japan, lying concealed in caves, and coming out by night only to encourage the Christians in the time of persecution. Being taken, he was condemned to the death of the fosse, and suspended with his head downwards, in which torment he expired on the third day of his sufferings. He had as companions in his martyrdom Father John Bilondo and Brother John Kidera, both Japanese.

3. At Smolensk, in Russia, in the year 1635, Father Laurence Bartil, a Pole, a man of extraordinary piety and devotion to the Virgin Mother of God, whose life he had divided into the several days of the week, and made the sweet subject of his meditation. Even when Provincial he insisted on making his own bed, saying that works of humility are never to be laid aside. Before giving advice to others he took counsel with God. He governed gently but firmly. In prayer his countenance assumed an air of Heaven, and he was sometimes seen raised in the air. He prophesied many things. After his death a Lay-brother went to the vault and cut off some of his hair, but the Father appeared to him in the night, and bade him restore what he had taken.

AUGUST 29.

1. At Rome, in the year 1541, died Father John Codure, a Savoyard, the ninth of the first ten companions of St. Ignatius. Whilst making the Exercises for the first time at Paris, he passed three days without eating or drinking, so greatly was he affected by them; nor did he afterwards relax from his first fervour, but rather greatly increased in it. He was born and ordained on St. John Baptist's Day, and died on the day of

his martyrdom, at the same age as the Baptist. St. Ignatius crossing the Sistine bridge, to say Mass for him at St. Peter's, learned by revelation the news of his death, and saw his soul carried by Angels to Heaven.

2. At Ximabara, in Japan, in the year 1633, John Kidera, or Guindora, a Japanese, the companion of Father Gianni, who suffered long imprisonment, and then hung head downward in the fosse, died a glorious martyr on the fourth day.

3. At Montereggio, in the year 1637, Father Christopher Ferreri, an Italian. He was remarkable for the love of his vocation and for the forgiveness of his enemies. His aged Father had sent him a copy of his will, desiring him to alter it to suit himself, in which was written—"If Father Christopher Ferreri, my only son, through sickness or any other reason, should not persevere in Religion, but return to the world, in that case I revoke all I have willed, and make him heir of all my property." Father Christopher sent it back corrected as follows—"If Father Christopher Ferreri, my only son, through sickness or any other reason, should be so mad, ungrateful to God, and wicked, as to leave his Religious State and return to the world, in that case I declare him unworthy to succeed me and be my heir." He not only pardoned the assassin who killed his only brother, but prayed daily for him in the Mass, and obtained for him by prayer a sincere sorrow and repentance for the crime.

August 30.

1. At Treves, in Germany, in the year 1587, died Father Peter Clutz, a Belgian. Deliberating on a state of life, and hesitating between the Society and another Religious Order, and petitioning for light from God with many tears, he heard distinctly a voice saying—"Peter, Peter, blessed is he whom I have called to the Society of My Name."

2. At Prague, in Bohemia, in the year 1660, Father Adam Krawarski, a Silesian, moulded by many adversities into an apostolic man. He brought back to the fold of the Catholic Church more than thirty thousand heretics in various parts of Bohemia. He was an indefatigable preacher and missioner amidst many perils to his life. The method he pursued in his sermons was usually as follows. He first knelt, and called God and Heaven to witness, that he was going to say what was necessary for the salvation

of his hearers, for which he was ready to answer at God's tribunal, and that he was willing to be punished for ever if he knowingly deceived them. He then proceeded to prove from Scripture and the Fathers the articles of the Catholic Faith. He spoke in this manner very movingly, and as one having authority. Expelled from Prague by the heretics, he returned in the disguise of a collier, and secretly assisted the Catholics with spiritual aid. When he was abused and beaten he returned thanks for the insults and blows, and offered the Holy Sacrifice for his persecutors when he could. He heard two Masses to prepare for his own, and then two more as a thanksgiving. For this holy and laborious life he was prepared by sacrifice and victory over himself. He was at first considered useless for other things, and was put among the Lay-brothers, and given the care of the stoves in winter. Being afterwards admitted among the Scholastics, although not a young man, instead of being sent to his philosophy he was ordered to teach a class of grammar for four years. By mistake he was then set to study moral theology instead of his philosophy; and when at last he went to his philosophy, in which he was found clearly proficient, he was again by mistake sent back to his moral instead of proceeding to dogmatic theology. Through all these trials of his patience, though naturally he felt a severe struggle within, he persevered with Spartan silence and Christian fortitude; nor ever showed a desire for his four years of theology, nor found fault with the arrangements concerning him.

3. At Logrono, in Old Castile, in the year 1564, Father Peter Martin, Rector of the college, a victim of charity. The rich having fled, and the poor not venturing to ask for the assistance of the Fathers in the plague, he promised from the pulpit that, of the six Fathers in the college, three should be employed in their service, with three Lay-brothers. And the same day, the Feast of the Visitation, he traversed the quarters of the city with the aid of two other Fathers, administering the Sacraments to the dying, while the three Brothers collected alms for the sick. The three Fathers and two of the Brothers soon fell victims of the plague. Thirty others of our Fathers died that year in Spain in the same service. Father Martin was a man of great talents and of constant prayer. He had a great aversion to the Society before he entered it. After his admission he declared that were he allowed to create a vocation for himself to his own liking, he would have chosen no other than that to which God had called him.

August 31.

1. At Châtelet, in Belgium, in the year 1629, died Father Florence Tennier, a Belgian. Being the seventh of seven brothers in succession, he enjoyed a privilege as was commonly believed in that country, of curing the king's evil. He was, as he was called, an Israelite without guile, and was remarkable for his contempt of self, and his devotion to the Blessed Virgin Mary.

2. At Lima, in Peru, in the year 1618, John Gonzalez, a Spanish Lay-brother. Even as a shepherd, before entering the Society, he was greatly given to prayer, and would turn with tears to pray in the direction of a church. In the Society he was for twenty years employed in the kitchen, was exquisitely cleanly in his office, always joyful, and ever sending up ejaculations to Heaven. A nobleman of Peru, observing the wonderful neatness of the kitchen, declared that if he were free from ties, he would make choice of a Society which made and kept men like him. Asked for a brief formula of perfection, the Brother replied, "Obedience."

3. At Tarragona, in Spain, in the year 1604, Father Peter Villar, a Spaniard. He was wonderfully ingenious in afflicting his body. Whilst Superior at Valencia, he often spent the whole night before the tabernacle, where he poured forth his soul in prayers and sighs, adding a most severe discipline. On his journeys he gave his mule to his Lay-brother and followed on foot. God recompensed him with supernatural lights in the guidance of souls and with the gift of healing. His nephew, Brother Paul Villar, an Augustinian Father, being grievously sick in India, calling to mind Father Peter, his uncle, immediately seemed to behold him present with him, and was restored to health.

4. At Vienna, in Austria, in the year 1709, Brother Andrew Pozzo, an Italian. As he was endowed with an extraordinary talent for painting and architecture his Superiors called him to Rome that he might perfect himself in these arts. But first they thought it fit to exercise him in entire self-abnegation, and put him to assist the cook in the Roman College. He was thus employed for five months, during which he made no complaint nor showed the least repugnance. He was known in all Rome for his piety; and when on the point of leaving Rome for Vienna, Brother

Andrew presented himself with his pupils before His Holiness to ask his benediction. Pope Clement XI. exhorted the pupils to imitate the piety of their master much more than to profit by his lessons in painting. He never took his pencil in hand until he had made his hour's meditation and heard Mass; and a Cardinal one day seeing the modest air with which he exposed for the first time a picture, said, that it was easy to see that the Brother did not seek his own glory but that of JESUS CHRIST. He died at the age of seventy, and his funeral was attended by persons of the highest rank.

SEPTEMBER.

September 1.

1. At Pekin, in China, in the year 1654, died Father Nicolas Longobardi, a Sicilian, a pillar of the Church in China. He spent nearly fifty-eight years in the cultivation of that vineyard, refusing no labour and shrinking from no danger where there was question of the salvation of souls. He used no seasoning with his food, slept without mattrass or pillow, and kept the fasts of the Church when past ninety. He spoke the Chinese language with such eloquence that it was a matter of surprise to the Mandarins. His apostolic labours were highly appreciated by the Father General, Mutius Vitelleschi, who raised him from being a Spiritual Coadjutor to a Professed of four vows. He was held in high esteem by the Emperor of China, who gave three hundred gold pieces for his funeral, which were not refused, that the honour paid him might further the advance of Christianity.

2. At Valencia, in Spain, in the year 1596, Father Martin d'Alberro, a Spaniard. For many years he spent a great portion of the night in prayer, and was often favoured with visits of the Blessed Virgin. On one Saturday, when he was occupied in the humblest offices of the house, she appeared to him and said, "My son, in this you please me very much. A painter, told by him to represent her as she appeared to him, brought a picture to him with which the Father was much dissatisfied, saying, that it was very far from any true resemblance; that the most pure Virgin would not, and could not, be painted by any but a pure hand in such a manner as she ought to be represented. "Cleanse your soul," he said, "and again apply to the task." He obeyed, purified his soul, and so corrected the picture that it seemed like an inspired painting. This picture is in the Professed House in Valencia, and many copies have been dispersed throughout the Christian world. The Blessed Virgin

again appeared to him and said, "After thirty more, you shall receive from my Son the reward of your labours." Whilst joyfully relating the vision to a friend, he was asked whether it was thirty months, or weeks, or days. "I shall soon know," he said; and having recourse to prayer to the Blessed Virgin, he soon learned that it was thirty days. When the days had passed he died.

3. At Nancy, in Lorraine, in the year 1644, Father Erard Mainbourg, a Frenchman. After the death of his pious wife, he followed the example of his son, whom he had already given to the Society, by entering it himself and becoming a Lay-brother; but after his first year's noviceship the Father General wished that on account of his great benefactions to the Society he should be ordained. He died thirty days after his first Mass. So great was his liberality to the Society that he doubled the foundation of the College of Nancy, and entirely founded that of St. Nicholas. There were some however even of the Society who disapproved of his benefactions; but so far were he and his pious wife from being disturbed, that they said they had given what they had given for the glory of God, and that they should not cease to love the Society though all its members should spit in their face.

4. In the month of September, in the year 1567, Father Andrew Oviedo, the Patriarch of Abyssinia, finished his course of indefatigable labour at Fremona, a small Abyssinian town. He was a perfect Religious, and gave eminent proofs of his virtue in his missions, in France, Flanders, Italy, Portugal, and Spain. Raised against his will by the Holy See to an Ecclesiastical dignity, he was an admirable Prelate. Passing to the Indies and from thence to Abyssinia, he lived there for nearly twenty years in the strictest poverty, in the midst of extreme dangers, cruel persecutions, and constant sufferings. The schismatics themselves so admired his humility, charity, and zeal for souls, that they revered him as if he had been one of the Fathers of the Primitive Church. Many extraordinary things are related in his life, and his tomb was frequented by the people of the country with veneration after his death.

SEPTEMBER 2.

1. At Coimbra, in Portugal, in the year 1589, died Dominic Juan,

a Portuguese Lay-brother. He was indefatigable in labour, saying that in the world he would have had to work harder, and with incomparably less gain. His soul was seen after death by a holy Priest, presented to our Lord adorned with many precious virtues. The Priest was recommended by Brother Juan to give himself to the Society.

2. At Barcelona, in Spain, in the year 1585, Martin Apparitias, a Spanish Lay-brother, exceedingly devout to the Blessed Virgin. She appeared to him as he was dying a martyr of charity in service of the plague-stricken.

3. At Cusco, in Peru, in the year 1624, Peter Martinez, a Portuguese Lay-brother. He was an industrious and skilful manager of the farm, while at the same time he was no less intent upon his spiritual duties. He was thrice at least exposed to dangerous trials in his out-door employment, but armed with the recollection of the presence of God he was always superior to them. He rose in the night to pray—even when on journeys—and received many illustrations from God. As he was thus occupied in prayer at night Father John Sebastian, who had lately died, appeared to him, and told him to prepare for his death. Falling sick at the farm, he grieved at dying without the comfort of being surrounded by his Brothers in Religion, and he revived so far as to be able to return to the house, where he came, he said, to die. He died as he had lived, in a most holy manner, amid the prayers of his Religious Brethren.

4. At Montreal, in Canada, in the year 1656, Father Leonard Garreau, born at Limoges. He was mortally wounded by the Iroquois while in a canoe instructing the Algonquin Hurons, after thirteen years spent on the missions amid dangers by land and water. He was put on shore, and remained bleeding for three days, praying for the savages, to whose fort he dragged his body, to hear the confessions of some captives, and prepare them to endure with Christian courage their death in torments. Carried to Montreal, he received the last Sacraments with extraordinary fervour and consolation of his soul amid extreme pains of body. His memory is in veneration; and his tomb, visited from all parts, was made famous by miracles.

5. At Paris, in the year 1792, Fathers Peter and Robert Francis Guérin du Rocher, natives of Falaise in Normandy, were massacred by the Republicans in the Seminary of St. Firmin, out of hatred to the Faith.

Father Peter was the author of "The True History of the Fabulous Times," and his brother had been missioner in the East, from whence he had brought memorials which he intended to publish.

SEPTEMBER 3.

1. At Cranganor, in the East Indies, in the year 1659, died Father Francis Garcia, Archbishop of Malabar. After having been Professor in the Society of philosophy and theology, which he taught with great talent, learning, and solid virtue; and having ruled with universal satisfaction as Rector and Provincial, he was ordered to accept of the Archiepiscopal dignity, at the announcement of which he fainted away. Among other surpassing gifts, he brought to this charge a knowledge of Hebrew, Greek, Chaldaic, Syriac, Tamul, Hindostanee, Latin, Portuguese, and the language of the Canary Isles. He always called the Society his mother, and kept before his eyes the pictures of those who had been made Prelates or Cardinals out of it. He was a great restorer of Ecclesiastical worship, and the Father of the poor, leaving by will an institute for the advance of loans. He was publicly bewailed, and buried with civil and military pomp, not only as a pious Prelate, but as a good governor and defender of Cochin against the wrongs of the Dutch.

2. At Naugasachi, in Japan, in the year 1632, Father Antony Yxida Pinto, a Japanese. He preached the Faith by word and example for forty-five years amid continual dangers to his life, with great fruit in the salvation of souls. Being taken, he avowed himself a Christian and a Priest; and solicited to apostatize, he challenged them to try with all their torments his Christian fortitude. He was tortured in various ways by the sulphurous waters, suspended in such a manner that all his joints were dislocated; and boiling water was poured upon his shoulders. For thirty days he endured these and all other torments they could devise, and was at last burned by a slow fire.

3. At Milan, in the year 1601, Peter Stopelli, an Italian Lay-brother, admirable for his peace of soul, love of prayer, self-conquest, and assiduous labour. Our Lady appeared to him when in sickness and apprehensive of death, and told him that he had yet a long time to live, and much work to do in the service of God. He lived ten years more, most assiduous

in every kind of labour, so as to give satisfaction to his patroness, who again appeared to him at the time of his death.

4. At Paris, in the year 1792, Father Alexander D'Enfant, a native of Lyons. He taught rhetoric at Marseilles; but his talent for preaching being discovered, he was applied to this duty. At the suppression of the Society he lived with such regularity, sweetness, and charity, that he was beloved by all. Seized at Paris on the 30th of August, he was brought before the Revolutionary tribunal, and at the demand of some of the bystanders was about to be released, when a cry was raised that he had been the King's confessor. He offered with joy the sacrifice of his life, and falling on his knees with hands uplifted to Heaven, expired under the blows of his assassins.

5. At Paris, in the year 1680, Father Ragueneau, formed in virtue under Father Louis Lallemant. He was a man of a great soul, singular penetration, solidity of judgment, courage, holy simplicity, and confidence in God. Sent on the missions of Canada, he laboured for many years among the Hurons and Iroquois, and deserved the title of Apostle of Canada. Recalled to France to be Procurator of that mission, he displayed consummate experience in spiritual things and the direction of souls, and died at the age of seventy-five.

SEPTEMBER 4.

1. In Nigritia, in Africa, in the year 1627, died Father Antony Macciado, a Portuguese. He laboured and suffered much to promote the Faith in the Kingdom of Angola, with great fruit in the salvation of souls, and at no less peril of his life. By a Divine interposition he escaped death, being preserved by God, Who kept him for further labours. He died a martyr of charity attending on the plague-stricken Negroes.

2. At Catania, in Sicily, in the year 1637, Father Vincent Raimondo, an Italian. His singular modesty attested the purity of his virginal soul. Before entering the Society he had given strict orders that no beggar should be ever sent away from his house without an alms, and every day he invited to his table the first poor man he met, and ate with him from the same dish and drank from the same cup. Every Tuesday, in honour of the Queen of Angels and her crown of twelve stars, he gave large alms

to twelve poor men. He adorned by his extraordinary virtues a high Ecclesiastical state, and was designated for advancement to a Bishopric, when preferring humility and obscurity, he hid himself in the Society. The severity with which he afflicted his body with different penitential austerities not only caused edification but exited compassion.

3. At Tongres, in the year 1653, Father Sidronius Hosch, born in the Diocese of Spres. His feeble health during the noviceship nearly occasioned his dismissal, but he begged to be retained at least among the number of the Lay-brothers. He became distinguished for his many virtues; he was a good poet; and he took great delight in publishing his humble extraction. He meditated daily on the Passion, and was devout to the Blessed Virgin, especially to her Immaculate Conception, which he loved to celebrate in his poems. Being in danger of death by sickness, he engaged to write a poem in her honour if he recovered, which after his recovery he fulfilled, and placed it on her altar. He journeyed on foot, and often fasting; and from his great charity was called the "Father of the poor." He died Superior of the Residence of Tongres.

SEPTEMBER 5.

1. In China, in the year 1631, died Father Andrew Rudomina, a Lithuanian. He asked for the mission of China, being moved to do so by a vision of Angels wiping with handkerchiefs the sweat from the faces of our missioners in the four quarters of the world, and God giving to each one a crown in return. Moreover, Father Andrew saw himself conducted by his Angel Guardian to Christ as a labourer on the mission, and our Lord accepted him and gave him to understand that he should die in the East. Having obtained the mission of China, he hastened thither, not to labour, but to receive his reward. St. Ignatius, whom he loved with a filial devotion, appeared to him on his death bed. He said to a Father beside his bed, "My Father, pay honour to our holy Father Ignatius, who has come to take me. See how beautiful his countenance is, and what a glorious company is with him! Look, he calls me!" His body, exposed in the church, is said to have filled all the place with a most sweet fragrance.

2. At Granada, in Spain, in the year 1648, Father Alphonsus de

Medrada, a Spaniard. Three years before he finished his life of innocence and labour spent in the West Indies and in Spain, as he lay in a grievous sickness he saw the heavens open and beheld our Lord, St. Ignatius, and others of the Society; and turning with confidence to Christ, he asked, "Lord, is it time that I come to Thee?" and Christ replied, "Not now, but in a few years." Then as he prayed for himself and for all in the College of Granada he heard, "that all these were predestined to glory." At which Alphonsus delighted, and wished to hear it again repeated. "What! All, Lord?" "All, My son," replied our Lord, "now in this college shall be saved."

3. At Ghent, in Flanders, in the year 1621, Charles de Paro, a Scholastic of strong and tender piety. He fought perseveringly on his knees against sleep coming over him during prayer. Before going to schools he always made a visit to the Blessed Sacrament. He desired the Indian mission, but was called away to Heaven. In his sickness it was necessary to take away his Crucifix lest he should exhaust himself with too ardent colloquies with it. He often broke out into the words, "O sweet JESUS! how good a mother is the Society of Jesus!" When the doctors were consulting whether there was any hope. He cried out with joy, "O Sirs, there is no hope! To Heaven! to Heaven!" and thither shortly he departed, as we may with full confidence believe.

4. At Tonquin, in the year 1675, Father Francis Pimentel, a Portuguese. Disembarking in Tonquin, he met Father Philip Marin, condemned to exile. Both were in disguise as merchants. At the same time they were recognized by two Portuguese, one of whom out of revenge denounced them to the Mandarins. They were soon taken and led to the capital, and condemned to be publicly beaten with rods. By the intercession of a lady of the court they were spared this punishment; but the King, who forbade the Christian religion, commanded them to be exiled. They left the port, but were privately conveyed on shore in a boat, and conducted to a place of safety by the neophytes. Father Pimentel lived two years in Tonquin, revered as an Apostle and a Saint, and converted many to the Faith. His death was brought on by his labours. In his last moments he was visited by our Lord and His Blessed Mother, attended with other Saints.

September 6.

1. At Nangasachi, in Japan, in the year 1627, died Father Thomas Tzugi, a Japanese. After thirty-four years of glorious toil, spent in the conversion of his countrymen, he was seized and condemned to death by fire. In the midst of the flames he spoke with great power and eloquence on the Passion of Christ and faith in Him. Then changing his tone to singing, he chanted the psalm, *Laudate Dominum omnes gentes*, and expired as he sung. Both Portuguese and Japanese witnessed a miracle which followed. They saw his breast part asunder, and from it issue a purple flame which flew upwards to Heaven surrounded by a brilliant light. The hearts of all the Christians who were present were inflamed with a holy zeal at the sight.

2. On the voyage from Peru to Spain, in the year 1622, Father Paul Joseph Arriaga, a Spaniard. He was very devout to the Blessed Virgin, by whom he was specially called to the Society, and to his Angel Guardian. He laboured many years in Peru. He had a particular gift of inspiring the young with a love of learning and of Christian virtue. For forty years he was favoured with a great gift of prayer and union with God, and received many extraordinary graces. He spent the interval between Maundy Thursday and Easter Sunday without food, and slept leaning against a tree or on a plank, with a billet of wood for a pillow. He preserved his baptismal innocence till death. Called by obedience to Spain, and overtaken by a furious tempest on the way, having heard the confessions of his companions, leaning against the mast, and pressing his Crucifix to his lips, he calmly waited until the ship went down.

3. At Drepano, in the year 1630, John Laparo, an Italian Lay-brother, and the model of his order. He united wonderful assiduity in labour to great abstemiousness. Thus with no other precaution than scanty sustenance and continued active toil, he prolonged his labours in Religious life to his hundred and seventh year.

4. At Rome, in the year 1649, Father Damian Strada, an Italian, one of the greatest of modern historians, and a worthy rival of the ancients. He was Professor of Rhetoric for fifteen years at Rome. His "History of the War in the Netherlands" is praised most highly even by non-Catholic

men of learning, and its excellence is shown by the many editions it has passed through, and by various translations of it into other languages. The King of Poland, Ladislaus, on reading the first part, was so delighted, that he wrote to the Father General Vitelleschi to urge Father Strada to hasten to publish the second. Within ten years the Latin went through ten editions, and was translated into five languages. Most modest amid all this applause, Father Strada was never heard to commend his own or criticize the works of others.

5. At Rome, in the year 1731, Father Francis Mary Galluzzi, born at Florence. For twelve years he was Prefect of the Oratory of St. Francis Xavier at the Roman College, and Director of many other congregations among the students. His confessional was visited with an ever-increasing crowd of penitents, and he effected innumerable conversions. He devoted day and night to his labours, visiting the sick and dying, and promoting in many various ways the glory of God. He was looked upon as the Apostle of Rome; and Clement XII., confirming by Brief an hospital for women without a home, founded by Father Galluzzi, called him "a man full of zeal for the glory of God and the salvation of souls." It was wonderful that with a broken constitution he could endure such labours with little sleep and but one poor meal a day. When he sank beneath them, the whole city was so moved, that the same Pope Clement declared that nothing like it had been known before. It was necessary to place guards to restrain the people who came to venerate his remains, and miracles were wrought by his intercession.

SEPTEMBER 7.

1. At Lancaster, in the year 1628, Father Edmund Arrowsmith, an Englishman, when he was forty-three years of age. After fifteen years of missionary life, the last five of which he spent in the Society, he was condemned to be hanged, disembowelled, and quartered, as a Priest and a Jesuit, and because he taught that out of the Catholic Church there was no salvation. He died with great constancy, cheerfulness, and charity, praying for his murderers; rejecting with generous indignation the life which was offered him at the foot of the ladder as the price of apostacy. He had the consolation of dying in company with a good thief whom he had converted

in prison, and who refused the pardon offered him on condition of returning to heresy. He appeared on the following day to Father Ambrose Barlow, a Priest of the Order of St. Benedict, and told him how well it had been with him at Lancaster, and bid him prepare for a similar good fortune. His hand, preserved with great veneration, has been the instrument of a multitude of cures. We may mention here that the father of Father Arrowsmith also died in prison, a confessor of the Faith.

2. At Tyburn, in London, in the year 1644, Father Ralph Corbie, hanged and quartered for the Faith. He was born in Ireland, whither his father had fled to avoid persecution, and educated abroad. He joined the Society in 1626. Five years later he began his missionary career at Durham, and after labouring there nearly twelve years, he was taken while at the altar, thrown on board a vessel at Sunderland, and conveyed to London. He was there offered the means of escape, which he renounced in favour of another prisoner. He was dragged from Newgate to Tyburn, where he suffered martyrdom, kissing the scaffold, and being cut down before he was dead. He was an innocent, holy, and humble Religious man.

3. At Cassau, in Transylvania, in the year 1639, Father Stephen Pongracz, a Hungarian, and Father Melchior Grodec, slain by the Calvinists out of hatred to the Faith. After three days' imprisonment without food, they were condemned to death. Father Stephen coming out of his cell, was struck down with a blow of a spiked club; a rope was then passed round his head, and twisted so tight that he was left for dead. He spent the following night in torments, his fingers and other extremities being cruelly crushed between gun-wheels. He was offered his liberty if he would become a Calvinist, which when he constantly refused, his breast was scorched with fire; and he was finally strangled together with Father Grodec and a Canon of Graïn. Their bodies were cast into a sewer, from whence they were taken out by the most noble wife of the Viceroy of Forgach, Catharine Palfia. Songs of Angels were heard at their death, and miracles were wrought at their tomb.

3. At Xeres, in Spain, in the year 1616, Father Joseph de Escalza, a Spaniard. When he was Minister of the college he took upon himself some of the duties of the Lay-brothers, and especially those of the humblest kind. Once when he was wearied with labour Christ appeared to him

loaded with a heavy cross, and said—"My son, if the cross seem heavy to thee, look on Mine, and do not imagine that thou art without Me on thine."

SEPTEMBER 8.

1. At Carthagena, in the West Indies, in the year 1654, died Blessed Peter Claver, a Spaniard, and great friend of Blessed Alphonsus Rodriguez. This holy Brother, when praying fervently for the Blessed Peter, saw a bright throne in Heaven, and heard an Angel say, "This throne is for thy disciple Claver, on account of his virtues and the souls he shall convert in the Indies." He is renowned as the Father and consoler of the negro slaves, of whom he converted and baptized many thousands. He practised every kind of mortification, great as well as small; in the intense heats not wiping away the sweat from his face, nor driving away the mosquitoes which drew blood from his face and hands. At prayer he placed upon his head a crown of thorns, and a rope round his neck. In reciting the Divine Office he was most attentive to every word. His patience, charity, and mortification in the service of the slaves were wonderful. He was enrolled in the number of the Blessed by Pope Pius IX. in the year 1851.

2. At Spires in Germany, in the year 1609, Father John Magirus, a German. He had an especial call from God to the Society; still he hesitated. His brother lately dead then appeared to him in his sleep, and upbraided him with his tepidity and carelessness of life. He pointed to our Lord crucified, and seemed to sprinkle upon John some Blood drawn from the Sacred Side. Whilst he did so he said—"Look to it, that this Blood be not shed for thee in vain." Hereupon, leaving a rich inheritance, he entered the Society, in which he lived as a holy Priest. He was finally taken with a fever of which he died. During his sickness he was consoled with the sight of our Lord and St. Ignatius, whereupon he exclaimed with joy, "Such a fever was better than all the health in the world;" and so exhorting all to the great virtue of the Society, Obedience, he happily expired.

3. At Wratislaw, in Silesia, in the year 1653, Father John Vazin, a German, a famous preacher for the space of twenty-three years, and surnamed the Gospel Trumpet. Father Henry Pfeischmid, lately dead,

appeared to him from Heaven, of whom he asked whether his labours were pleasing to God. Father Henry replied, "They are, they are." And being asked whether he had suffered a severe Purgatory, he answered that it had been light and short, God rewarding the charity with which he had helped others during his life. He added, that the apostolic labours of the Society at Wratislaw against heresy were pleasing to God.

4. In the year 1633, died Brother John Yama, a Japanese, by the death of the fosse. He was a learned catechist, and laboured for forty-seven years in promoting the Faith. In the same year, Father Francis Baldini, a Roman, died of his sufferings in Japan during the persecution. He had long lived concealed in caves and woods. He had been Professor of philosophy and theology, and asked for the mission of Japan. The day and month of the death of both are unknown.

SEPTEMBER 9.

1. At Polosk, in Russia, in the year 1620, died Father Andrew Leoman, a Lithuanian, Rector of the College of Derpat in Livonia. He was taken by the Swedes, chained hand and foot, and carried into Sweden, where for seven years he wasted away in prison, after suffering intense pains from the cold and the rack. At length when set at liberty, he returned to his country enriched with the patient endurance of his sufferings, and bearing in his hands and feet the marks of his fetters. At Polosk he showed the extent of his great charity, serving twenty sick companions with wonderful care and diligence; being an example of that perfect charity that can do all things, and endure all things.

2. At Verdun, in Lorraine, in the year 1651, Father John Parisot, a Frenchman, remarkable for his zeal and deep humility. His daily life carried out the vow or promise which he had written and signed with his own blood as follows—"Hear me, dear JESUS, my Guide, Teacher, and Master in the school of most profound humility. In the sight of Thy Divine Majesty I have chosen, and again choose, to be an abject in Thy house, and in the most holy Society of Jesus, for the whole course of my life, and promise that I will not turn aside from the path of holy humility in which I have begun to walk. From my whole heart I renounce every high grade or dignity of every kind in it, being ready to perform the

meanest offices, and teach boys in the lowest classes of grammar, as far as health will permit; and for the glory of Thy Name to undertake with willingness, and execute while I live, whatever is most contemptible in the eyes of men. Thus I promise, resolve, and from my heart desire. At Avignon, before celebrating my first Mass, in the year 1644. John Parisot. So help me Christ, the pattern of humility." And so he lived most humble in his own sight and that of God; nor would he make the profession of the four vows until he was commanded to do so by obedience.

3. At Burgos, in Spain, in the year 1599, died Father Christopher Ribera with six others, in service of the sick. Also in 1625, a fatal year in Belgium, Father John Chisaire, a Belgian, a man of great note, died in the same service; two others at Douay, six at Dinon, two at Lille, one at Artois, fifteen at Antwerp—twenty-seven in all. The following year, 1626, nine others died in the same manner in Belgium.

4. At Florence, in the year 1672, died Father Francis Joseph Bresciani. After teaching humanities and philosophy for many years, he asked for the mission of Canada, where he laboured with signal success. He was taken prisoner by the Iroquois, and suffered most cruel tortures at their hands. They scourged him severely, cut off two fingers of his right hand, and the thumb of his left; they then burned off his nails and dislocated his feet. The next day they exposed him to be mangled by dogs. After some days, covered with wounds, he was sold to the Dutch colonists, who, touched with compassion at his misery, healed his wounds, and, when he was able to bear the voyage, sent him to Rochelle. Thence the brave warrior returned to his mission, and the joy with which he was received by his neophytes compensated him for his sufferings. But some years after, his Superiors recalled him to Europe on account of his health, where for a long time he fulfilled the duties of a preacher, his wounds and mutilated hands making a yet deeper impression on his hearers than his words. He died full of merits and of years.

5. In Japan, in the year 1633, died three Lay-brothers, Thomas Riocan, Louis Cafucu, and Denis Yamomoto, Japanese. They were martyred by a slow fire some time in September, but the precise day is unknown.

SEPTEMBER 10.

1. At Nangasachi, in Japan, in the year 1622, died the Blessed Charles Spinola, an Italian, burned to death by a slow fire. He was born of noble parentage at Genoa. At his own request he was sent to Japan, where he arrived after a protracted voyage, having been detained a prisoner in England. For seven years he was Minister of the College of Meaco, and he fulfilled the office with a most loving charity. He prepared himself for martyrdom by daily disciplines, and by making the Exercises every year for thirty days. In the time of the most cruel persecution of Daifusama, under the name of Joseph of the Cross, he secretly assisted the Japanese Christians, and baptized five thousand souls. At last, captured on the 14th December, 1618, he was thrust with his eight companions into the terrible prison or cage of posts at Omura. They were so closely packed that the captives had not a space of three spans width each; and they endured hardships and sufferings almost worse than death for full four years. The brave soldiers of Christ not content with these sufferings, added to them voluntary afflictions of the body, fasts, watchings, and disciplines. The Blessed Spinola declared that "prison seemed to him like Paradise." Besides these nine Confessors of the Society, there were in that prison eight Dominicans, four Minorites, and thirty other Christians. When they were led out to die by fire, they sang psalms shedding tears of joy. At the place of execution thirty thousand Christians are reckoned to have assembled. Bound to the stakes, they chanted the Psalm, *Laudate Dominum omnes gentes*, Father Charles acting as precentor. As they were being burned, after the space of half an hour some sparks flew to the breast of Father Spinola, and setting his clothes on fire, he died before the rest of his companions in martyrdom. Their names are, Father Sebastian Chimura, nephew of the first neophyte baptized by St. Francis Xavier in Japan, and the first Japanese Priest; Antony Kiuni, Gonzales Fusai, Louis Cavara, Michael Xumpo, Peter Sampo, Thomas Acafoxi, and John Ciongocou, Novices; the last named was beheaded, because no stake could be procured to which to bind him to be burned.

2. At Rome, in the year 1661, Father John Rho, a Milanese, of rare talents and eloquence. Having asked but not obtained the mission of the

Indies he devoted himself to preaching in Italy, in which he spent thirty-seven years with such success that few have equalled him. The virginal purity and innocence which shone in his countenance added a heavenly lustre to his eloquence.

3. At Catanzaro, his native place, Father Alexander Ferrara, surnamed for his modesty and virtues, an Angel, and a Saint. He threw himself at the feet of an angry man who had struck him, and kissed them. The votes having been lost at his last examen, he made a vow never to say a word concerning the profession of the four vows which it was sure he had deserved. God recompensed his humility by many gifts and favours. He moved the most hardened hearts, cured maladies by his touch, or by the sign of the cross. By his prayers he miraculously filled a vessel with oil; and the necessitous and afflicted had recourse to him in all their wants, and he was called the Father of the poor. Burning with a desire to shed his blood for Christ, he embarked for India, but was recalled in the midst of his voyage, to return to the country he had already evangelized, and he laboured to the age of eighty, never ceasing to toil and bring back multitudes of sinners to the way of salvation. At his funeral it was impossible to conclude the Dead Office on account of the numbers that crowded to it, and it was necessary several times to renew the habit, which was torn away by the multitudes. His body remained flexible and without sign of corruption, and his memory is in benediction.

SEPTEMBER 11.

1. In Aquila, in Italy, in the year 1608, in the repute of sanctity, died Father Sertorius Caputo. His mortifications were almost excessive. His labours for the salvation of souls were such as three other active missioners could scarcely fulfil. His countenance was often seen surrounded with a halo of light. When he was making a visit to the Blessed Sacrament, our Lord coming forth from the tabernacle tenderly embraced him. His virginal body was found incorrupt after the lapse of five years, flexible, and emitting a fragrant odour. He was the originator of many practices of piety at Aquila.

2. At Rheinberg, in Germany, in the year 1639, Father Hermann Hugo, a Belgian, renowned for the sweetness of his manners and the elegance

of his compositions. His tender love of God is attested by the ardent longings expressed in his sweet elegies which have been printed more than once. He was Superior of Ours in the camp missions to the army of the King of Spain, and his charity was so boundless that he took a vow never to refuse any act of charity to any one, either of Ours or externs. Hence he caught the disease which caused his death, attending on the sick. When about to receive the Viaticum, he addressed our Lord with great confidence—"Lord, Thou knowest that I have truly sought Thee, loved, and served Thee! Give me the crown of justice."

3. At Posen, in Poland, in the year 1637, Father Stanislaus Domaniewsky, a Pole. He rose from sleep thrice during the night to give three hours to prayer. During the Octave of *Corpus Christi* he almost lived in the church. His Mass, preparation, and thanksgiving occupied two hours. Each night he took three disciplines so severe that he would fall at the foot of the Crucifix exhausted, and ask pardon for himself and the souls in Purgatory, to whom he had devoted his good deeds and sufferings. For his sweetness in government he was called the Rector of Charity.

4. At Antwerp, in the year 1681, Father Godfrey Henschenius. Having taught humanities with great repute in several colleges of Flanders he was sent to his theology, and had only finished half his course when he was joined to Father Bollandus, his former master, to aid him in compiling the "Acts of the Saints." To this work he devoted himself with such zeal as nearly to cost him his life. His was restored to health by a vow which Father Bollandus made in honour of St. Francis of Paul. In spite of his labours and delicate health he reached his eighty-first year. His gaiety and obliging character, which he preserved in his infirmities, made him dear to all. Helpless at eighty from paralysis, he would pleasantly say—"Here I am a child again; I must be fed, put to bed, dressed, and assisted in all my wants. May God give me grace to find again the innocence of children, to whom He promised the Kingdom of Heaven." He died confiding himself to the prayers of the Saints, to whose glory he had consecrated his life, and repeating in his last moments—"*Misericordias Domini in æternum cantabo.*"

SEPTEMBER 12.

1. In Paraguay, in the year 1632, died Father Marcellus de Lorenzana, a Spaniard. He nobly fulfilled his apostolical calling, laboured much, and endured very many hardships. He was honoured with many gifts and graces of God, was a prophet of future events, and healed the sick by the imposition of his hands.

2. At Marchena, in Spain, in the year 1637, Father Michael Sanchez, a Spaniard. For the sake of forming youth to virtue he spent more than forty-two whole years in teaching grammar. He caught the plague whilst attending the sick, but recovered, and thereupon immediately returned to the same field of holy warfare, binding himself by vow to that service as often as there was an opportunity for so doing. He daily gave five or six hours to prayer, supplying in the night the time which his occupations in the day would not allow him.

3. At Antwerp, in Belgium, in the year 1665, Father John Bollandus, a Belgian, the beginner of the compilation of the great work of the *Acta Sanctorum*. Father Herbert Rosweyd had collected much matter with a view to set on foot this vast design, and upon his untimely death Father Bollandus put it into shape, began the laborious execution of it, and gathered materials for it from all parts of Europe. He published five volumes of the months of January and February, which were received with great admiration by the learned world and the lovers of piety, and left other matter for the continuation of the work. In his gigantic labours, he was most exact in all spiritual duties and in prayer, devoting half an hour to thanksgiving after Mass, and reciting the Divine Office at the appointed hours. He practised great mortifications. He wore a hairshirt which covered half his body, and his discipline was armed with iron points, and these were found stained with blood after his death. He found time to hear confessions and direct a congregation committed to his charge. During his latter years he suffered from the pains of asthma, hernia, and gout, all which he bore with indomitable patience. He died at the age of sixty-nine, having entered the Society at sixteen. The honours rendered to his memory proved how much he was loved and esteemed by all Religious Orders in every part of the world. His obsequies were celebrated with great solemnity not only at Antwerp but in other countries, and even at Rome.

SEPTEMBER 13.

1. At Cashel, in Ireland, in the year 1647, died Father William Boyton, an Irishman, killed by the soldiers of Cromwell at the storming of the town. Pardon was offered to all except Priests. Father Boyton deserted not his post, and when he was killed was engaged in hearing the confessions of the Catholics.

2. On the voyage to Brazil, in the year 1571, Father Peter Diaz, a Portuguese, and four companions, Gaspar Goez, Francis de Castro, Michael Aragona, and Francis Pauli, were flung by French Calvinist Corsairs into the sea. These five with seven others had been part of the company of missioners which the Blessed Ignatius de Azevedo had taken with him, and from whom they had been separated at sea by the violence of a storm. They thus suffered a similar martyrdom with their leader. One only, Gaspar Gonsalvez, not having courage enough to die a martyr, put off the habit of the Society and mingled with the crowd in the taking of the ship. But the pirates afterwards threw him overboard; and so he lost his martyr's crown.

3. At Como, in Italy, in the year 1630, Louis Schiesa, an Italian Scholastic. He died of the pestilence whilst engaged in the labours of teaching a school. Shortly before his death, after a long silence, he drew a deep sigh, and then foretold the calamities impending on the town. He gave the names of those who were to die of the plague in the college, and the day and hour on which they would each die. One of the Masters, Guido, asking him how he knew what he said, he replied that it was useless curiosity to inquire how he knew it. Shortly after, fortified with the Sacraments, he expired, and all things came to pass as he had predicted.

4. At Palermo, in Sicily, in the year 1676, Father John Marchese, a Sicilian, with two others. He died a martyr of charity in serving the plague-stricken.

SEPTEMBER 14.

1. At Rome, in the year 1596, died Father Francis Toleto, a Spaniard,

a Cardinal of the Holy Roman Church. Soto, his master in the world, called him a prodigy of learning, and considered him the first man of the age. He was sent to Rome to teach philosophy and theology by St. Francis Borgia; and Saint Pius V. appointed him preacher in the Apostolic Palace. He fulfilled this office for twenty-four years, and was greatly admired for his piety and learning. He also executed several important commissions in Poland and Germany, and was made Cardinal by Clement VIII. In this high dignity he was a lover of poverty, lived usually on vegetables, and on Saturdays fasted on bread and water in honour of the Blessed Virgin; and in all weathers went on foot from the Vatican to St. Mary Major's to say Mass on every Saturday. He prepared himself for the Feast of the Assumption by a fast of forty days. He died at the age of sixty-four, after having been three years Cardinal, and was buried at St. Mary Major's. Appearing after death he said, "By the help of the Blessed Virgin I am saved."

2. Upon the sea, on the coast of Brazil, in the year 1571, the remaining seven of the company of Father Azevedo and of Father Peter Diaz, of whom mention was made yesterday, were flung into the sea by Calvinist pirates and drowned, while on their way to preach the Faith in Brazil. They were Peter Fernandez, John Alvarez, Alphonse Fernando, Andrew Paz, Ferdinand Alvarez, Peter Diaz, and Diego Carvalho.

3. At Paris, in the year 1562, Father Paschal Broet, one of the first ten Fathers of the Society, and called by St. Ignatius the Angel of it. He was the first Provincial of Italy, and was sent by the Pope as Apostolic Nuncio to Ireland. On his return from Ireland he was passing through Lyons where he was thrown into prison as a spy. When at Paris he was appointed Patriarch of Abyssinia, but before he could set forth he sickened of the plague and died.

4. At Neswich, in Lithuania, in the year 1694, Father Andrew Damajewickz, a Pole. He was led to enter the Society by a melancholy prediction of Father Sierakowski, Prefect of the College of Olmutz. And the prophecy was this—Whilst yet a boy he was at play with thirty-nine companions when Father Sierakowski suddenly burst into a flood of tears. The boys pressed the Father to tell them the cause of all his grief, and he told them: "Out of you forty now at play, seventeen only shall be saved." Andrew, more terrified than the rest, broke out into tears, and refused

to be consoled until the Father told him that he was one of the seventeen. Still, to make his salvation more secure, he asked most earnestly for admission into the Society, and lived in it as an excellent Religious, remarkable for the greatest meekness, and adorned with extraordinary graces from God.

SEPTEMBER 15.

1. At Tabira, in Japan, in the year 1622, died Father Camillus Constanzi, an Italian. After many labours and sufferings endured for the Faith, he was banished, but he returned in the disguise of a soldier, and during the night time employed himself in the assistance of souls. Apprehended, and condemned to die by fire, he gave a noble example of Christian fortitude. In the midst of the flames he discoursed in a sublime manner to the people on the immortality of the soul and the happiness of being a Christian. Then he sang the Psalm *Laudate Dominum omnes gentes*, and after the *Gloria Patri* exclaimed thrice in the Japanese language—"O how well it is with me!" And when his body was now nearly consumed, he sang aloud five times *Sanctus, Sanctus, Sanctus*, so that even the unbelievers were amazed at his indomitable courage.

2. At Jafanatapa, in the East Indies, in the year 1628, Father Matthew Fernandez, a Hindoo, and Father Bernardine Pe-che, a Chinese, killed by the natives out of hatred to the Faith. They were first pierced with spears and then beheaded. They had laboured much in that country; Father Matthew alone had baptized five thousand.

3. At Turin, in Savoy, in the year 1618, Cæsar Boscho, an Italian Scholastic. Having resolved to enter the Society, he called his relations into a room where he had collected all his instruments of music, and having played a pretty piece with exquisite taste and feeling, he said—"Farewell, old friends, instruments of my pastime and passing pleasure; I bid you good bye, to give myself and all I have to the standard of Christ and the Society of Jesus." He did as he had said, conforming his life to such perfect harmony with the Rules, that he was never known even inadvertently to break them.

4. At Flushing, in Zealand, in the year 1641, Father John Suffren, a Frenchman, a preacher of great fame throughout the whole of France, and universally beloved, for he inveighed against vice without personality.

He was thirty-one years preacher and confessor to the Dowager Queen Mary, widow of Henry IV., and her son, Louis XIII.; yet in all that time he was not tainted by the atmosphere of the Court. If any one asked his influence with royalty he replied, that "the thing had no connexion with the Prince's conscience." Suffering acutely from a disease which compelled him to undergo a severe operation, he bore the pain without sigh or groan, only repeating—"Yes, Father, for so it has seemed pleasing in Thy sight." When accompanying the Queen to England he was taken with a sickness which obliged him to turn back, and he died on his way at Flushing. He published two volumes of sermons, and some excellent books on spiritual perfection.

5. At Bordeaux, in the year 1625, Father Louis Richeaume, surnamed the Cicero of France. He was yet more illustrious for his virtues than for his learning. He was honoured with the esteem of the most distinguished persons, and even of King Henry IV. himself. He wrote an Apology for the Institute of the Society, and his affection for it was so great, that he could not hear it named in his latter years without shedding tears. Conformity to the will of God was his special devotion. His thoughts were all of God, and he spoke and wrote only for the glory of God. At the age of eighty, when he could no longer walk, he would be carried to the kitchen and be employed in washing the plates. He died full of years and merits in his eighty-first year, having lived sixty years in the Society. His funeral was attended by the magistracy of the city.

SEPTEMBER 16.

1. At Arras, in Belgium, in the year 1633, died Father John Carlier, a Belgian, a model of a holy and successful missioner. Albert and Isabella, then governing the Netherlands, hearing of his fame, sent for him, and gave him the greatest encouragement and praise. The Father General, Mutius Vitelleschi, not only commended him, but bid him write out his method of giving a mission, and send it to Rome for the instruction of others. The common subjects of his discourses were Death, Judgment, Heaven, and Hell. He would often add a sharp discipline to his sermons in presence of the people, to awaken penitence in the hearts of his hearers. He gave three or four sermons in the day with such intense fervour that

September 16.

he sometimes burst into something similar to a sweat of blood. He had the surname of "John that neither ate, nor drank, nor slept."

2. At Huy, in Belgium, in the year 1636, Father Henry Carlier, a Belgian, nephew to the above-mentioned Father John. Most severe to himself and gentle to others, he died in the service of the plague-stricken, to which work of charity he had more than once devoted himself. The Minister of the college, lately dead, appeared to him to warn him of his death, and to invite him to the Society of the Saints in Heaven.

3. At Rome, in the year 1580, Januarius Duchi, an Italian Scholastic. When he approached to Holy Communion he was filled with such heavenly sweetness that his tears bedewed all the ground around him. He heard a voice after Communion on the Nativity of the Blessed Virgin bidding him be of good hope, for his sins were forgiven him.

4. At Tchao-tse, in China, in the year 1591, Father Antonio Almeida, a Portuguese. As entrance to China was otherwise impossible on account of the edicts of Mandarins, he asked permission to be sold as a slave, that thus he might preach the Gospel at the expense of his liberty for life. He was the first of the Society to be buried in Chinese ground. In his last sickness he suffered great pains, which he prayed might be increased, if only his patience and his love might be also increased. In addition to the Divine Office he also daily recited that of the Blessed Virgin, which he had been accustomed to from his childhood. To the journeys and hardships of a missioner's life he added fasts, hairshirts, and disciplines, saying ever with St. Francis Xavier—"More, O Lord, yet more."

5. Among the Moxes, a tribe of Indians, Father Cyprian Barase, a native of Navarre, martyred in the year 1702. He was the first to preach the Gospel among them, and baptized with his own hand more than forty thousand of the savages during the space of twenty-seven years. He founded among them numerous fervent congregations at the cost of immense labour and fatigue. His zeal was unbounded, and in his travels his food was chiefly roots. He always wore a hairshirt, took severe disciplines, and usually slept but four hours a night. During a discourse to an unconverted tribe, he was first shot with arrows and then dispatched with the stroke of a hatchet. He was sixty-one years of age when he met his glorious death.

September 17.

1. At Rome, in the year 1621, died Father Robert Bellarmine, Cardinal of the Holy Roman Church, and Archbishop of Capua. He was obliged to accept of these high dignities under pain of excommunication if he refused. Pope Clement VIII. gave the reasons for his election to the Cardinalate as follows—"We elect him, first because the Church of God has not his equal in learning; and secondly, because he is the nephew of a most excellent and holy Pontiff," namely, Marcellus II. He was the first of Catholic controversialists, and if any should be disposed not to award him the first place, the Protestants would give it him by holding him to be their chief enemy. Theodore Beza said of a certain volume of Bellarmine's, "This book alone completely prostrates us to the ground." In Cambridge, and afterwards in Oxford, lectureships were founded to refute if possible the arguments of Bellarmine. Cardinal Perrone, the great opponent of heresy in France, declared that he esteemed the Controversies of Bellarmine the best defence of the Faith published in the Church for the space of a thousand years. And Baronius calls him the tower of David hung around with a thousand shields, all arms of the valiant. In the northern parts of Europe alone the work has gone through twenty editions. His sanctity is attested by the evidence of his published life and by common repute, as well as by miracles wrought both before and after his death, and by the process of his Beatification, which has been begun. At the age of seventy-nine he retired to the Noviceship of S. Andrea, where he closed his holy and meritorious life in sentiments of the most tender piety.

2. At Rome, in the year 1599, Father John Teller, a Frenchman. He established two excellent confraternities; one for the living, called "The Archconfraternity of Charity," for assisting and relieving those in prison, in sickness, and in pleading the causes of the poor; another for the dead, by which the Parish Priests were led to agree to give a signal every night after the *Angelus*, by the church bell, for prayers to be offered for the suffering souls in Purgatory. He laid the united consent of the Priests before the Pope, Gregory XIII., who promoted the good work by granting indulgences it.

SEPTEMBER 18.

1. At Valencia, in Spain, in the year 1617, died Father John Sanchez, a Spaniard, a great lover of poverty and humility. All the furniture of his room was a bed, table, chair, wooden crucifix, and paper picture of the Blessed Virgin Mary. He was wont to carry baskets of food to the poor at the gate, and he served them on bended knees, remembering that he was serving Christ our Lord.

2. At Metz, in Lorraine, in the year 1657, Father John Fagot, a native of Lorraine. He was a man of a modest and religious gaiety, and was both active and laborious. He preached at Paris and elsewhere for forty-six years with applause and great success. The devil, enraged against him, threatened, by a person possessed at Nancy, that he would put him to signal shame and confusion. Shortly afterwards, as he was beginning a discourse in some other city, his memory suddenly failed him and he had not a word to say. That this was by the agency of the devil, was evident from what he insultingly declared at Nancy—"Now Fagot is nonplussed." The Father having begged the prayers of his auditors for an afflicted person, received assistance, and was able to proceed with his sermon.

3. At Presburg, in Hungary, in the year 1665, Father Zachary Trinkel, a Hungarian, adorned with great gifts both of nature and of grace. He undertook and carried through many works for the glory of God and the good of the Society. He gave public proof of his great humility, by asking and obtaining the school of elements the year after he had taught philosophy with great applause in the University of Gratz. This act of humility was a step to dignity, for he was raised to the chair of theology, and was afterwards Provincial. He bore for thirty years the grievous pain of the gout with undisturbed serenity of soul.

4. At Pekin, in China, in the year 1704, Father Charles de Broissy, of the Province of France. Before going on the Chinese mission he bound himself by vow to do all he should know to be for the greater glory of God. He preserved an intimate union with God and great serenity of mind amid the cares of six new establishments, founded by his labour in that Empire. His mortifications were so great that they required to be moderated

by his Superiors. He was remarkable for his patience and sweetness, though naturally of a hasty temperament; and for his perfect obedience. He was a great lover of prayer, and was indefatigable in the study of the Chinese language, to which he devoted much time for the good of the souls committed to his care. He died of fever on board a bark on the way to Pekin, whither he was brought, and buried in the place of the graves of the missioners.

September 19.

1. At Marchena, in Spain, in the year 1636, died Father John de Herrera, a Spaniard. He felt himself called to the Society, but was hesitating to obey the call from a too fond affection for his mother, when he seemed to hear these words from a picture of Christ bound to the pillar, "And how did I leave My Mother?" and then, "I will raise thee to great love." And certainly great love did inflame his heart towards God, his neighbour, and the Society, and incited him to labours of great utility for the service of God and the good of souls. What he could not accomplish by his own efforts, he besought for others who labour for souls among Christians or infidels by many prayers and many penances. Extraordinary things are said to have been done through his prayers both while he lived and after his death.

2. At Bologna, in Italy, in the year 1649, Father Alphonsus Gianotti, an Italian. He not only never relaxed the spirit of fervour he acquired in the noviceship, but he continually added to it; and there were many who declared that the sight of him gave them the idea of what true fervour is, and of the spirit of the Society, and incited them to perfection. He was Master of Novices at Novellara, and Rector of several colleges, offices which he filled in the most exemplary manner. He was subsequently devoted to giving country missions, wherein he gave signal proofs of his zeal. He kept strict guard over his chastity, and kept with great exactitude the rules of modesty. He died lamented by the city of Bologna, and revered as a Saint, at the age of fifty-three, having spent thirty-four years in the Society.

3. At Krems, in Germany, in the year 1634, Father Paul Langemantel, a German, a victim of charity in the service of the sick. With him died

two others who were similarly engaged. He thus closed a life spent in the charitable instruction of poor children in the streets, to whom he was known in every by-way in the city, and thus crowned his labours with a precious death.

SEPTEMBER 20.

1. At Lisbon, in Portugal, in the year 1597, died Father Peter Mascareña, a Portuguese. He was a member of one of the first nobility of the Kingdom. He died a martyr of charity with seventeen others, in the service of those who were infected with the plague. He thus found a short passage to Heaven. He had previously asked and obtained the African mission, but on the breaking out of the plague in Portugal he thought it superfluous to seek elsewhere the palm which was offered him in his own country.

2. At Lisbon, in the year 1604, Father Francis Cardosa, a Portuguese. He was a brilliant preacher, but he preferred the humbler office of teaching Christian doctrine to children and the ignorant, and therefore he gave more time and attention to it than to sermons. It was impossible to see him thus engaged in the public squares in Lisbon without being edified at the sight. He was wont to show his cane, saying that he had guided more to Heaven with that sceptre than by his sermons. The day before his death he had discoursed upon death with more than usual fervour, both in the sermon in the morning and the catechism in the afternoon. On the following day he was found dead sitting at his table in his room, with his finger pointing to the text in an open book, "Blessed are the dead who die in the Lord." His death under such remarkable circumstances made a great impression on the whole city, and caused many conversions. Religious and nobles vied for the honour of bearing his corpse to the grave.

3. At Marino, in Italy, in the year 1556, John Mendoza, a Spanish Novice, son of the Marquis della Valli, and Governor of the Citadel of Naples. He asked permission from Philip, King of Spain, to enter the Society; and in the meanwhile prepared for it by so exemplary a life that his servant, a young Mahometan, struck by his example, embraced the Christian faith. In the Society he humbled himself to the lowest offices; and once, on a time when he was visited by the Duke of Pagliano,

he came from the kitchen girded with his linen apron to receive his illustrious visitor. This life of humility quickly rendered him ripe for Heaven, and after a half a year of meritorious labour he received the reward of eternal recompense.

September 21.

1. At Calatagirone, in Sicily, in the year 1611, died Father Angelo Sibilla, an Italian. He was looked upon as the Angel of Sicily for his modesty, innocence, and great love of prayer. After having taught the lower classes of Grammar for eighteen years, he was appointed to be Master of Novices, which office he fulfilled for thirty years with admirable skill. He never taught any method of mortification or self-conquest which he had not himself put in practice. He died a holy death at the time which he himself had predicted.

2. At Rome, in the year 1620, Father John Amadée, a Frenchman. Many men of keen observation said they could not discover anything in his life to find fault with. He meditated with tender devotion on the Passion of Christ, from which he drew his heroic patience in affliction and suffering. He had recommended himself to a holy person's special prayers without giving his name; and as these prayers were being made for him, Christ manifested Himself as it were with five cords, representing His five Wounds, drawing Father John to Heaven, and saying—"I am with him in tribulation; I will rescue him and glorify him." In his last sickness he feared much to lose his senses, and he consequently recommended himself to the same holy person's prayers, who heard the words—"He shall sleep in peace and shall rest." And he died most peacefully.

3. At Lisbon, in Portugal, in the year 1590, Father Vasco Pirez, a Portuguese. He was wont to examine his conscience after each action. He was so great a lover of poverty, that he went on foot from the College of Oporto to Lisbon, to the Provincial Congregation, begging all the way. He was most devout to the Blessed Virgin, and received many favours from her. She even appeared to him; and he said that on the Feast of her Nativity he usually received some special favour from her. He penetrated the secrets of hearts, had the spirit of prophecy, and was seen surrounded with heavenly light.

4. At Coimbra, in Portugal, in the year 1596, Father Vasco Ballesti, a Portuguese. His modest and venerable exterior exhibited a true portrait of the Rules of the Society. His conversation was most pleasing, while it was ever directed to the glory of God. As he was very devout to the Blessed Sacrament, he made frequent visits to It in the day, and obtained permission to spend before It a portion of the night. His devotion to the Blessed Virgin was no less admirable. To spread her devotion, he traversed country villages to teach it to the people. On Fridays he fasted on bread and water in memory of the Passion. He died a victim of charity by his having caught a pestilential disease from a poor and nearly naked man, whose confession he had heard, and whom he covered with his cloak, that he might receive decently the holy Viaticum.

SEPTEMBER 22.

1. At Nangasachi, in Japan, in the year 1633, died Father Michael Pineda, a Japanese. After having laboured much for the good of souls in his own country, he was banished from it, and retired to the Philippine Islands. But his apostolic zeal prompting him to return to Japan, every cunning act was employed to discover him in order to put him to death. But the man who entertained him not daring to keep him, though he would not betray him, turned him out of his house at midnight in the most severe frosts of winter. This and other hardships which he endured brought on his death at the end of three days. His only grief was that he had not the happiness of shedding his blood for the faith.

2. At Yendi, in Japan, in the year 1637, John Yama, a Japanese Lay-brother. At the daily risk of his life he spread the Gospel through the kingdoms of Japan by his zeal and eloquence. Being taken and imprisoned for some years, he promoted the faith by writing when he could no longer preach it among his countrymen, until at length he died a glorious martyr, suspended by the feet with his head downwards in the pit.

3. At Madrid, in Spain, in the year 1611, Father Peter Ribadeneira, a Spaniard. He was very young when he attached himself to our Holy Father St. Ignatius, by whom he was regarded with special affection for his sprightly and lively temperament and excellent natural gifts. Father Ribadeneira became a celebrated missioner, and he laboured with much

fruit to souls in Italy, Sicily, Belgium and Spain. He displayed great prudence and charity in the government of colleges and provinces, and twice filled the post of Assistant for Spain. In the midst of these active duties he published so many learned works that he might seem to have had no other occupation all his life but this. He lived a holy Religious man, exact in observance of Rule, beloved by his brethren, agreeable to others, esteemed by the great, and without offence to any, and he died a holy death.

September 23.

1. At Loretto, in Italy, in the year 1590, died Father Nicholas Bobadilla, a Spaniard, one of the first ten companions of St. Ignatius. He laboured with indefatigable zeal in the cause of the faith in Italy, Germany, and Dalmatia; assisting, by the orders of the Sovereign Pontiffs, at the Diets of Nuremberg, Spire, Worms, and Ratisbon. He refused the offer of a Bishopric made him by the Emperor Ferdinand. In his apostolic career he suffered much; he was seized with the plague while serving the sick, was wounded in the head while defending the true faith, was stripped of his clothes, and his enemies attempted to poison him while he was contending for a cause of justice. Having caused some disturbance in the first General Congregation after the death of St. Ignatius, he acknowledged his fault, and lived a good Religious, watchful, modest, and simple, with his mind fixed upon Heaven, and a bridle on the tongue, dead to the world, severe to himself and sweet to others. He died at the age of eighty, having seen the Society spread throughout the world.

2. At Alcalà, in Spain, in the year 1604, Father Gabriel Vasquez, a Spaniard, a man of extraordinary talent, and of no less diligence and labour in study, by reason of which he acquired so great a fame among theologians that he has been styled by great authors, "the Augustine of Spain," "the Light of the Schools of Theology," "the Master of Masters," and an "Angel in life and intellect." He joined the study of Religious perfection to the learning of the schools, and so has deserved the title of the "Religious Doctor." While Spain admired his learning, he himself desired to live unknown, and asked to be sent into a far off country to teach catechism to the heathen. His funeral was attended by the Religious Orders and Magistrates of Alcalà. His works on Scholastic Theology and Holy Scripture are published in ten folio volumes.

3. At Antwerp, in Belgium, in the year 1626, Father John Callant, a Belgian, a martyr of charity whilst attending upon the plague-stricken. Anne of Jesus, the Superioress of the Nuns of St. Teresa, saw his soul ascending to Heaven surrounded with light.

September 24.

1. On the Indian Ocean, in the year 1680, died Father George Fernandez and Father Gomez Damarales, Portuguese, slain in the voyage from Goa to Amboyna by the natives of Java, while they were hearing the confessions of those on board ship.

2. At Mayence, in Germany, in the year 1626, Father John Falck, a German, a fervent preacher, and an indefatigable attendant on the sick in the hospital. He would sometimes preach six or seven discourses in the day, in different churches or chapels of the towns, or in the villages and neighbouring hamlets, whilst his only food was bread and cheese. He made a vow of never taking meat or drink for pleasure, but only for support of nature, and he avoided every appearance of any superfluity, and chose the more common kinds of food. At the beginning of every month he presented himself to the Rector, and on his knees renewed his vow of Obedience, promising to obey him exactly in all things. When he was in want of little things, he asked them as an alms from the Father Minister for the love of the Blessed Virgin. Taking off his shoes at night he would place them on his head, as worthy to be trodden under foot by all. It was his custom to take a severe discipline before he gave a sermon.

3. At Rio Janeiro, in the year 1653, Father John Almeida, whose true name was Mede, an Englishman. He was more famous for his virtues than for the miracles he wrought. He seemed a second Anchieta. More than once he was seen elevated from the ground in prayer. One day when he was unable to prevent some discourse injurious to the character of others, he was so deeply afflicted, that drops as of blood burst from his forehead and flowed down to the ground. The miracles wrought by him after death have been duly put on record. He died at the age of eighty-two, after having spent sixty-one years in the Society.

SEPTEMBER 25.

1. At Lisbon, in Portugal, in the 1617, died Father Francis Suarez, a Spaniard, the greatest of modern theologians, entitled by Paul V. in four different letters, "*Doctor Eximius*—the Excellent Doctor," and praised by the eulogies of all the learned world. He filled, with extraordinary talent and repute, the chair of theology for forty years either at Rome, or in Spain, or at Coimbra, whither he was invited with expressions of the greatest honour by Philip II., King of Spain and Portugal. He wrote twenty-four volumes in folio on philosophy and theology with such erudition, that he is thought not without reason to have received his knowledge infused from Heaven, since it is so sublime and universal; and yet when he first applied himself to the study of philosophy, he laboured with such little success, that he begged to be removed from it as wanting in talent. Shortly afterwards such a flood of light burst upon him, that he who was the last quickly became the first of the students. His sanctity was equal to his learning, and he was seen raised in prayer several feet from the ground, while rays from the Crucifix darted upon his face and breast. When dying he exclaimed with gladness, "I did not know it was so sweet to die."

2. Upon the Rhine, in Germany, in the year 1620, Godfrey Thelen, a German, taken and maltreated by heretical soldiers, as a disseminator of Popish idolatry. After receiving six deep wounds he was shot dead with a musket ball. He was so much given to prayer, that he was called by some who did not know his name, "The Father who prayed so continually and fervently."

3. At Cadiz, in Spain, in the year 1651, Father John Armenta, a Spaniard. For more than forty years he was a highly esteemed preacher in the chief cities of Andalusia. Although so great a preacher, he loved to teach the catechism to the poor. Thirty-six English corsairs having been taken captive and condemned to die, remained obstinate in their heresy; but the magistrates applying to the Society for a Father to assist them, so great was the earnest zeal and powerful persuasion of Father Armenta, that they abjured their heresy, and died it is hoped good Catholics.

SEPTEMBER 26.

1. In Spain, in the year 1641, died Father Peter Continente, a Spaniard. He was a man whose life accorded with his name not only in all purity, but in the government of that unruly member, the tongue, of which he was a perfect master. It was his wont to salute each picture or statue of our Lady in the corridors, and he had the habit of reciting a kind of rosary composed of acts of contrition. He endured without flinching most acute pains in a surgical operation by keeping his eyes fixed upon his Crucifix.

2. At Bahia, in Brazil, in the year 1654, Gaspar Almeida, a Portuguese Lay-brother, a pigmy in stature, but a giant in virtue. He gave himself with all the force of his mind and body to the maceration of his little frame, which was spent with fastings, disciplines, and watchings. He would rather take much from his sleep than a little from his labour, to give time to protracted prayer. He often spent whole nights before the Blessed Sacrament. He foretold many things that were to happen. His daily food was two crusts of bread and two apples; the rest, whether fish or flesh, he gave with permission to the poor. The Porter of the house being sick and in bed, Brother Gaspar bid him rise, telling him that he had yet a long time to live. The sick Brother rose, and for many years continued in his charitable office of serving the poor at the College gate.

3. At Augsburg, in Germany, in the year 1627, Father Tobias Paumbgartner, a German, one of six martyrs of charity in service of the plague-stricken.

4. At Münster, in Westphalia, in the year 1656, Father John Fabricius, a German, a man of singular gentleness and mercy. He made an offering of all the prayers and Masses to be said for him by the Society at his death to the souls in Purgatory, by whom he was often visited and petitioned for succour. In winter it was his custom to go about in quest of alms to buy wood to distribute to the poor. The plague, caught in attending the sick, closed his career of charity.

5. At Tournay, in the year 1673, Peter Bertoult, a French Laybrother. When first admitted into the Society he heard the words of our Lord—"Know that it is to the merits of My Blood that thou owest thy entrance

into Religion. The memory of these words made so profound an impression on him that he daily kissed his habit as he put it on, whilst he shed abundant tears of gratitude. He spent three hours in prayer every night. In the first he prayed for the conversion of sinners; in the second he poured out his soul in thanksgiving for the benefit of our Redemption; in the third he prayed for the suffering souls in Purgatory. His room was beneath a staircase, his bed a truss of hay and a poor blanket. Though suffering from two violent diseases he constantly wore a hairshirt. In his last illness he was ever repeating prayers of thanksgiving to God; and his death was accompanied with great consolations.

September 27.

1. At Ingolstadt, in Bavaria, in the year 1606, died Father Theodore Canisius, a Belgian, brother of the Blessed Peter Canisius, who once said to him, "Theodore, observe what the news of my death will bring you." He was at table in the refectory when the death of the Blessed Peter was announced. On the instant he fell suddenly into a stupor as from a stroke, and his memory so failed him for eight years, till his death, that he forgot even his own name, and he could neither read nor speak except to pronounce the holy names JESUS, Mary. These he could repeat as often as he pleased without difficulty. Just before his death he articulated "To Heaven! To Heaven!" to which he added "JESUS!" and expired as he began to utter "Mary." He often made the sign of the Cross on his forehead while in sickness, and the bystanders say they saw it imprinted there when he was dead.

2. At Cracow, in Poland, in the year 1612, Father Peter Scarga, a Pole. From a Prelate he became a Novice of the Society at Rome. He kept its Rules to the letter, while he preached its spirit to the world. He is the first of Polish preachers, and his published sermons for long years afterwards were read in the Refectory every year. He lived at Court for the long period of twenty-four years without injury to his poverty of spirit or relaxation of religious discipline. Eight years before his death, as he lay sick, Father Stanislaus Warsewitch, some time dead, appeared to him, and told him to ask of God a few years longer life. In his last sickness, having made himself a candle of wax in honour of the

Blessed Virgin of Clermont, he sent it thither to be lighted, and as soon as it was consumed he expired.

3. At Nissa, in Silesia, in the year 1633, Father Stephen Todor, a Bohemian. He freely gave his life, together with seventeen others of the Society, to the service of the plague-stricken.

4. At Pekin, in the year 1741, Father Dominic Perennin, a Frenchman, an accomplished missioner, and one of the most zealous workmen ever sent to labour in China. He was of a robust constitution and of a venerable and majestic appearance; he possessed a great facility in languages, was quick in intellect, and a man of great erudition. To these gifts he added great purity of conscience, love of poverty and suffering and labour. He was forty-three years on the missions, and so won the esteem of the Emperor Chang-hi, that he would converse with the Father for long hours on religious and scientific subjects. He died at the age of seventy-seven, and was honoured with a magnificent funeral, such as is the custom for a great Mandarin.

SEPTEMBER 28.

1. On their way to Abyssinia, in the year 1625, died Father Francis Macciado and Father Bernard Pereira, Portuguese. They had sanguine hopes of promoting the good of the Church in Abyssinia, owing to the conversion of the Sultan Seged to the Catholic faith; but being taken on their journey by a Mahometan Governor they were put to death out of hatred to the faith.

2. At Cocyra, in Japan, in the year 1633, Thomas Riocan, Lewis Cafucu, and Denis Yamomoto, Japanese. They were banished, but returning to their country to preach the Gospel, they were again taken, and won a crown of eternal recompense by being burned alive at a slow fire.

3. In the Isle of Tatacuran, on the coast of Florida, in the West Indies, in the year 1566, Father Peter Martinez, killed by the savages the very moment he set foot upon it, for he was dragged from the boat in which he was landing. He knelt down, and raising his hands to Heaven, received a mortal blow from a club, and thus gained the martyrdom he had desired. He was the first to preach the Gospel in the Western Indies that were subject to Spain, and by his blood opened the door to the

conversion of these countries. After his death many cures were wrought by his intercession.

4. At Ettingen, in Germany, in the year 1634, Father Matthew Maile, a German, who, after a life spent in educating the young Princes of Bavaria, died a martyr of charity in assisting the plague-stricken; in which service eighty of the Society died in different parts of Germany. While he lived amid the honours of the Court he used to make and mend shoes for the use of the poor.

SEPTEMBER 29.

1. At Rome, in the year 1609, died Father Francis Folian, a native of Valtelina, in the Tyrol. He was a man of great humility and mortification, and of extraordinary devotion to the mystery of the Blessed Trinity. His practices in Its honour are worthy of all admiration, though some of them may perhaps appear to us rather minutious. His chamber at Rome was triangular; three boards formed his bed; he arranged his knife, fork, and spoon at table in a triangle; he ate only of three dishes, drank only three times, and used a rosary of three decades on a string woven of three colours. He would often say, "All things are in three." Gazing on the sun he saw a likeness of the Blessed Trinity in its light, colour, and heat. With leave from the Pope he added daily to the Mass the Preface of the Most Holy Trinity. On the Eve of Trinity Sunday he stood the whole night vested at the Altar, and in the morning said Mass with incredible delight, being an hour in its celebration. That these devout affections were pleasing to God was evidenced by three tongues as of flame, united at the base, found in his heart when dead, to the astonishment of the physicians and all the bystanders. When he was dying he placed three fingers in the form of a triangle on his breast, to signify his love of the Blessed Trinity to the last. His praises were publicly recited in the Refectory, so great was the opinion of his sanctity.

2. At Lima, in Peru, in the year 1626, Father Ferdinand Monrois, a Spaniard. From his earliest years he was remarkable for his fervent piety. After entering the Society he asked to be sent on the mission of Peru, where he led an apostolic and holy life for twenty-seven years. He rose at midnight to pray till sunrise, spending two hours in his preparation

for Mass and his thanksgiving after Mass, and this practice he continued for thirty-three years. He received an injunction from our Lord often to give thanks to the Eternal Father for the gift of the Blessed Sacrament to us, and he was ever afterwards specially consoled and illuminated at those words of the Preface, *Domine sancte, Pater omnipotens.* He was tenderly devout to the Blessed Virgin Mary and his Guardian Angel. He died on the Feast of St. Michael with great calmness and sweetness, leaving by an act of heroic charity all the suffrages to be offered for himself for the relief of the souls in Purgatory.

SEPTEMBER 30.

On the Baltic Sea, in the year 1598, died Father Martin Laterna, a Russian Pole. He entered the Society at Brunsberg, out of admiration for the piety, learning, and conversation of our Fathers. He imitated in this the example of his master, and he became a truly apostolic man, and wonderful as a preacher of penance. He preached for three years in the camp of the renowned King Stephen Bathorius, and eminent was the fruit done to souls by his pious eloquence. After the death of Stephen he was invited by King Sigismund to Sweden. When he was returning thence back again to Poland, the ship in which he sailed was taken by heretics, and the Catholics most cruelly maltreated. Father Martin exhorting them to fortitude, was discovered to be a Priest and a Jesuit. He was immediately mortally wounded and then flung into the sea. After his death he appeared to a Polish nobleman, Laurence Bienczowski, a prisoner among the Tartars, in a splendid chariot drawn by four horses. He freed the captive from his chains and slavery, and transported him to Russia, a distance of fifty miles, as the same nobleman deposed on oath at Rome. Many others also did he succour with his kindly aid.

2. On the Indian Sea, in the year 1639, Father Maurice Moureira, a Portuguese. When the Portuguese ship in which he sailed was burned by the heretics, he leaped with the others into the sea; and while they picked up the rest in their boats, recognizing him by his tonsure for a Priest, and by his habit for a Jesuit, they beat him to death with their boating poles.

3. At Sciki, in Japan, in the year 1633, Father James Antony Tacu-

sima, a Japanese, a man of heroic zeal and eloquence. He refuted the errors of the Bonzes in many public disputations, and wrought many conversions by his preaching and holy example. He was condemned to the stake, and burned by a slow fire.

4. At Barcelona, in Spain, in the year 1607, Father Vincent Martrese, an Italian. He is the same whom Brother Laurence Mola, a holy Capuchin, called to him in his last sickness and said—"Father, I have had you called to tell you the message God has commanded me to deliver to you, namely, that all who die in the Society are saved." When Father Vincent would have qualified somewhat the general terms of this expression, the sick man said, "My Father, the truth is as I have said it, and God charged me to declare it, and therefore I had you sent for." Filled with joy at this announcement, Father Vincent so lived as to end his life in the Society by a happy and holy death.

OCTOBER.

1. At Rome, in the year 1572, died St. Francis Borgia, third General of the Society; receiving an immortal crown in reward for a life of signal and meritorious sanctity. He gave an example of perfection in every state of life. A holy Prince, a faithful Minister, a chaste consort; in youth, a pattern of integrity; in Religious life, a model of humility, contempt of the world, and Priestly devotion; he showed Prelates how to fly from honours, and was a model to all of fervent charity towards God and man. The solemn commemoration of his happy death was transferred by the authority of the Apostolic See, first to the third and afterwards to the tenth of October.

2. At Castel Gandolfo, near Rome, in the year 1757, Father Aloysius Centurione, the seventeenth General of the Society; of lofty mind, rare talents, and tender love for the Society. He was distinguished for the wisdom of his undertakings; but the short duration of his government and the weakness of his health did not allow him to mature all his projects.

3. At Vienna, in Austria, in the year 1558, Father Theodoric Gerard, a Belgian. Such was the holiness of his life at Rome, that Father Martin Olave said of him, that "many virtues shone in the Roman College, but that in Father Theodoric not one was wanting." When about to die, he said to Father Theodoric Canisius, who stood by him: "Dearest Canisius, I hear the songs of Angels; come with me and listen. I hear the Angels' songs." Extolling the happiness of a Religious vocation, he used to say, that any thought or suggestion of the devil against it should be put away like a temptation against the faith.

4. At Syracuse in Sicily, in the year 1575, Father Michael Ochoia, a Spaniard. He had the gift of miraculous cures, which he exercised not only in Spain but at Rome, curing Father Polanco of the fever. He made use of this power to effect spiritual cures in souls, while he restored

health to the body. By this gift a great efficacy accompanied his sermons and his other labours in the Apostolic ministry.

5. At Cologne, in Germany, in the year 1655, Father Adrian Horn, a German. He was found dead in the morning, having been in good health the previous day; seeming like one who had fallen asleep, holding his rosary in his left hand, as was his custom at night. He was preeminent for piety, angelic purity, and a pleasing affability; his discourses breathed of God, and his government was gentle, prudent, and very liberal, especially to strangers exiled from various provinces in the disturbed times; whom he supplied with every necessary, though the house was poor. Once, being anxious to provide for these, he heard a voice bidding him "be of good heart;" and shortly after, being called to attend a rich sick person, he received an abundant alms. He was no less attentive to religious poverty, and a favourite saying of his was; "Pray let us be careful not to infringe on holy poverty."

October 2.

1. In Japan, in the Isle of Xiqui, in the year 1570, died Father Cosmo de Torres, a Spaniard, a zealous Apostle of the faith. He lived on scanty food; without bread, wine, milk, or flesh, but abounding in heavenly delights: regarded by all as an Apostle, and beloved as a father. He baptized the King of Omura, and left at his death nearly thirty thousand Christians.

2. At Nangasachi, in Japan, in the year 1633, Father Benedict Fernandez, a Portuguese, and Father Paul Saito, a Japanese, suffered for the faith by the torment of the pit. Father Paul endured it, hung with his head downwards, for seven whole days. Father Benedict was taken out somewhat sooner, to be put to more lengthened tortures in presence of the Emperor; but died in prison on hearing that Father Paul had expired. The amazed executioners declared that they distinctly heard the words in the Portuguese and Japanese tongues with which the bodies of these two Fathers saluted one another as they were being carried to be burned, and congratulated one another on their blessedness.

3. At Lerena, in Spain, in the year 1677, Father Francis Pardos, a Spaniard, a zealous and indefatigable missioner. Promoted to the chair

of Professor of Theology, on account of his great talents, he obtained by his incessant prayers leave from the Father General to abandon the schools, and devote himself entirely to Apostolic labours. To these he gave himself with such ardour, that neither fatigue, nor length of journeys, nor fastings and hunger, nor grievous sickness, could detain him from them. He was eagerly demanded by Bishops and Archbishops to give missions in their dioceses. Accordingly, when he died, the bells of the whole city were tolled, and he was followed to the grave by the Canons of the three Chapters.

OCTOBER 3.

1. At Cork, in Ireland, in the year 1602, died Dominic Collins, an Irish Lay-brother. He was of good family, and had served with honour and reputation in the armies of France and Spain. Having entered the Society as a Lay-brother, he was sent to accompany one of our Fathers to Ireland, where he was captured by the heretics at Dunboyne Castle, and executed at Cork, after cruel treatment and imprisonment. From the scaffold he exhorted the Catholics to persevere in the faith, and not to allow themselves to be perverted by any hope of reward or fear of punishment. "Look up to Heaven," he said; "and, as worthy sons of your fathers, keep the ancient faith which they professed, and for which you now see me die." He was then thrown off the ladder, and quartered.

2. At Cracow, in Poland, in the year 1591, died Father Stanislaus Varsewitch, a Pole, illustrious for his embassy to the Turks, his Senatorial rank, and office of Chancellor; also for his refusal of a Bishopric offered him by King Sigismund. He entered the Society at Rome, together with some other members of his family, and was fellow-novice with St. Stanislaus Kostka. He rendered great and extraordinary service to the Catholic faith by his learning, preaching, and example of life. His love of prayer was great, and he was often seen in ecstasy. He laid down his life as a martyr of charity, attending upon the plague-stricken.

3. At Naples, in the year 1588, Pompeio Capuano, an Italian Novice, of the illustrious family of the Viceroys, of which he was the rising hope. By constant prayer, the skin was callous on his knees. All attempts to induce him to embrace a secular life were vain. But when he asked permission of his father to enter the Society, he was closely confined in

a dark room, as mad; and many persons, amongst whom were some Religious, were employed to deter him from his purpose; but in vain, for he overcame all obstacles. The Society, however, was not permitted to enjoy him long; as he was already ripe for Heaven, which claimed him for its own.

4. At Cracow, in Poland, in the year 1662, Laurence Chodorowicz, a Polish Lay-brother, remarkable for his love of prayer, his patience, and charity. During the night, when all was still, he would betake himself to the church, and continue in prayer till the dawn. He once upset a cauldron of boiling water upon his right leg and foot, scalding them in a shocking manner. He bore the pain for three days without examining the hurt, or taking off his stockings. Then he saw that it was his duty to conceal it no longer; and the doctors were amazed at his unflinching endurance, when, in drawing off his hose, the skin and flesh adhered to them. He was never known to be angry, or to refuse any labour. He gave his life in service of the plague-stricken, and died a martyr of charity.

OCTOBER 4.

1. In the East Indies, in the Isle of Mariduque, died Father John de las Missas, a native of the Manillas, martyred by the savages and the Mahometans out of hatred to the faith: being first shot with a bullet and then beheaded. After the martyrdom, they turned their rage against the church; desecrating all the holy things, and treating the corpse of the Father with barbarous indignities, making a drinking-cup of his skull. A high opinion of his sanctity was entertained from the very commencement of his Religious life; and it is said that he was spoken to by a Crucifix before which he prayed.

2. At Wenden, in Livonia, in the year 1620, Father Ertman Tolgsdorff, a Prussian, a native of Wörms; an indefatigable missioner, and styled by the Bishop Otto Schenking, "the Father and Apostle of Livonia." Resigning a Canonry at Gutstadt, he gave himself to the Society, together with a deserted monastic house, which was his property at Riga. Having made his Noviceship at Cracow, he was sent to Riga, where he devoted himself to the salvation of souls and the restoration of the Catholic faith; inviting youths from Prussia, whom he educated upon alms which he

begged: he prepared them for the Priesthood, and thus supplied the churches. So great was his charity towards poor simple people, that he was known among them by the name of "the honoured old Master," or "the Father," and even "the 'Bishop' of Livonia." To extreme old age, he continued to give the hours before day-break to hearing confessions, then preached in German, after which he received petitions and applications and performed the duties of a Parish Priest, said Mass, and then addressed the people in Livonian; after which he again heard confessions till midday. In the afternoon, he catechised the children and ignorant, sang the Vespers, and, if required, visited the sick; so that all were amazed at his strength for such labours at so great age: but the fervour of his charity sustained him.

3. At Cazorla, in Spain, in the year 1596, Dominic de Onate, a Spanish Lay-brother. While yet in the world, he was tried on some light unfounded suspicions, condemned, and deprived of all his goods, and, though innocent, thrown into prison. He there made his first noviceship; and being afterwards found innocent and discharged, he resolved to put no more trust in the world. His constant subject of meditation in the Society was on the expectation of death. On being once asked by a Superior what he was thinking of, he replied: "Of being carried out, feet-foremost; and of the strict account that must be rendered." At night he seemed to hear his Guardian Angel say, "Life is short; the labour is little; the reward is great; prepare to give thy account." And in this manner he died, not taken unprepared.

4. In Tonkin, in the year 1723, Father Francis Mary Bucherelli, a Florentine, beheaded for the faith after cruel sufferings in prison. He exposed his life for six years in preaching, after the proclamation of the Imperial edicts against the Christian faith. Ten neophytes suffered with him, companions of his martyrdom. These, animated by his words and example, gave their lives with great constancy, to the astonishment of the idolaters, to whom it seemed a kind of miracle.

5. At Moulins, in France, in the year 1635, Father Charles Mallean, of the Diocese of Belley. Having been Rector and Professor, he devoted himself to the service of the plague-stricken at Lyons. He was Provincial when he was summoned to the Court of Louis XIII., as the King's Confessor. He lived in Religious poverty as regards food and clothing; saying, that a lover of Religious life can find no pleasure at Court; and remained

at his post only from obedience, and love of the Society, which required of him this service for the good of France and of the King. He expired in sentiments of profound humility, asking pardon of God, of the Church, of the Society, of the Lay-brother, his companion; and even of the servants who had waited on him: being assisted by the Rector of the College of Moulins.

October 5.

1. At Amacusa, in Japan, in the year 1583, died Father Louis Almeida, a Portuguese. He was a surgeon of note on board a Portuguese ship; and, having made the Spiritual Exercises, entered the Society, in which he became remarkable for the supernatural gift of curing all diseases, but still more so for the cure of souls, and for his zeal in preaching the Gospel, and his insatiable thirst for sufferings and labours. Of these he received an abundance, being often sought for by the Bonzes to take his life, maltreated by the idolatrous pirates, and by agency of the devils; on one occasion he was seized, stripped of his clothes, scourged, put in an open boat out to sea; from all which he escaped. Another time, banished from Cangoxima, he lay concealed for a year in a hut upon a desert shore, living upon wild herbs. He was greatly mourned for at his death by the Church of Japan, which he had wonderfully spread and defended for twenty-seven years.

2. At Syracuse, in Sicily, in the year 1590, Father Michael Lætavalle, an Italian; a man of great mortification and labour in the salvation of souls. Even on his death-bed he would not receive the Holy Viaticum without his accustomed discipline, as far as his sickness and advanced age would permit. He was seen in prayer raised three hands' breath from the ground; and, for the forty years he lived in the Society, was molested by no bad thought. The Blessed Virgin, and St. Michael with other Angels, visited him while dying. After his death, Joseph Saladini, Bishop of Syracuse, commanded inquiry to be made into the virtues and miracles of Father Michael, and sent the processes, attested upon oath, to Pope Paul V., with a petition for his Beatification.

3. At Dijon, in France, in the year 1654, Father Nicholas Condé, of Lorraine, a great and zealous preacher throughout France. In his room

he had no book but the Holy Scriptures, which he read daily upon his knees; but the power of his memory was so extraordinary that his mind was filled with erudition of all kinds; and he retained in it, without writing, sermons which he had preached many years before. A zealous observer of the Rules, he loved most and practised that which enjoins the ready undertaking of those offices in which humility and charity are more particularly exercised.

4. At Antwerp, in Belgium, in the year 1629, Father Herbert Rosweyde, a Belgian. From his very noviceship he showed of what service he would be to the Saints and to the Church. As a student of philosophy, on recreation days, when others betook themselves to the pleasant fields or gardens, he withdrew to the Libraries, and searched for and examined old manuscripts, especially on the lives of the Saints; collecting materials for the vast work which, after the death of Father Herbert Bollandus, he undertook and commenced. More than twenty volumes on various matters, as Southwell reckons, were published by this most laborious man.

5. At Monaco, in Italy, in the year 1595, Father Bonaventure Paradinas, a Spaniard. Three years after his entrance into the Society, he was appointed Master of Novices; and held the office for twenty-three years, first at Monaco, and then at Landsberg on the Upper Rhine. He was a man of great detachment from the world, of great enlightenment and prudence in the direction of souls, and wonderful calmness and resignation. His care of the Novices was not limited to the time they lived under him, but he continued to aid them by his counsels in their after life; and he was regarded and beloved as the common Father of the province. Leaving Landsberg, by order of the Provincial, for the purer air of Monaco, he bade farewell to his Novices, recommending specially to them five things: Pure intention, mortification, conformity to God's will, love to one another, and devotion to the Blessed Virgin. On his death-bed he spoke to the Fathers around him on the happiness of persevering and dying in the Society; in which, he said, all are either preserved from mortal sin, or quickly arise from it, if, by misfortune, any one falls. Having received the last Sacraments with tender devotion, he died at the age of sixty-two.

October 6.

1. At Rome, in the year 1583, died George Gilbert, an English Novice. Born of a wealthy and noble family in England, he was considered one of the first gentlemen of his time at the University and the Court. The heresy in which he was born was the only stain upon his life; and this Father Robert Persons removed, by receiving him into the Church. From that time forward, he devoted himself to the furtherance of the Catholic faith; relieving the Catholic poor, sustaining the wavering, and supporting the missioners. In this he spent all his revenues, to this he devoted all his labours; and more than once even stripped himself of his own clothes to relieve the needy. Leaving the noble lady to whom he was married, he attended our missioners, Father Campion and Father Persons, in the capacity of a Lay-brother. By such great zeal he incurred the hatred of the heretics, who diligently searched for him throughout the Kingdom, in order to imprison him; but by the advice of Father Persons he went over to France, and from thence to Rome, where he lived some time a holy life in the English Seminary, and was in his last sickness admitted to the Society and took his Religious Vows, which he had long desired. In his sickness, when his stomach revolted at a nauseous dose, upon the suggestion of the Rector of the College that he should take it out of obedience, he promptly swallowed it; and joyfully exclaimed to a Father who shortly afterwards visited him: "O Father, how happy you find me! In reward of my obedience and the little violence I offered to myself, the Blessed Virgin has appeared to me with such a calm, benign, and sweet countenance; whereas before she appeared with a stern expression, because I was too obstinate and nice in my palate." In his happy death his only grief was that he died in his bed, and not on a blood-stained scaffold. He was buried at the Novitiate of S. Andrea.

2. At Bazain, in the East Indies, in the year 1551, Father Melchior Gonsalvez, a Portuguese, appointed Rector of the College of Bazain by St. Francis Xavier. By his apostolic zeal he very much promoted the Catholic faith, and destroyed many idols. The idolatrous people, enraged at the progress of Christianity, hastened his death by poison.

3. At Ximoxima, in Japan, in the year 1628, Michael Xucan, a

Japanese Catechist, who by his constant zealous exhortations induced many of his countrymen to forsake their idols. Banished to Macao, and returning thence to Japan, he exposed his life to constant peril in the propagation of the faith. He died a victim to hardship and toil, desirous of suffering martyrdom by fire.

4. At Wilna, in Lithuania, in the year 1677, Father Albert Kojaloniez, a Pole. Having been Rector of the University of Wilna, he was appointed Superior of the Professed House, in which office he gained the love of the whole Community. The Lay-brothers were particularly the objects of his solicitude, and he omitted nothing to advance them in perfection. He composed a Menology of the Brothers who had lived and died in repute of sanctity. Himself a model of poverty, patience, and obedience, he passed much of the day in prayer; hearing two Masses before his own, and visiting the Blessed Sacrament seven times a day. He had great devotion to the Passion, and practised often the devotion on Fridays in honour of St. Francis Xavier, to obtain a happy death. He offered his life for the recovery of two Fathers attacked by pestilence, and shortly after their recovery died at the age of seventy, having spent fifty years in the Society.

OCTOBER 7.

1. At Toledo, in Spain, in the year 1588, died Father John Peralta, a Spaniard. In whatever he did he aimed at perfection and exactness. All his life he was a most strict observer of silence, and thus had abundance of time for prayer and labour. It was a saying, that he who conversed with Peralta came away redolent of piety. When Rector of Villa Real, he was slandered by some seculars, against whom he had stood in defence of the College property, and was deposed by Superiors from his office. He kept heroic silence; but afterwards his innocence shone forth with greater splendour, when the clouds of calumny were dispersed.

2. At Bologna, in Italy, in the year 1630, Father Angelo Orimbello, an Italian, a martyr of charity in assisting the plague-stricken Bolognese. He had petitioned for this service by a letter to the Father General, and obtained it; and moreover, at the request of the Governor of Bologna, made through Cardinal Spada, he was appointed over a very large newly

erected double hospital. He was welcomed with the greatest joy by the medical men, and confessors of the sick of various Religious Orders, on account of his well known prudence and charity. He fully answered all their expectations; and by his suggestion, inspired from Heaven, the city of Bologna, choosing by a public decree St. Ignatius and St. Francis Xavier for its Patrons, experienced their most efficacious aid in deliverance from the pestilence. The Father himself, after the loss of nine of the Society in the same service, fell a victim to his labour of charity.

3. At Paris, in the year 1651, Father James Sirmond, a Frenchman, a most learned antiquarian, who in his laborious researches ransacked not only the libraries of France, but the Vatican. He was an excellent Greek and Latin scholar: Southwell reckons thirty-six ancient authors whom he illustrated with learned notes. He was highly praised by Cardinal Baronius, Grüther, and other learned men. He published ten volumes of *Opuscula*, and was sixteen years Secretary to the Father General, Claudius Acquaviva, and moreover confessor to Louis XIII.; yet amid such constant labours he lived to the protracted age of ninety-three, and so vigorous in health that he kept the fast of Lent as rigorously as when young. He lived seventy-five years in the Society.

4. On the mission of Peru, at the College of Santa Cruz, Father Angelo Monitola, an Italian. For twenty-five years he laboured with indefatigable zeal in the mountains of the Cordillera, enduring heat and cold, and traversing vallies and rivers for the salvation of souls. His only desire was to sacrifice his life in so holy a cause. He would often beg alms in the streets, and receive with sweetness and patience the ill treatment of the populace. God always recompensed him by granting the conversion of some sinners. He obtained by his prayers a victory of the Spaniards over the savages, and delivered them from other dangers. He died at the age of fifty-three, having spent thirty-three years in the Society.

OCTOBER 8.

1. At Nangasachi, in Japan, in the year 1633, died Father John d'Acosta, a Portuguese, a glorious martyr, after twenty-nine years of labour and hardships endured for the salvation of souls. He had been banished for the faith, and returned disguised as a sailor: on being discovered

he was taken, and hung by the feet in the torment of the pit, and on the fourth day completed his victorious career, giving up his soul to God.

2. At Sassari, in Sardinia, in the year 1571, Father Antony Boscho, a Spaniard. He entered the Society on account of its favouring the practice of frequent Communion. After a life of great piety, lying upon his death-bed, he broke out into expressions of great joy, saying: "Our fleet has gained a great victory over the Turks," and he invited all present to sing the *Te Deum*; two days after which he departed full of happiness to the Lord. His prophecy was confirmed afterwards by news of the victory gained at Lepanto.

3. At Valencia, in Spain, in the year 1579, Father Gaspar Loarte, a Spaniard. Even before entering the Society, he was noted for learning and probity, and gave four hours daily to meditation on holy things. When he was Rector at Genoa, he was in great mental affliction, but was consoled by a vision of Christ on the Cross, Who said to him: "Be of good courage; throughout life I will not abandon you." And Father Gaspar experienced the truth of this sweet promise. He was so great a lover of prayer that when sick he would join his hands and raise them to heaven during the usual time of morning meditation, and give himself to fervent prayer.

4. At Naples, in the year 1726, Father Martin Mastorelli. To an entire detachment from earthly things he joined an intimate union with God in prayer, to which he consecrated the greater portion of the day. In his far advanced old age, when his infirmities and years would no longer permit him to go down to the church, he loved to drag himself to the domestic chapel or the tribune, and remain long in prayer. This constant communication with God merited for him the graces of discernment of spirits and of prophecy. Cures were often wrought by the touch of his cap, or the mere sound of his voice. Painful infirmities and a long agony increased his merits, and at the age of seventy-two he went to receive the crown of justice. He was seen shortly after his death, by a person who much esteemed him, admitted to the company of Heaven; as before, when entering the Society, he had been seen by his aunt, a holy Religious, accompanied by two Angels.

October 9.

1. At Nangasachi, in Japan, in the year 1633, died Father Xystus Tocuum and Brother Damian Fucaye, Japanese, suspended head downwards in the pit, martyrs for the faith, after great and zealous labours in the conversion of their country. They expired at the close of the fifth day.

2. At Mons, in France, in the year 1639, Father Balthasar Belli, a Frenchman, a man of great innocence and exact religious life. Ten years prior to his death, he had devoted himself at Lyons to the service of the sick, but escaped contagion; entering again upon the same conflict, he was seized with the plague after fifteen days attendance on the sick, and went to receive the reward of his labours.

3. At Rome, in the year 1659, Wenceslaus Kolowrat, a Bohemian student of theology, illustrious for noble birth and virtue. Having received permission to enter the Society from the Emperor Ferdinand III., and from his mother, whose only son he was, he exclaimed: "I rejoiced when it was said to me, we will go into the house of the Lord! How lovely are Thy tabernacles, O Lord of Hosts." He endeavoured to conceal as much as he could from others the nobleness of his birth, out of true humility and love of poverty; and disposing of all his patrimony, when it was suggested that with leave of Superiors he might retain something for his own private use, he exclaimed with holy horror, "May God forbid it! He certainly will provide me, in whatever college I live, with a bit of cloth to make me a habit as a Religious." In reply to the suggestion of another, that he should not offend the eyes of his noble family by too old a dress, he answered with St. Aloysius' dilemma: "Either those who see me are strangers to me or are not; if they are strangers, it is no matter; if they are not, they will be edified." When he fell sick, a noble lady who was related to him sent him some nice food, suitable for the sick. He would not take it, as being too delicate; saying, it was fit for one Count Kolowrat who was now no more, but too good for a poor Religious. Though he had given to the Society more than was sufficient to found a college, he would not accept the honours of a Founder. He often asked his friends to pray for him, that he might become a great Saint; and as such he lived and died, though he was not aware of it. His body was laid under

the tomb of St. Aloysius, near to that of the Blessed John Berchmans.

4. At Paris, in the year 1708, Father Charles Le Gobien, a native of St. Malo, Secretary of the Missions, to which he gave his assiduous care. At the same time, the gift he had in the guidance of souls drew to him a great number of persons; and he may be said to have been the victim of his zeal, for the sickness that carried him off had no other cause than his excessive labour. His equability of soul, his sweetness, patience in sufferings, and great charity, made him dear to all. He died at the age of fifty-five.

OCTOBER 10.

1. At Oviedo, in Spain, in the year 1591, died Father Garcias de Alarcon, a Spaniard. Whilst yet a boy, he persuaded his younger brother, for the love of Christ's Passion, while at table, to set aside, with himself, at a signal which he gave, whatever was most pleasing to their palate. Moved by the example of St. Francis Borgia, he asked to be admitted to the Society, in which he discharged the offices of Master of Novices, Rector, Provincial, and Visitor, with admirable and conscientious attention to his duties. For many years he never touched the evening meal, rose at midnight for prayer, after which he rested for an hour, and then rose for meditation with the rest. He said to the Fathers who stood around his death-bed, and whom he saw lamenting: "You have no reason to grieve at my death, for I enjoy more comfort now than I ever had in life." He appeared to one at Valladolid who was grieving over his death, and said that he was now living with his good God in eternal glory.

2. At Saragossa, in Spain, in the year 1593, Father Honoratus Abella, a Spaniard, remarkable for the greatest modesty, and for innocence of life. His very appearance was so full of purity and virginal modesty, that it was sufficient to repel attempts made against his virtue.

3. At Straubingen, in Germany, in the year 1634, after the loss of five others, martyrs of charity, Father Adam Straub, a German, fell the last victim in service of the plague-stricken; a man illustrious for religious virtue and for his skill in government, having been Rector of three colleges and of two residences. Thirteen of the Society died at Munich in the same glorious cause of charity.

4. At Cracow, in Poland, in the year 1666, Father Gabriel Kacski, a Pole, for thirty-two years Socius to the Master of Novices. He had a great love for prayer, to which he gave each day two hours more than the Rule prescribes for Novices. He often said that his most ardent desire was to die in the Society; in return for which he received the gift of strengthening those whose vocation was in danger. Towards the end of his life his intellect became weak; but his life-long habits of obedience made him as submissive and docile as a child. He died at the age of seventy-two, after fifty-two years spent in the Society.

OCTOBER 11.

1. On a desert isle, in the Indian Ocean, in the year 1555, died Father Nicholas Pasqual, Father Andrew Gonzalez, and Alphonsus Lopez. They were on their way to Abyssinia, to devote themselves to the teaching of youth and the promotion of Christianity; but their ship was wrecked on the shore of a desert island. A great portion of the crew escaped in the boats, and invited the Fathers to come with them; but they preferred to remain on shore with the ship's company, who were left to die of hunger, that they might be a consolation to the living and assist the dying. Thus, after the others had died of famine, they also for want of food fell victims of their heroic charity.

2. At Naples, in the year 1569, Father John Pedelongo, an Italian. He had been a Doctor of Law, and of great skill in his profession; but having one day seen a man condemned by the judges whom he knew to be innocent, he resolved to quit the world, and having distributed his goods to the poor, he entered the Society. He asked out of humility to be allowed to study merely what was sufficient to hear confessions; and being charged to this ministry, he acquitted himself of it with most edifying fervour and assiduity; being confessor to great multitudes of seculars, and charged with the confessions of Ours, so that he was commonly called the "Father Confessor." He was greatly noted for modesty of eyes, which he never seemed to raise from the ground. He was appointed Master of Novices; and in his last sickness gave an admirable example of invincible patience. He died a holy death at the time he himself had predicted.

3. At Lomza, in Poland, in the year 1624, Nicholas Gruda, a Lay-

brother, with four others, died a martyr of charity attending upon the plague-stricken.

4. At Cracow, in Poland, in the year 1591, Father Stanislaus Warsewich. In Germany, as a student, he had learned heresy from Philip Melancthon. Returning to his country he repented of his error, and coming to Braunsberg he recognized the place, as shown to him in a dream when a boy, became acquainted with the Society, and entered it at Rome on the 24th of November, 1567, being then thirty-seven years old. He lived in the Society twenty-four years, leaving a bright example of modesty, charity, obedience, humility, and zeal in combating vice and heresy. He was Rector of the College of Wilna for eight years, then of the College of Lublin for six years. He brought back to the bosom of the Church many heretics among the first nobility of Poland. In Sweden, whither he was sent by Gregory XIII., he sustained by his labours the faith which was falling; and there he was tutor to the Prince who was afterwards Sigismund III., King of Poland. He yearly commemorated the day on which he resolved to enter the Society, saying, "that every good had come to him together with it." In the year 1590, being elected Procurator of the Province, he came to Rome; and on his return to Cracow, where the pestilence was raging, asked to be allowed to devote himself to the care of the sick, and in this duty died a martyr of charity. Some years after his death, he is said to have appeared to Father Peter Scarga, who was on his sick-bed, and bade him ask of God ten more years of life, which Father Scarga obtained.

OCTOBER 12.

1. At Madrid, in Spain, in the year 1600, died Father Louis Molina, a Spaniard, of great name among later theologians, and whose authority, though by many assailed, remains still unshaken, Paul V. having decreed in 1606 that all that Molina taught should stand uncondemned. Besides learned commentaries on the First Part of St. Thomas, and the entire concord between Grace and Free Will, which was the much disputed dogma, he published six volumes *De Justitia et Jure*, showing such knowledge of Civil Law, that it is quite a marvel how a man who spent his life in the study of theology should have acquired such familiarity with it.

Nor was Molina less remarkable for his virtue as a Religious than for his learning as a theologian. When past sixty, and constantly engaged in study, he strictly adhered to common life in food and clothing; and the Breviary which he used was so worn that the Little Hours were scarcely capable of being read. He was as prompt as the most exact Novice to hasten to perform the humblest offices of the house.

2. At Ingoldstadt, in Germany, in the year 1618, Father James Rhem, a German, remarkable for innocence, which he guarded by custody of eyes and severe mortification. He was very devout to the Blessed Virgin, in whose honour he instituted a Sodality of the "Conferences of Mary," in which the Sodalists held pious discourse on our Lady. While the choir in the Chapel was singing the Litany of the Blessed Virgin, he was desirous to know which title was most pleasing to her. She appeared to him and gave him to understand that the title of "Mother most admirable" was the most pleasing to her. He therefore ordered this to be repeated three times. He was more than once seen raised from the ground during Mass, and knew what was passing at a distance, or foretold the future.

3. At Mexico, in the year 1637, Father John de Ledesma, a native of America, of Spanish descent. He entered the Society at the age of fifteen, and in the novitiate was a model of piety. Afterwards he applied himself to his studies, so as to be accounted an oracle, and to be consulted from all parts, being cited by his fellow professor among other authors. In his old age, as Rector of the College of Mexico, he loved to act as Sacristan, attending to the altars, sweeping the church, and even lighting the candles in public. He wore pointed iron chains, and his disciplines were so severe, that his books, table, and walls were besprinkled with his blood. His affection for the native Indians was very great. He instructed, fed them, and defended their interests; and in a great inundation he was seen in a canoe carrying provisions to them which he had begged. For three years during a pestilence he devoted himself to their care. The Canons, Religious Orders, and Magistrates of the city attended his funeral.

OCTOBER 13.

1. At Rome, in the year 1574, died Father Sebastian Romeo, an

Italian. For nineteen years he was Superior of the Roman College with singular prudence and great humility, on account of which he was especially beloved by our Holy Father St. Ignatius. Although he was distracted with many laborious occupations, he would not be relieved, but sought labour after labour, saying, "that the men of the Society should never rest except when sick." Hence he appeared after death to Father Julius Mancinelli, reclining on a rich couch under a snow-white canopy, to signify the happiness of eternal rest which he had gained after his constant labours. St. Ignatius often tried him, with extraordinary orders to advance him in perfection, and to give others an example of blind obedience. He was grave, affable, and kind to all; of great devotion to the Blessed Virgin, which he promoted in the Roman and German Colleges. He suffered a martyrdom from his infirmities, which he bore with the greatest patience; and was full of joy and contentment at the approach of death.

2. At Huy, in Belgium, in the year 1653, Philip Francis Pennant, a Belgian, Master of the schools. After lying for six months, deprived of the use of hands and feet by paralysis, the Virgin Mother of God, to whom he had earnestly prayed, appeared to him in his sleep, with the Infant JESUS, and accompanied by St. Francis Xavier on the one side, and Father Mastrilli on the other. He learned from her that his cure was to be wrought by St. Francis Xavier: and upon the application of the medal, representing St. Francis in the act of curing Father Mastrilli, he gradually recovered the use of his hands, so as to be quite well at the Feast of St. Francis Xavier. But as some doubted, and ascribed the miracle to other causes, he fell sick again; and again applied the medal to the parts affected, and again immediately recovered the use of them. In gratitude he always wore round his neck that medal of St. Francis Xavier.

3. At Zagrabe, in Hungary, in the year 1621, Father Alexander Dobokay, a Hungarian. He reckoned among other favours received from God, the circumstance that, when a secular, after Holy Communion, he heard these words whispered in his right ear: "Enter the Society." A ball of bright light was seen by a certain nobleman over the head of Father Alexander as he preached on Christmas Day. It was remarked, with admiration, that during his long and varied exercise of government, though severe and stern in preserving religious discipline, he never admonished any one sharply. He was so fervent in prayer, that he was more than once seen raised from the ground.

OCTOBER 14.

1. At Toulouse, in France, in the year 1621, died Father William Trebosic, a Frenchman. When Minister of the College, he was attentive to every want, and watchful over every duty. If any one had not complied with the rule of sweeping his room, he would sweep it in his absence; leaving the sweepings at the door, to admonish him. He toiled in arduous and on distant missions, with little sustenance for the body; and many severe disciplines. He vowed, a little before death, for the conversion of a certain gentleman, to wear a hairshirt for a week, with discipline to blood. He obtained his petition, though prevented by mortal sickness from accomplishing his vow.

2. At Lisbon, in Portugal, in the year 1369, Jerome de Silva, a Portuguese Lay-brother; an excellent Religious man, and a great observer of rule. It was he who often saw the Venerable Father Suarez absorbed in prayer and surrounded with a heavenly light; and who received Holy Communion from Father Suarez, after death, appearing to him in an unfrequented chapel. He had been taken by the Rector as his companion on the Feast of the Presentation; and, the Rector riding forwards, he turned into a chapel by the roadside, and there lamented that he could not receive Communion, as he was used always to do on that day, when he saw Father Suarez coming to him with a pyx of gold, and heard him say that he was sent by divine appointment to give him the happiness of receiving, and at the same time gave him Holy Communion from the pyx. He then overtook the Rector, who, on returning to the house, received by letter an account of all that had befallen Brother Jerome, from a Nun of the Order of St. Clare.

3. At Rennes, in France, Father William de la Rongère, native of that place. Entering the Society at the age of twenty-eight, he showed particular talent for the direction of souls, whom he drew to God by holy industries and sweetness of manner. He used to say, that to enjoy great peace in the Society, it was necessary, after the maxim of St. Francis of Sales, to ask for nothing, and to refuse nothing. Twice he devoted himself to the service of the plague-stricken and escaped the infection. In his last sickness, he reproached himself, as if it had been by cowardice

that he had not given his life in that heroic work of charity. His funeral was attended by a great concourse of people.

OCTOBER 15.

1. At Cilia, in Styria, in the year 1646, Father Paul Cyrian, a Hungarian, a martyr of charity. When the plague was raging in that city, and the sick were dying without a Confessor, Father Paul, then at Grüin, eagerly asked for the post, but found the people of the town, to whom the Society was little known, so ill-minded towards him, that he could get no lodging, nor so much as a piece of bread, except from the sick of the plague. Notwithstanding this, the Father took possession of a house, the inmates of which had all died from the plague, and there, destitute of all supplies, began to visit the sick, to search for them in the neighbouring hills and valleys, to rouse the people by his discourses to a sense of their spiritual destitution, and to give them a respect for the Society—with regard to which, by his apostolic labours he brought about a change in their feelings and a great esteem for himself; but they did not long enjoy the good they were too long in discovering, for he was speedily carried off by the plague.

2. In the Philippine Islands, in the year 1650, Father Francis Puche, a Spaniard. He asked to be sent on a Mission of the most arduous kind. His clothing was mere patchwork. Once having found an old sick man, he carried him to his room, covered him with his cloak, gave him food, and instructed him in the Faith, baptized him, and sent him to heaven, to which, shortly after baptism, he departed. The gain of this soul gave him great joy, and he wore the cloak he had put on him only on festivals. One morning an official of the place came in haste to the house, to give notice that flames were seen issuing from it. After diligent inquiry, nothing else was discovered, except that at the time Father Francis was pouring out ardent affections in prayer while he took a severe discipline.

3. At Lyons, in France, in the year 1628, Father Ignatius Pompon died a martyr of charity, in service of the plague-stricken, with nine others. In the following year, twenty-one of the province of Lyons died in the same noble cause in various parts, and thirteen more in France, not of that province. The following year, 1630, gave France twenty-one crowns of martyrs in the same labour of charity.

October 16.

1. At Liége, in Belgium, in the year 1675, died Joseph Lowick, an English Lay-brother. The parents of this holy Brother were poor, but had suffered persecution for the Faith, and his mother was in prison when he was born. He made his perfection in the Society consist in exact obedience to the rule which recommends to Lay-brothers humility, industry, and obedience. It was his delight to undertake the humblest and most laborious occupations and those most repugnant to others. In the office of Porter, he became the advocate of the poor with the Rector, who, admiring his tender charity and solicitude for the suffering members of CHRIST, willingly acceded to his petitions. He excelled in entire conformity to the will of God, and this virtue was the source to him of imperturbable peace during life and at the moment of his holy death.

2. In a forest near Trêves, in the year 1588, died Richard Biler and John Sopp, Novices, both Germans, slain by the heretics out of the hatred they bore to Jesuits. Their bodies were left naked exposed to the wild beasts, but after some days were found intact, though the place was infested by packs of wolves.

3. At Douay, in Belgium, in the year 1652, Father Martin L'Hermite, a Belgian, a great lover of prayer and of great corporal austerity. All his prayers were full of fervour, but most fervent for those who had wronged him; and when he suffered calumny or other injuries from any ill disposed towards him, he betook himself to his room, and prostrate before the Crucifix, he would exclaim, "Lord, forgive them, for they know not what they do! By Thy tender mercies and Thy wounds, lay not this sin to their charge!" He was filled with such sweet joy as he thus prayed, that nothing gave him greater pleasure than to suffer some calumny. No task was so arduous, or so disagreeable, in the eyes of the world, that he would not undertake it without the least human respect, when enjoined by Superiors. On greater feasts he took a public discipline in the Refectory. He was seen on his knees creeping for a whole day among files of sick soldiers, lying at Armentiers in the open air, listening to their confessions and whispering to them consolation.

4. At Crumlow, in Bohemia, Father John Jähn, a German, in the

year 1625, a martyr of charity. Such was his ardent zeal in devoting himself to the service of the plague-stricken, that when the Rector would have interred him by night, the Magistrates interposed, and his funeral was solemnized with great magnificence by day, the Council carrying the coffin, and the clergy following with torches.

5. At the College of Limoges, in 1618, Father Ignatius Balsamon, a native of La Ponille. Of signal love of prayer, during which his face was often bathed with tears. Of great humility in the performance of the humblest offices; and of prompt obedience, so that one day, being vested for Mass, and being told that the Rector wanted him, he immediately quitted the sacerdotal vestments and went. It was remarked that none of those whom he formed in the Novitiate left the Society. He tenderly loved the Institute, and had the spiritual advancement of Ours much at heart, saying, that by the progress of a single one more glory is procured to God than by that of a great number of others. He was very exact in requiring observance of silence. He expired calmly, amid sufferings, in his poor and hard bed, which he would not allow to be changed, at the age of seventy-five.

OCTOBER 17.

1. At Nangasachi, in Japan, in the year 1637, died Father Marcellus Francis Mastrilli, a Neapolitan; miraculously cured of a mortal wound by the apparition of St. Francis Xavier, by whom he was commanded to take a vow of the Indian mission. He was a man of great innocence, and burned with a fervent desire of shedding his blood for Christ; and received many favours from the Blessed Virgin, St. Eustachius, and other Saints. On his way to Japan, he worked miracles and foretold the future. Scarcely had he set foot upon the land which he had so earnestly desired, than he was seized and imprisoned. A light was seen shining round his head while he prayed in his prison; and he appeared surrounded with glory, as the Saints are depicted, and was raised from the ground. He first suffered the torment of water poured down his throat, and then forced out by violence; afterwards he was burned with red hot irons; and then suspended by the feet, head downwards in the pit, according to the manner of tormenting in Japan. On the fourth day, being still alive,

he was taken out to be beheaded. The two first blows took no effect; at the third he uttered the names of JESUS and Mary, and his head was struck off. He was seen in glory immediately after his death by various persons in Europe, and healed the sick of their diseases.

2. At Granada, in Spain, in the year 1556, Father Alphonsus, or Basil de Avila, a Spaniard; a powerful preacher and labourer on the mission. His sermons were called the thunder and lightning and trumpet of God; for before mounting the pulpit he stirred the fire of charity by taking a discipline to blood. Yet, being requested to say something on his deathbed, for the edification of his brethren, he said: "Would that this tongue, Fathers, which has discharged the office of preaching, had been rather a clout in the kitchen to scour the pots and wipe the dishes." In a public sermon on a Sunday, he cited some unjust judges, who had condemned to public punishment a Priest and a Religious, to appear before the tribunal of God; and as they refused to listen to his admonitions here, declared that he would confront them there. A few days after, the Father died a holy death; and the same night one of the unjust judges died, and the other shortly after followed him. The families of both were reduced to beg their bread.

3. At Kalisch, in Poland, in the year 1605, Father John Cnaps, a Pole; a martyr of charity attending on the plague-stricken. He was a man of fervent zeal and exact religious life.

4. In the year 1628, Father Francis Bouton, a Frenchman. He entered the Society at the age of eighteen, and preserved until death his baptismal innocence. To virginity he added the merit of a Doctor, by the many excellent works he wrote; and the crown of a martyr, first by slavery, which he endured among the infidels, and then by giving his life in the service of the plague-stricken. Nine other Fathers died with him martyrs of charity.

OCTOBER 18.

1. At Goa, in the East Indies, in the year 1553, died Father Gaspar Barzeus, a Belgian, a truly apostolic man, the disciple of St. Francis Xavier in the preaching of the Gospel, and the emulator of his labours, being always much esteemed by him. He endured toil sufficient for the zeal of ten

active Missioners. He converted great numbers of idolators to the Faith, and brought back multitudes to penance, the chief scene of his labours being the great city of Ormuz. He was fearless in dangers, and full of confidence in Him Whose grace is strength in weakness. He was of great austerity of life, and many miracles are recorded of Him.

2. At Urgel, in Spain, in the year 1605, Father John Rico, a Spaniard, an excellent preacher. When Rector of the College of Majorca, contrary to the custom there, he preached in the polished dialect of Castile, and Blessed Alphonsus Rodriguez, who was his Companion, heard these words from God—"Your Rector will suffer in the fire of Purgatory for this sermon." On hearing this, Father John never afterwards used the language of Castile, and was assiduous in prayer and chastisement of his body. When Blessed Alphonsus prayed for him after his death, he saw him surrounded with rays of light, but especially with glory round his head, with which he was, as it were, crowned.

3. In America, among the Iroquois, in the year 1646, Father Isaac Jocques, a Frenchman. He burned with an incredible desire of suffering, and once, when he had spent the whole night prostrate before the Blessed Sacrament, and had asked for many and great sufferings, he heard a voice in reply—"Thy prayer is heard, it shall be granted to thee as thou hast asked. Take courage, and be stout of heart." Accordingly, when he was on the Mission instructing the Hurons in Canada, being taken by the Iroquois, most cruel savages, he suffered torments of the most excruciating kind with admirable fortitude, equalling the courage and endurance of the martyrs of antiquity.

OCTOBER 19.

1. At Lorraine, in the year 1637, died Father Laurence Worthington, an Englishman. He joined the Society in Spain, and taught philosophy at Cordova and Seville. He landed in England in 1612, and after three years on the Mission was apprehended and committed to the Gate House, whence he wrote a letter to Rome, saying that he heard more confessions in prison in one week than he would have heard in six or seven if free. After three years' imprisonment, he was banished, and died, worn out with labours, at Lorraine. He left a translation of Coster's *Life and Passion of Christ*.

2. At Bivona, in the year 1564, Father Peter Venusti, an Italian. Sent by our holy Father St. Ignatius into Sicily, he was there Master of Novices, and showed an apostolic zeal. Among others, he visited a certain Priest who was giving public scandal, and gently but firmly admonished him to change his life. In requital for his charitable admonitions, which were more than once repeated, he came upon Father Peter as he returned from the country, and with an axe struck him from behind three blows, the last of which gave him his death-wound upon the head, and stretched him on the ground. Being found by the people of Bivona weltering in his blood, and asked if he knew the murderer, he replied that he did, but would not give his name, saying—"Let him be: may God forgive him." And pronouncing the holy name of JESUS, he expired, leaving behind him a great reputation for sanctity.

3. At Louvain, in Belgium, in the year 1608, Father Martin Delrio, a Belgian. Of honourable parentage, he left the office of Chancellor of Brabant, and of the Exchequer, to embrace religious poverty. He brought to the Society not only the highest repute, knowledge of languages, and a mind stored with erudition in all the profane sciences, but an exemplary character as a Christian man. Becoming a child again in the Society, he showed himself as humble and docile as a Novice, as before he had been learned and celebrated as a Doctor. After his theological studies, he employed his acute mind in speculative theology and the interpretation of Holy Scripture. Candour of soul, and innocence, which he had preserved from his earliest years, shone in his countenance. His religious life may be summed up in two things; most humble obedience, and most obedient humility. For obedience he showed that he was ready to sacrifice his life. He wrote many works, both before and after his entrance into the Society. Amongst others, six books of disquisitions on Magic.

4. On the coast of Gallicia, in the year 1596, Father Francis Ronsillo, a Spaniard, and Father George Blancr, a Belgian. The ship in which they sailed was wrecked off Neri, and a few escaped by swimming, or on planks, while others were dashed to pieces on the rocks. The vessel heaving on one side, made a bridge with its mast to the shore, by which some of the chief of the crew escaped, and exhorted the Fathers to follow them and save their lives. They refused so long as any remained in the ship, and there were still three hundred in it. Whilst they heard the confessions of

these, a huge wave sunk them all. Their bodies were thrown on shore, and buried in a neighbouring chapel.

5. At Avignon, in France, in the year 1791, Father Anthony Nolhuc, born at Puy in Velay; at the time of the suppression of the Society, Rector of the Novitiate at Toulouse. He often spoke to the Novices on the happiness of martyrdom, for which he sighed. After the suppression, he undertook the care of a parish in Avignon, and to supply the wants of his numerous poor, lived a frugal and austere life, thus preparing for his glorious combat. Arrested by the Revolutionists, he was shut up with a crowd of captives, amongst whom he was massacred, after two days' confinement, by the blows of an iron crowbar. Before his death, he gave the aids of religion to sixty of his fellow captives who died with him. The body of the Father, when the corpses were removed, was found by the people, who eagerly sought for it, covered with fifty wounds, and only identified by the crucifix and ecclesiastical dress. His gown was pulled to pieces for relics, and his body lay eight days exposed for the veneration of the people.

October 20.

1. At Baden, in Germany, in the year 1573, died Father George Schorick, a German, who was received into the Society by our holy Father St. Ignatius, and being ordered to transfer his talents to the study of literature from the office of cook, wrought such wonders for the faith in Germany, that he was selected by the Duke Albert, to accomplish the task of bringing back Bavaria to the Catholic Faith. In this he was so successful, that he was sent to Baden for the same purpose, where he died of poison, administered to him by the heretics.

2. At Constance, in Germany, in the year 1635, Father Balthasar Weguelin, a German. For thirty years he was an exact Procurator of the College, and, at the same time, an indefatigable Missioner. He died a martyr of charity, in service of the plague-stricken, together with twenty-one companions, in different parts of Germany.

3. At Posen, in Poland, in the year 1655, Father Stanislaus Woysza, a Pole. Born a shapeless mass, without head, and scarce a human form, he was wholly restored to shape by St. Stanislaus Kostka, to whom he had been

offered. None could be more prompt in attending the sick and hearing their confessions, or those of others in health. He was also most devoted to the aid of the souls in Purgatory, from which he had frequent visits, to ask for help. Most forgiving of injuries, he offered to God, for the space of thirteen years, on fixed days every week, certain prayers and mortifications for one who had done him wrong. Ripe for Heaven, he died a martyr, in the service of the plague-stricken.

4. At Louvain, in Belgium, Francis Gruythusen, a Belgian Scholastic. Not yet a Priest, he anticipated his time, devoting his youth to the service of the plague-stricken, and died a martyr of charity, with nineteen others, in various parts of Belgium.

5. At the College of Puy, in the year 1680, Father James Montal, at the age of eighty-four and full of merits, the successor of St. John Francis Regis in his missions, and imitator of his Apostolic virtues. He divided his time between prayer and works of mercy. Full of sweetness to others, and severe to himself, he lived on uncooked vegetables, and often passed many days without food. His devotion to the Blessed Virgin and his Guardian Angel obtained for him many extraordinary graces, and he worked many miracles during his life and after his death. His severity to himself occasioned wounds, the neglect of which hastened his death. The repute of his sanctity was very great; and the people were so eager to obtain relics of him, that it was necessary to inter the body with doors shut. Many graces were obtained by his intercession, and his memory has remained in benediction.

OCTOBER 21.

1. At Nangasachi, in Japan, in the year 1633, died Father Julian Nacaura, born of a princely family in Japan, and who had been Ambassador from the King of Bungo to Pope Gregory XIII., to declare his obedience to the Apostolic See. On his return from Rome, he was admitted into the Society; and having led the life of a good Religious and an active missioner, he was taken and suspended in the torment of the pit, used in Japan. As he was being led to it, he addressed the people who followed him, and said that he was that same Julian who had gone as Ambassador from Japan to Rome, when Japan was wiser and more humane, and that he now laid down his life for that true faith, the faith of Rome. After three days torment, he went to

receive the crown of eternal glory. Two Japanese Novices, Peter and Matthew, suffered with him by the same death of the pit.

2. At Palermo, in Sicily, in the year 1656, Father Aloysius La Nuza, a Sicilian, of noble parentage, the Apostle of his country, illustrious for the gain of innumerable souls, and for his prophecies and miracles. He piously fulfilled the duty of a preacher for the space of nearly forty years. Some persons saw bright rays of light streaming from his forehead, and illuminating his hearers as he spoke; others beheld an Angel standing by his side as he preached. While he prayed, light was seen issuing from his mouth towards Heaven, and his soul was beheld mounting thither in company with St. Ignatius, St. Francis Xavier, and others of the Society, together with innumerable souls, the fruit of his labours.

3. In the College of La Plata, in South America, Father Emmanuel Ortega, a Portuguese, a great labourer for the glory of God and salvation of souls, in Portugal, Brazil, Paraguay, and the Province of Peru. He was the faithful companion of Father Joseph Anchieta, who foretold that he would suffer great things for the saving of souls. At the peril of his life, in a great inundation, he swam to baptize the Indians who were being drowned. He was often in similar perils from floods, in the darkness of night, in hunger, and amid the savages. A large thorn, which had pierced his leg, caused him much suffering, and after some years brought about his death. He died at the age of sixty-nine, a Spiritual Coadjutor, having refused the profession of the four vows which was offered him after he had taken his grade, lest any relaxation should be made in the Institute on his account.

4. At Koningsberg, in Prussia, in the year 1653, Father John Kihn, a Prussian, who, in that populous city of heretics, during the time of the fearful plague, administered the Sacraments to Catholics, and gave to heretics what help he could, to the amazement of the Protestants, and died a martyr of zeal and charity.

OCTOBER 22.

1. At Nangasachi, in Japan, in the year 1633, Father John Matthew Adami, an Italian. Having suffered many and great hardships in the preaching of the Gospel and the salvation of souls, he was at last taken and starved for a time in prison, then hung with his head downwards in the

torment of the pit, in which he survived five days, and then went to receive a martyr's crown.

2. At Kalisch, in Poland, in the year 1634, Father Blasius Plozzins, a Pole. Being a most virtuous youth, he was ordered by his Superior to pray to God for rain during a drought. He obeyed, and a copious rain fell. In the Society he was a most exact observer of the rules and a holy Religious. He said that he had asked two things of God; that his sickness might be severe and short, so that he should give little trouble to the house, and that he might die soon. He obtained both his requests, and a foreknowledge of the time of his death.

3. At Brünn, in Moravia, in the year 1648, Father Samuel Richter, a Moravian. Thirsting for the salvation of souls, he was most prompt in assisting them at all times; and, on one occasion, took the cup from his lips, with which he was about to quench his thirst when weary with labour. He looked upon the words of the Psalmist as addressed to himself—"The poor is left to thee, thou shalt be the helper of the orphan." He was indeed their zealous helper, until he fell a glorious martyr of charity, in assisting the plague-stricken.

October 23.

1. At Liége, in Germany, in the year 1634, died Ralph Russell, an English Scholastic. In order that he might adorn his soul, which had never been sullied by grievous sin, with more admirable virtue, he added two practices to the most exact observance of the rules; namely, to allow of no moment of time to elapse without fruit, and never to break a firmly fixed resolution of speaking always on pious subjects.

2. At Cassari, in Sardinia, in the year 1635, Father John Andrew Manconi, a Sardinian; celebrated for his great virtues, and for the gift of preaching. Being most devout to the Blessed Virgin, he was often favoured with visions of her; but always at the foot of the Cross. Once, however, when troubled with an importunate imagination, and dejected on account of it, he had the happiness of beholding the Queen of Heaven, accompanied by St. Catherine and St. Cecilia, who appeared in wonderful beauty, and said: "See whether beauty that decays can in any way be compared with this." Being asked, just before he died, what gave him

most consolation at that moment; he replied: "It is, that I never sought for myself any consolation."

3. At Seville, in Spain, in the year 1647, John de Soria, a Spanish Lay-brother. He left his employment as a merchant, and when he was on the point of being married, to enter the Society; being moved to it by hearing a sermon of one of our Fathers. His fervour in Religious life was increased by a miraculous cure through the intercession of St. Ignatius. He rose several hours before the Community to pray. Twice a day he gave some time to the careful reading of the Rules. He bound himself by vow to commit no deliberate venial sin; confessed frequently in the week, and made a general confession of the week every Saturday; being permitted to communicate daily. He fasted twice a week in honour of the Blessed Virgin, and the eves of her Festivals on bread and water; and took every day a discipline, and even three times in the day when he desired to obtain a particular grace.

OCTOBER 24.

1. At Coimbra, in Portugal, in the year 1604, died Father Jerome Carvalho, a Portuguese. He daily gave six hours to prayer, and genuflected a hundred times. He loved poverty so dearly that, out of curiosity, some one counted in his habit ninety patches. Once, when anxiously thinking on the pains of Purgatory, he saw the Virgin Mother of God, who appeared to him and said, "that he should lay aside his fears, for that she was the advocate of the afflicted, not only in this life but also in Purgatory." Being forty-five years of age, he put in writing that he had fifteen years yet to live, and so it proved to be.

2. At Rouen, in France, in the year 1626, Father John Le Sec, a Frenchman, who, full of charity and zeal, twice devoted his life to the service of the sick of the plague. Being very devout to the Blessed Virgin, he constantly implored her, that as she had obtained for him the grace to enter the Society, so she would also obtain for him perseverance in it. About to make the Spiritual Exercises, he foretold that it would be for the last time, and mentioned the day on which he should die, which proved to be true.

3. At Murcia, in Spain, in the year 1558, Father Mark Antony Fontova, a Spaniard. He was Vice-Provincial of Aragon, in the absence of

the Provincial at Rome, when the plague broke out in some parts of Spain, and he offered himself with heroic zeal for the service of the sick, and died, with two others, a martyr of charity. The same year, two Lay-brothers died in the same service at Valencia, and several others at Barcelona, with their Rector, Father John Gesti, and in the following year, at Murcia, Father Gaspar Lopez. At Gandia, in the year 1560, four others died in the same service of charity.

4. At Alcala, in Spain, in the year 1593, Father Michael de Torres, a Spaniard. Before he entered the Society he was Rector of the University of Alcala, and much prejudiced against the Society, and being sent to Rome to defend the rights of the University, avoided the conversation and the very sight of ours, and could not even endure to hear mention made of them, being set against them by the assertions of the ill-disposed towards them; so much so, that with difficulty John de Vega, the Spanish Ambassador, prevailed on him to see Father Salmeron by night. By much entreaty, Father Salmeron induced him to see St. Ignatius. De Torres came to meet him prepared with prayer, as against a wizard. St. Ignatius saluted him in his usual kindly manner, so that, struck with his appearance and affability, and by the "Spirit which spoke in him," he embraced him, saying, "I am yours; what would you have me to do?" St. Ignatius admitted him to the Society, and called him the "Apple of his eye." Shortly afterwards he sent him to found the College of Salamanca. He was afterwards Visitor and Provincial of Portugal. He joined great prudence to rare simplicity, rose every night to pray and take a discipline to blood, though for forty years he had no consolation in prayer. It is said that St. Francis Borgia saw his name written in the Book of Life. He was suffering from a swelling, which stopped the passage of his throat, but it was freed on the day that he died, so that he could receive the Viaticum. He died a holy death, at the age of eighty-five.

OCTOBER 25.

1. At Neti, in Italy, in the year 1637, died Father Michael Montalto, a Sicilian. From his entrance into the Society, he applied himself especially to the love of suffering, of poverty, and to the pursuit of perfection, as a means to which he sought to detach himself from all earthly affections,

October 25, 26.

and had recourse to the Blessed Virgin, towards whom he had a tender devotion from his infancy. He fasted on the eves of her Festivals on bread and water, and watched through the night, passing it prayer and pious reading. On her Feasts he put flowers before her picture in his room, and renewed his vows, adding one of devoting himself to her service. He made frequent use of chains and disciplines, was a man of few words, and seldom seen except at the altar, pulpit, and confessional; he slept, wrapt in a cloak, in a chair. He gave as a token of gratitude to the Father who attended him in his last sickness an iron discipline, saying—"It is all the riches I had in this world."

2. In Brazil, in the year 1645, Father Antony de Mattos, a Portuguese. Having been for two years wasting in a Dutch prison, he acquired there the reputation of a Saint. He used to take his sleep at night standing, resting on his stick, that he might wake more easily to give praise to God. When Rector or Provincial, he gave no answer to the questions put to him until he had collected his thoughts, by fixing his eyes on the crucifix, or looking on the ground. To some who begged his prayers, while he said that he would pray for them, he at the same time bid them avoid such and such a hidden sin. To one who was afraid of trusting himself to a sea voyage for fear of pirates, he gave advice to make confession of some secret sins, and perform some devotions, promising a secure voyage. And so it turned out to be.

3. At Landsperg, in Germany, in the year 1636, Magnus Augerer, a German Lay-brother. For twenty-two years he was a model of industrious labour as baker, gardener, and man-of-all-work, without any cessation of toil, or diminution of piety. As he worked, he held his rosary by his teeth in his mouth, and while his hands were employed thus, told his beads, and invoked the Blessed Virgin with his tongue. A rare example of industry seldom equalled.

October 26.

1. At Toledo, in Spain, in the year 1584, died Father Francis Strada, a preacher of such zeal, that the Society has seldom had his equal. By the wonderful force of his eloquence he moved, softened, and turned men's hearts as he pleased, even when young and not yet a Priest, and before he had made his higher studies. By his sermons, and the Exercises which

he gave with great skill, like one endued with the double spirit of an Elias, he stirred all Italy, Belgium, France, Portugal, and Spain, appeasing deadly discord among citizens and between states, filling religious houses with inmates, and establishing many Colleges of the Society. Being asked by Father Ribadeneira whence his eloquence came, he frankly replied that as he preached, a kind of impulse and light from heaven came into his soul, with which his whole heart was moved. Intent on labour and prayer, he slept little, and while he was sleeping, he found such knowledge of the homilies of St. John Chrysostom infused into his mouth from heaven, that he could preach from him as if he were all familiar to him, though he had not read him. Though he was so great a man, he always thought himself, and from his heart, an unworthy instrument of the Society.

2. At Cologne, in Germany, in the year 1574, Father Leonard Kessel, a Belgian; gained to the Society by the discourses of Father Strada. He was a man of great weight in word and deed, especially in preserving the city of Cologne from heresy. While assisting the plague-stricken, he not only cured their souls, but, by a special grace, their bodies also; so that it was commonly said, that all who confessed to Father Kessel got well quickly and amended their lives. He had an intense desire of seeing our holy Father St. Ignatius, who was still living, and of speaking to him; and on that account asked permission to go to Rome. The holy Father, complying with his pious wish, gratified him to the full, by appearing miraculously to him at Cologne.

3. At Nangasachi, in Japan, in the year 1633, Father Antony de Sousa, a Portuguese; who being banished for life from Japan, returned; and first suffered the torture of water poured into the mouth and forced out by violence; then was hung with his head downwards in the pit. On the eighth day, having consummated his course, he expired a glorious martyr.

4. At Rome, in the year 1556, Father Andrew Frusia, a Frenchman, no less renowned for learning than for innocence, so that he was accounted by St. Ignatius and by others as an Angel. He was learned in the Latin, Greek, and Hebrew tongues, a great theologian, lawyer, physician, mathematician, and excellent musician, eloquent speaker, a poet of the highest order, and with the gift of composing improviso. He translated the *Spiritual Exercises* of our holy Father from Spanish into Latin, and this was the first work printed in the Society. He was Professor of Scripture

in the Roman College, and then Rector of the German College, in which he died full of patience and joy after protracted suffering.

OCTOBER 27.

1. At Rome, in the year 1705, died Father Thyrsus Gonzalez, a Spaniard, the thirteenth General of the Society. He governed the Society for eighteen years; in the opinion of all, and of the Court of Rome, a man of exalted piety and learning. He was in his method exact according to the Institute, of great diligence in his office, regardless of all human respect, and constant and courageous in adversity. Distinguished by devotion to the Saints of the Society, he erected in the Gesù the magnificent Chapel of our holy Father, deposited in a rich urn the relics of St. Aloysius under the High Altar, and converted into a Chapel the room consecrated by the death of St. Stanislaus Kostka. He was an ardent propagator of the faith, and promoter of the missions, and crowned a long life by invincible patience in his sufferings during his last illness. He died at the age of eighty-four, having been sixty-three years in the Society.

2. At Valencia, in Spain, in the year 1615, Father Peter Belido, a Spaniard. Besides the usual hour, he gave two others to prayer in the morning, and in the evening as many as the nature of his duties and obedience allowed him. He used to begin his meditation with the Passion of Christ, then he would elevate his mind to the Divine attributes, and finally offer his will as a holocaust in Sacrifice to God. He was seen to come from prayer with his face all radiant. He admonished many persons of most hidden secret things. At his death, when some one said, "Lift up your heart to Heaven," he answered, "It is already there." A holy person, of repute for sanctity, being asked whether all ours in that College would be saved, and whether they would suffer Purgatory, replied, that all would be saved, but only three without Purgatory one of whom was Father Bellido. When the Superior told this to Father Peter a little before his death, he joyfully exclaimed, "Glory be to the Father, and to the Son, and to the Holy Ghost," and happily expired.

3. At Bourdeaux, in France, in the year 1620, Father William Baile, a Frenchman. He possessed a wonderful power in dealing with heretics, so that few of them who treated with him, went away unconverted. When

called to prepare the sick for death, before going out of the house he gave himself a merciless discipline for them. He would not ascend the pulpit without taking first a severe discipline, wearing a hairshirt, and touching his tongue with holy water. He reclaimed the people of Saintoigne from the heresy of Calvin, with which they were much infected, and with such zeal, that from the time of St. Eutropius, the Apostle of Saintoigne, no one is thought to have so much advanced religion in those parts. He discovered without fail the arts of sorcerers and witches. In the Holy Sacrifice, when, about to communicate, he held the adorable Host in his hand, he would say, "Lord JESUS, give me souls, for which Thou art the Saving Victim." He was so famed for the zeal of souls that his name was applied proverbially to all in general who were conspicuous in the labour of saving souls.

OCTOBER 28.

1. In the East Indies, in the year 1568, died Father Francis Lopez, a Portuguese. After many and great labours for the salvation of souls, he was taken by the Moors on the voyage from Cochin to Goa, and for a long time urged by many solicitations to apostatize and become a Mahometan. He rejected with abhorrence the impious proposal; at length his breast was pierced through with a spear, his head cleft asunder with a scimitar, and his body thrown into the sea.

2. Upon the British Sea, in the year 1596, Father George Vallier and Father Francis Rosillo, Spaniards. Being ordered to sail with the armament of Martin de Padilla against England, they were caught in a fearful storm at night. All hope of safety being lost, the Fathers aided the perishing with all the means in their power, until they themselves were swallowed up in the sea. A few who by some means escaped, declared that in the darkness, so dense that they could not see one another, the Fathers' faces, as they ran to and fro with the Crucifix uplifted, shone so bright that it seemed like the light of day.

3. At Mexico, in America, in the year 1572, Father Francis Bazain, a Spaniard. He asked for the Indian Mission, to see, as he said, whether a useless tree transplanted thither would produce fruit. In the Society he sedulously concealed the nobility of his family, which was that of

the Marquisate of Santa Cruz, and his learning, under the name of Francis Arana and amid the labours of an humble and industrious Lay-brother for the space of five years. When this was all discovered, he was put to his studies, and being ordained Priest, crossed the sea to America, and on his voyage thither, and on the mission there, gave evident proofs of Apostolic zeal and virtue.

4. At Aquila, in the year 1656, Father Januarius Pisa, a martyr of charity. During the plague he carried the sick in his arms, collected alms, and provided them with food, being sometimes miraculously aided in supplying them. In the midst of his labours he strove to avert the anger of God by fasts and disciplines to blood. He was seen surrounded with light while serving the plague-stricken or saying Mass. His death was revealed to him beforehand, and he had his grave prepared, from which his body was afterwards removed to the Church; and though buried seven months in quicklime, was found incorrupt.

OCTOBER 29.

1. In Japan, near Fuxima, in the year 1633, died Father Matthew de Couros, a Portuguese; a truly apostolic man in his labours and sufferings. He was not only an indefatigable missioner, but for nine years governed the Church of Japan as Vicar-Apostolic, and was twice Provincial in most difficult times and in the midst of a fierce persecution. Providence protected the servant of God in many wonderful ways through his constant dangers, for the consolation of that afflicted Church. Sometimes he wandered over unfrequented mountains, through forests and thickets, to escape the scouts in search of him; at other times he passed seas and rivers, hastening from province to province. Once he lived eight months in a dark subterranean cavern; and again, flying from his pursuers, hid himself in a narrow place of concealment, covered like that of St. Felix, by the suddenly spun webs of spiders. Thus, amid so many dangers, and dying daily, he was worn out, and resolved to comply with the original desire which he had in coming to Japan, and to give himself up to the Magistrates of Meaco, that, if it were the will of God, he might die a martyr by fire. But such was not the divine will; for briefly afterwards a messenger came to summon him to attend a sick leper, lying

in a hut, out of the city, in a retired spot: whither, when he was brought, he himself fell sick, broken with his labours, and peacefully expired in the forty-third year of his missionary life in Japan.

2. At Antwerp, in Belgium, in the year 1625, when the plague was raging with the greatest fury, Thomas Verleyn, a Belgian Lay-brother, died a martyr of charity, together with fifteen others who died in the same glorious service, attending the plague-stricken.

3. In America, among the Iroquois, in the year 1646, Father Isaac Jogues, a Frenchman. He burned with an incredible desire of suffering; and once when he had spent the whole night prostrate before the Blessed Sacrament, and had asked for many and great sufferings, he heard a voice in reply—"Thy prayer is heard; it shall be granted to thee as thou hast asked. Take courage and be stout of heart." Accordingly, when he was on the mission instructing the Hurons in Canada, being taken by the Iroquois, most cruel savages, he suffered torments of the most excruciating kind with admirable fortitude, equalling the courage and endurance of the martyrs of antiquity.

October 30.

1. At Mentz, in Germany, in the year 1620, died Father John Sylworst, a Belgian; who, with no less fruit than labour, gave assistance to the Catholics of Groeningen. Being on this account carried off to prison by the heretics, upon seeing it from a distance, he fell upon his knees and gave thanks to God for so great an honour. Before the judges he answered boldly, that he dared no less freely come there to convert the heretics, than they dared go to Antwerp to pervert the Catholics. In his perils and trials he was wont to ejaculate, with great confidence in God—"I am Thine, O save me."

2. At Presburg, in Hungary, in the year 1634, Father George Kaldi, a Hungarian; of great abilities, eloquence, and virtue. He preached, and wrote much and excellently against the heretics. He published the Bible in the Hungarian tongue, restored to its purity from their corruptions. At Tyrnau he openly rebuked the Prince of Transylvania, Gabriel Bethlehem, in the pride of his victories, because he had given over to the Turks so many thousands of Christians. His friends feared that on that account

it would go hard with his life, but he received greater honour and esteem from that Prince for his freedom, and was presented by him with a large sum of money for printing his Bibles. He was a Religious of great perfection and a model of exactitude, and a preacher of great force and eloquence.

3. At Caltagirona, in the year 1622, Father Francis Tarsia, an Italian. While living in world rather a free life, he happened to meet the Blessed Sacrament carried through the streets, when a ray of light issuing from It, so touched and altered him, that being suddenly changed into another man, he betook himself to the Society, and by his example brought many others to a better life. He was thenceforward remarkable for his devotion to the Holy Eucharist, and especially for frequent renewal of Spiritual Communion; and it pleased God to grant him from time to time heavenly consolations and visions, and delightful taste and odour in the reception of the Blessed Sacrament.

OCTOBER 31.

1. At Majorca, in the year 1617, Blessed Alphonsus Rodriguez, a Spanish Lay-brother; renowned for sanctity, most tenderly beloved by Christ our Lord and his most holy Mother, and by them adorned with many singular graces. They visited him when sick and suffering excruciating pains, and, sitting at the foot of his bed, comforted him with sweet conversation and completely cured him. He once in pious simplicity exclaimed: "O Mother of God, if you only loved me as much as I love you." To which the Blessed Virgin replied: "Alphonsus, you are mistaken; I love you more than you love me." At another time, when he was accompanying a Father, and bathed in sweat, was giving himself to prayer, the Blessed Virgin is said to have wiped away his sweat and tears. Many hidden and future things were revealed to him, and scarce anything he prayed for was refused. He merited these favours of Heaven by his profound humility and rigorous mortification. He took cruel disciplines, fasted much, took food without salt, and was continually on the watch for every opportunity of mortifying himself.

2. At Lyons, in France, in the year 1663, Father Theophilus Raynand, a Frenchman, born at Nice. His learning was most extensive, as is shown

by the nineteen volumes in folio, which he wrote on subjects the most
various, and by the eulogies of writers of the greatest repute and ability.
He added to learning extraordinary virtue. He was exact in observance
of rule, abstemious, and watchful over himself in conversation, and a great
lover of his Religious vocation, from which attempts were made to allure
him by splendid offers, but his fidelity remained unshaken.

NOVEMBER.

November 1.

1. At Ximabara, in Japan, in the year 1622, died the Blessed Peter Paul Navarro, an Italian, with two Lay-brothers his companions, Denys Fugixima and Peter Onizucca, Japanese, suffering martyrdom by fire. Father Peter prepared himself for so glorious a death by a general confession and the Exercises of our holy Father. His life was very austere, and he had studied the language of the country so well, that he was ready to preach at a moment's notice, and published many works in Japanese. He went to the stake, where he was burned by a slow fire, with his rosary round his neck and wearing a hairshirt, which was found afterwards unconsumed. He sang the Litanies alternately with his companions and brothers in labour and in martyrdom. A secular named Clement, who was a religious all but the habit, shared their happy lot.

2. At Lima, in Peru, in the year 1592, Father John Atiença, a Spaniard. As he was praying with much fervour at Valladolid, he felt upon his shoulders a load as of an Indian resting on him, and repeatedly saying in his ears, "Come and help me, come and help me." He did so effectually without delay, devoting himself to the missions of Peru, where he laboured for the conversion of the Indians, and braved the greatest difficulties with extraordinary courage, prudence, and zeal. Almost the whole city followed him to the grave, and venerated him as a Saint.

3. In France, near Beziers, in the year 1629, Father Claude à Sainte Colombe, a Frenchman. Being most devout to the Blessed Sacrament, he visited It almost every hour in a private chapel, and there he passed the night, taking scarcely any sleep. If at any time he could not say Mass, he endeavoured to repair the loss by making Spiritual Communion a hundred times in the day. He died a martyr of charity assisting the sick of a certain village, to whom he devoted himself when attacked by a pestilential sickness.

4. At Douay, in the year 1618, Father Gerard Vervian, after long and laborious service of the sick, and after having twice recovered from the disease, gave his life in the same happy service.

November 2.

1. At Douay, in France, in the year 1609, died Father George Colibrant, a Belgian, and a man of singular mortification. When commanded to moderate his numerous austerities, he replied with obedience that he would do so, but that God would replace them instead. Shortly after this he began to suffer from the stone. His familiar maxim was, "For Life Eternal"; and to this he directed all his life and actions.

2. In Germany, in the year 1642, Father Lawrence Passoki, a Silesian. He received the reward of his great services as Chaplain of the Catholic soldiers, in a glorious death; for, as he was hearing the confession of a wounded officer in the battle of Leipsic, he was taken by a heretic of the victorious party, and being asked who he was, replied a Catholic Priest. Being required to blaspheme the Blessed Virgin, he not only refused, but broke out into her fervent praise. He was accordingly first cut down with the stroke of a sword and then shot through the body, and so happily died. In the same battle, and occupied in the same duty, Father Matthew Cramer, a Bohemian, met with a similar death, and received a like reward.

3. At Granada, in Spain, in the year 1611, Father Aloysius Ponce, a Spaniard, son of the Duke of Arcos. The nobleness of his birth, enhanced the true spirit of humility, with which he offered himself for the most abject offices in the service of all. He so completely renounced the use of all earthly objects that he would neither receive nor give the least thing without first asking and obtaining leave. He was so close an occupant of his confessional, that he used to say, this was the only score on which he was entitled to his daily bread. Being warned by the physician of his approaching death, he exclaimed, "Blessed be God, Who has thought me worthy of so great a happiness as to see the hour for which I have longed when I shall die in His house."

NOVEMBER 3.

1. At Evora, in Portugal, in the year 1608, died Father Anthony Pinas, a Portuguese. Being very delicate, and expected to live only three or four years, as the physicians declared, he was not admitted into the Society. He positively maintained in spite of the physicians, that he should live long in the Society and survive them all. This proved true, and he thrice exposed his life in service of the plague-stricken, going through the greatest labours. One of his duties was to hear confessions any hour when summoned day or night. He preserved his vigorous health to the age of seventy-one. He kept his brother's letters for three years unopened and used them for the cover of his inkstand.

2. At Seville, in Spain, in the year 1609, Father Melchoir de Sanivan, a Spaniard. It was found necessary to send him away from the Noviceship, to appease the anger of his father, a man of high rank; but he bound himself by vow to return, which he did. The greater part of his life was spent in the government of Colleges and Provinces, and he was remarkable for the suavity with which he governed, while at the same time he was severe in punishing any infringement of religious discipline. He closed each day with a meditation on the remembrance of death, and the necessity of being on the watch for it.

3. At Ingolstadt, in Germany, in the year 1634, Michael Alber, a German Lay-brother. He died a happy death in service of the plague-stricken with four others, amongst whom was Father Thomas Resch, notable for his zeal, and for having in the space of thirteen years heard the confessions of a hundred and eleven thousand penitents.

NOVEMBER 4.

1. At Lisbon, in Portugal, in the year 1599, died Father Peter de Fonseca, a Portuguese; a pillar of the Society in Portugal, for his sanctity and religious wisdom, his learning and published works, also for his conduct, as well in his private capacity, as in that of Rector of the College of Coimbra, Provincial of Portugal, and Assistant at Rome. Philip the Second of Spain employed him in most important affairs. He established

by his unwearied industry, Refuges for orphans and converts, and a Seminary for Irish students. He commenced a house for persons reclaimed from bad life, founded hospitals, and invited into Portugal the Brothers of St. John of God, besides other works for the public good, set on foot by his indefatigable zeal. He was of admirable modesty in submitting his judgment to the opinion of others, and of wonderful power in tranquillizing troubled minds, and himself most imperturbable in the midst of troubles and afflictions. If he had received a wrong from any one, he used to say, "At any rate I will do him good whether he wishes it or not." All his life was as regular as clock work, so exactly was everything fixed at stated hours.

2. In Japan, in the year 1614, Father James de Mesquita, a Portuguese, after forty-eight years of missionary labour there. He conducted to Europe the three Ambassadors deputed by the Princes of Japan to make their submission to Pope Gregory XIII. Having returned to Japan during the time that a furious persecution was raging, he was banished the Kingdom, and died in exile, worn out with hardships, in a poor fisherman's hut.

3. At Syracuse, in Sicily, in the year 1621, Michael Fiori, an Italian Lay-brother. Though every day employed in cultivating a most beautiful garden, he never tasted of its fruits. To his extreme old age he disciplined himself every night to blood. While he was in his agony a stranger came to the door of the College, and illuminated with a number of lights the part of the house where Michael lay dying.

November 5.

1. At Tchao-tche, in China, in the year 1593, died Father Francis de Petris, an Italian. He preached Christianity in China amid labours and dangers. To a Lay-brother who needed strengthening in his vocation, he said that he had been called to the Society by the Blessed Virgin with these express words—"Enter into the Society of my Son, and persevere in thy vocation." He had prophetic knowledge of the time of his death, and having a slight attack of fever, sent for Father Ricci, whom he embraced with much affection, and said—"Farewell, my Father, God calls me;" and a few hours afterwards expired.

2. At Lima, in Peru, in the year 1613, Father Stephen Paez, a Spaniard. He was, at the time he died, Visitor and Provincial of Peru,

and united consummate prudence to sanctity. He was surnamed the Angel, and was remarkable for devotion to the Blessed Virgin, in whose honour he fasted every Saturday on bread and water, and was assisted by her in promoting the salvation of souls in those parts. He pushed forward to religious perfection by heroic victories over himself, and was most uniform and regular in all, even the smallest observances. When his body was being carried to the church after his death, St. Ignatius was seen coming from the high altar to meet Father Stephen and to bid him a joyful welcome.

3. At Valladolid, in Spain, in the year 1642, Father Louis de Valdivia, a Spaniard. Having crossed the sea to Peru, he was first Master of Novices in that Province, and then Professor of Theology. Sent thence to found the Province of Chili, he suffered much in behalf of the Indians, in protecting them from their oppressors. Afterwards he returned to Spain, to inform the King of the unhappy condition of the poor natives; and the King, perceiving his prudence and ability, offered him the Bishopric, which, when he refused, he insisted that he should accept of the office of Visitor Royal in that country, and, invested with royal authority, should ordain whatever he thought necessary for the peace and religious welfare of the people. With the consent of the General, Claudius Acquaviva, Father Valdiva accepted this most arduous office; and, crossing the seas, inspected the whole Province by regal authority, and rescued from iniquitous slavery more than ten thousand Indians, curbing the tyranny of their Spanish masters; and having arranged things according to his desire for the good of religion, returned to Spain to give an account to the King. He, to show his approval of the Father's work, endeavoured to force dignities upon him, which the humble Religious firmly declined.

4. In Persia, in the year 1660, Father Alexander de Rhodes, a Frenchman. He was the first to penetrate, with one companion, into the Kingdom of Tonquin, bordering on China, and there converted to Christianity more than five thousand souls, and among them not a few of the nobles and Mandarins. Ordered by the King to leave the country, he promoted Christianity by means of good Catechists, so that in three years' time the number of the faithful amounted to thirty thousand. He spread the faith with similar success in Cochin China, and, expelled from thence, returned to Europe. Again, with some companions, he passed into Persia, where, after some years of glorious toil, he passed to a better life, and rested from his labours in the Lord.

5. At the College of Syracuse, Father Michael Lætavalle; of great repute for virtue and sanctity, which God confirmed by miracles.

6. In the year 1666, Father John d'Aglozza, a Spaniard; a most exact observer of the rules, so that he was never known to violate one of them. Many years before he died he made a vow to commit no deliberate venial sin. He was admirable for his fervour and mortification. A close hairshirt was found on his body after death. His virtues were recompensed by great favours from our Lord and the Blessed Virgin during his life.

November 6.

1. In Syria, in the year 1653, died Father John Amieu, a Frenchman. For eighteen years he laboured much upon the Syrian mission. He established at Aleppo two sodalities of Maronites, one of Armenians, and restored the French one. He founded the Missions of Damascus and Tripoli, and a third at Sidon, where he erected a French confraternity at the cost of much suffering and labour. He converted whole families from Mahometanism and from the schism of the Greeks. By his prudence he tranquillized the Maronite outbreak, and was of great service to the Roman Maronite College; a man of truly Apostolic labours, and of great ability in the conduct of important affairs.

2. At Lima, in Peru, in the year 1614, Alphonsus Ovando, a Novice, born in Spain. From his earliest years he was a model of virtue, and regarded as an Angel. To preserve Angelic purity, he covered his body with hairshirts, and converted it into one wound by disciplines. His devotion to the Blessed Virgin was so tender, that at the very thought of her he dissolved into tears of devotion. He offered to her all his actions, endeavouring to make them acceptable to her as his Queen and Mother. In observance of the rules he was most exact, and was never known to utter an idle word. His death much resembled that of St. Stanislaus, whose virtues he had imitated. He died at the age of seventeen years and six months.

3. At Madrid, in Spain, in the year 1669, Father John Anthony Velasquez, a Spaniard; after having governed well and worthily the Colleges of Montfort, Segovia, Avila, Medina, Valladolid, and Salamanca, and having also filled the office of Provincial. He was sent for by Philip IV. to Madrid, and made the Consultor of the Congregation for the defence of the Immacu-

late Conception of the Virgin Mother of God, which office he filled for some years excellently, and published two volumes in folio on the Immaculate Conception of the Blessed Virgin, and a third on Mary our Advocate. He was the author of three other learned works, "On the Psalms," "The Epistle of St. Paul to the Philippians," and "On the most august Sacrament of the Altar." King Philip, delighted with his prudence, learning, and virtue, bid him come to him once a week, and admonish him of anything to be done for the good government of the Kingdom; but no less wise than humble, he declined the task as unsuitable for one of the Society.

NOVEMBER 7.

1. In the Campagna, in the year 1717, the Venerable Antony Baldinucci; called from his infancy to the Society, the Holy Name appearing miraculously on his breast. He laboured for thirty years on the missions in more than thirty dioceses, in spite of weakness of health and a natural repugnance. He lived on vegetable diet, travelling on foot, and taking a discipline several times a day. In spite of interior sufferings and exterior persecutions, he preserved a sweetness and equanimity of soul, which was depicted in his countenance. He worked numerous conversions, spreading everywhere devotion to the Blessed Virgin, and was signalized by many supernatural graces and favours. He concealed as far as possible these gifts of God; preserved until death his baptismal innocence, and died in the exercise of his missions at the age of fifty-three. His body was found many months after his death incorrupt, and miraculous cures were obtained through his intercession. By Clement XI. he was called, "a saintly man, an indefatigable labourer, and Angel of the Lord."

2. At Genoa, in Italy, in the year 1657, died Father Augustine Centurione, an Italian. After having filled with applause the office of Doge of the Republic of Genoa, and acquitted himself worthily of other important tasks in embassies to royal personages, he entered the Society when more than seventy years old. He preferred coming into the vineyard at the eleventh hour, rather than not to come at all. Whilst yet a secular, and fulfilling the duties of Doge, he daily received the Bread of Angels, that he might derive thence grace and strength for the due administration of his office. He deemed it, nevertheless, safer to die in Religion than in the world. His

whole family may be said to have been composed of religious; for his father and mother, brothers, sisters, sons and daughters, all, with a rare example of virtue, devoted themselves to various Religious Orders. He lived in the Society scarcely two years, but by his virtues was ripe for Heaven.

3. At Messina, in Sicily, in the year 1622, Father Cæsar Cosso, an Italian. He gave only four hours to sleep, the rest of the night to prayer. For fifteen days before the Assumption of the Blessed Virgin, and before the Feast of St. Michael the Archangel, he fasted. Even in the greatest heats he never drank out of the accustomed times, nor took oil or salt at any meal whatever; and on Saturdays ate nothing cooked with fire. To augment his merit, in his extreme old age he suffered blindness for two years with no less cheerfulness than fortitude.

4. In Andalusia, in the year 1621, John de Aquilar, a Spanish Lay-brother. He preferred to be a Lay-brother in the Society rather than to be a Priest in another illustrious order to which he was invited. He was bailiff of the farm for thirty years, and acquitted himself of his office no less religiously than laboriously. He spent two hours in prayer before the usual time of rising. His food was a little bread. He tilled the ground, sowed the seed, and thrashed the corn himself; and before he took refection at night, recited the Rosary of the Blessed Virgin. Thus, returning to the house from his labours, he looked for severity of fasting instead of his meals, and lived in constant self-abnegation.

5. In Germany, in the year 1661, Father Maurice de Buren, President of the Imperial Chambers in Spire; he renounced the world to enter the Society. He preserved till death the vow of chastity he had made in his infancy, and was remarkable for his severe penance, and love of humiliations, and for the admirable courage with which he supported contempt and injuries from persons of the highest rank. During his life in the Society he became so emaciated from the little food he took, that, like St. Francis Borgia, he could double his skin round his body. He died in the Province of the Lower Rhine, which he had edified by his rare virtues and example.

November 8.

1. At Tivoli, in the year 1612, died Father Bernardin Piccio, an Italian. When death overtook him he was teaching the lowest class of

grammar, an office his humility had asked for. He inflicted on his body the utmost severities which his conscience allowed him. He used to say that man was the tongue of all other creatures, and ought therefore to perform their part as well as his own, in praising God. If at any time from infirm health he was unable to say Mass, he would often recite the Rosary of the Blessed Virgin, and then he would soon get well again. He told a lady, who wished for the gift of tears, to meditate on the Sorrows of the Blessed Virgin Mary, and offer them to her Son. She followed his counsel and obtained her desire. Father Bernardin was seen sometimes while at prayer raised in the air, whilst his soul was ravished with the songs of Angels.

2. At Ghent, in Belgium, in the year 1634, Father Nicholas Jannot, a Belgian. Having taught philosophy with applause, he aspired to a nobler crown, and he devoted himself to the service of the plague-stricken in the city of Ghent, and thus died a victim of charity.

3. At Utrecht, in Belgium, in the year 1571, Father Henry Denis, a Belgian; celebrated as a Professor in the schools and a preacher in the pulpit. Among other fruits of his zeal, was the conversion of Nicholas Strat, Dean of Utrecht, from a life of wickedness to a life of holiness. The Dean, to show his gratitude to his master, provided by his will that they should be both buried in the same grave. It is said that two years afterwards, on the very night on which the Dean died, the grave of Father Henry opened spontaneously to receive the body of the Dean. They slept together in death, as their minds had been united in life.

November 9.

1. In England, in the year 1648, died Father Edmund Neville. He was heir to an estate in Westmoreland, which he quitted, and went to Rome, where he was ordained Priest at the English College. Having obtained permission to enter the Society, he was sent on the mission to England. He laboured for nearly forty years, and at the age of eighty-eight fell into the hands of the Parliamentary soldiers, by whom he was dragged from his room, thrown into a cart, and carried to gaol, where he died after nine months of illtreatment. Another account says that he lingered under his afflictions for two years longer, and died at last in the hold of a vessel.

2. At Madrid, in Spain, in the year 1656, Father John de Guadarrama,

a Spaniard. Although of great talents and learning, he wished nevertheless to be employed in teaching grammar only, and by all the means he could lawfully use, strove to avoid the Profession of the four vows. He wore a broad chain full of points, night and day, well or ill, at home or employed on arduous missions, which he used to give travelling on foot and begging his way. To all this he added daily a discipline to blood for the space of half an hour. During the hour of meditation he held his arms extended in the form of a cross or lay prostrate on the ground. A fragrant odour was often perceived to breathe from him as he prayed. When he was sick and suffering from thirst, he refused even a cup of water, saying: "It is against the rule to drink out of meal time, and I wish to be faithful to God in the smallest thing." The Cardinal of Toledo held him in such high estimation, that he gave eighty days' indulgence to all who confessed to him.

3. At Coimbra, in Portugal, in the year 1553, Alphonsus Vaz, a Portuguese Scholastic, whose chief attention was fixed upon the one object, of ever keeping himself in the presence of God. He reverenced Christ in his Superior, the Apostles in the Fathers, and in all others the disciples of our Lord. He passed whole hours in prayer, shedding abundant tears of devotion. During the five months he was confined to his bed, he never omitted an hour's meditation in the morning and a second hour's meditation in the evening, nor the two examens of conscience. In these holy occupations he slept in the Lord.

4. At Calais, in France, in the year 1606, Brother Remigius Croiseé, a Belgian. Calais having been taken by the Spaniards, the Governor requested that some of ours should be sent thither to serve and assist the citizens who were sick of pestilence. It was in the midst of these labours, to which he devoted himself unsparingly, that Brother Remigius fell a glorious martyr of charity.

NOVEMBER 10.

1. At Cambrai, in France, in the year 1623, died Father Anthony Suffren, a Frenchman. He had been Rector of several Houses and Provincial of his Province, duties which he fulfilled in the most exemplary manner. He fell grievously sick; prayers were ordered for his recovery. A Lay-brother was earnestly praying for him, when the Blessed Virgin Mary appeared to him and said, "Father Anthony will not die of his present

sickness; he will be restored to health again." And so indeed it came to pass. Years afterwards, when Father John Suffren, his brother—well known for the excellent spiritual books he has written—was in danger of death, Father Anthony offered his own life while he was saying Mass for his brother's. No sooner had he left the altar than he was seized with fever and died. Father John recovered.

2. At Antwerp, in Belgium, in the year 1626, Father William de Pretere, a Belgian. Devoted with his whole heart and soul to the love and honour of the Blessed Virgin Mother of God, he governed with the greatest wisdom for twenty years three of her sodalities, and afterwards added to them a fourth. He used to say that he was ready to put off the happiness of his own eternity, if by the delay he could the better defend the honour of Mary. He brought to the bosom of the Church many converts from the highest ranks, some of whom he led to a life in Religion. He was ever indefatigable in the salvation of souls even at the peril of his life.

3. At Florence, in Italy, in the year 1630, Father Marcellinus Albergothi, an Italian. Meditating upon venial sin, and perceiving that it could not be always avoided in this life, he conceived an ardent desire of dying, and begged to be employed in the service of those who were sick of the plague, that he might end by death the possibility of sinning. He obtained both these desires, leave from his Superiors and death from God.

4. At Lecce, in the Kingdom of Naples, Angelo Valentino, an Italian Lay-brother. From his Noviceship he was looked on in fact, as he was by name, an Angel. He was a model of labour at the country farm, of devotion, observance of rule, obedience, sweetness, mortification, and charity.

NOVEMBER 11.

1. In Germany, in the year 1631, died Father John Arnoldi, a German; an active labourer in the vineyard of God and an eradicator of all heresy. As he was returning one day to his house after having said Mass and preached, the sacred vessels of the altar were torn from him by the heretics among whom he was dwelling. They next attacked him with heavy bludgeons, broke his back, and cleft his head open with a hatchet.

2. In the Philippine Islands, in the year 1649, Father Vincent Damiani, an Italian. He sought out the more remote and savage parts of the islands.

Among the Jubiges and people of Bacera he performed actions and endured sufferings worthy of a hero and an Apostle. At last, clasping his crucifix to his heart he was run through with a spear out of hatred to the faith, and purpled the white robe of innocence which had never been stained by grievous sin with his own blood and the Blood of the Lamb.

3. At Cosenza, in Italy, in the year 1653, Father Theodore Massimano, an Italian; remarkable for many extraordinary virtues, and more especially for an incessant prayer before the Holy Sacrament of the Altar. On the night on which he died, a Religious of known sanctity beheld in sleep a bed-room adorned with flowered hangings woven in silk and gold, and asking for whom it was prepared, a voice answered—"For a saintly man then departing this life." Upon this she awoke, and heard the sound of the bell tolling for one who had passed away. It was tolling for the death of Father Theodore.

November 12.

1. In the Tower of London, in the year 1606, died Nicholas Owen, (otherwise known as Little John,) an English Lay-brother, twenty years attendant on Father Henry Garnett. He rendered great service to religion by his ingenuity in contriving hiding-places for Priests and church furniture. Father Gerard writes of him—"No one can be said to have done more good than he, of all who laboured on the English mission." He was a man of great judgment, discretion, and constancy. He thus gained the well merited esteem and confidence of all who knew him. Being taken at Henlip with Father Garnett, he was placed on the rack several times for seven hours together; but grace was so abundantly given to him, that he never showed the least sign of impatience, nor ever uttered a word by which any one could be compromised. They tortured him even unto death. A hairshirt was found on his body when he died.

2. At Rome, in the year 1615, Father Fabius del Fabii, a descendant it is said of the renowned Fabian family of old Rome. He adorned his birth by extraordinary virtues as a Religious, and the exemplary manner in which he discharged the various offices he filled, of Master of Novices, Rector, Provincial, Secretary, and Assistant. Diminutive in stature, he showed a soul for the greatest undertakings. He was gored by a savage

bull and on being recommended to make a vow for his recovery, in honour of the arm of St. Francis Xavier, at that time brought from the Indies, he replied that he did not desire to have his health restored by asking for a miracle, and that he would rather choose whatever God should appoint for him.

3. At Brünn, in Germany, in the year 1643, Father Philip Streidt, a Bohemian. He was reckoned commonly by the people as a saint. Father Martin Stredonius, his Provincial, a man of consummate perfection and the highest repute, wrote of him—"That he knew for a certain fact, that never an hour of the day elapsed that he did not turn all the powers of his soul towards God." He paid so strict an attention to his particular examen, that he considered himself unworthy of eating his bread as a son of the Society if he ever neglected it. He honoured the Blessed Virgin with many ingenious devices of piety, and through her protection is believed to have kept his baptismal innocence.

4. At Goa, in the year 1642, Father Anthony Fernandez, a Portuguese. On account of his virtue he was judged fit for the office of Master of Novices. He asked and obtained his request, to go to the Indian Mission. He laboured in Abyssinia during the space of thirty years. He accompanied the Patriarch Mendez in his visitations, and was chosen by him as spiritual guide, on account of the high esteem he had for his virtue. This esteem was increased yet more by seeing him raised two cubits from the ground in prayer. The Patriarch being banished from Abyssinia, Father Fernandez accompanied him to Goa, where he devoted himself to the labours of the ministry, and where he died worn out with the fatigues of the mission.

NOVEMBER 13.

1. At Petrikoff, in Poland, in the year 1607, died Paul Kostka, the brother of St. Stanislaus Kostka, who behaved harshly to him while they studied at Vienna. God seems to have granted to the merits and prayers of the blessed youth that his brother Paul should come to himself, and esteem heavenly things above earthly vanities. Converted to a better life, he wholly devoted himself and all his goods to the glory of God, building a church and monastery for the Franciscan Fathers at Presnitch, and endowing the parish church and hospital with yearly revenues, and

distributing his wealth with such liberality to the poor, that he showed himself to be already ripe for the Kingdom of Heaven. Having obtained permission from the Father General Claudius Acquaviva to enter the Society, which he had long and earnestly desired, while he was making preparation to do so, he departed, to join as we trust the society of Saints in Heaven.

2. At Vienna, in Austria, in the year 1669, Father John Bucellini, native of Brescia in Italy. He was Rector of various Colleges, and was Provincial of Austria; highly esteemed for his sweetness mingled with strength of government. He celebrated Mass with such fervour that many externs waited for the hour at which he said it. He usually said his Office prostrate before the Blessed Sacrament. He fasted the day before he began his annual Retreat, from which he always came forth still more holy than before. He was ingenious in practices of mortification on every little occasion, where necessity did not require the contrary; being never seen for thirty years to lean back in a chair either in the Refectory or elsewhere, and using in his room a seat without a back to it. During the winter he did not protect his hands from the cold. He allowed of no delicacy in his food; and even in his old age, and as Provincial, would have no assistance in his room. Freed from office, he took care of the Library, and swept it and dusted the books, which he kept well arranged, every week. God repaid his humility and mortification with extraordinary favours.

3. At Constance, in Germany, in the year 1625, Father Paul Layman, a German; a man as celebrated for profound learning as he was humble and modest. How well he was versed in Moral Theology and Canon Law his published volumes fully declare, to which such recourse is had by the learned. He was consulted from all parts of the world, even the most remote, and his answers were regarded as oracles of wisdom. He himself seemed ignorant of his own great learning, and lived as if unconscious of it.

NOVEMBER 14.

1. At Ferrara, in Italy, in the year 1598, died Father Benedict Palmio, an Italian; received into the Society by our Holy Father Ignatius, and celebrated in its Annals. He was so excellent a preacher, that he seemed to be able to move at will the minds of his hearers, and was once for

his eloquence saluted with the words "Blessed is the womb that bore thee." He was the first Italian Father professed of the four vows, and the first of the Society appointed by the Pope to be preacher at the Vatican.

2. In Bengal, in the East Indies, in the year 1602, Father Francis Fernandez, a Portuguese. While devoting himself entirely to the salvation of the Hindoos, he ran to appease a quarrel which arose between them and the Portuguese. The mob in their passion abused him and beat him cruelly, and hurried him off to prison, where he died in chains of the injuries he received, if not for the faith, at least for the sake of peace and charity of which he was a martyr.

3. At Nankin, in China, in the year 1628, Father Nicholas Trigault, a Belgian. Although of a weakly constitution he petitioned for the arduous mission of the Indies. Having obtained permission, he suddenly gained strength sufficient not only for his journey but to travel on foot to Portugal, and to return again as Procurator of the Province from China. After three years spent in Europe in procuring assistance for the mission, he returned, and there traversing on foot two and sometimes three Provinces as large in extent as France or Spain, at length, worn out with fatigues, he rested from his labours. He advanced Christianity by many books written in Chinese and Latin. He died at the age of fifty-two, having lived thirty-four years in the Society, eighteen of which were spent in China.

NOVEMBER 15.

1. At Rome, in the year 1811, died the Venerable Joseph Mary Pignatelli. From his noviceship he was remarkable for rare modesty and recollection, virtues which were enhanced by gaiety of disposition, liberty of soul, and easy manners. While Master he asked for the missions in America, but God reserved him for greater trials in Europe. In 1767 he rendered great services to the members of the Society banished from Spain, procuring them subsistence in Corsica and Genoa. The Suppression of the Society in 1773 caused him bitter grief, but he continued, in the dress of a Secular Priest, to be the refuge of his companions in sorrow. The Pope having assured him that the Society still existed in Russia, he applied for readmission; and though it was impossible for him to travel to that country, he obtained his request, and in 1799 was appointed Master of Novices in the first house

of the Society since its suppression, established by the Duke of Parma at Calormo, and on the expulsion of the Jesuits from thence was made Provincial of Naples. Father Pignatelli's confidence in God was rewarded by the miraculous multiplication of money in his hands, and he received many other extraordinary favours from Heaven, as is attested upon trustworthy evidence. He died at the age of seventy-four, and his body lies in the vault of the Generals of the Society in the Professed House at Rome. The memory of this venerable Father will always be dear to the Society, both on account of the rare example of his virtues, and because he was a glorious link of union joining the old Society with the new.

2. In Paraguay, South America, in the year 1618, Father Roche Gonzalez de Santa Cruz, an American Indian. Wholly devoted to the salvation of souls, he civilized and made subject to Christ several nations of his people. He with his own hands helped to build them huts, gave them laws, divided out the lands, and taught them agriculture, settled the form of government with its officers, and was the common farmer, master, father, governor, and everything to all. He had just finished saying Mass, when some savages who had conspired against him broke in upon him, and with the blows of a wooden club set with flint stones cleft and dashed his skull to pieces. Fifty-three natives declared that they heard these words coming from his mutilated corps—"You have killed him who loved you. You have killed my body and broken to pieces my bones, but you have not killed my soul which is now with the blessed in Heaven. Many calamities shall befall you on account of my death, for my children will come and take vengeance on you for the injuries you have done to the image of the Mother of God." "What!" they exclaimed, "is this sorcerer still able to speak?" and tearing out his heart from his breast, they threw it together with the spear on which it was fixed into the fire. The spear was consumed, but the heart was found entire, and in the year 1633 was taken to Rome.

3. At the same place and at the same time, Father Alphonsus Rodriguez, a Spaniard, fell a victim to the fury of the Indians, massacred by their wooden swords. The bodies of both the Fathers were dragged round the church and twice thrown into the fire, together with two crucifixes, one of ivory and the other of lead. But the bodies as well as the images of Christ were found the next day entire amid the ashes of the church which was consumed.

4. At Antwerp, in Belgium, in the year 1624, Father Adrian Mangot, a Belgian. He was an ardent promoter of the good of souls by his words, by his writings, and his example. In extreme old age he so completely lost his memory that, though in complete possession of his senses, he could not remember his own name. He had however a few phrases which he used as occasion served. If any one praised him he said, "I am a poor wretch;" if any one pitied his infirmities, "It is the Lord"—meaning that he resigned himself to the will of God; if he heard any disputing or contending he would say, "We are brothers." Otherwise he kept unbroken silence, speaking only with his tears.

NOVEMBER 16.

1. In America, among the Tepeguans, in the year 1616, died Father Ferdinand de Tovar, an American Indian, born of a noble native family of New Spain, which had been very friendly to the Society. He saw his mother when he was yet a child ornamenting a case for the preservation of the head of Father Gonsalvo de Tapia, lately martyred for the faith, and the case being too small, Ferdinand said to her—"It is too little, mother, for it; but keep the case for my head, for I will be killed in the same way." In the Society he devoted himself to the conversion of the Tepeguans, and when a sorcerer excited them against him and against Christianity, Father Ferdinand was struck down with a tomahawk and pierced through with a lance, and so died; while the savages insulted over him, and bid him now repeat his *Pater noster* and *Ave*.

2. At Madrid, in Spain, in the year 1629, Father Gaspar Sanchez, a Spaniard. He taught humanities with singular perseverance for thirty years, twelve uninterruptedly even during the three years he was Rector of the College. He was never seen angry, or uttered a falsehood, or was guilty of grievous sin, and was ever remarkable for humility and religious simplicity. At the command of an Exorcist, the devil in a possessed person flung himself at the feet of Father Gaspar and kissed them, acknowledging his sanctity. In his youth he appeared to have little intellect, and it was doubted whether he could learn the elements of grammar. Afterwards, being enlighted from above, he surpassed in learning, and applied to the explanation of Holy Scripture in the College of Alcala. He wrote ten

volumes of Comments, for which he is said to have received the thanks of the Choir of the Holy Prophets. He was of a most mortified life, exact in the keeping of the rules, often seen in ecstasy, and predicted the hour of his death. He is said to have received visits from our Lord, the Blessed Virgin, St. Ignatius, and St. Francis Xavier, and to have been shown the place prepared for him in Heaven.

3. In Friesland, in the year 1651, Father Daniel Stull, a Belgian. By his apostolic zeal and labours he worked much good in Friesland. In the midst of his arduous toil he encouraged himself with this stimulating thought—"Courage, Daniel; there is a happy futurity for thee, but that great glory must be purchased at a great price." He had the courage to receive the Holy Eucharist which had been vomited by a sick person. Ministering with evangelical charity to a sick man who had done him injury, he caught his death, and died a martyr of charity.

November 17.

17. In Paraguay, in the year 1638, died Father John de Castillo, a Spaniard. Whilst he was zealously labouring in promoting Christianity, by the order of a Cacique who claimed divine honours, he was attacked by a savage multitude, beaten with clubs, dragged naked through wild and pathless places, hacked to pieces with wounds, pierced with spears, and tied in the form of a cross to a tree, and despatched by the beating out of his brains with stones. The impious tyrant, to purify as he said those baptized by the Father, poured boiling water upon their heads and scraped the skin off their tongue with shells, as being infected with the blessed salt, and the profession of the Christian faith.

2. At La Plata, in Peru, in the year 1626, Father Alphonsus Cortes, a Spaniard. Troubled with scruples, he earnestly besought a remedy of the Blessed Virgin, and received an admonition from her, to be more devout in assisting the souls in Purgatory. When he expressed his anxious fear whether he was working out his salvation, she replied that he was; but that he should endeavour to perform his actions with still greater perfection. Moreover she visited him on his deathbed and poured the sweetest consolation into the heart of her servant. He laboured with zeal for the conversion of the Indians, and died in repute of sanctity.

3. At Rome, in the year 1638, Peter Angelo Boncristiano, a Scholastic. It was his daily delight to study the lives of St. Aloysius and Blessed John Berchmans, to excite in himself the love of perfection by their example, and imitate their modesty, silence, and mortification. He carried in his bosom the life of St. Aloysius, and read a chapter before and after Holy Communion. During the three days of Carnival he eat no meat. As death approached he was heard often repeating—"Lord, I rejoice that Thou art incomprehensible, infinite, almighty, merciful, and the Supreme Good. What Thou willest I also will. I exult in the thought that Thy Majesty is so great, so good, so deserving of all love." Occupied in these thoughts he entered into life eternal.

NOVEMBER 18.

1. At Rome, in the year 1575, died Father James de Ledesma, a Spaniard; celebrated for his literary and theological acquirements. Having entered the Society at Louvain, he went from thence to Rome. On his way Christ our Lord appeared to him at Acosta, bidding him be of good courage, and promising him perseverance. At Brescia the Blessed Virgin accompanied by St. Mary Magdalen, St. Catherine the Martyr, and St. Catherine of Sienna, promised him their protection at the hour of death. He heard these Saints sing the praise of chastity, saying—"O how great a gift is chastity, which the God of mercy gives! Chastity is a thing divine, and divine are its rewards, which God bestows on the continent soul." He was appointed by Father Laynez to explain St. Thomas in the Roman College, and he discharged this duty with much applause for learning, and at the same time was distinguished for a spirit of fervent piety. Exercising the laborious office of confessor to the pilgrims at the time of the Jubilee of Gregory XIII., he contracted a sickness of which he died, at the age of fifty-five, to the regret and sorrow of Rome.

2. In Mexico, New Spain, among the Tepeguans, in the year 1616, Fathers Diego de Orosco, Bernard de Cisneros, and Louis de Alabes, slain out of hatred to the faith. They were prepared for their glorious death by extraordinary virtues, mortification, and apostolic zeal. A singular fact is connected with Father Louis; that when the Priest, a Religious of St. Dominic, was registering his name after baptism, as if in a prophetic

anticipation of his martyrdom, he wrote his name alone of all the rest in large red characters. It is said that our Blessed Lady three times spoke with him, and distinctly informed him of the manner of his death and of the day on which it would take place. To prepare himself for a martyr's death he took frequent disciplines, and gave himself to much prayer, which was often prolonged to three or four hours.

3. Companion of these in martyrdom was Father John de Valle. He was an indefatigable labourer in the conversion of the Indians. To teach them to plough and prepare their food, he became farmer, cook, father, servant, brother, and all in all. He had a wonderful gift of pacifying those at variance, and was surnamed Father John of Peace. He was beyond all expression devout to the Blessed Virgin, and continually intent on honouring and praising her by every means, and he was in like manner most dear to her. Three months before his death he wrote that he should die martyred by the hands of the Tepeguans.

NOVEMBER 19.

1. In Mexico, New Spain, among the Tepeguans, in the year 1616, died Father John de Fuente, a Spaniard; put to death by the savages out of hatred to the faith, together with Father Jerome Moranta, also a Spaniard. Father John was indefatigable in enduring privations and labours. He made bricks for the Indians to build their houses; made and drove the ploughs; was servant to them in health; and cook, physician, nurse, father, and everything to them when sick. Father Jerome was the salvation of many, being an eloquent and laborious missioner, and in one discourse converted five hundred. He was observed on one occasion, in a place remote from witnesses, holding in one hand his crucifix and with the other giving himself a severe discipline, shedding abundance of tears, while he prayed for the salvation of the Indians and for the efficacy of his discourses. The Blessed Alphonsus Rodriguez predicted that he would die martyred for the faith. His body and those of his companions, who died for the faith on the previous day, were found after the lapse of three months lying stretched on the ground, covered with haircloths, quite fresh, and guarded by two dogs.

2. At Rome, in the year 1672, Father John Baptist Giattini, born at

Palermo in Sicily. He was a man of such superior talents, that he was well versed and taught with repute in every department of science that the schools of the Society embrace. He was learned in Greek, Hebrew, Syriac, Chaldaic, and Arabic. He was very skilful in every kind of handiwork. He translated with elegance into Latin the "History of the Council of Trent," written in Italian by Cardinal Pallavicini. He composed several tragedies and comedies, which the youths of the Roman College act almost every year, and which while they please are instructive to the audience. He was no less devout as a religious man than eminent in letters; was full of zeal for the salvation of souls, often preaching to the people and ever assiduous in the confessional.

3. At Rome, in the year 1750, Father Francis Retz, in the year 1750, fifteenth General of the Society. Having worthily discharged the offices of Rector of several houses, and Provincial of Bohemia, he was appointed Assistant of Germany, then Vicar General, and in the sixteenth Congregation unanimously chosen General. In this post he was remarkable for profound humility, sweetness, and modesty, and was esteemed and beloved by the Sovereign Pontiff. He was full of zeal for the exact observance of religious discipline, and was particularly active in promoting the missions, and in the establishment of houses of Retreat for the laity. It was owing in a great part to his exertions that the Canonization of St. Francis Regis was obtained. In the midst of the solicitude of the duties of office, he never failed to consecrate many hours daily to prayer with a tender devotion, and his peace of soul was never disturbed by his grievous infirmities or multifarious occupations. He suffered much from a painful sickness, borne with amazing patience, and died at the age of seventy-eight. His death was revealed the same day to a Father in Germany, and the glory he enjoyed in Heaven.

4. At Avignon, in the year 1697, Father Honorius Chauvrand, a native of Provençe. He was a model of a missioner, and friend of the poor, for whom he established one hundred and twenty-six houses of refuge, in various cities. Pope Innocent XII. summoned him to Rome to establish an hospital of this kind. After fifty years of constant labour he retired to the Novitiate at Avignon, where he spent his last years in prayer and practices of penance, and died at the age of eighty-one.

November 20.

1. In Spain, in the year 1581, died Father Diego Borassa, a Spaniard. He taught philosophy in Rome, Dilingen, and Paris with such great repute, and to such large audiences, that he was surnamed "the Philosopher," and his school was attended by five hundred scholars. He was still more deservedly famous for religious simplicity and blind obedience. Being bidden by his Superior to catch a swallow which was perched, he went and easily caught the bird, and put it into the hand of his Superior, by a miracle in reward of obedience, similar to those of the ancient Fathers.

2. At Tenerapa, in Mexico, in the year 1616, Father Ferdinand Santaren, a Spaniard; slain by the Tepeguan savages out of hatred to the faith, after many toils endured for their sakes. Full of hunger and thirst for sufferings, he used to say that, to wish to be without toil and suffering, was the same as to wish to turn one's back upon Christ, and to leave Him alone to carry the Cross. For twenty-three years he laboured in that thorny vineyard with indefatigable zeal, and God gave increase equal to his labours. He built more than forty new churches, and baptized with his own hand more than fifty thousand Indians. Enraged at the progress of the faith, the devil inspired his agents to plot his death, and he, with several companions of whom mention has been made in the previous days, suffered martyred at their hands. Father Ferdinand prepared himself for this death by frequent disciplines to blood, not only by his own hands, but sometimes he would be bound to a tree and be scourged cruelly by two Indians. Before his death he asked the savages why they were about to kill him. They replied that it was more than reason enough that he was a Christian Priest. His head was split open and his brains dashed out with a tomahawk.

3. At Paris, in the year 1624, Father John de la Bretesche, a Frenchman. His devotion to the Blessed Virgin gained for him the grace of a Religious vocation, and from her he learned that it was the will of God that he should enter the Society. He wore continually a hairshirt, and rose two hours before the Community to pray and take a sharp discipline; and though so severe to himself, was full of sweetness to others. He was twice appointed Master of Novices, and acquitted himself of the charge with admirable success, being distinguished for prudence and gentleness in government. He died at the age fifty-five.

NOVEMBER 21.

1. At Rome, in the year 1584, died Father Francis de Torres, a Spaniard. He assisted at the Council of Trent as the Pope's Theologian with great repute for learning, and was regarded as a high authority on the gravest questions. After this he entered the Society somewhat advanced in years, but in a green and useful old age, giving great edification by his humble conversation among the youthful novices. He received this special reward for his erudition and laborious researches among libraries, that when Pius V. gave permission that the Feast of the Presentation of the Blessed Virgin should be expunged from the Breviary, as a modern invention, he so well proved the antiquity of the Feast from ancient records and writings of the Fathers, that it was again restored. It seems to have been in recompense for this, that he died happily on this very feast of the Virgin Mother of God. He added to his virtues and piety the fruit of labour in publishing various excellent works, of which Southwell reckons more than fifty.

2. At Ingoldstadt, in Germany, in the year 1634, Nicholas Martin, a German Scholastic; distinguished for his innocence of life, his desire of the Indian missions, and heroic charity. In his third year of philosophy, when the plague was furiously raging, and he saw that he could compensate for the loss of the Indian mission which he could not yet obtain, by devoting himself to the charitable service of the sick, he obtained leave to sacrifice himself for the salvation of his brethren, which he did by vow; and after two days, seized with a violent affection of the lungs, expired a martyr of charity.

3. At Smolensk, in Russia, in the camp of Sigismund III., King of Poland, in the year 1609, Father Frederic Bartsch, a Prussian. Having joined the Society at Rome, studied at Vienna, and taken his degree at Wilna, he was appointed confessor to King Sigismund. For his extraordinary virtue, learning, and agreeable conversation, he was beloved and revered by the nobles of the Court and by the very heretics. He followed the King's army to Smolensk in Russia, where, in assisting the soldiers attacked by the plague, he was taken with the pestilence and died. His body was conveyed to Wilna by the royal order, and honoured with solemn obsequies and a panegyric in the presence of the Queen Constance and the Prince her son.

4. At Brussels, in Belgium, in the year 1658, Father Jodoc Andriès, a Belgian; an excellent and indefatigable preacher for nearly forty years—sometimes called upon to preach two or three times in the day. It is stated on good authority that he was seen surrounded with light as he spoke, and with a bright star above his head. Observing the great utility of small tracts and flying sheets for distribution among the people, he wrote many such, especially with the title "Christ's continual Cross," and the "Perpetual Sorrows of the Virgin, Queen of Martyrs"—reaping a rich harvest from his labours. Dying, he tenderly kissed the Crucifix, and exclaiming joyfully, "To Heaven! to Heaven!" he expired at the age of seventy.

NOVEMBER 22.

1. At Oporto, in Portugal, in the year 1656, Father Nicholas Nugent, an Irishman. It is said of him that, when a child, hearing his elder brother discourse on the enormity of mortal sin, he conceived such a horror of it, that he never in the course of a long life offended God grievously. He was admitted to the Society in Rome, and was sent to Dublin in the year 1615. He laboured on the mission for near forty years, and suffered imprisonment for four years of that time by order of the English Governor. At length he was banished to Portugal, where he promoted the interests of religion, and edified all as Superior; but was so little content with his own success, that when he resigned his post he never could recall the memory of his office without tears. He cured many sick by offering for them the Holy Sacrifice.

2. At Guadix, in Spain, in the year 1601, died Father Peter Bernal, a Spaniard. He was in repute of sanctity, for continual prayer, mortification, zeal for souls, and virtue. He preached so zealously against the vice of swearing, that the children used to say they would not swear, lest Father Bernal should be angry with them. He spoke many things prophetically of the future, and cured dangerous distempers by the imposition of his hands.

3. At Monte Frio, in Spain, in the year 1607, Father Ferdinand de Adamo, a Spaniard. Being invited by the Provincial to go upon the foreign missions, he declined under plea of feeble health. But afterwards making the Spiritual Exercises of St. Ignatius, and meditating upon the

Sacred Wound opened in the Side of Christ, he received such light from Heaven, that with shame and tears he begged to be sent on the missions, which he entered upon with apostolic zeal, and gained a multitude of souls; so that a devil was heard to declare that "Allamell" (so he called him in scorn), was one of his greatest enemies.

NOVEMBER 23.

1. At Prague, in Bohemia, in the year 1613, died Father Mark Soldano, an Italian; a martyr of charity in service of the plague-stricken, together with fifteen others in the same service throughout Bohemia. He did much for the comfort of the miserable, and was therefore called "the Father of the poor." He had three times already descended into this arena and came forth safe and victorious; but the fourth combat was the last, in which he won his crown, and to this St. Ignatius and St. Francis Xavier invited him, appearing to him in a vision a few days before his death, with a company of the Society in glory. By his death he seems to have obtained security for those of the Society who were engaged in the same work, for after him no one died.

2. At Castiglione, in Italy, in the year 1621, Father Hector Lupatino, an Italian. He was noted for his modesty and guard over his chastity from his earliest years. As a student at Padua before entering the Society, he was remarkable for his care and preservation of this angelic virtue; and in the Society was a model in keeping guard over his senses in the duties of the confessional, to which he gave his ears but not his eyes, dismissing his penitents with equal edification and brevity. He excelled in charity, patience, and obedience, undertaking nothing either in sickness or in health except at the intimation and wish of the Superior; the slightest intimation of this sufficed to make him leave off any work that he had begun.

NOVEMBER 24.

1. At Rome, in the year 1775, died Father Lawrence Ricci, eighteenth General of the Society. After distinguishing himself for strict application to study, he was received into the Society in 1718, at the age of sixteen. He taught philosophy at Sienna, and afterwards with great applause filled

the Chairs first of Philosophy and then of Theology in the Roman College. Remarkable not only for learning but for solid virtues, he was appointed Spiritual Father in the year 1751; and then, by the Father General Centurione, Secretary; and in the year 1758, at the Nineteenth General Congregation, unanimously elected General. His life as General was as glorious for him as it was mournful for the Society, and from its commencement to the end he was a stranger to tranquillity; but his severe trials only served to render more conspicuous his resignation, constancy, equanimity, and admirable serenity; his mildness, spirit of conciliation, and profound humility. To him we are indebted for the celebrated Bull of Clement XIII., "Apostolicum," which thoroughly cleared the Society, at that time exposed to the blackest calumnies. But the storm was not averted, and Father Ricci received with heroic patience the blow struck on August 16th, 1773; and went with perfect resignation to his prison, which was first the English College and afterwards the Castle of S. Angelo, where he remained until his death. When about to receive the Holy Viaticum, Father Ricci read before a crowd of witnesses a solemn protestation of his innocence and that of the Society of all the crimes laid against them. A splendid funeral was ordered in his honour by Pope Pius VI., and his body was placed in the vault of the Generals in the Church of the Gesù.

2. At Salamanca, in Spain, in the year 1601, Father Francis Ribera, a Spaniard; an excellent preacher and zealous labourer for souls. This he was already before entering the Society, to which he was drawn by hearing Father Martin Guttierez say that "we must consecrate to God that which we hold most dear, namely, our free will." Under Father Balthasar Alvarez as Novice Master he made such progress in perfection as to become the model of a religious. St. Teresa, who had him for her Confessor, saw him once when preaching surrounded with light, and Christ our Lord beside him leaning on his shoulder and embracing him, and saying these words to her—" Soul, this is he who explains My Scriptures in their real sense, and in the truth which I infuse. He knows how to appreciate the value of them, purchased for men by My most precious Blood. Rejoice that you have him for your confessor; obey him, and so you will satisfy My wishes." He was seen the third day after his death, distinguished with great glory, before the throne of God, from Whose sacred Breast proceeded a bright ray of light, covering Father Francis with exceeding glory and filling him with

joy. Hence we may gather how great authority is due to the learned commentaries he published on the Epistle to the Hebrews, and the Gospel and Apocalypse of St. John.

3. At Villagarcia, in Spain, in the year 1621, Father Bartholomew Perez, a Spaniard. He was a most exact observer of the rules, which he always carried in his bosom. Almost every time he left his room he made a visit to the Blessed Sacrament. When at the point of death and feeble, he asked whether he could with a safe conscience omit his usual making of marks in his particular examen book. He shed copious and continued tears that he had not employed his time in the Society according to the best of his ability.

NOVEMBER 25.

1. At Aviz, in Portugal, in the year 1590, died Father Louis Alvarez, a Portuguese. He gained such celebrity for preaching, that the Pope said to Father General that he was told that a new St. Paul had arisen in Portugal, so fervent were his discourses, and such power to penetrate the inmost soul. Even in his old age he would cross the Tagus and travel on foot, carrying his books and a little provision; and if he had none, he lived on alms, taking his lodging at the hospital. Preaching against female vanity in dress, he foretold that they would soon have to part with their foolish finery to redeem their husbands from captivity among the Moors. This was the case after the fatal defeat of King Sebastian in Africa. Father Louis is supposed to have died of poison, administered by one whose immoral life he had endeavoured to amend.

2. At Madrid, in Spain, in the year 1627, Father Roderic Niño de Guzman, a Spaniard. He adorned his noble birth with extraordinary virtue and zeal for the salvation of souls. To live hidden and unknown he asked to teach the lowest class of grammar, although very capable of teaching the higher sciences. He obtained his request, but his light could not thus long lie hid. Being appointed preacher he was heard with great admiration and moved every heart, so that being once heard by King Philip IV., he was shortly after selected as Preacher at the Court. In this he was singularly deserving of admiration, that whether as Rector of a College, or Superior of the Professed House, or as Provincial, he with

the same assiduity sat in the confessional, preached in the pulpit, served the sick in hospital, gave exhortations, catechised the ignorant, visited and prepared the sick for dying; so that it became a saying that Father Roderic was a whole college in himself, for he preformed alone the duties of all.

3. At Naples, in the Professed House, in the year 1613, Father John Andrew Terzo, after sufferings for forty years, of various diseases, and amongst them of leprosy, with which he begged our Lord to afflict him, that he might more securely preserve his chastity. His body all disfigured, and lame both in hand and foot, he contrived by his address to manage without the assistance of others. He was most zealous and exact in observances of common life and obedience, and thought himself happy when called to the confessional to hasten thither on his crutches, thus to employ himself in the sanctification and salvation of souls.

NOVEMBER 26.

1. At Rome, in the year 1681, died Father John Paul Oliva, a Genoese, seventeenth General of the Society. His grandfather and uncle were Doges of the Republic of Genoa. He was for many years celebrated as a preacher, and appointed by four Popes, Innocent X., Alexander VII., Clement IX., and Clement X., Preacher at the Vatican. His written works attest his greatness and excellence. He was remarkable for serenity of mind and countenance, wisdom in giving counsel, sweetness of manner, goodness even to those of whom he had reason to complain, and fervour of devotion even in the midst of business. He united gentleness with firmness in the maintenance of the Institute in its integrity. Father Goswin Nickel having laid down the office of the government of the Society from feebleness of health, he was appointed by the General Congregation to take his place with full powers, and right of succession. He governed the Society for twenty years, with a combination of singular sweetness, vigour, and prudence, deserving praise of all.

2. At Modena, in Italy, in the year 1629, Father John Argento, an Italian. He was an example of a perfect Religious for prudence, zeal, and union with God, in Italy, Austria, Poland, and Transylvania; and held everywhere in such high estimation, that upon the death of Father Claudius Acquaviva, though absent, he had twenty-nine votes for the office of General.

He was of great sincerity and mortification, taking but one meal a day, sleeping on a lion's skin, bearing a paternal affection to all; he had a wonderful devotion to the Blessed Virgin and to our holy Father St. Ignatius; and with reason is believed to have received visits from them. He filled the offices of Provincial of Transylvania and of Austria, and Visitor of Lithuania and Poland.

3. At Rome, in the year 1572, Father John Baptist Sanchez, a Spaniard. Severe upon himself, he was equally severe in exacting the observance of religious discipline from others. Accordingly having noted some faults in members of the Society, he attributed them to the Society itself, as though it had fallen into a state of relaxation. He was on this account summoned to Rome, and came obedient to the summons, though sick and infirm, and there learned to think better of the Society. He once said to Father Balthasar Alvarez, that it would be enough to make him die of grief to know for certain that he had to live a whole day, so ardent was his desire to be dissolved and to be with Christ.

NOVEMBER 27.

1. At Mexico, in America, in the year 1695, died Father James Herrera, a Spaniard; of great humility, piety, and zeal for the salvation of souls. He had guided with so much wisdom and holiness souls which had given themselves to his direction, that among other excellent fruits of his ministry, he sent into various religious orders three hundred young persons of the other sex who had been under his instructions.

2. At Douay, in France, in the year 1617, Mathias de la Saulx, a Belgian Lay-brother. He entered the Society at the age of twenty-one, and was an excellent infirmarian; but having some knowledge of Latin he nearly fell a victim to a temptation which seized him, of a desire of the Priesthood. He persisted in his pretension in spite of the advice of his Superior; and remonstrance being useless, he was about to be dismissed on the following day, when in the night he saw as he thought, in his sleep, our holy Father St. Ignatius, who stood at the foot of his bed, and with a menacing gesture threatened him with eternal perdition if he left the Society. In the morning, bathed in tears, he hastened to the Superior; and, renouncing his error, he most earnestly begged to be retained in the Society,

and obtained his request; living ever afterwards in it with great perfection, and beloved by all. He afterwards died a martyr of charity in the service of the plague-stricken.

3. At Seville, in Spain, in the year 1611, Father Peter Fontano, a Spaniard. From his earliest years he was most devout to the Blessed Sacrament and the Virgin Mother of God; and to make himself pleasing to our Lord and to her, he studied how to preserve his heart not only chaste but as pure as possible from every stain. Fearing that through human frailty he might contract some faults, he prayed earnestly that he might rather die. For this purpose he made a novena to the Blessed Virgin; and thinking that he had not obtained his petition, resigned himself entirely to the divine will. But the accomplishment of his hopes was nearer than he thought, for within a few days death carried him whither he so much desired to go.

November 28.

1. In Japan, at Nangasachi, in the year 1629, died the Lay-brother, Blessed Leonard Chimura, a noble Japanese. Though well versed in literature he preferred the condition of a Lay-brother. After the banishment of the Society from Japan, he continued in secrecy in the country to the comfort and support of the Christians. At length, being captured, he was thrown into a close prison, of which he bore the hardships for nearly three years with courage and joy. Under him the prison became like a religious house, with regular hours for prayer; and he converted ninety-six persons to the Christian faith. Being interrogated by the judge why he remained in Japan contrary to the edict of the Emperor, he replied, "To preach the Gospel of Christ." "Then," said the judge, twice repeating the sentence with a loud voice, "you shall be burned alive by fire." The Blessed Leonard gave thanks to God when bound to the stake, and displayed the greatest courage without any sign of pain; and when the bonds with which his hands were tied were consumed and left them free, he was seen to gather with them the burning embers, with which he crowned his head as if with roses, and heard to chaunt aloud the *Laudate Dominum*; and thus rejoicing he gave up his soul to God by martyrdom.

2. At Tournay, in Belgium, in the year 1614, Father Oliver Manareo,

a Belgian. He derived from St. Ignatius himself the first spirit of the Society, and persevered in it with ever increasing fervour. He first governed the Roman College and then that of Loretto, where, by reading the letter of St. Ignatius, he freed a room from the infestation of evil spirits which had caused much trouble to the inmates. There also he experienced more than once the aid of the Blessed Virgin in miraculous supplies of food and money. When filling the highest offices of the Society he never permitted any one, even a Novice, to remain long in his presence with his head uncovered, retaining always that humility and charity which endeared him to all.

3. At Bruges, in Belgium, in the years 1621, Father John Maus, a Belgian. When the plague was raging, the Bishop and the magistrates applied to him as Rector for aid. Father John did not suffer so glorious a palm to fall to the lot of another, but offered himself; and after great services, gained for himself the reward of a martyr of charity.

4, At Benevento, in Italy, in the year 1729, Father Cajetan Guiro, a Neapolitan. He obtained leave to devote his rare talents and learning to the salvation of souls on the mission at Benevento, where by his preaching, holiness, and austerity of life, he was held in opinion of sanctity, and was honoured by extraordinary divine favours both during his life-time and after his death.

NOVEMBER 29.

1. At Valladolid, in Spain, in the year 1611, died Father Anthony de Padilla, a Spaniard. He divested himself of great titles and the fortune of a nobleman to put on the livery of Christ in the Society. Humility was his first nurture in religious life, and the seasoning with which he made all adversities palatable. In his noviceship Father Balthasar Alvarez, his Superior, bid him on one occasion rise from table, and eat with beggars at the doors of the house. He obeyed with alacrity; and on Saturdays went out with the dispenser and carried home on his shoulders the meat that was bought. In the pulpit he was heard with the greatest attention, and Philip II. used to say of him, that it was quite enough to move an audience to see Father Anthony in the pulpit, glorious for so great contempt of the world. When he was offered the Archbishopric of Burgos, he said

that all he needed was one poor old bed to die on. And though he had led a life of such ascetic practice of virtue, he was seen to tremble at the hour of death for fear of the approaching judgment. But having received the Holy Viaticum he said—"Why should I fear, dear Lord, when Thou hast said to me that Thou carriest me within Thy Heart? And since it is so, I need not fear to go whithersoever Thou willest." He peacefully expired at the hour he had predicted.

2. At Militch, in Germany, in the year 1633, Father Peter Ximenes, a Spaniard; famous in the annals of Austria. At Gratz, where he was appointed Chancellor of the University, and at Olmutz, he laboured with courage and success against the heretics who were in great power and influence there, and had the happiness to see the fruit of his toils. In the cause of the faith and of God he feared the face of no man. And thus at Vienna, he took by the hand and led out of the church some men who were conversing by signs with women, saying that that place was consecrated to God, and was not to be defiled with these impurities. Angelic purity shone in his countenance, and he was often rapt from his senses in prayer. He heard two other Masses after celebrating his own with great attention and devotion. He died at the age of eighty-one.

3. At Rome, in the year 1694, the Venerable Father Paul Segneri, an Italian; celebrated for his missionary labours and apostolic preaching throughout Italy. About the year 1663, when he was making the Spiritual Exercises at Perugia, he heard the voice of God speaking in his heart and saying—"It is my will that we love one another." From that moment being changed into another man, though he had always been an exemplary Religious, he began to advance with rapid strides to perfection, being everywhere accounted and publicly reputed a saint, and requested by the Popes for Preacher at the Vatican. He spoke not to please the ear, but to convert the hearts of men, in the power and spirit of God.

NOVEMBER 30.

1. At Alcala, in Spain, in the year 1597, died Father Milan or Æmilian Garcia, a Spaniard; an ardent preacher and indefatigable missioner, and very successful in the conversion of sinners. As he spoke, on more than one occasion his face was seen to shine with light; and on the Feast of

Pentecost a dove was seen over his head while he was preaching. When dying he earnestly besought the attendant Fathers to preach with St. Paul, JESUS only, and JESUS crucified.

2. At Osnaburg, in Germany, in the year 1630, Father John Teinzer, a German. He brought many to the Catholic faith, and not a few to religious life, by his wonderful power in speaking of religious things. When Procurator of the house at Osnaburg, and afterwards Rector, during a trying period and the difficulties into which ours were thrown by the heretics, he advised the saying of the Litany of the Blessed Virgin with the daily Litanies, a custom which has continued, and the assistance of the Mother of God was soon manifestly experienced.

3. At Polosk, in Lithuania, in the year 1650, Father Adam Ciecierski, a Pole. Of great piety and with a gift of abundant tears, he was most skilful in delivering souls from the mire of sin, and on this account experienced the devil's enmity, whom he nevertheless easily overcame. Being seized with paralysis, he was thought to be near his end; but the Blessed Josaphat, the martyred Archbishop of Polosk, appeared to him and promised him three more years of life. At the expiration of that time he died a holy death, often turning his eyes to that side of his bed where the blessed martyr had on the former occasion appeared, and who perhaps was also then present.

4. At Bologna, in the year 1548, Father James Loste, native of Douay. While Professor at Louvain, he was led to enter the Society by the sermons of Father Strada and conversations with Blessed Peter Faber. Formed by St. Ignatius at Rome, he was sent to Sicily. After preaching with great zeal and working numerous conversions, he was ordered to return to Louvain where his presence was earnestly demanded. Exhausted by fatigues he stopped on his road at Bologna, and there after a brief illness expired.

DECEMBER.

DECEMBER 1.

1. At Tyburn, in the year 1581, died Father Edmund Campian, an Englishman; esteemed throughout the world as a glorious martyr. Born at London of Catholic parents in the year 1540, he was educated first at Christ's Hospital, and then St. John's College, Oxford. He quitted his fellowship at the University at the age of twenty-nine. After two years which he spent in Ireland, he crossed to Douay, where he studied some time. Thence he went to Rome, where he was admitted into the Society, and sent to make his noviceship at Brünn. Ordained at Prague, he was summoned to Rome by Father Everard Mercurian, and sent in company with Father Parsons on the English Mission. He arrived at Dover in June, 1580. In a short time he converted many to the faith, confirmed Catholics in their constancy, and raised up many imitators of own Apostolic zeal, especially by the publication of a Treatise called the *Decem Rationes* or "Ten Reasons," which was privately printed at Henley. He was apprehended in July, 1581, and cruelly put to torture. After a while he was brought out from his prison to dispute in public with the chiefs of the sectarians. Though at first his humility, modesty, and weakness from the rackings he had endured, were the subject of their scoffs, he put them to shame and silence by the power of his arguments. He was condemned to be hanged and quartered at the age of forty-one.

2. At Tyburn also on the same day, Father Alexander Briant, an Englishman, received his crown; in countenance an Angel, and in spirit an Apostle. After studying at Hart's Hall in Oxford, he went to Douay and Rheims, and was sent on the English Mission in 1579. He was taken in April, 1581, and put in prison, where he endured most cruel tortures on the rack. He was at length led out to martyrdom. He carried with him to his trial the cross, which he was commanded to throw away; he

refused, and said—"It is the banner under which I fight, and I will not desert my colours till death. I go to die for Him Who first died for me." He was admitted into the Society whilst he was in prison. It was the accomplishment of a resolution he had taken two years before. He was hanged and quartered at the age of twenty-eight, in company with Father Campian.

3. At Medina, in Spain, in the year 1633, Father Ferdinand de Castro Palao, a Spaniard. He passed his early years in such innocence that he was commonly called, "a child of predestination." In the Noviciate of the Society he gained the title of "an Angel" and a "Saint." He confirmed his right to such high titles by a life adorned with the virtues of the most profound humility, strict poverty, unwearied progress in perfection, and laborious study. Having completed his course of Dogmatic Theology with great reputation for learning, he devoted himself to Moral Theology, on which he published seven volumes in folio. He was listened to by so numerous an audience at Compostella, that no one before or after him had the like attendance.

DECEMBER 2.

1. In the Island of Sancian, on the coast of China, in the year 1552, died St. Francis Xavier, the great Apostle of the Indies, and wonderful worker of miracles. He gave up his great soul to his Creator lying alone upon a desert shore, clasping his crucifix to his heart, after ten years of labour in the East Indies, and after having baptized more than twelve hundred thousand heathens. He died on the second of December, but Pope Alexander VII. commanded that his Feast should be kept on the third of this month. The number of astounding miracles wrought by him has gained him the name of "the wonder-worker." He has been solemnly chosen as the special Patron of the Kingdom of Navarre; of the Cities of Naples, Bologna, Parma, Placentia, Massa, Aquila, Trieste, Goritz, and of the Diocese of Worms; of Goa, Macao, and Mexico. Moreover, he has been chosen as the protector of voyagers in the Pacific Ocean, and of the armies in Chili. Very many churches have been built in his honour at Rome, Naples, Palermo, Messina, Genoa, Bologna, Trent, Rimini, in Italy; at Trenchin in Hungary; Spital in Corinthia; Bruges in Flanders; Paris,

Lyons, and Embrun in France; Madrid in Spain; and in many other dioceses, provinces, and kingdoms. And so our good God is glorified throughout the world in his great and glorious servant, St. Francis Xavier.

2. At Brisac, in Alsace, in the year 1635, Father Godfrey Teller, a Belgian; who freely gave away his life in the service of the plague-stricken. He died a martyr of charity with nine others in various parts of Germany.

3. At Prague, in the year 1638, Father George Aquitar, a Silesian; a worthy emulator of the virtues of St. Francis Xavier. He twice exposed his life in the service of the plague-stricken. When asked by his Superior as he was dying, whether he were prepared to sacrifice his life for God his Creator, he replied—"Am I ready to give this my *one* life to God? O that I had a thousand times a thousand, I would give them all as willingly as the one I am now sacrificing."

4. In Paraguay, in the year 1614 (the precise day being unknown), Father Martin Xavier Urtaso, a native of Pampeluna, and a relative of St. Francis Xavier. He descended from a high estate in the world, and quitted a tender mother, that he might walk in the footsteps of the Apostle of the Indies. Though his health was delicate, he asked to be sent upon the missions among the Indians. He laboured two years in Paraguay, and then died of the plague, caught in attendance upon the sick. This martyr of charity was remarkable for his zeal, patience, and spotless innocence.

DECEMBER 3.

1. At London, in the year 1641, died Father John Fisher, or Piercy, an Englishman, and a native of Durham. An early convert to the Faith he studied at Rome, and was ordained before the Canonical age by dispensation. He joined the Society at Tournay. At Flushing he was stopped by the English soldiery, by whom he was put to the horrible torture of having a knotted cord twisted round his head by the aid of the butt end of a pistol. Shortly after his arrival in England he was imprisoned in Bridewell, or Gatehouse, during the space of four years. The torture to which he had been put by the brutal soldiery at Flushing delivered him from severe head aches to which he had been long subject. When he effected his escape from prison he found refuge with Father John Gerard. During his many years of missionary life he wrought many conversions, and amongst

others that of the mother of George Villiers, Duke of Buckingham. He was also the author of many able controversial works. He died peacefully and happily after two years of patient suffering when he was upwards of seventy years old.

2. At Mindanao, one of the Philippine Islands, in the year 1634, Father John del Carpio, a Spaniard; a zealous missioner among the tattooed Indians. The King of the island falling sick, had taken an impious vow that in the event of his recovery he would sacrifice to Mahomet all the Christian preachers he could lay his hands on. Father John was the first who was taken. Offering himself a victim to the glory of God, he fell upon his knees, and was martyred by a stroke from a scimitar.

3. At Sienna, in Italy, in the year 1608, early in December, Father Francis de Benavides, a Spaniard. The riches he had possessed in the world as son of the Count St. Stephen, only endeared to him the more the poverty of the Society. He afflicted his body (already broken in health,) with voluntary mortifications so severe, that Father Jerome de Florentia said of him, that he never knew a body in a more pitiable condition and a soul in a more desireable state than were the body and soul of Father Benavides.

4. At Bologna, in Italy, in the year 1644, Father George Justiniani, a Greek, born in Chios, of the principal family in the island. He was a man of great industry and zeal for the salvation of souls. While teaching Humanities at Rome he inflamed his scholars with such a love of virtue, that upwards of sixty of them entered religious life. Being an excellent preacher, he advanced the cause of Christianity much both in Chios and Constantinople. He displayed his zeal with so much fervour at Bologna for forty years, that he gained for himself the name of the Apostle of Bologna. He instituted there thirteen different sodalities, and at his death a magnificent cenotaph was erected in his honour.

5. At the College of Billom, in the year 1675, Father John Chambord, of the Province of Toulouse; celebrated for his labours in the mountains of Auvergne. He was a worthy emulator of St. John Francis Regis both in his apostolic labours and his saintly life. He added to his missionary toils great bodily austerities, often fasting the whole day whilst he travelled on foot. He ceased not from such holy practices when he was far advanced in years. His preaching moved the most obstinate sinners. He was a

man of singular modesty and humility, and is reputed to have worked many miracles. The Bishop of Clermont received his crucifix with a veneration due to a relic; and he assured the Rector that at the moment of his death Father Chambord had appeared to him all brilliant with glory.

December 4.

1. At Yendi, in Japan, in the year 1623, died the Blessed Jerome de Angelis, an Italian; and Blessed Simon Jempo, a Japanese; burned alive through hatred of the Faith. The Blessed Jerome made a fervent address to the people from out of the flames of the fire. He had carried the light of the Faith into five provinces and four kingdoms, into which no Priest had yet penetrated, and baptized more than ten thousand heathens. In the prison itself he converted forty prisoners. The Blessed Simon, his companion, as he had been the assistant of his labours in life, so was he joined with him in death, suffering as he had desired a glorious martyrdom by a slow fire.

2. At Lima, in Peru, in the year 1613, Peter de Salazar, a Spaniard. Once when he was meditating on Heaven, and praying fervently, invisible Angels sang to him strains of celestial music, whilst St. Barbara (to whom he had a special devotion) appeared to him in company with other holy virgins. She asked him whether he wished to depart to Heaven, where there is peace and repose and life everlasting? The holy man spoke and said—"It is my earnest prayer." In a little while after he was seized with sickness, and died on the very feast day of his blessed Patroness, St. Barbara.

3. At La Flèche, in France, in the year 1644, Father John Chevalier, a Frenchman. From his childhood he watched with the most jealous care over his chastity. His earnest and continual prayer to the Blessed Mother of God and his Angel Guardian was, that he might die without a stain on his purity. His prayer was not in vain; for one night after he had entered the Society, his Guardian Angel girded his reins so tightly that from very pain he broke out into loud cries. From that night until his death he had an easy mastery over the flesh and its temptations. He loved our Blessed Lady with a filial affection, for she was his Mother; and she often appeared to him, bestowing on him favours which he asked

of her for the sick and many others. So great was the ardour of divine love with which he burned, that unable to endure the excess of it, he often exclaimed—"O Love! O Fire! Oh, my heart in flames!" Nor was it a love that remained idle and inert, but a love that was spread abroad and blessing his fellow-men.

DECEMBER 5.

1. At Mazua, an island of the Red Sea, in the year 1596, died Father Andrew Gualdanes, a Portuguese, companion of Father Andrew Oviedo, Patriarch of Abyssinia. After zealous and fruitful missionary labours in Abyssinia he was taken prisoner by the Mahometans; and having been pierced by their lances he died a martyr for the faith.

2. At Rome, in the year 1653, Father Octavius Bonini, an Italian. He often excited Himself to diligence in spiritual things by those words of Christ—"What doth it profit a man if he gain the whole world and lose his own soul?" He used to show to the Spiritual Father the domestic exhortations he was about to give that they might be corrected by him. Having obtained a private interview with a man of rank, he drew from his bosom a crucifix, and falling on his knees besought the nobleman with such earnest prayers, that he totally changed the manner of his life. He spoke with such evangelical unction to the preachers and confessors of a certain city, that the scandalous indecency of the women's dress in that place was changed to a becoming propriety and modesty.

3. At Choynetz, in Poland, in the year 1656, Father Stephen Staroscirski, a Pole; an active missioner and zealous preacher. He fulfilled the duty of warning and exhorting his neighbour not only in life but in death, appearing to one of the Society who was suffering a slow martyrdom in the filth of a Swedish prison and encouraging him to gain by patience the rewards of everlasting life.

DECEMBER 6.

1. In the island of Ceylon, in the East Indies, in the year 1616, died Father John Metella, a Portuguese, and Father Louis Polingotti, an Italian. They were both transpierced by the lances of the natives, through a hatred of the faith.

2. At Brussels, in Belgium, in the year 1619, Father Francis Coster, a Belgian. He was three times Provincial, and was the first to erect sodalities of the Blessed Virgin Mary in the provinces which he governed. At Antwerp he had a large statue of our Lady placed in front of the Town Hall instead of a profane one which stood there before. Consecrated from his childhood to the Mother of God, he was her zealous servant. Being once asked what devotion was the most pleasing to her, he replied—"Any, however little, *if constant*." He was much beloved by St. Ignatius, who seeing him when a young man at Rome always laughing, said to him—"Courage, my child; I recommend to you always to preserve joy and peace in your heart." In after life he recommended to a noble youth, Charles Grobendonque, this spirit of joy together with obedience and humility, saying that after this advice of our holy Father he had made it a matter of earnest thought. He had also asked of the Blessed Virgin to show him how he should compass this end of being always joyful even in painful infirmities, and she replied to him—"Francis, do *you* promise me that you will be always humble and obedient, and *I* promise you that you shall never fall sick, and thus you may be always joyful." "And so," added he, "if you should ever hear it reported that Father Coster is sick, be sure it is not true, and that it would be a wrong to the Blessed Virgin to believe it. Death will be my first sickness." And so it was. He died of mere exhaustion at the age of eighty-eight. He preserved his virginity unspotted, often taking severe disciplines and wearing a hairshirt. His great delight was to speak about spiritual things. When about to die, he was asked whether he accepted death willingly, he replied—"I have I trust so lived, that I am not ashamed of my life; and I am not afraid to die, for we have a good Master."

3. At Rome, in the year 1686, Father Nicholas Avancino, a native of the Tyrol; a man of great learning and religious perfection. He was Rector of the colleges of Passau, Gratz, and Vienna, where he was also Superior of the Professed House. He was also deputed by the Father General Visitor of the Province of Bohemia. Being sent to Rome first as Procurator and then as Elector by the Austrian Province, he was chosen in the Twelfth Congregation Assistant of Germany. He wrote several works, both in poetry and in prose, which are much read and admired for their excellence.

December 7.

1. At Rome, in the year 1549, died Father Peter Codacio, an Italian. He was the first Italian to join the Society. He was already a wealthy Priest and highly esteemed, and one of Pope's own household. He was an ornament to the Society by his extraordinary virtues, and so great a benefactor to it in temporal things, that our holy Father decreed to him a Founder's honours, and besides the suffrages usually made for Founders when they die, ordered a tablet with an inscription to be set up in his memory. By his means the Society obtained its first house and church in Rome, and so great was his love of it as his mother, that St. Ignatius said of him, " Blows could not drive him out of it."

2. Among the Hurons, in America, in the year 1649, Father Charles Garnier, a Frenchman; celebrated for his apostolic labours as missioner to that tribe. In assisting the dying, he used especially to commend himself to their Guardian Angels and earnestly implore their aid. An Angel was once seen standing by the side of Father Charles and admonishing the sick man whom he attended to obey the counsel and advice of the Father. The savage tribe of the Iroquois falling upon the Christian Hurons and putting them to indiscriminate massacre, Father Garnier was in the midst of his Christians, going about hearing the confessions of the dying and baptizing the neophytes, and so was pierced with three musket balls; yet even then he dragged himself to confess and absolve the wounded till his head was cleft in twain by a hatchet.

3. On the same mission, about the same time, Father Noel Cabanel, a Frenchman. He was slain by a renegade neophyte. Having a natural repugnance to live among the savages, he had bound himself by vow to pass the rest of his life among them.

4. At Tournay, in Belgium, in the year 1621, Ignatius de Raffinghem, a Belgian Lay-brother. Though of a very noble family, and with knowledge of the Latin tongue, he chose by preference the condition of a Lay-brother. He was always cheerful, but his joy was greatest when he was employed in the meanest offices. Throughout his life in religion he undertook no work of any importance without first asking on his knees the blessing of the Superior; yea even before entering into his last agony, he asked and obtain leave to do so. He then happily expired.

DECEMBER 8.

1. At Cagliari, in Sardinia, in the year 1594, died Father Peter Espiga, a Sardinian, called the Father of the captives and the poor, and the Apostle of Sardinia. Small in body he was great in soul. He refused both a Bishop's and an Archbishop's mitre. It is incredible with what tender, solicitous, and ingenious, charity he was alive to every opportunity of aiding the poor, the imprisoned, and the afflicted of every class. By his example and well-timed admonitions he led the Secular Clergy to the practice of heroic virtue, especially in the care of the poor. He had such power over the hearts of the opulent that he bent them at his will to give succour to the indigent. On his death-bed being asked by the Rector of the college, who feared the house might suffer from paying what he owed, what sum his debts amounted to, he replied, "A thousand and five hundred pounds;" and seeing him alarmed he said, "Do not fear, Father; it is a debt upon God's account, and he is bound to make it good—do not doubt He will do so speedily." When the reply of the Father was heard of in the city, the same day the Viceroy with the Archbishop paid a visit to the sick man, and freely undertook to pay all the debt. Thus God by this and many other marks of favour approved and assisted the Father's magnanimous charity.

2. At Salamanca, in Spain, in the year 1559, Alphonsus de Prato, a Spanish Lay-brother. On hearing of the entrance of St. Francis Borgia into the Society, he earnestly begged for and obtained the same favour. He wished to enter as a Lay-brother, though he had learning enough to fit him to be a Professed Father. He had just paid his visit to the Blessed Sacrament of the Altar, and joined his Brothers at recreation, when, as was his custom, he began to speak about Mary Immaculate, on a sudden his countenance became radiant with light, he leaned his head upon the shoulder of him who sat next, and so yielded up his holy and humble soul to God.

3. At Rome, in the year 1694, Father Paul Segneri the younger; a faithful imitator of the apostle whose name he bore. He spent twenty-six years on the missions, converting very many sinners, and practising the most severe penances both in public and in private. His writings, translated

into many languages, show with what force and eloquence he preached the word of God and treated of spiritual things. He had the gift of prophecy and of miraculous cures, and was seen during prayer raised from the ground. He was held in veneration by the Pontiffs Innocent XII. and Clement XI., who while Cardinal had his life written, and when Pope had it printed. The holy man died at the age of seventy.

December 9.

1. At Manilla, in the Philippine Islands, in the year 1681, died Father Francis Calderon, a Spaniard. For thirty years he was a laborious and active missioner in Japan. He used to wash the feet of our Fathers on their return to the house from their missionary labours, repeating with sweet devotion the words, "How beautiful are the feet of those that evangelize peace." He was so great a lover of poverty that he would not have even a Breviary of his own. His particular examen was found under his pillow noted up to his death. When dying he requested to be left by himself without interruption, asking, "whether it seemed an employment of little moment to be in one's agony. My business now," he said, is with God and the Angels.

2. At Placenza, in Italy, in the year 1620, Father Julius Orsini, illustrious by his family, but still more so by his angelic purity, a virtue which he preserved unstained through life by the special protection of the Blessed Virgin Mary. He entered the Society at the age of twenty-two and died at the age of forty-six. Being appointed Rector of the College of Florence, he prostrated himself before a statue of our Lady and confided the care of the house to her as his Mistress and Queen. He had recourse to her protection in every want, and he never did so in vain. When he was sick, one who was praying for him saw a hand gathering a beautiful lily, and was given to understand by this that the dying man had bloomed like a fair lily, and was now not so much to be cut down by the scythe of death as plucked by God's own divine hand. When the same person was again in prayer after the death of Father Orsini, and wished to know for what virtue he had been most noted, a voice replied, "He lived dead to this world. Before his death he assured his confessor that the Blessed Virgin had appeared to him when young, and said—"Know, that I will watch with care over the preservation of your innocence."

December 10.

1. At Münster, in Germany, in the year 1655, died Peter Schmidt, a German Lay-brother. He had so perfectly united constant prayer with labour, that prayer was an assistance to his labour, and his labour did not hinder his prayer.

2. At Aleppo, in the year 1740, Father Peter Fromage, a Spaniard. He rendered important services to the suffering Churches in Syria, and by a discourse delivered in an assembly of Maronite Bishops he secured the abolition of many abuses which had crept into Ecclesiastical discipline. Unalterable meekness was his characteristic virtue, and he was uniformly tranquil and gay in spite of all the cares of business and the contradictions he had to indure. During his last sickness no deliberate movement of trouble or impatience was seen in him, and the sweet serenity of his countenance edified all who visited him. "Ah," he often exclaimed, "God Whom we serve is a good Master." His burial seemed more like a triumphant procession than a funeral, and the crowd was so great that the body was obliged to be protected by Turkish soldiers from those who pressed to see. He translated into Arabic no less than thirty-seven of the best French works, established catechetical instructions in three churches at Aleppo, and taught the Maronite Priests to preach to their people.

December 11.

1. At Rome, in the year 1686, died Father Charles de Noyelle, the twelfth General of the Society, a Belgian. He was twenty years Assistant of Germany, and was unanimously elected General in the Twelfth Congregation. He governed the Society for five years with great wisdom, diligence, and indefatigable zeal. His very accurate knowledge of the Institute was of great service to him in this duty. He was the living expression of all our rules and customs, and he would never allow himself any dispensation from them, either on account of his employments or his infirmities. He died at the age of seventy-one in sentiments of great piety. His obsequies were honoured by a great concourse of people of the highest rank, who manifested a singular veneration for his person and his virtues.

2. At Milan, in Lombardy, in the year 1612, Louis Visconti, an Italian Scholastic. He graced the nobility of his birth by the singular innocency of his life and by his many virtues. He had to overcome a host of difficulties in order to obtain leave to enter the Society; and when at length the religious habit was brought to him, he threw himself from excess of joy at the feet of him who brought it, and tenderly kissed it, as the robe of salvation. He dearly loved the virtue of humility, and he was moved especially to cultivate this virtue by those words of the Pontifical Bull—"This Institute requires men truly humble in Christ." He burned with an ardent desire of serving God in some excellent manner, and as the sickness, with which he was slowly wasting away, would not allow of the accomplishment of his desire, he was consumed with a great grief. When he was bidden by his master in philosophy to disclose the cause of his sorrow, he burst into tears and said—"Because through the weakness of my body I cannot serve God as I know he should be served and as I wish to serve Him.

3. At Paris, in the year 1652, Father Denis Petaux, a Frenchman; of an extraordinary learning and piety. He is justly reckoned among the brightest lights of the Society. Philip IV. invited him to his newly founded University of Madrid, and Urban VIII. more than once summoned him to Rome, but Louis XIII. opposed his leaving the Kingdom lest it should be deprived of so great a man. Moreover, he himself was loth to go to Rome lest he should be made a Cardinal. Besides five folio volumes on Dogmatic Theology, he published many other works on various subjects, and translated many Greek writers into Latin, and Latin writers into Greek. He was a man of great mortification, and most devout to the Blessed Sacrament and to the Blessed Virgin. In his last sickness, when attacked by many complicated and painful diseases, he heard a voice comforting him as he made complaint to God—"Thou thinkest of Me as man, but I think of thee as God." Consoled and enlightened, he expired at the age of seventy-four, having been fifty-two years in the Society.

DECEMBER 12.

1. In the Philippine Islands, in the year 1626, Father Emmanuel

Martinez, a Spaniard. For his purity he was honoured by the sight of Christ our Lord appearing to him; and for his attention at prayer (especially when he recited the Canonical Hours) the miraculous favour was granted him that his Breviary falling into the sea did not sink. A friend present at his death, who was too much involved in the vanities of the world, seeing the calm and fearless manner in which Father Emmanuel prepared for death, most earnestly besought him that when he entered into eternal happiness he would obtain for him of God an efficacious grace to break through the bonds of the world, and to gain a complete victory over himself. Scarcely had the Father expired when this friend was touched with the greatest grief for his sins. Bathed in bitter tears, he made a general confession of his whole life, and took the resolution of following the standard of Christ.

2. At Suld, in Belgium, in the year 1597, Father Francis Fabricius, a Belgian; a martyr of charity in attendance on the plague-stricken, whose confessions he used to hear amid bodies putrifying around him.

3. In China, in the year 1660, Father Andrew Savier, a Viennese. He was sought as a mathematician by the Mandarins, and thus obtained access to the Empress Mother, whom he converted to the faith, and afterwards the wife of the Emperor and her mother. The Emperor himself would have probably embraced the faith, but was obliged to fly before the Tartars. Father Savier fell into their hands, and making the sign of the cross was cut to pieces by them.

December 13.

1. At Mindanao, in the Philippine Islands, in the year 1655, died Father Alexander Lopez, a Spaniard, and Father John Montiel, an Italian. They were put to death through hatred of the faith by order of King Coralat. He had agreed to a treaty by which he was to permit the free exercise of the Christian religion in his dominions. Father Alexander trusting to the long acquaintance that had existed between them, modestly urged the King to embrace the Christian faith. He grew enraged at the request, and the two Fathers narrowly escaped being sacrificed to his fury. Departing from his palace they were recalled to the King's presence and, upon their way, pierced through with spears, the King openly declaring

that they were put to death by his officers for having preached to him Christianity.

2. At Ruremond, in Belgium, in the year 1630, Father Arnold Cathie, a Belgian, notable for great and solid piety. He let no hour pass without recalling to mind some mystery of the Passion, and venerating it with suitable affections. His charitable zeal engaged him more than once in the service of the plague-stricken, and he more than once was seized with the infection. After a laborious missionary life in Holland, he made an agreement with his brother that whichever of the two first departed this life should obtain for the other a quick release if it were for the good of his soul. His brother died on the 13th of October, and Father Arnold followed on this day of the following December.

3. At Omultz, in Moravia, in the year 1655, Father Gaspar Hildebrand, a Silesian, died a martyr of charity, taking the infection while serving the plague-stricken.

4. At Flushing, on his return from England, whither he had accompanied the Queen, in the year 1641, Father John Suffren, confessor for twenty-six years to Mary of Medicis, consort of Henry IV., and preacher at the Court. He was famous for his eloquence and for his sanctity of life. He was also confessor to Louis XIII. for five years, and fulfilled his task with scrupulous fidelity, preserving great union with God, and practising such austerities that it was necessary to charge one of his Religious Brothers with the care of his health. He expired discoursing sweetly with God. The Queen inconsolable for his loss, ordered his body to be embalmed and brought to Paris.

DECEMBER 14.

1. Among the Elicuran Indians, in Chili, in the year 1621, died Father Martin de Aranda Valdivia, a Spaniard, and Father Horatio Vecchi, an Italian, and Diego Montalto, a native Lay-brother, slain in hatred of the faith. Father Martin, born of a noble family, was already a distinguished captain of cavalry, and was preparing for taking the post of a commander by making the Exercises of St. Ignatius, when he received a light from heaven which led him to enter the Society and become a zealous labourer on the foreign missions. Brother Diego was the first to suffer, Fathers

Martin and Horatio were struck down by tomahawks and then pierced with spears. At last they were bound to the trunks of trees, were embowelled and had their hearts torn out, and so gave up their souls to God.

2. At Rome, in the year 1615, Father Peter Antony Spinelli, an Italian. When a child of seven years of age, amid the splendours of a ducal palace, he vowed virginity to God; and at eight he was wont to rise at night and recite the Office of the Blessed Virgin Mary. His face was often seen radiant with heavenly light, and once the Infant JESUS was seen in his hands as he administered the Holy Communion. Exceedingly devout to the Blessed Virgin, he devoted his talents to celebrate her privileges, and wrote beautiful pieces in her praise, and for two whole nights together he watched and prayed in the Holy House of Loretto, and his prayer was to escape some honourable distinction which he feared. He wore for eighteen years one old ragged inner vest. The earth or a board was his customary bed.

3. At the Professed House, in Naples, in the year 1642, Father Evangelist de Gallis; remarkable for an unalterable patience in a long and painful sickness, for his continual mortification, great austerities, profound humility, and an intimate union with God. In recompense for his virtues he received extraordinary graces, being often visited by our Divine Lord, by his Guardian Angel, and by the Blessed Virgin, who appeared to him when he was deliberating on a state of life to determine him to enter the Society.

DECEMBER 15.

1. At Forli, in Italy, in the year 1589, died Father Mark Antony Mustoni, an Italian; remarkable for piety, silence, poverty, and obedience. He received a previous knowledge from Heaven of the time of his death, for as he returned from a visit to a sick lady he said to his companion— "She will not die, but in a few days I shall go hence." And so it fell out. He departed full of joy with a sweet song of praise in his mouth.

2. On Mount St. Gothard, in the year 1654, Father Thomas Werner, a German; beloved by the people, the soldiery, and by his religious Brethren as a preacher, a confessor, and a superior. Ever ready for every arduous duty, he was no less resolute and indefatigable in accomplishing what he

undertook. Applying the relics of St. Francis Xavier to a swelling on his leg, and taking a vow to go on the mission of the East Indies, he rose from bed sound and whole; but he could not fulfil his heroic vow, for he was overwhelmed as he started on his journey by an avalanche of snow.

3. At Palencia, in Spain, in the year 1595, Father Antony de Torres, a Spaniard. (Given on this day by Father Nadasi.) His apostolical zeal displayed itself both in Spain and in the Indies. He introduced the custom of giving a pious story or narrative on Friday evenings and taking a discipline, and established it in many places. When Rector of Palencia, having found a poor sick man outside of the city unable to enter it, he took him upon his shoulders and carried him to the hospital. He also established there a Confraternity of Charity (chiefly of gentlemen) for the assistance of the poor who were ashamed to beg. He prayed four hours daily. In heat after preaching he changed his hairshirt, but only to put on an equally rough one. When he returned late from his sermon at noon, he gave a full quarter of an hour on his knees to the examen of conscience. When preaching upon Hell his face was once seen by many to shine like the face of an Angel.

4. At Dantzic, in Poland, in the year 1631, when the outbreak of the plague gave an opportunity to the Society to exercise apostolical charity, Father Nicholas Piwnichi, a Prussian, died a martyr of charity, with eleven others in various places at different seasons of the year.

5. At Bourges, in the year 1782, Father William Francis Berthier, a Frenchman. He entered the Society at the age of seventeen, and after employments in teaching he was requested to write a continuation of the History of the Gallican Church. After the suppression of the Society he was appointed Royal Librarian, and charged with the education of Louis XVI. He died aged seventy-eight. The whole city of Bourges attended his funeral.

6. At Paris, in the year 1811, Father John Baptist Bourdier Delpuits; celebrated for giving Retreats to the Clergy and Religious Communities. He suffered imprisonment during the Revolution, but afterwards resumed his labours and had numerous auditors among the young, whom he assembled and instructed. He died beloved and regretted by them, and crowds of them gathered together to do him honour at his funeral.

December 16.

1. At Palermo, in Sicily, in the year 1614, died Father Vincent Reggio, an Italian; remarkable for modesty. He is said never to have looked on the face of his own sister. He was especially devout to St. Ignatius, in whose honour he paid the most exact attention to the observance of every rule, and is said to have been favoured on that account with an appearance of the Saint at the hour of his death.

2. At Rome, in the year 1624, Father Francis Sacchini, an Italian; the historian of the Society and its Secretary, no less distinguished as an exact and good Religious than as a writer. To find time for his continual labours he was most careful not to lose a moment of it, so that Father Mutius Vitelleschi, the General, used to say of him that, "Father Sacchini never wasted an ounce weight of it." He was equally careful with regard to religious poverty, both because he knew that it was commended to us as a Mother by our holy Father, and because he was born in the bosom of it, having a muleteer for his father. Father Francis delighted to point him out to his companions as often as he came to the Roman College, saying, "Yonder is my father." One day as he came from saying Mass, meeting the Brother who attended on the Father General, he said—"Go to Father General and tell him I am going to the Infirmary and shall shortly die." Four days after he died a holy death.

3. At Placenza, in Italy, in the year 1644, Lawrence Ortega, a Spanish Lay-brother. He took great care of the sick, especially of one old Father for five years, who after death appeared to Brother Lawrence, and thanking him for his long and affectionate service, bade him continue his kindly duty of charity. He then gave him the kiss of peace on the forehead and disappeared.

4. At Ashaffenbourg, on the Upper Rhine, John de Merle, an imitator in purity and innocence of the Blessed John Berchmans. He died while a Master, and his life was written as a model for the imitation of Novices and Scholastics.

DECEMBER 17.

1. At Ingolstadt, in Germany, in the year 1608, died Father Paul Hoffeus, a German; a most courageous champion of the faith. Hence that most wise Prince, Albert Duke of Bavaria, used to say of him and the Blessed Peter Canisius, what the Church sings of the Princes of the Apostles—"Peter Canisius and Paul Hoffeus, these have taught us Thy law, O Lord." He was successively Rector, Provincial, Visitor, and Assistant, and was present at four General Congregations. Being very devout to the souls in Purgatory he often had them coming to his room door to ask for prayers. When he saw any of our younger Brothers allowing themselves some indulgence out of strict rule, he would pleasantly say—"You too will come some day to me knocking for prayers." After his death he was seen in great glory, in company with Father Claudius Aquiviva.

2. At Alcala, in Spain, in the year 1625, Father John Suarez, a Spaniard. His continual occupation of mind and heart was the praise and love of God. He confessed to one who was familiar with him that he often at every step made an act of divine love. He spoke almost always of God, and had great tact in withdrawing himself from other subjects of conversation. Being in expectation of an order from a Superior to which he had great repugnance, he betook himself to the Chapel and before the Blessed Sacrament bound himself by vow to execute the order without excuse. He received as a reward for this great victory over himself the heavenly gift of great and extraordinary graces and consolations for the space of twelve years.

3. At Glattow, in Bohemia, in the year 1648, Father George Pelinga, a Moravian; an ardent preacher of the word of God, and a zealous and successful missioner especially as an army chaplain.

DECEMBER 18.

1. At Cracow in Poland, in the year 1629, died Father Adam Gorski, a Russian, at the age of thirty-seven. He was most wonderfully exact in celebrating the Holy Sacrifice and in reciting the Canonical Hours. He used to say—"Oh, how little do many Priests know of the sweetness

there is in this their duty." He spent many hours before the Blessed Sacrament as motionless as a statue. His favourite among the rules was that in which we are bidden to seek our mortification in all things. He never allowed his body to be without some severe penitential suffering. He laid it down as a general rule for himself to live as he had lived in his third year of probation.

2. At Ingolstadt, in Germany, in the year 1648, Father Sebastian Schaller, a German; remarkable for a most wonderful exactness in observance of rule. He was inflamed with so ardent a zeal for the salvation of souls that he made a vow to sacrifice his life in gaining them in whatever manner obedience should allow him. He sacrificed it, falling a victim of charity in the service of the plague-stricken.

3. In the course of this month, in the year 1715, Father Joseph D'Arcé, born in the Canary Isles. Sent to Spain for his education, he joined the Society, and at his earnest desire was sent upon the missions on the confines of Peru. He spent some years among the Guaranis and then among the Chiriguanes, whose indomitable nature rendered his labours almost fruitless. Learning the language of the Chiquitos, he went and lived amongst them in the forests. He there went through incredible fatigues. Aided by some other missioners he formed of them five reductions. While he was descending the river of Paraguay with six neophytes he was massacred by the Guayeurus. He died at the age of sixty-five. He is justly regarded as the first apostle of the Chiquitos.

December 19.

1. At Granada, in Spain, in the year 1610, died Father John de Torres, a Spaniard. Neither labour nor sickness nor any other difficulty could turn him aside where he had the prospect of gaining a soul. The devil is said to have given some one the advice to have nothing to do with that enemy of his. He spent whole days in the confessional and nights in meditation. Death found him in these occupations, and he exclaimed—"I did not think it was so sweet a thing to die, and this I doubt not is a grace of my vocation.

2. In Holland, in the year 1620, Father Peter de Hollandre, a Belgian. Seeing that he was about to die, he wrote a letter to his Provincial declaring

that during the whole time he had lived in the Society he had derived such sweet and solid happiness from the union of his own will with that of his Superiors, that all the delights of the world could not be compared to it.

3. At Paris, in the year 1748, Father William de Ségand, a Frenchman; famous for preaching missions and retreats during the space of forty years. He asked for the foreign missions, but was kept to labour at home. Ever faithful to his exercises of piety, severe to himself and mortified, he was in all things much sought for as a director, even by those who felt a certain fear of him. He expired calmly at the age of seventy-four.

4. In the West Indian isles, in the year 1650, Father James de Valliére, a Frenchman, born of a noble family at Tours. Sent on the mission to the isle of St. Christopher, he learned that the French in a neighbouring island were attacked with a pestilential disease and dying without the Sacraments. He devoted himself to their assistance, and after two months of labour died a martyr of charity.

DECEMBER 20.

1. At Goa, in the East Indies, in the year 1562, died Father John Nugnez, a Portuguese, the Patriarch of Abyssinia. As he was deliberating upon entering a religious life, the Blessed Virgin appeared to him accompanied by Father Peter Faber and Father Francis Strada and asked of him—"Do you wish to serve my Son even to extreme fatigue?" and when he assented she replied, "Then follow these men," and disappeared. Shortly after falling in with Father Faber at Coimbra, he recognized him as the person whom he had seen in company with the Blessed Virgin; and when Faber addressed him in almost the same words spoken by our Lady—"Do you wish to serve Christ even to faintness and weariness," he gave himself to the Society; and after having given proofs of extraordinary virtue he was chosen Patriarch of Abyssinia, and adorned the dignity by his virtues and talents.

2. In Sicily, in the year 1592, Father Jerome Domenceo, a Spaniard. He promoted the welfare of the Society in Sicily. A kind Father, an exact Superior, and wise admonitor, he was called the Angel of the Society in that Province. He made so much account of prayer, that he used

to say, "that even St. Francis would have fallen from his high sanctity if he had not supported it by prayer." At night he laid himself down to rest as if he were about to die that very night.

3. At Cagliari, in Sardinia, in the year 1623, Francis Ortolano, a Spanish Lay-brother. He was no sooner born into the world, than he joined his hands as if in prayer, and clearly and distinctly pronounced the words, "Mary, Mary." He lived her ever devoted servant. Whilst he was attending one of ours who was sick, he saw our Blessed Lord stretch out His arms to him from the crucifix, and heard Him promise never to forsake him. He was a man of great humility, patience, and mortification, and was often visited by Christ and His Blessed Mother. He learned by revelation the canonization of St. Ignatius on the very day it was decreed at Rome.

December 21.

1. At Freiburg, in Switzerland, in the year 1589, died the Blessed Peter Canisius, a Belgian; the great support of the Catholic cause in Germany, the irrefragable confuter of heretics. He was called by them in mockery, "the Austrian watch dog," because he was employed continually by the Emperor Ferdinand to baffle the sectaries. By Catholics he was entitled the Apostle of Germany. He laboured in Italy, Austria, Bohemia, Germany, and above all in Bavaria, and accompanied the Apostolic Nuncio of Paul IV. to Poland, where he strengthened the Clergy in the faith. He was praised by Pius IV. as an indefatigable defender of the faith, and summoned to Rome by Gregory XIII. to give His Holiness an account of the state of Germany. By his advice the Pope re-established and endowed the German College. His life for fifty-five years was a continual succession of catechising, preaching, writing, disputing with heretics, and answering communications from Catholics requiring instruction or spiritual direction; of visiting the poor and sick, giving missions, founding colleges and seminaries. Prudent, modest, and humble, attacked by calumnies, he ever preserved an unalterable sweetness of temper, and prayed for his persecutors. Loving the humblest of offices, he refused the Archbishopric of Vienna. He was venerated as a saint, and multitudes of graces were obtained through his intercession at his tomb.

2. At Rome, in the year 1577, Father John Polanco, a Spaniard. He was of great assistance to our holy Father St. Ignatius in the government and advancement of the Society, being as prudent and learned as he was eminently religious. Although as Secretary of the Society he was burdened with an immense amount of necessary business, he nevertheless preached and catechised. He was the Procurator General of the Society, and yet he found time to serve both in the refectory and kitchen. He filled the office of Secretary to St. Ignatius, Father Laynez, and to St. Francis Borgia, and ever with the same wonderful, imperturbable serenity of mind and countenance. After the death of St. Francis Borgia he presided as Vicar General at the third Congregation. His last office was Visitor of Sicily. Having accomplished this work religiously and well, he died a holy death.

3. At Cordova, in Spain, in the year 1576, Father Francis Gomez, a Spaniard; a man of dove-like simplicity and sweetness both in his dealings with externs and in the government of ours. It is written that a snow white dove settled on his head at Mass on the day of Pentecost.

4. At Antwerp, in Belgium, in the year 1624, Father John Isenbrant, a Belgian; noted for his promptness to every call of obedience. His reply to every wish of any Superior was ever the same—"Most willingly." He was carried off by a disease caught in attending on the sick, and shortly afterwards seen in the glory of Heaven.

DECEMBER 22.

1. At Tyburn, in London, in the year 1642, died Father Thomas Holland, an Englishman; a laborious and successful missioner. He died the common death of Catholic Priests in those days of persecution. The judge himself on the bench openly avowed that no other charge lay against Father Thomas than that of being a Catholic Priest. When the sentence of death was pronounced upon him, he said with a loud voice, *Deo gratias!* and invited his companions in the prison to sing with him the *Te Deum*. As he was about to suffer he said, "that he was a Catholic Priest and a Jesuit, and that he was ready to lay down for God and His holy religion as many lives as he had hairs on his head, or as there were drops of water in the sea, or as there were wonders and perfections in God." Conversing with externs or discoursing with ours he spoke with so much

grace and singular learning on spiritual matters, that he was said to breathe spirituality, and was called "the Library of spiritual books."

2. At Munich, in Germany, in the year 1634, Father Matthew Roder, a Tyrolese. With remarkable perseverance he taught Rhetoric for two and twenty years. He was praised for his surpassing skill in the Greek and Latin tongues, erudition, and elegance in composition, by the most learned men of the age, Justus Lipsius, Martin Delrio, Velser, and many others. He retained a vigorous memory and the gentlest of manners when his health was broken by his labours. His innocence of life, sweetness and humility, from the commencement of his life even to the end of it, showed the perfect religious man. The volumes he published, especially in illustration of Greek and Latin classic authors, of which two and twenty are enumerated, are witnesses of his erudition.

December 23.

1. At Mauriac, in Auvergne, in the year 1601, died Father Robert Cuissot, a Frenchman. A great lover of interior life, he passed the greatest part of his life in obscure employments. At the Altar his ecstasies were frequent, and at times his server at Mass was obliged to recall him to his senses. He forgot to take his food, and was found in the garden half covered with snow, having gone thither to pray. He laboured much among the poor in the mountains of Auvergne; and the Bishop of Rhodez said of him that his very look inspired the beholders with the love of God. He was so well grounded in humility, that he did not fear being puffed up with pride by any arts of the Devil. At the point of death, after teaching a small class during his latter years of life, he repeated with great sweetness the words of the Apostle—"Whether we live, we live unto the Lord; or whether we die, we die unto the Lord."

2. At Carpentras, in France, in the year 1658, Father Balthasar de Bus, a Frenchman. From his entrance into the Society, a blessing he received through the prayers of his Jesuit uncle, he gave his whole attention to the subjugation of the flesh to the spirit, and for this purpose collected examples of heroic acts of penance from the old Fathers and from more modern writers, and strove to emulate them as far as Superiors would allow him. His flesh being thus subdued, God poured into his soul such

spiritual delights that they seemed to him so excessive that he sometimes looked on them with a sort of suspicion. His thoughts and affections were in such union with God that he found it difficult to turn them to creatures. Just before death he said with great emotion the *Dies Iræ*, and then added the *Te Deum* in thanksgiving for dying in the Society. Thus with mingled sentiments of fear and love of God he longed to pass from earth to a blessed eternity.

3. At Liège, in the year 1767, Father Charles Joseph Perrin, in repute of sanctity. His sweetness, simplicity, and obliging manners endeared him to all who saw or conversed with him. He was a zealous and indefatigable missioner, passing his time in the pulpit and the confessional, at the sick bed and in the hospitals. He died in retirement at Liège after the suppression of the Society.

DECEMBER 24.

1. In Brazil, in the year 1554, Peter Correa and John Sosa, both Portuguese, were slain by the natives from their hatred of the faith. Peter had been captain of a troop of horse, which was engaged in taking captive and enslaving the native Indians; but receiving an inspiration from Heaven, he resolved to redeem these poor savages from the thraldom of the Devil and make them free with the freedom of the children of God. He therefore entered the Society, in which he laboured with an indomitable energy and an indefatigable zeal for their conversion. He was at last seized together with Brother Sosa, and both were shot to death with arrows. His Christian converts lamented over him as their master, friend, father, and brother.

2. At Ancona, in Italy, in the year 1587, Father Claude Matthée, a Frenchman. He was born of poor and humble parents, but his virtue and talents were so eminent that Henry III., King of France, would willingly listen to him as he spoke for two or three hours together. The Duke of Guise was often in his company, and under his direction made the Spiritual Exercises of St. Ignatius for the space of forty days. When Provincial he knew by revelation whenever any of his subjects died. He also foretold that Father Claudius Aquaviva would be elected General of the Society, and would hold that office for a long period. On his last

journey to Rome he daily gave exhortation for half an hour either to his companions or some of the attendants. He died at Ancona on his way home to France.

3. At Seville, in Spain, in the year 1584, Father George Alvarez, a Spaniard. He was a fervent missioner, and had great power in moving the hearts of most obdurate sinners. He was seen by many at the altar surrounded with light; was regarded as the Father of the poor; and when the city was attacked with pestilence, was the foremost in the ranks of charity. When Brother Rodrigo Flores was dying, Father George asked him to obtain for him a speedy death. "Cannot you obtain of God for me," he said, "that I may keep the coming Christmas in Heaven?" Rodrigo promised that he would ask it for him, and shortly after Father George fell sick on the eleventh of December, and on this day departed this life as he had desired.

December 25.

1. At London, in the year 1625, died Father John Bennet, a Welshman; born at Comb, near St. Asaph, in North Wales. He was one of the first seven missioners sent from Douay to England to labour, and was apprehended in North Wales by Sir Thomas Mostyn, carried before William Hughes, Bishop of St. Asaph, an apostate priest, and committed to Flint gaol. He was tried at Holywell, but as he was much beloved in all the country round, his life was spared and he was sent to Ludlow Castle. There while he was on the rack a minister proposed to dispute with him, to which he agreed if his opponent were also put on the rack, that they might thus argue on equal terms. In the year 1585 he was banished, and entered the Society at Verdun at the age of thirty-six. After his noviceship he returned to Holywell, where the people, who held him to be a saint, flocked to him at midnight as many as a hundred at a time. After fifty years of labour he closed his apostolic career by dying at London a martyr of charity to the plague-stricken.

2. At Nangasachi, in Japan, in the year 1628, Michael Nacaxima, a Japanese; martyred for the faith. He was often bastinadoed, was put to the torture of water, then exposed to the burning heat of the sun, **when he was refreshed by a gentle breeze from Heaven; and at length**

was plunged into sulphurous and burning waters, and so suffering gave up his blessed soul to God.

3. At Fremona, in Abyssinia, in the year 1593, Father Emmanuel Fernandez, a Portuguese, Socius of Father Andrew Oviedo the Patriarch, the companion of his labours and sharer in his dangers. He foretold to a Nestorian Monk who was inciting the Emperor against the Catholics, that the Catholics would suffer nothing from the Emperor, but that the false Monk would shortly be summoned to the tribunal of God: and so it fell out. He was forewarned of his death, and died in inexpressible sweetness of soul, the Blessed Virgin appearing to him while he exclaimed— "Ah, my Lady; my dear Lady." And when Brother Francis Lopez asked of him why he cried out so, he replied—"I have seen the Blessed Virgin robed in an admirable and divine beauty; let me go and follow her: and so saying he departed.

4. In Belgium, in the year 1690, Father Cornelius Hazart, a Belgian. For more than twenty years he was a celebrated preacher in Antwerp. He was also a writer of considerable repute. He published seven volumes in folio of ecclesiastical history, and thirty-seven books of controversy.

December 26.

1. At Rheims, in France, in the year 1654, died Father Peter Cellot, a Frenchman; a most exact observer of all the rules and customs of the Society. He is praised in an especial manner in the Annual Letters, for that in explaining Holy Scriptures to three or four auditors he prepared his lectures as willingly and carefully as if he had a most numerous audience.

2. At Carpentras, in France, in the year 1628, James Vasserot, a French Lay-brother. During the raging of the plague he obtained leave from his Superiors to assist the sufferers. The day before he went out to aid the sick he saw in his sleep our Lord JESUS CHRIST walking before him, with His back turned to him. Full of fear at the sight, he followed Him on his knees, and humbly begged pardon for his sins, upon which he saw our Lord presently turn His face towards him and say—"Thy sins are forgiven thee." He attended the infected in the hospital with such care that he seemed the father of all, until he himself fell a victim of charity at the age of forty-one.

3. At Ratisbon, in Germany, in the year 1649, Mark Grandl, a German; a laborious and careful Lay-brother. The more effectually to keep death before his eyes, he had made his own coffin and set it in his cell. One day while yet in good health, as he was making a careful and exact confession to a Priest, of the sins of his whole life, he was struck with apoplexy, and died almost in an instant of time.

December 27.

1. In London, in the year 1656, died Father Andrew White, an Englishman. He entered the Society at the age of twenty-eight at Louvain, and in the year 1634 was sent at the request of Lord Baltimore to labour in Maryland, where his zeal earned for him the title of "Apostle." Assisted by five other English Fathers, he rendered great service to the colony until he was seized and carried off by some English invaders, and imprisoned in London. Even in his old age he continued his custom of fasting on bread and water twice in the week. His keeper told him to moderate his austerities that he might have strength to appear at Tyburn. He replied—"My fasting will give me strength enough to bear anything for the sake of my Lord JESUS CHRIST; but my time," he added, "is not come until St. John the Evangelist's day." On that festival he heard a voice—"This day shalt thou be with Me." And fortified with the holy Sacraments, he departed as he had desired, both from the prison of the flesh and the prison of persecution, at the age of seventy-eight.

2. At Gandia, in Spain, in the year 1570, Peter Alden, a Scholastic Novice, a Spaniard. He was advancing rapidly in perfection when he was called away to Heaven.

3. At Vienna, in Austria, in the year 1634, Father John Hitzettea, a native of Lorraine, died a martyr of charity with three companions. This was a fatal year to multitudes of Germans. No less than sixty-four of ours died this year in the service of the plague-stricken.

4. At Landsperg, in the year 1596, James Birura, a Flemish Lay-brother, died in the odour of sanctity, confirmed by miracles. He was received at Rome by Father Laynez, and sent first to Dillingen, and then to Landsperg to be Socius to the Master of Novices, an office which he filled for twenty-three years with consummate perfection. His prayer was

continual; his devotion to the Blessed Sacrament most tender. He died at the age of eighty-two.

DECEMBER 28.

1. At Valencia, in Spain, in the year 1583, died Father Michael Governo, a Spaniard. His calm and gentle style of preaching as well as solid reasoning made his advice acceptable both at the Court and everywhere else. He was remarkable for his fervent love of the Infant JESUS, and the images of the Holy Infant were wont to draw from him abundance of sweet tears. He used to say that from Him he learned his sermons and everything else besides. Once when he was entering the Library the Infant JESUS met him and said—"Go and ask permission to speak with Me." He went, and returning with all due leave obtained, he held for a while most sweet converse with the Divine Child.

2. In France, in the year 1623, Father Nicholas Pollieni, a Savoyard; a great lover of silence and a devout servant of the Mother of God. He was not very learned, but of great repute for sanctity. Lying on his bed of sickness, he asked of two Fathers who were going to Annecy to visit the tomb of St. Francis of Sales, to implore of him the favour of dying on the same day on which that holy Bishop died, the feast of the Holy Innocents. The petition was made and granted.

3. At Brussels, in Belgium, in the year 1630, Father John à Gouda, a Belgian; an apostolic preacher both by word and example. He was a great lover of silence. His room was a model of poverty. He used one pen for ten years, with which he wrote several controversial works. He wished for three things in death: to die quietly, on a day dedicated to our Lady; and, as he used to express it, "in harness." He obtained all three petitions; for, fatigued with preaching through Advent, sitting at table on a Saturday he suddenly fainted, and being immediately anointed, peacefully expired.

DECEMBER 29.

1. At Lisbon, in Portugal, in the year 1616, died Father John Nugnez, a Portuguese. His intercourse with God was uninterrupted by day, and

he protracted it long into the night before the Blessed Sacrament. Employed as confessor at the Court, he would neither partake of their dainty meats, nor allow any honour to be paid him. He always walked thither on foot although it was a distance of three or four miles. He brought about great practice of morality and virtue at the Court, both by his preaching and example. When he died, his body was laid on a bier which was decorated by persons of rank, and carried to the grave by six of the highest grandees.

2. At Prague, in Bohemia, in the year 1651, Father Bernard Oppel, a Moravian. Before he entered the Society he was a Canon, and a zealous and fervent preacher and catechist. When a student he obtained permission to go in surplice to various quarters of the city and collect the children, whom he led in procession to a church to teach them the Christian doctrine. He was also a frequent visitor of prisons, hospitals, and the sick poor, and was revered as a saint. When Rector of the College of Prague he gave his own clothes to the needy, and melted down the church plate to be enabled to aid the plague-stricken. Having given to a decayed gentleman the last ten pieces of money in the house, he found in lieu of them ten gold pieces in his desk.

3. At Mons, in Belgium, in the year 1652, John Daniel, a Lay-brother; a great servant of the Blessed Virgin, by whom he was miraculously delivered from a painful disease, as she appeared to him in a vision by night.

December 30.

1. At Arona, in Italy, in the year 1596, died Father Emmanual Sa, a Portuguese; illustrious among the great men of the Society for admirable learning combined with no less admirable piety. When he was scarcely seventeen years of age he taught with applause philosophy in the new university of Gandia, and was honoured with having as his private pupil the founder of that university, St. Francis Borgia, then Duke of Gandia. He gave a course of sermons at Rome for several years, without rhetorical flourish, and almost purposely inelegant, but still always pleasing for sound reasoning and solid spirituality, and therefore productive of great good. He is said to have been blessed with the sight of the Infant JESUS and His Blessed Mother on more than one occasion. She also appeared to him on his death bed accompanied by our holy Father.

2. At Seville, in Spain, in the year 1644, Father Peter de Urteaga, a Spaniard. He preached to the people with wonderful spirit and success for forty-five years, even while he was Rector of Colleges and Superior of Professed Houses. He had an especial care of prisoners and sick people. When by chance, as Rector, he met with any of the house unoccupied in the afternoon, he would pleasantly say—"What are you doing here, my Father? How will you earn your supper of our Lord unless before night you bring Him some gain of souls?" Our Lord rewarded his apostolic labours more than once by miraculous supplies for the temporal wants of the house.

3. At Evora, in Portugal, in the year 1600, Father John Stremos, a Portuguese. Two extraordinary things are related of him—one, that he lived to the age of a hundred and ten; the other, that he took a daily discipline at that extreme old age.

4. Also at Evora, in the year 1582, Father Emmanuel Alvarez, a Portuguese. He was of singular prudence and innocency of life. He is the author of the Grammar and Prosody so generally received and esteemed throughout the world, and adopted by the whole Society in its schools.

5. At Potosi, in Peru (the day unknown), Father John de Montoya, a Spaniard. After having been Rector of various colleges, he obtained leave of Father Everard Mercurian to go upon the missions of Peru. He travelled on foot over unknown regions, enduring every privation in the conversion of the natives, until his legs became so swollen and ulcerated that he could walk no more. He died at the age of eighty.

DECEMBER 31.

1. At La Louvesc, in France, in the year 1640, died Father John Francis Regis; renowned for his zeal for the salvation of souls, and for innumerable miracles. He spent his life with wonderful success in giving missions, erecting and governing sodalities, and assisting the poor. In his missions, after preaching several sermons in the day, he went into the confessional, taking no food until evening, and then only a little milk, fruit, and bread, which he obtained by begging. When in the house he gave scarcely three hours to sleep, and on the mission only two; the rest of the night was consecrated to prayer. Foreknowing the time of his death,

and asking out of humility to be carried to a stable to die, he had a vision of Christ and the Blessed Virgin. To celebrate the funeral of the man of God in the village of La Louvese in which he died, the Priests of eighteen parishes flocked together through the deep snow, bringing with them numerous congregations, though it could not be ascertained by what means they received the news of the Father's death. All wept for him and deplored his loss as their common and saintly Father. Many cures were wrought with the very dust from his tomb. Beatified by Clement XI. in the year 1716, he was canonized by Clement XII. in 1737, and his feast is kept on the 16th of June.

2. At Messina, in Sicily, in the year 1630, Marcellus Scaglione, an Italian Lay-brother. He was of a good family in Calabria, and called miraculously to the Society by a light from Heaven, which indicated that in it he was to live and die. Although by birth and education fitted for the Priesthood, he preferred the humbler condition in the house of God. He was favoured more than once with apparitions of the Blessed Virgin and the Saints. All his life at dinner and at supper he presented an offering to Heaven of something of the best, abstaining from it for the love of God. It was his custom daily to ask for perseverance in the Society through the intercession of the Saint of each day. Having the gift of tears, and giving an admirable example of patience in his last painful sickness, he died a holy death, having spent in the Society fifty-two years.

INDEX.

A.

NAME.	COUNTRY.	PLACE OF DEATH.	DAY AND YEAR.	PAGE.
Alagona, James de *Coad.*		Cagliari	Jan. 3, 1624	3
F. Alvarez, Ven. Bartholomew	Portugal	Tonkin	,, 12, 1737	14
F. Alven, Ven. Emmanuel de	Portugal	Tonkin	,, 12, 1737	14
F. Accentra, Ven. Vincent d'	Portugal	Tonkin	,, 12, 1737	14
F. Adorno, Francis		Genoa	,, 13, 1606	15
F. Alfaro, D. de		Paraguay	,, 17, 1559	19
Alvarez, Vincent *Schol.*		Dabul, East Indies	,, 18, 1606	20
F. Auger, Edmund	France	Novocomo in Italy	,, 19, 1591	21
F. Albenosa, Matthew		Bilboa in Spain	,, 22, 1585	24
F. Almeida, John	Brazil	Lima	,, 22.	24
F. Aubergeon, William	France	Isle of St. Vincent	,, 23, 1654	25
F. Albert, Francis	France	Isle of Naos	,, 28, 1651	29
F. Araos, Antony	Spain	Madrid	,, 30, 1573	32
F. Aquaviva, Claudius *General.*	Italy	Rome	,, 31, 1615	33
F. Amico, Francis	Italy	Grain in Styria	,, 31, 1651	34
F. Auseld, Jerome	Italy	Rome	Feb. 2, 1652	38
F. Aix, Francis d'	France	Lyons	,, 10, 1656	47
Ausa, Sancho de *Schol.*	Spain	Valladolid	,, 13, 1585	49
F. Acosta, Joseph	Spain	Salamanca	,, 15, 1599	51
F. Antonio, Francis	Portugal	Madrid	,, 15, 1601	52
Andrada, Francis de *Schol.*	Portugal	Coimbra	,, 16, 1569	54
F. Arias, Anthony	Spain	Wilna	March 2, 1591	69
F. Aloysius, Peter	Malabar	Malabar	,, 5, 1596	72
F. Albizi, Peter		Naples	,, 11, 1610	77
F. Andrada, Antony de	Portugal	Goa	,, 19, 1634	85
F. Arnaya, Nicholas	Spain	Mexico	,, 21, 1622	87
F. Alvarez, John Paul		Placencia in Spain	,, 23, 1564	89
F. Aguasco, Peter d'	Spain	Peru	April 12, 1605	110
F. Alvarez, Roderic	Africa	Seville	,, 14, 1587	111
F. Avila, Stephen		Lima	,, 14, 1601	112
F. Azevedo, Gaspar de	Spain	Burgos in Spain	,, 23, 1565	122
Arteaga, Emmanuel de *Coad.*	Spain	Lima	,, 24, 1654	124
F. Abercrombie, Robert	Scotland	Brunsberg, Prussia	,, 27, 1613	127
F. Abraham, George		Coast of Red Sea	,, 30, 1595	130
F. Achilli, Paul		Palermo	May 7, 1586	139
Arrogo, Gregory de *Coad.*		Seville	,, 13, 1649	147

Index.—A.

NAME.	COUNTRY.	PLACE OF DEATH.	DAY AND YEAR.	PAGE.
F. Altobodos, John	Spain	Seville	May 14, 1578	147
F. Arnoux, John	France	Toulouse	„ 14, 1636	148
F. Armano, Angelo	Italy	Manilla	„ 31, 1621	168
F. Almeida, Apollinaris *Bishop*.	Portugal	Abyssinia	June 1658	169
F. Almarza, John de	Spain	Alcala	„ 4, 1669	172
F. Arriaga, Rodriguez de	Spain	Prague	„ 7, 1667	176
F. Anchieta, Ven. Joseph	Canary Isles	Reritiba, Brazil	„ 9, 1597	177
Antonio, Mark *Coad*.	Italy	Quito	„ 11, 1612	180
F. Annat, Francis	France	Paris	„ 14, 1670	183
F. Andrada, Alphonsus do		Madrid	„ 20, 1672	190
Apicella, Brother St. *Coad*.		Naples	July 6, 1695	210
F. Aragona, Alphonsus de		Paraguay	„ 10, 1619	213
F. Aubas, Bernard	France	Haguenau	„ 11, 1617	214
F. Arents, Joachim	Belgium	Brussels	„ 12, 1614	216
F. Aicha, Gaspar	Bohemia	Brüln, Moravia	„ 13, 1659	216
F. Azevedo, Blessed Ignatius de	Portugal	Palma, Canary Isles	„ 15, 1570	218
F. Aquaviva, Ven. Rudolph	Italy	Salsette Isles, Goa	„ 15, 1583	219
F. Alvarez, Gonsalvo	Portugal	Japanese Sea	„ 21, 1573	225
F. Alemanni, Cosmo	Italy	Milan	„ 24, 1634	228
Angelini, Gerard *Coad*.	Italy	Novellara	„ 24, 1656	228
F. Alvarez, Ven. Balthasar		Belmonte, Spain	„ 25, 1580	229
F. Ascensias, Andrew		Palença, Old Castile	„ 26, 1580	231
Alvarez, Michael *Schol*.	Portugal	Evora	„ 27, 1597	232
F. Antonio, Mark		Granada	Aug. 1600	240
Antonio, Brother John	Italy	Messina	„ 7, 1551	244
F. Aubenton, William d'	France	Madrid	„ 7, 1723	244
Alvaro, Bartholomew *Coad*.	Portugal	Lisbon	„ 24, 1614	263
F. Androti, Fulvius	Italy	Ferrara	„ 27, 1575	266
F. Alberro, Martin d'	Spain	Valencia	Sept. 1, 1596	272
Apparitias, Martin *Coad*.	Spain	Barcelona	„ 2, 1585	274
F. Arriaga, Paul Joseph	Spain	Voyage from Peru	„ 6, 1622	279
F. Arrowsmith, Edmund	England	Lancaster	„ 7, 1628	280
Acafoxi, Blessed Thomas *Schol*.	Japanese	Nangasachi	„ 10, 1622	285
Alvarez, John *Schol*.		Coast of Brazil	„ 14, 1571	290
Alvarez, Ferdinand *Schol*.		Coast of Brazil	„ 14, 1571	290
F. Almeida, Antonio	Portugal	Tchao-tse, China	„ 16, 1591	293
F. Amadée, John	France	Rome	„ 21, 1620	298
F. Almeida *alias* Mede, John	England	Rio Janeiro	„ 24, 1653	301
F. Armenta, John	Spain	Cadiz	„ 25, 1651	302
Almeida, Gaspar *Coad*.	Portugal	Bahia, Brazil	„ 25, 1654	303
F. Almeida, Louis	Portugal	Amacusa, Japan	Oct. 5, 1583	314
F. Acosta, John d'	Portugal	Nangasachi	„ 8, 1633	318
F. Alarcon, Garcias de	Spain	Oviedo	„ 10, 1591	321
F. Abella, Honoratus	Spain	Saragossa	„ 10, 1593	321
F. Alphonsus, or Avila, Basil de	Spain	Gaunda	„ 17, 1556	330
F. Adami, John Matthew	Italy	Nangasachi	„ 22, 1633	335
Angerer, Magnus *Coad*.	Germany	Landsperg	„ 25, 1636	339
F. Atiença, John	Spain	Lima	Nov. 1, 1592	347
Alber, Michael *Coad*.	Germany	Ingolstadt	„ 3, 1634	349
F. Aglozza, John de	Spain		„ 5, 1666	352
F. Amien, John	France	Syria	„ 6, 1653	352

Index.—A, B.

NAME.	COUNTRY.	PLACE OF DEATH.	DAY AND YEAR.	PAGE.
Aquilar, John de *Coad.*	Spain	Andalusia	Nov. 7, 1621	354
F. Albergothi, Marcellinus	Italy	Florence	,, 10, 1630	357
F. Arnoldi, John	Germany	Germany	,, 11, 1631	357
F. Alabes, Louis de		Mexico	,, 18, 1616	365
F. Andriès, Judoc	Belgium	Brussels	,, 21, 1658	370
F. Adamo, Ferdinand de	Spain	Monte Frio	,, 22, 1607	370
F. Alvarez, Louis	Portugal	Aviz	,, 25, 1590	373
F. Argento, John	Italy	Modena	,, 26, 1629	374
F. Aquitar, George	Silesia	Prague	Dec. 2, 1638	382
F. Angelis, Blessed Jerome de	Italy	Yendi, Japan	,, 4, 1623	384
F. Avancino, Nicholas	Tyrol	Rome	,, 6, 1686	386
F. Arcé, Joseph d'	Canary Isles	Paraguay	,, 1715	398
F. Alvarez, George	Spain	Seville	,, 24, 1584	403
Aldea, Peter *Schol.*	Spain	Gandia	,, 27, 1570	406
F. Alvarez, Emmanuel	Portugal	Evora	,, 30, 1582	409

B.

NAME.	COUNTRY.	PLACE OF DEATH.	DAY AND YEAR.	PAGE.
F. Barréna, Alphonsus		Cuzco, Peru	Jan. 1, 1598	1
F. Balbas, Peter	Spain	Alcala	,, 2,	3
F. Bartoli, Daniel	Italy	Rome	,, 13, 1685	15
F. Brent, James		Vilna	,, 15, 1657	17
F. Benassai, Stephen		Rome	,, 16, 1620	18
F. Bresciani, Laurence		Forli in Italy	,, 24, 1608	26
F. Becan, Martin	Belgium	Vienna	,, 24, 1624	26
F. Bonvet, John		Nancy	,, 28, 1643	29
F. Bradley, Richard	England	Manchester	,, 30, 1645	32
F. Busenbaum, Herman	Germany	Münster	,, 31, 1668	34
F. Barcira, Baltassar	Portugal	Guinea	Feb. 2, 1612	38
Bracco, Joseph *Coad.*	Italy	Novellara	,, 3, 1620	39
F. Bonipar, Marcelline	France	Le Puy	,, 4, 1623	40
F. Barrett, Alphonse Nunhez		Lisbon	,, 12, 1571	48
F. Baving, Herman	Germany	Cologne	,, 14, 1656	50
F. Bovillet, Louis	France	Montelimar, France	,, 16, 1630	54
F. Boecop, Arnold	Belgium	Cologne	,, 19, 1622	58
F. Brun, Peter le	France	Verdun	,, 19, 1656	59
F. Boym, Benedict		Vilna	,, 28, 1670	67
F. Basile, James Anthony	Italy	America	March 1, 1652	68
Bastus, Peter *Coad*	Portugal	East Indies	,, 1, 1645	68
F. Beizama, John Ignatius		Peru	,, 5, 1654	72
F. Brebœuf, John		Canada	,, 16, 1649	82
F. Brignolo, Antony	Genoa	Genoa	,, 20, 1662	86
P. Bordese, John	France	Bearn	April 2, 1620	98
F. Bonis, Emeric de		Naples	,, 10, 1595	107
F. Barradas, Sebastian		Coimbra	,, 14, 1615	112
F. Bernel, Peter		Cadiz	,, 18, 1601	117
F. Bruner, Andrew	Germany	Innspruck, Tyrol	,, 20, 1650	118
F. Barnuevo, Gonzalvo	Spain	Peru	,, 23, 1620	123

NAME.	COUNTRY.	PLACE OF DEATH.	DAY AND YEAR.	PAGE.
F. Barma, John Bapt.	Spain	Murcia	May 3, 1650	135
F. Bausech, Adalbert	Bohemia	Vienna	„ 3, 1571	135
F. Brunow, Stanislaus	Poland	Poland	„ 5, 1642	137
F. Baeza, Ven. John Bapt de	Spain	Nangasachi	„ 7, 1626	139
F. Buteux, James	France	Canada	„ 10, 1652	142
F. Bourdaloue, Louis	France	Paris	„ 13, 1704	146
F. Baeza, Gabriel de	Spain	Peru	„ 15, 1614	149
F. Bobola, Blessed Andrew	Poland	Janow	„ 16, 1657	150
F. Berens, Simon	Prussia	Brunsberg, Prussia	„ 16, 1650	151
F. Bischoff, Valentine	Belgium	Courtrai	„ 17, 1636	152
F. Bordese, Francis	France	Periqueux, France	„ 19, 1596	155
F. Beauvais, Anne Francis de	France	Dijon	„ 23, 1669	159
F. Buri, Nicholas	Belgium	St. Omers	„ 26, 1597	163
F. Busæus, John	Belgium	Mayence	„ 30, 1611	167
Baptista, Br. *Coad.*	Spain	Granada	June 13, 1610	182
F. Burckhurst, Florence	Belgium	Louvain	„ 14, 1610	183
Buceri, Simon *Coad.*	Sicily	Palermo	„ 16, 1617	186
F. Bustamante, Bartholomew	Spain	Triqueros	„ 21, 1570	191
F. Bredane, John	Belgium	Ratisbon	„ 25, 1609	195
F. Bonvet, James	France	Pekin	„ 28, 1732	199
F. Bucelin, Paul	Belgium	Neustadt	July 2, 1600	204
F. Binet, Stephen	France	Paris	„ 4, 1639	207
F. Brevedent, Francis Xavier de	France	Abyssinia	„ 9, 1699	213
Bretrand Brother		Pont-a-Mousson	„ 15, 1685	219
F. Bottelberg, Andrew	Belgium	Mechlin	„ 17, 1613	222
F. Boddey, John Baptist		Utrecht	„ 20, 1638	224
F. Benedict, Martin	Moravia	Prague	„ 25, 1649	230
Beechnert, Martin *Schol.*	Belgium	Louvain	Aug. 3, 1621	240
F. Bellavia, Antonio	Italy	Pernambuco	„ 4, 1633	241
F. Bertenda, Ximenes	Spain	Marchenas	„ 8, 1662	245
F. Burnat, Matthew	Germany	Bohemia	„ 9, 1629	246
F. Bazier, Matthew Grimes	France	England	„ 11, 1650	248
Bitter, John *Schol.*	Germany	Paderborn	„ 12, 1629	250
Berchmans, Blessed John *Schol.*	Belgium	Rome	„ 13, 1621	251
F. Baëza, Diego de	Spain	Valladolid	„ 15, 1647	254
F. Bath, John	Ireland	Drogheda	„ 16, 1649	254
F. Borges, Emmanuel	Portugal	Nangasachi	„ 16, 1633	254
Browne, William *Coad.*	England	Liege	„ 20, 1637	258
F. Brilmacher, Peter	Germany	Mayence	„ 25, 1595	264
F. Baker, Chas. *alias* David Lewis	Wales	Usk, England	„ 27, 1616	265
F. Bartil, Laurence	Poland	Smolensk, Russia	„ 28, 1635	267
F. Buldini, Francis	Italy	Japan	Sept. 8, 1633	283
F. Bresciani, Francis Joseph	Italy	Florence	„ 9, 1672	284
F. Bollandus, John	Belgium	Antwerp	„ 12, 1665	288
F. Boyton, William	Ireland	Cashel	„ 13, 1647	289
F. Broet, Paschal	France	Paris	„ 14, 1562	290
Bosgho, Cæsar *Schol.*	Italy	Turin	„ 15, 1618	291
F. Barase, Cyprian	Spain	America	„ 16, 1702	293
F. Bellarmine, Robert *Cardinal*	Italy	Rome	„ 17, 1621	294
F. Broissy, Charles de	France	Pekin	„ 18, 1704	295
F. Ballesti, Vasco	Portugal	Coimbra	„ 21, 1596	299

NAME.	COUNTRY.	PLACE OF DEATH.	DAY AND YEAR.	PAGE.
F. Bobadilla, Nicholas ...	Spain	Loretto	Sept. 23, 1590	300
Bertoult, Peter *Coad.* ...	France	Tournay	,, 26, 1673	303
F. Borgia, St. Francis *General*	Spain	Rome	Oct. 1, 1572	309
F. Bucherelli, Francis Mary ...	Italy	Tonkin	,, 4, 1723	313
F. Boscho, Antony	Spain	Sassari, Sadinia	,, 8, 1571	319
F. Belli, Balthasar	France	Mons	,, 9, 1639	320
Biler, Richard *Schol.* ...	Germany	Trêves	,, 16, 1588	328
F. Balsamon, Ignatius ...	France	Limoges	,, 16, 1618	329
F. Bouton, Francis	France		,, 17, 1628	330
F. Barzens, Gaspar	Belgium	Goa, East Indies	,, 18, 1553	330
F. Belido, Peter	Spain	Valencia	,, 27, 1615	341
F. Baile, William	France	Bourdeaux	,, 27, 1620	341
F. Bazain, Francis	Spain	Mexico	,, 28, 1572	342
F. Baldinucci, Ven. Antony ...		Campagna	Nov. 7, 1717	353
F. Buren, Maurice de ...	Germany	Germany	,, 7, 1661	354
F. Bucellini, John	Italy	Brescia	,, 13, 1669	360
Boncristiano, Peter Angelo *Schol.*		Rome	,, 17, 1638	365
F. Borassu, Diego	Spain	Spain	,, 20, 1581	368
F. Bretesche, John de la ...	France	Paris	,, 20, 1624	368
F. Bartsch, Frederic	Prussia	Smolensk, Russia	,, 21, 1609	369
F. Bernal, Peter	Spain	Guadix, Spain	,, 22, 1601	370
F. Briant, Alexander	England	Tyburn, London	Dec. 1, 1581	380
F. Benavides, Francis de ...	Spain	Sienna	,, 1608	383
F. Bonini, Octavius	Italy	Rome	,, 5, 1653	385
F. Berthier, William Francis ...	France	Bourges	,, 15, 1782	395
F. Bus, Balthasar de	France	Carpentras	,, 23, 1658	402
F. Bennet, John	Wales	London	,, 25, 1625	404
Birura, James *Coad.* ...	Belgium	Landsperg	,, 27, 1596	406

C.

F. Cames, Peter le		Verdun	Jan. 3, 1684	4
Cuvillon, Baldwin *Schol.* ...		Tournay	,, 3, 1592	4
F. Castro, Alphonso de ...	Portugal	Moluccas	,, 6, 1558	7
Carrera, John *Coad.* ...		Burgos in Spain	,, 7,	8
Cuidad Real, Francis de *Coad.*		Mexico	,, 8, 1599	8
F. Cavalieri, Januarius ...		Loretto	,, 11,	13
F. Cratz, Ven. Gaspar ...	Germany	Tonkin	,, 12, 1737	14
F. Cravina, Peter		Yamorita, New Spain	,, 15, 1635	17
F. Coloncel, John	Germany	Vienna	,, 18, 1627	20
Cecotti, Paulinus *Coad.* ...		Rome	,, 21, 1612	23
F. Costens, Martin	Poland	Warsaw	,, 22, 1614	24
F. Cassarribios, John		Ategnex, Spain	,, 23, 1646	24
F. Cornier, Thomas	England	Baston, France	,, 24, 1639	26
F. Crasset, ——	France	Paris	,, 24, 1692	27
F. Cordova, Antony	Spain	Oropesa, Spain	,, 26, 1567	27
F. Campo, John del	Spain	Mindanao Is.	,, 27, 1621	29
F. Cruz, Francis de la ...	Portugal	Lisbon	,, 29, 1706	32

NAME.	COUNTRY.	PLACE OF DEATH.	DAY AND YEAR.	PAGE.
F. Cayron, Peter John	France	Toulouse	Jan. 31, 1754	34
Cenardi, Jerome *Schol.*	Italy	Cremona	,, 31, 1608	35
F. Clavius, Christopher	Germany	Rome	Feb. ·6, 1612	42
F. Chaussée, John de la	France	La Fleche	,, 6, 1654	42
F. Criminali, Antonio	Italy	Punchal, E. Indies	,, 7, 1549	43
F. Carlantini, Charles		Novocomi	,, 10, 1610	46
Caray, Gaspar de *Coad.*	Spain	Zebu, Philippines	,, 14, 1627	50
F. Columbière, Claude de la	France	Paray-le-Monial	,, 14, 1682	50
F. Cerqueyra, Louis de *Bishop*		Japan	,, 15, 1614	52
F. Cardim, Ven. John	Portugal	Braga	,, 18, 1615	57
F. Carvalho, Blessed Diego	Portugal	Japan	,, 22, 1644	61
F. Crispian, Adrian Kundde	Belgium	Paraguay	,, 25, 1651	64
F. Cortho, Alexander	Portugal	Lisbon	,, 27, 1580	66
F. Consalez, John		Alcala	March 10, 1570	76
F. Cornœus, Melchior	Germany	Mayence	,, 13, 1665	80
F. Coparius, Virgil	Italy	Rome	,, 14, 1631	80
F. Coton, Peter		Paris	,, 19, 1626	85
Cladera, Joseph *Coad.*		Majorca	,, 21, 1621	86
Colet, Peter *Coad.*		France	,, 22, 1628	88
F. Capeti, Antony	Italy	Japan	,, 25, 1643	90
F. Chicoff, Nicolas	Poland	Cracow	,, 27, 1669	92
F. Cussola, Julius	Spain	Majorca	,, 28, 1583	93
F. Cavell, Henry	Ireland	Ireland	April 8, 1643	105
F. Castillo, Ven. Francis de	Portugal	Lima	,, 11, 1673	109
F. Caldeira, Ven. Louis	Portugal	Abyssinia	,, 12, 1640	109
F. Croce, Ven. Bruno de Santa	Italy	Abyssinia	,, 12, 1640	109
F. Cusan, Nicholas	Germany	Germany	,, 20, 1636	118
Cajetano, Francis *Schol.*	Italy	Messina	,, 20, 1601	118
F. Colnago, Ven. Bernard	Sicily	Catania in Sicily	,, 22, 1611	121
F. Cardenas, Antony de	Spain	Xeres in Spain	,, 22, 1615	122
F. Ceruto, James	Italy	Rome	,, 28, 1575	128
F. Castillo, John de	Spain	Valladolid	May 4, 1599	136
·F. Carnostaw, Christopher	Poland	Poland	,, 5, 1642	137
F. Carvahal, George	Portugal	Ikizuki, Japan	,, 5, 1592	138
F. Colin, Francis		Philippines	,, 6, 1660	138
F. Cerda, John Louis de la		Madrid	,, 6, 1643	138
F. Chessoy, Adrian	France	Auxerre	,, 9, 1613	141
Cuñha, Dominic da *Coad.*	Portugal	Lisbon	,, 10, 1644	142
Coussi, Matthias le *Coad.*	France	Ponta-a-Mousson	,, 12, 1631	145
F. Cornforth, Thomas	England	Liege	,, 14, 1649	147
F. Cordés, Antony	Spain	Seville	,, 16, 1601	150
F. Cuevas, Peter	Spain	Spain	,, 18, 1575	153
F. Cardoses, Gonzales	Portugal	Abyssinia	,, 22, 1573	158
F. Czyzowski, Nicholas	Poland	Posen	,, 23, 1625	159
F. Coelho, Gaspar	Portugal	Canzuca in Japan	,, 25, 1590	162
F. Corneille, John *Coad.*		Cologne	,, 26, 1627	162
Coetho, Francis *Schol.*	Portugal	Portugal	,, 27, 1607	164
F. Cottam, Thomas	England	London	,, 30, 1582	166
F. Corbinelli, Louis	Italy	Rome	June 2, 1591	170
F. Cazorla, Andrew de	Spain	Seville	,, 2, 1649	170
F. Cousin, Quintin	Belgium	On the way to India	,, 3, 1618	171

NAME.	COUNTRY.	PLACE OF DEATH.	DAY AND YEAR.	PAGE.
F. Carafa, Ven. Vincent *Gen.*	Italy	Rome	June 8, 1649	176
F. Cataldini, Joseph	Italy	Paraña, Paraguay	,, 10, 1653	179
F. Castañeda, John	Spain	Valladolid	,, 12, 1575	181
F. Carminata, John Baptist ...		Palermo	,, 16, 1619	185
Cannoni, Thomas *Coad.* ...	Sicily	Palermo	,, 17, 1611	187
F. Caunas, John de		Malacca, E. Indies	,, 19, 1596	189
F. Coutzen, Adam	Germany	Munich	,, 19, 1635	189
Caun, Blessed Vincent *Schol.*	Corea	Nangasachi	,, 20, 1626	190
F. Corderius, Balthasar ...	Belgium	Rome	,, 24, 1650	195
F. Campens, Otho	Belgium	Neustadt	July 2, 1600	204
F. Caussin, Nicolas	France	Paris	,, 2, 1651	205
F. Cornelius, John	England	Dorchester	,, 3, 1594	205
Carillo, Peter *Coad.* ...	Spain	Oropesa	,, 5, 1615	208
Cassui, Peter *Coad.* ...	Japan	Yendi,	,, 7, 1639	210
F. Christynen, Charles ...		Ghent	,, 7, 1634	211
F. Cluselle, Claude	France	Bourdeaux	,, 9, 1636	212
F. Cabarasi, Sebastian ...	Sicily	Syracuse	,, 13, 1605	216
F. Calatayud, Joseph ...		Gandia	,, 15, 1636	219
F. Corciono, Francis	Italy	Naples	,, 20, 1656	224
F. Costa, James à	Spain	Cuidad Real	,, 21, 1585	225
F. Corquera, Christopher ...	Spain	Bari in Apulia	,, 21, 1639	226
F. Cochez, Bartholomew ...	Spain	Majorca	,, 22, 1587	226
F. Charlart, Quentin	Belgium	Tournay	,, 28, 1556	233
F. Cordova, Francis de ...	Spain	Villagarcia	,, 28, 1580	233
F. Collignon, John	France	Pont-a-Mousson	Aug. 1, 1633	238
F. Carrion, Francis	Spain	Ikizuki, Japan	,, 2, 1590	238
F. Croix, Francis de la ...	Belgium	Tournay	,, 2, 1644	239
F. Cansfield, Brian	England	York	,, 3, 1645	239
F. Cuellar, Francis de ...		Granada	,, 1600	240
Cajetan, Cæsar *Schol.* ...	Italy	Palermo	,, 5, 1651	241
F. Campo, John Sabastian à ...	Sardinia	Sassari	,, 6, 1608	243
F. Castillo, Diego de	Spain	Madrid	,, 7, 1662	243
Caguin, Francis *Coad.* ...	France	Lyons	,, 11, 1617	248
F. Campo, John à	Spain	Mindanao, Philipp.	,, 11, 1596	249
F. Coture, Jules César ...	Belgium	Wurtenberg, Silesia	,, 11, 1651	249
F. Crutz, Adrian	Flanders	Antwerp	,, 13, 1619	251
Czaplinski, Ladislaus ...	Poland	Kalisch	,, 18, 1639	256
F. Crevilly, Thomas de ...	Normandy	Coast of Cayenne	,, 18,	256
F. Carnero, Melchior *Bishop* ...		Macao, China	,, 19, 1583	257
Correa, Peter *Coad.*	Portugal	Brazil	,, 24, 1554	262
F. Carvalho, Blessed Michael ...	Portugal	Omura, Japan	,, 25, 1624	264
F. Codure, John	Savoy	Rome	,, 29, 1541	267
F. Clutz, Peter	Belgium	Troves, Germany	,, 30, 1587	268
F. Corbie, Ralph	Ireland	Tyburn, London	Sept. 7, 1644	281
F. Claver, Blessed Peter ...	Spaniard	Carthagena, W. Ind.	,, 8, 1654	282
F. Chisaire, John	Belgium	Belgium	,, 9, 1625	284
Cafucu, Louis *Coad.*	Japan	Japan	,, 9, 1633	284
F. Chimura, Blessed Sebastian	Japan	Nangasachi	,, 10, 1622	285
Cavara, Blessed Louis *Schol.* ...	Japan	Nangasachi	,, 10, 1622	285
Ciongocou, Blessed John *Schol.*	Japan	Nangasachi	,, 10, 1622	285
F. Caputo, Sertorius		Aquila	,, 11, 1608	286
Castro, Blessed Francis de ...		On the way to Brazil	,, 13, 1571	289

BBB

NAME.	COUNTRY.	PLACE OF DEATH.	DAY AND YEAR.	PAGE.
Carvalho, Diego		Coast of Brazil	Sept. 14, 1571	290
F. Constanzi, Blessed Camillus	Italy	Tabira, Japan	,, 15, 1622	291
F. Carlier, John	Belgium	Arras	,, 16, 1633	292
F. Carlier, Henry	Belgium	Huy	,, 16, 1636	293
F. Cardosa, Francis	Portugal	Lisbon	,, 20, 1604	297
F. Callant, Francis	Belgium	Antwerp	,, 23, 1626	301
F. Continente, Peter ...	Spain	Spain	,, 26, 1641	303
F. Canisius, Theodore	Belgium	Ingolstadt	,, 27, 1606	304
Cafucu, Lewis *Schol.* ...	Japan	Cocyra, Japan	,, 28, 1633	305
F. Centurione, Aloysius *General*	Italy	Rome	Oct. 1, 1757	309
Collins, Dominic *Coad.* ...	Ireland	Cork	,, 3, 1602	311
Capuano, Pompeio *Schol.* ...	Italy	Naples	,, 3, 1588	311
Chodorowicz, Laurence *Coad.*	Poland	Cracow	,, 3, 1662	312
F. Condé, Nicholas	France	Dijon	,, 5, 1654	314
F. Cyrian, Paul	Hungary	Cilia in Styria	,, 15, 1646	327
F. Chaps, John	Poland	Kalisch	,, 17, 1605	330
F. Carvalho, Jerome	Portugal	Coimbra	,, 24, 1604	337
F. Couros, Ven. Matthew de ...	Portugal	Fuxima, Japan	,, 29, 1633	343
F. Colombe, Claude à Sainte ...	France	Beziers, France	Nov. 1, 1629	347
F. Colibrant, George	Belgium	Douay	,, 2, 1609	348
F. Centurione, Augustine ...	Italy	Genoa	,, 7, 1657	353
F. Cosso, Cæsar	Italy	Messina	,, 7, 1622	354
Croisée, Remigius	Belgium	Calais	,, 9, 1606	356
F. Castillo, John de	Spain	Paraguay	,, 17, 1638	364
F. Cortes, Alphonsus	Spain	La Plata	,, 17, 1626	364
F. Cisneros, Bernard de ...		Mexico	,, 18, 1616	365
F. Chauvrand, Honorius ...	France	Avignon	,, 19, 1697	367
Chimura, Blessed Leonard *Coad.*	Japan	Nangasachi	,, 28, 1629	376
F. Ciecierski, Adam	Poland	Polosk	,, 30, 1650	379
F. Campian, Edmund	England	Tyburn, London	Dec. 1, 1581	380
F. Carpio, John del	Spain	Mindanao, Philipp.	,, 3, 1634	383
F. Chambord, John	France	Billom	,, 3, 1675	383
F. Chevalier, John	France	La Flèche	,, 4, 1644	384
F. Coster, Francis	Belgium	Brussels	,, 6, 1619	386
F. Codacio, Peter	Italy	Rome	,, 7, 1649	387
F. Cabanel, Noel	France	America	,, 7, 1649	387
F. Calderon, Francis	Spain	Manilla	,, 9, 1681	389
F. Cathie, Arnold	Belgium	Ruremond	,, 13, 1630	393
F. Canisius, Blessed Peter ...	Belgium	Freiburg	,, 21, 1589	400
F. Cuissot, Robert	France	Maurine	,, 23, 1601	402
Correa, Peter *Schol.*	Portugal	Brazil	,, 24, 1554	403
F. Cellot, Peter	France	Rheims	,, 26, 1654	405

D.

NAME.	COUNTRY.	PLACE OF DEATH.	DAY AND YEAR.	PAGE.
F. Decker, John	Belgium	Griiin in Styria	Jan. 10, 1619	11
F. Dunn, Edmund	Ireland	Cork	,, 30, 1580	33
Davitia, John Peter *Coad.*		Ferrara	Feb. 3, 1607	39
F. Dicconson, Robert	England	Liege	,, 14, 1693	51
F. Druzbicki, Thomas	Poland	Posna	April 2, 1662	98
F. Darbyshire, Thomas	England	Pont-a-Mousson	,, 6, 1604	102
Domagalski, John *Schol.*	Poland	Poland	May 5, 1642	137
F. Delgado, John	Portugal	Guinea	,, 25, 1610	162
F. Dario, John	Italy	St. Iago	June 8, 1633	177
F. Daniel, Antony	France	Canada	July 4, 1649	206
Dominique, Gerard *Coad.*	France	Pont-a-Mousson	,, 14, 1654	217
Doligier, Peter *Coad.*	France	Avignon	,, 18, 1604	222
F. Duvergier, Francis	France	Bourdeaux	Aug. 3, 1720	240
F. David, John	Belgium	Antwerp	,, 9, 1613	246
Domyne, John *Schol.*	France	Pont-a-Mousson	,, 23, 1622	261
F. Domaniewsky, Stanislaus	Poland	Posen	Sept. 11, 1637	287
F. Diaz, Blessed Peter	Portugal	On the way to Brazil	,, 13, 1571	289
Diaz, Blessed Peter		On the coast of Brazil	,, 14, 1571	290
F. Damajewickz, Andrew	Poland	Neswich	,, 14, 1694	290
Duchi, Januarius *Schol.*	Italy	Rome	,, 16, 1580	293
F. Damarles, Gomez	Portugal	On the Indian Ocean	,, 24, 1680	301
F. Dobokay, Alexander	Hungary	Zagrabo	Oct. 13, 1621	325
F. Delrio, Martin	Belgium	Louvain	,, 19, 1608	332
F. Denis, Henry	Belgium	Utrecht	Nov. 8, 1571	355
F. Damiani, Vincent	Italy	Philippines	,, 11, 1649	357
F. Delpuits, John Bapt. Bourdier		Paris	Dec. 15, 1811	395
F. Domeneco, Jerome	Spain	Sicily	,, 20, 1592	399
Daniel, John *Coad.*		Mons, Belgium	,, 29, 1652	408

E.

F. Elleniz, Luke		Treves	Jan. 1, 1607	2
F. Enzinas, Francis de		Manilla	,, 2, 1632	2
F. Espinoza, d'		Ezega, Spain	Feb. 4, 1638	40
F. Ertmer, Martin	Germany	Gratz in Styria	,, 22, 1612	61
F. Engelgrave, Henry		Antwerp	March 8, 1670	74
Emerson, Ralph *Coad.*	England	St. Omers	,, 12, 1604	78
F. Everard, James	Ireland	Ireland	April 13, 1647	110
Elphinston, William *Schol.*	Scotland	Naples	,, 16, 1548	114
F. Everard, Thomas	England	London	May 17, 1633	151
Espalza, Simon de *Coad.*	Spain	Bilboa	June 11, 1623	180
F. Eguia, James	Spain	Rome	,, 15, 1555	184
F. Everard, Laurence	Belgium	Neustadt	July 2, 1600	204
F. Entrecolles, Francis Xavier de	France	Pekin	,, 2, 1741	205
F. Espinosa, Peter de	Spain	Paraguay	,, 3, 1637	206
F. Esquéra, Alphousus	Spain	Alcala	,, 17, 1637	221

NAME.	COUNTRY.	PLACE OF DEATH.	DAY AND YEAR.	PAGE.
F. Evans, Philip	Wales	Cardiff, S. Wales	July 22, 1679	227
F. Esquiel, Gonzalez	Spain	Seville	Aug. 18, 1575	256
F. Enfant, Alexander de	France	Paris	Sept. 3, 1792	276
F. Escalza, Joseph de	Spain	Xeres	,, 7, 1616	281
F. Espiga, Peter	Sardinia	Cagliari	Dec. 8, 1594	388

F.

NAME	COUNTRY	PLACE OF DEATH	DAY AND YEAR	PAGE
Francisco, Adam *Schol.*		Cape Comorin	Jan. 2, 1549	2
F. Fuentes, Michael de		Valencia	,, 4, 1609	4
Fernandez, Blessed Ambrose *Coad.*	Portugal	Omura	,, 7, 1620	8
F. Francisci, John		Courtrai	,, 7, 1579	8
F. Funes, Raymond de		Huesca, Spain	,, 21, 1646	23
Fernandez, Francis *Coad.*		Gandia	,, 25, 1570	27
F. Fernandez, Emmanuel	Africa	Evora	Feb. 18, 1555	57
Fréredoux, Louis *Schol.*	France	France	,, 23, 1620	62
Fort, Philip le *Coad.*	France	Marseilles	,, 25, 1655	64
F. Filcox, Roger	England	London	,, 27, 1601	66
Fonseca, Gaspar *Schol.*		Portugal	March 1, 1561	68
F. Fernandez, John	Spain	Valentia	,, 9, 1595	75
F. Florens, —		Antwerp	,, 21, 1616	86
F. Fernandez, Matthew		Paraguay	,, 22, 1645	87
F. Fonseca, Ignatius de	Spain	Seville	,, 23, 1677	123
F. Fernandez, Diego		Brazil	,, 28, 1607	128
F. Furlanetto, Joseph	Italy	Arima, Japan	April 30, 1595	130
F. Fernandez, Dominic	Portugal	Goa	May 2, 1583	133
F. Four, Anthony du	France	Rouen	,, 2, 1610	133
Fernandez, Dominic *Coad.*		Madrid	,, 8, 1577	140
F. Fevre, Stephen le	France	Hang-tcheou-fou	,, 10, 1657	142
F. Fischer, Jerome	Bohemia	Silesia	,, 23, 1634	160
F. Frias, John	Spain	Cordova	June 20, 1597	190
Fernandez, John *Coad.*	Spain	Firando, Japan	,, 26, 1587	197
F. Ferrer, Raphael	Spain	America	,, 27, 1610	179
F. Fenwick, John	England	London	,, 30, 1679	201
Flores, Gregory		Leon	July 1, 1599	203
F. Ferrer, Peter Paul		Lisbon	,, 4, 1618	207
F. Fröes, Lewis	Portugal	Nangasachi	,, 8, 1597	211
F. Fröes, John	Portugal	Hang-tcheou-fou	,, 11, 1638	215
Fernandez, Br. Sebastian		China	,, 1627	228
F. Faber, Blessed Peter	Savoy	Rome	Aug. 1, 1546	237
Flores, Rodriguez de *Coad.*	Spain	Seville	,, 19, 1584	257
F. Ferreri, Christopher	Italy	Montereggio	,, 29, 1637	268
Fusai, Gonzales *Schol.*	Japan	Nangasachi	Sept. 10, 1622	285
F. Ferrara, Alexander	Italy	Catanzaro	,, 10,	286
Fernandez, Blessed Peter		Coast of Brazil	,, 14, 1571	290
Fernando, Blessed Alphonse		Coast of Brazil	,, 14, 1571	290
F. Fernandez, Matthew	Hindustan	Jafantapa, E. Indies	,, 15, 1628	291
F. Fagot, John	France	Metz	,, 18, 1657	295

NAME.	COUNTRY.	PLACE OF DEATH.	DAY AND YEAR.	PAGE.
F. Fernandez, George	Portugal	Java, Indian Ocean	Sept. 24, 1680	301
F. Falck, John	Germany	Mayence	„ 24, 1626	301
F. Fabricius, John	Germany	Münster	„ 26, 1656	303
F. Folian, Francis	Tyrol	Rome	„ 29, 1609	306
F. Fernandez, Benedict	Portugal	Nangasachi	Oct. 2, 1633	310
Fucayo, Damian *Coad.*	Japan	Nangasachi	„ 9, 1633	320
F. Fontova, Mark Antony	Spain	Murcia	„ 24, 1558	337
F. Frusia, Andrew	France	Rome	„ 26, 1556	340
Fugixima, Denys *Coad.*	Japan	Ximabara	Nov. 1, 1622	347
F. Fonseca, Peter de	Portugal	Lisbon	„ 4, 1599	349
Fiori, Michael *Coad.*	Italy	Syracuse	„ 4, 1621	350
F. Fabii, Fabius del	Italy	Rome	„ 12, 1615	358
F. Fernandez, Anthony	Portugal	Goa	„ 12, 1642	358
F. Fernandez, Francis	Portugal	Bengal	„ 14, 1602	361
F. Fuente, John de	Spain	Mexico	„ 19, 1616	366
F. Fontano, Peter	Spain	Seville	„ 27, 1611	376
F. Fisher, or Percy, John	England	London	Dec. 3, 1641	382
F. Fromage, Peter	Spain	Aleppo	„ 10, 1740	390
F. Fabricius, Francis	Belgium	Suld	„ 22, 1597	392
F. Fernandez, Emmanuel	Portugal	Fremona, Abyssinia	„ 25, 1593	405

G.

Geronimo, Mary Joseph de *Coad.*	Italy	Naples	Jan. 4, 1713	5
F. Granada, James		Granada	„ 5, 1632	6
F. Gusman, Louis	Spain	Madrid	„ 10, 1605	11
F. Gardiner, Francis	England	England	„ 18, 1648	21
F. Geloso, Gaspar		Innspruck	„ 23	25
F. Gueymen, Francis	France	Isle of St. Vincent	„ 23, 1654	25
F. Gretser, James		Ingolstadt	„ 29, 1625	31
F. Gomez, Peter	Spain	Japan	Feb. 1, 1600	37
Goto, St. John de *Schol.*	Japan	Nangasachi	„ 5, 1597	41
F. Guttierez, Martin	Spain	Cadillac, France	„ 21, 1573	60
F. Gross, John	England	Lincoln	„ 27, 1645	66
F. Grodzicki, Stanislaus	Poland	Posen	March 4, 1613	71
F. Galvanelli, Andrew	Italy	Perugia	„ 6, 1557	73
F. Garcia, Ferdinand		Caravaga, Spain	„ 7, 1579	73
F. Gans, John		Vienna	„ 11, 1662	77
F. Gottifried, Alexander *General*	Italy	Rome	„ 12, 1652	78
F. Gonsalvo, Louis		Lisbon	„ 15, 1575	81
F. Gomez, Ferdinand		Mexico	„ 17, 1610	83
F. Gueror, Alphonsus		Mexico	„ 18, 1640	84
F. Gomez, Martin		Granada	April 15, 1567	113
F. Gordon, James	Scotland	Paris	„ 16, 1620	113
F. Gueret, John	France	Nancy	„ 24, 1630	123
F. Gelosse, Stephen	Ireland	Ireland	„ 26	126
F. Gaulbert, John	France	Poitiers	„ 29, 1626	129
F. Greef, Anthony de		Nimeguen, Belgium	May 1, 1636	132

NAME.	COUNTRY.	PLACE OF DEATH.	DAY AND YEAR.	PAGE.
F. Gérard, John	France	France	May 1711	133
F. Garnett, Henry	England	London	,, 3, 1606	134
F. Guzman, James de	Spain	Seville	,, 8, 1606	140
Goffetti, James *Coad.*	Italy	Rome	,, 17, 1658	152
F. Grillo, Hyacinth		Parma	,, 22, 1630	158
Gagliardi, Leonetto *Schol.*	Italy	Rome	,, 28, 1654	165
F. Godinez, Cornelius Beudin	Belgium	New Biscay	June 4, 1650	172
F. Gonzalez, John		Huete, Spain	,, 6, 1583	174
F. Goyssard, Michael	France	Lyons	,, 10, 1623	179
F. Gonzalez, Rodrigo		Madrid	,, 12, 1580	181
F. Garasse, Francis	France	Poitiers	,, 14, 1631	183
F. Gascon, Peter	Spain	Valencia	,, 18, 1583	188
Gonzaga, St. Aloysius *Schol.*	Italy	Rome	,, 21, 1591	190
F. Gedoyn, Claude	France	Alençon	,, 21	192
F. Garnett, Thomas	England	London	,, 23, 1609	193
F. Govéa, Francis	Portugal	Africa	,, 28, 1575	199
F. Gustapane, Joseph			,, 28, 1656	199
F. Gawen, John	England	London	,, 30, 1679	201
F. Geronimo, John	Spain	Seville	July 1, 1605	203
F. Good, William	England	Naples	,, 5, 1586	208
F. Gagliardi, Achilles	Italy	Modena	,, 6, 1607	209
F. Giedroycz, George	Lithuania	Wilna	,, 12, 1653	215
F. Graben, Adalbert	Poland	Resel	,, 18, 1693	222
Garcez, Br. Diego		Alcala	,, 23, 1599	227
F. Gerard, John	England	Rome	,, 27, 1637	231
Gomez, Peter *Coad.*	Spain	Alcala	Aug. 4, 1565	241
F. Ginkiewicz, Michael	Poland	Wilna	,, 4, 1663	241
Gorczyn, Laurence *Coad.*	Poland	Cracow	,, 8, 1636	245
F. Gruzewski, John	Lithuania	Warsaw	,, 12, 1646	250
F. Gravency, Wolfgang	Germany	Innspruck	,, 20, 1650	258
F. Gianni, James Antony	Italy	Ximabara	,, 28, 1633	267
Gonzalez, John *Coad.*	Spain	Lima	,, 31, 1613	270
F. Garreau, Leonard	France	Montreal	Sept. 2, 1656	274
F. Garcia, Francis *Archbishop*		Cranganor, E. Ind.	,, 3, 1659	275
F. Galluzzi, Francis Mary	Italy	Rome	,, 6, 1731	280
F. Gianotti, Alphonsus	Italy	Bologna	,, 19, 1649	296
F. Gerard, Theodoric	Belgium	Vienna	Oct. 1, 1558	309
Gilbert, George *Schol.*	England	Rome	,, 6, 1583	316
F. Gonzalez, Melchior	Portugal	Bazain, E. Indies	,, 6, 1551	216
F. Gobien, Charles le	France	Paris	,, 9, 1708	321
F. Gonzalez, Andrew		Indian Ocean	,, 11, 1555	322
Gruda, Nicholas *Coad.*		Lomza, Poland	,, 11, 1624	322
Gruythusen, Francis *Schol.*	Belgium	Louvain	,, 20	334
F. Gesti, John		Barcelona	1558	338
F. Gonzalez, Thyrsus *General*	Spain	Rome	,, 27, 1705	341
F. Guadarrama, John de	Spain	Madrid	Nov. 9, 1656	355
F. Gonzales, Roche	America	Paraguay	,, 15, 1618	362
F. Giattini, John Baptist	Sicily	Rome	,, 19, 1672	366
F. Guzman Roderic Niño de	Spain	Madrid	,, 25, 1627	373
F. Guiro, Cajetan	Italy	Benevento	,, 28, 1729	377
F. Garcia, Milan or Æmilian	Spain	Alcala	,, 30, 1597	378
F. Gualdanes, Andrew	Portugal	Isle of Mazua	Dec. 5, 1596	385

NAME.	COUNTRY.	PLACE OF DEATH.	DAY AND YEAR.	PAGE.
F. Garnier, Charles	France	America	Dec. 7, 1649	387
F. Gallis, Evangelist de		Naples	,, 14, 1642	394
F. Gorski, Adam	Russia	Cracow	,, 18, 1629	397
F. Gomez, Francis	Spain	Cordova	,, 21, 1576	401
Granal, Mark *Coad.*	Germany	Ratisbon	,, 26, 1649	406
F. Governo, Michael	Spain	Valencia	,, 28, 1583	407
F. Gouda, John à	Belgium	Brussels	,, 28, 1630	407

H.

NAME.	COUNTRY.	PLACE OF DEATH.	DAY AND YEAR.	PAGE.
F. Haywood, Gaspar	England	Naples	Jan. 9, 1598	10
F. Haye, John de la	Servia	Douay	,, 14, 1614	15
F. Hoffer, George		Edersburg	,, 16, 1621	18
F. Henriguez, Henry	Portugal	Punchal, E. Indies	Feb. 6, 1600	42
F. Havelland, John	England	Cadiz	,, 9, 1649	45
F. Hamel, John	Belgium	Louvain	,, 14, 1589	50
F. Hincza, Martin	Prussia	Posen	,, 23, 1667	63
F. Herbest, Benedict		Yaroslave, Poland	March 4, 1593	71
F. Huntley, Alexander	Scotland	Cambray	,, 28, 1606	93
F. Hayneuve, Julian	France	Paris	,, 31, 1663	96
F. Hozez, Diego		Padua	,, 31, 1538	96
F. Henriguez, Leo		Lisbon	April 8, 1589	105
F. Hurtado, Rodriguez	Spain	Berlanga	May 13, 1578	146
F. Holtby, Richard	England	England	,, 24, 1640	161
F. Huneken, Frederic	Germany	Iglau, Bohemia	,, 28, 1648	165
Herrera, Michael *Coad.*	Spain	Rome	June 2, 1593	170
F. Hubat, John	Bohemia	Prague	,, 13, 1661	182
F. Hart, John	England	Jaroslau	,, 18, 1586	187
Henrici, Antonio de *Coad.*	Italy	Tivoli	,, 24, 1602	195
F. Harcourt *alias* Whitbread, Th.	England	London	,, 30, 1679	201
F. Hernandez, Alphonsus	Spain	Barcelona	July 6, 1621	209
F. Henrici, Leo		Lisbon	,, 22, 1569	227
F. Halloix, Peter	Belgium	Liege	,, 30, 1656	234
F. Hurtàdo, Gaspar	Spain	Alcala	Aug. 5, 1646	242
F. Hurtàdo, Melchior	Spain	Philippines	,, 27, 1603	266
F. Hosch, Sidronius	Spres	Tongres	Sept. 4, 1653	277
F. Hugo, Hermann	Belgium	Rheinberg	,, 11, 1639	286
F. Henschenius, Godfrey		Antwerp	,, 11, 1681	287
F. Herrera, John de	Spain	Marcheña	,, 19, 1636	296
F. Horn, Adrian	Germany	Cologne	Oct. 1, 1655	310
F. Hermite, Martin l'	Belgium	Douay	,, 16, 1652	328
F. Herrera, James	Spain	Mexico	Nov. 27, 1695	375
F. Hildebrand, Gaspar	Silesia	Omultz	Dec. 13, 1655	393
F. Hoffeus, Paul	Germany	Ingolstadt	,, 17, 1608	397
F. Hollandre, Peter de	Belgium	Holland	,, 19, 1620	398
F. Holland, Thomas	England	London	,, 22, 1642	401
F. Hazart, Cornelius	Belgium	Belgium	,, 25, 1690	405
F. Hitzettea, John	France	Vienna	,, 27, 1634	406

I.

NAME.	COUNTRY.	PLACE OF DEATH.	DAY AND YEAR.	PAGE.
Ignatius, Martin *Coad.*		Bohemia	May 31, 1739	168
F. IGNATIUS, SAINT *Founder*	Spain	Rome	July 31, 1556	235
F. Ibannez, Antony	Spain	Saragossa	Aug. 17, 1594	255
F. Isenbrant, John	Belgium	Antwerp	Dec. 21, 1624	401

J.

F. Jacobi, Bartholomew		Potosi, W. Indies	Jan. 13, 1589	15
F. Juliis, Ignatius de		Theate, Italy	Feb. 13, 1626	49
F. Justinian, Austin	Genoa	Naples	March 2, 1590	69
F. Justinian, Fabius	Greece	Morica, Sicily	„ 13, 1648	79
Judkiewicz, Michael *Coad.*		Vilna	April 6, 1666	103
F. Jerome, St. Francis	Italy	Naples	May 11, 1716	143
F. Junceda, John		Spain	„ 31, 1598	168
F. Josiski, Ignatius	Poland	Vienna	June 11, 1655	180
F. Joanelli, Francis	Italy	Philippines	„ 25, 1622	196
Jucunanga, Nicholas Keyan *Schol.*	Japan	Nangasachi	July 31, 1633	236
F. Justinelli, Peter	Italy	Castiglione	„ 31, 1630	236
F. Jay, Claude le	Savoy	Vienna	Aug. 6, 1552	242
Juan, Dominic *Coad.*	Portugal	Coimbra	Sept. 2, 1589	273
F. Jühn, John	Germany	Crumlow	Oct. 16, 1625	328
F. Jocques, Isaac	France	America	„ 18, 1646	331
F. Jannot, Nicholas	Belgium	Ghent	Nov. 8, 1634	355
F. Justiniani, George	Greece	Bologna	Dec. 3, 1644	383

K.

F. Kuber, Matthew	Germany	Walz, Germany	Feb. 4, 1646	40
Kysai, St. James *Coad.*	Japan	Japan	„ 5, 1597	41
F. Kedd, Jodoc	Germany	Vienna	March 27, 1657	92
F. Kölick, Luke	Moravia	Transylvania	April 20, 1690	119
F. Keynes, John	England	Watten	May 15, 1697	148
F. Klatauski, Albert	Bohemia	Klatau, Bohemia	„ 16, 1643	150
Kisacu, Blessed John *Schol.*	Japan	Nangasachi	June 20, 1626	190
F. Klinka, Mathias	Moravia	Krems	July 2, 1658	204
Kostka, St. Stanislaus *Schol.*	Poland	Rome	Aug. 15, 1568	253
F. Kempis, John		Heilgenstadt	„ 26, 1626	265
Kidera, or Guindera, John	Japan	Ximabara	„ 29, 1633	268
F. Krawarski, Adam	Silesia	Prague	„ 30, 1660	268
Kiuni, Antony *Schol.*	Japan	Nangasachi	Sept. 10, 1622	285
F. Kojalonicz, Albert	Poland	Wilna	Oct. 6, 1677	317
Kolowrat, Wenceslaus *Schol.*	Bohemia	Rome	„ 9, 1659	320
F. Kacski, Gabriel	Poland	Cracow	„ 10, 1666	322

NAME.	COUNTRY.	PLACE OF DEATH.	DAY AND YEAR.	PAGE.
F. Kihn, John	Prussia	Koningsberg	Oct. 21, 1659	335
F. Kessel, Leonard	Belgium	Cologne	,, 26, 1574	340
F. Kaldi, George	Hungary	Presburg	,, 30, 1634	344
Kostka, Paul	Poland	Petrikoff	Nov. 13, 1607	359

L.

F. Lessius, Leonard		Louvain	Jan. 15, 1623	16
F. Laynez, James *General* ...	Spain	Rome	,, 19, 1565	21
F. Lallemant, Jerome ...	France	Quebec	,, 26, 1673	28
F. Lopez, Jerome		Valencia	Feb. 2, 1658	38
F. Leon, John	Spain	Triguera, Spain	,, 8, 1566	44
F. Leon, John	Belgium	Belgium	,, 8.	44
F. Liverza, Vincent		America	,, 20, 1693	60
Lazzari, Basil *Coad.* ...	Sicily	Catania, Sicily	,, 25.	64
F. Leleszy, John	Hungary	Loretto	,, 26, 1594	65
F. Landini, Silvester	Italy	Corsica	March 3, 1564	70
F. Levesque, William ...		Naples	,, 11, 1622	77
F. Lallemant, Gabriel ...	France	Canada	,, 17, 1649	83
F. Labbé, Philip	France	Paris	,, 17, 1667	84
F. Lee, Patrick	Ireland	Ireland	,, 24, 1650	89
F. Lorin, John	France	Dôle, France	,, 26, 1634	91
F. Lancicius, Nicholas ...	Poland	Cown, Lithuania	,, 30, 1652	95
Lechner, John Baptist *Coad.*		Vienna	April 3, 1654	100
F. Lallemant, Louis	France	Bourges	,, 5, 1635	101
F. Lesley, Alexander ...	Scotland	Rome	,, 7, 1760	104
F. Lorraine, Charles de ...	France	Toulouse	,, 28, 1631	127
F. Ledesma, Valerius de ...	Spain	Manilla	May 6, 1639	138
F. Lopez, Francis	Portugal	Abyssinia	,, 15, 1597	149
F. Laski, Martin	Poland	Cracow	,, 23, 1615	159
Loffredo, Antony *Schol.* ...	Italy	Naples	,, 26, 1619	163
F. Löhner, Tobias	Germany	Munich	,, 26, 1697	163
Lopez, Francis *Coad.* ...	Spain	Lima	June 5, 1610	174
Laskowski, John *Schol.* ...	Poland	Cracow	July 20, 1624	225
F. Lopez, Antony	Spain	Peru	,, 23, 1596	227
Lozan, Brother Peter ...		Alcala	,, 28, 1599	227
F. Leon. William	Belgium	Utrecht	,, 27, 1612	232
Laynez, Mark *Coad.* ...	Spain	Rome	,, 30, 1541	235
Leon, Antonio de *Coad.* ...	Spain	Seville	Aug. 6, 1627	243
F. Lecouteux, Stephen ...	France	China	,, 8, 1730	246
F. Lugo, John de *Cardinal* ...	Spain	Rome	,, 21, 1660	259
F. Longobardi, Nicolas ...	Sicily	Pekin	Sept. 1, 1654	272
Laparo, John *Coad.* ...	Italy	Drepano	,, 6, 1630	279
F. Leoman, Andrew ...	Lithuania	Polosk	,, 9, 1620	283
F. Lorenzana, Marcellus de ...	Spain	Paraguay	,, 12, 1652	288
F. Laugemantel, Paul ...	Germany	Krems	,, 19, 1634	296
F. Laterna, Martin	Poland	On the Baltic Sea	,, 30, 1598	307
F. Lætavalle, Michael ...	Italy	Syracuse	Oct. 5, 1590	314
F. Loarte, Gaspar	Spain	Valencia	,, 8, 1579	319

NAME.	COUNTRY.	PLACE OF DEATH.	DAY AND YEAR.	PAGE.
Lopez, Alphonsus … …		Indian Ocean	Oct. 11, 1555	322
F. Ledesma, John de … …	America	Mexico	„ 12, 1637	324
Lowick, Joseph *Coad.* …	England	Liege	„ 16, 1675	328
F. Lopez, Gaspar … …		Murcia	„ 24, 1558	338
F. Lopez, Francis … …	Portugal	East Indies	„ 28, 1568	342
F. Layman, Paul … …	Germany	Constance	Nov. 13, 1625	360
F. Ledesma, James de …	Spain	Rome	„ 18, 1575	365
F. Lupatino, Hector … …	Italy	Castiglione	„ 23, 1621	371
F. Loste, James … …	France	Bologna	„ 30, 1548	379
F. Lopez, Alexander … …	Spain	Mindanao	Dec. 13, 1655	392

M.

F. Maldonado, John … …	Spain	Rome	Jan. 5, 1583	6
Meseguer, John *Coad.* …		Majorca	„ 6, 1580	7
F. Mascaregnas, Peter …	Portugal	Manado, East Indies	„ 7.	7
Manuel, Louis *Coad.* …		Bahia	„ 7.	8
F. Madrid, Antony … …		Alcala	„ 12, 1563	13
F. Manrique, Peter … …		Alcala	„ 12, 1577	14
F. Mello, Martin de … …		Evora	„ 14, 1617	16
F. Musart, Charles … …	Belgium	Vienna	„ 17, 1653	20
F. Moro, Silvester … …	Italy	Rome	„ 17, 1687	20
F. Maunoir, Ven. Julian …	France	Brittany	„ 28, 1683	30
F. Mendoza, Sanchez de …	Spain	Cadiz	„ 31, 1649	34
F. Martinez, Emmanuel …	Portugal	Guadaloupe	Feb. 1, 1632	36
F. Morse, Henry … …	England	London	„ 1, 1645	36
Miki, St. Paul *Schol.* …	Japan	Nangasachi	„ 5, 1597	41
F. Martinon, John … …	France	Bourdeaux	„ 5, 1662	41
F. Montmorency, Francis de …	France	Douay	„ 5, 1640	41
F. Masie, Jaspar … …		France	Tournon	„ 9, 1617	46
F. Motta, Calixtus a … …			„ 11.	47
Mlocki, James *Schol.* …	Poland	Riga	„ 12, 1611	48
F. Mayering, James … …	France	Alsace	„ 15, 1634	51
F. Martinez, Peter de *Bishop.*	Portugal	Malacca	„ 18, 1598	57
F. Morales, Francis de …		Valladolid	„ 20, 1595	60
F. Malvése, Nervé … …	France	Clerac, France	„ 21, 1622	61
F. Metsch, Andrew … …	Germany	Glatz, Germany	„ 23, 1657	62
F. Martin, Ignatius … …		Coimbra	„ 28, 1598	66
F. Mumford, James … …	England	England	March 9, 1666	75
Mocchio, John Bapt. *Coad.* …		Piacenza	„ 10, 1651	76
F. Meczynski, Albert …	Poland	Nangasachi	„ 23, 1643	88
F. Moralés, Diego de …	Spain	Nangasachi	„ 25, 1643	90
F. Marquez, Francis … …	Japan	Nangasachi	„ 25, 1643	90
Mayr, Baltassar *Coad.* …	Germany	Brun, Germany	„ 26, 1627	91
Martinez, Francis Minore *Schol.*	China	China	„ 31, 1606	95
F. Martinez, Ven. Diego …	Spain	Lima	April 2, 1626	98
F. Medeiros, Gonzales de …		Lisbon	„ 4, 1552	101
F. Montaya, Ruez de …	Portugal	Lima	„ 11, 1632	108
F. Maignet, Louis … …		Pont-a-Mousson	„ 19, 1657	117
F. Moloto, Benedict … …	Italy	Messina	„ 21, 1634	119

NAME.	COUNTRY.	PLACE OF DEATH.	DAY AND YEAR.	PAGE.
Magni, James *Schol.*		Mantua	April 24, 1607	123
F. Melendios, Gonzalez	Spain	Naples	,, 24, 1580	124
F. Mendora, Christopher de	Spain	Paraguay	,, 25, 1635	124
F. Manfiti, Alfius	Italy	Sicily	,, 26, 1635	125
F. Monterey, Peter	Spain	Seville	,, 27, 1598	126
F. Mambrecht, John	Scotland	Warsaw	,, 28, 1670	128
F. Mercado, Jerome de	Spain	Mexico	May 2.	133
F. Mendoza, Francis de		Mindanao	,, 7, 1642	139
F. Miranda, Ildephonsus de	Spain	Peru	,, 11, 1609	144
F. Massé, Edmund	France	Canada	,, 12, 1643	145
F. Mello, Gonzalez Vas de	Portugal	Lisbon	,, 14, 1563	147
F. Maffon, Simon		Horodlo, Poland	,, 15, 1657	149
Martini, John *Coad.*	Spain	Saragossa	,, 18, 1617	153
Mendoza, Diego *Coad.*		Madrid	,, 19, 1578	155
F. Maccadio (Machado) Bl. J. Bapt.	The Azores	Nangasachi	,, 22, 1617	158
F. Mendoza, Antony de	Spain	Rome	,, 24, 1596	160
F. Montera, Diego	Portugal	Coimbra	,, 27, 1630	164
F. Marica, Simon		Cagliari, Sardinia	,, 27, 1656	164
Monier, Peter *Schol.*	France	Paris	,, 28, 1582	165
Martz, Michael *Schol.*	Silesia	Germany	,, 16, 1649	167
F. Meagh, John	Ireland	Bohemia	,, 31, 1739	168
F. Mendoza, Francis de	Portugal	Lyons	June 3, 1626	171
F. Martius, Martin	Germany	Hang-choo	,, 6, 1661	175
F. Macedonio, Francis		Naples	,, 16, 1656	184
F. Massari, Baptist		Tonquin	,, 15.	185
Marino, John *Schol.*	Spain	Bilboa, Spain	,, 21, 1625	191
Martini, Joseph *Schol.*	Italy	Parma	,, 22, 1578	192
F. Mettam, Thomas	England	Wisbeach, England	,, 28, 1592	199
Mathias, Brother	Poland	Stockholm	,, 28, 1610	200
F. Mendez, Alphonsus *Patriarch*	Portugal	Goa	,, 29, 1656	200
F. Martin, Peter	France	Rome	,, 29, 1716	201
F. Mantuano, Paul	Italy	Palermo	July 3, 1575	206
F. Marquez, Ferdinand	Spain	Ocaña, Spain	,, 3, 1584	206
F. Miranda, Alphonsus de	Spain	Peru	,, 3, 1609	206
F. Mendoza, Antonio de Escobar	Spain	Valladolid	,, 4, 1669	207
F. Moxica, John Paul		Saragossa	,, 6, 1564	209
F. Montoya, Thomas de	India	Manilla	,, 14, 1627	217
F. Mendoza, Ferdinand de	Spain	Seville	,, 16, 1648	220
F. Martinez, Antonio	Spain	Logrono	,, 17, 1564	221
F. Massoni, Laurence	Italy	Manilla	,, 19, 1631	223
Mariani, Christopher *Coad.*		Turin	,, 19, 1599	224
F. Marchienicz, George	Poland	Brunsberg	,, 19, 1657	224
F. Martinez, Emmanuel	Portugal	Malabar	,, 22, 1656	226
F. Manuel, John	Spain	Toledo	,, 29, 1586	234
F. Mercurian, Everard *General*	Belgium	Rome	Aug. 1, 1580	237
F. Mairhofer, Earnest	Germany	Halle	,, 2.	239
F. Molina, Peter de	Spain	Granada	,, 3, 1600	239
F. Miller, Sebastian	Belgium	Toulouse	,, 7, 1598	243
F. Menard, Renée	France	Canada	,, 10, 1661	247
F. Montmorency, Florence	Belgium	Lille	,, 12, 1659	249
F. Mancinelli, Julius	Italy	Naples	,, 14, 1618	252
F. Mendoza, Ignatius	Spain	Alcala	,, 15, 1602	253

NAME.	COUNTRY.	PLACE OF DEATH.	DAY AND YEAR.	PAGE.
F. Martincourt, John Francis ...	France	Aurillac	Aug. 18, 1628	256
F. Murdock, William ...	Scotland	Pont-a-Mousson	,, 21, 1616	260
F. Martez, Emmanuel ...	Portugal	Trichinopoly	,, 22, 1656	261
F. Miro, James	Spain	Rome	,, 25, 1590	263
F. Miroldi, Francis	Italy	Bivona	,, 26, 1611	265
Manriquez, Brother James ...		Barcelona	,, 26, 1589	265
F. Martin, Peter		Logrono	,, 30, 1564	269
F. Mainbourg, Erard	France	Nancy	Sept. 1, 1644	273
Martinez, Peter Coad. ...	Portugal	Cusco, Peru	,, 2, 1624	274
F. Macciado, Antony ...	Portugal	Nigritia	,, 4, 1627	276
F. Medrada, Alphonsus de ...	Spain	Granada	,, 5, 1648	277
F. Magirus, John	Germany	Spires	,, 8, 1609	282
F. Marchese, John	Sicily	Palermo	,, 13, 1676	289
F. Mascareña, Peter	Portugal	Lisbon	,, 20, 1597	297
Mendoza, John Schol. ...	Spain	Marino	,, 20, 1556	297
F. Macciado, Francis	Portugal	Abyssinia	,, 28, 1625	305
F. Martinez, Peter		Isle of Tatacuran	,, 28, 1556	305
F. Mailo, Matthew	Germany	Ettingen	,, 28, 1634	306
F. Monrois, Ferdinand ...	Spain	Lima	,, 29, 1626	306
F. Mourira, Maurice	Portugal	On the Indian Ocean	,, 30, 1639	307
F. Martrese, Vincent	Italy	Barcelona	,, 30, 1607	308
F. Missas, John de las ...	Spain	Is. of Mariduque, E.I.	Oct. 4.	312
F. Mallean, Charles	France	Moulins	,, 4, 1635	313
F. Monitola, Angelo	Italy	Santa Cruz	,, 7.	318
F. Mastorelli, Martin	Italy	Naples	,, 8, 1726	319
F. Molina, Louis	Spain	Madrid	,, 12, 1600	323
F. Mastrilli, Ven. Marcellus Franc.	Italy	Nangasachi	,, 17, 1637	329
F. Montal, James	France	Puy	,, 20, 1680	334
Matthew, — Schol.	Japan	Nangasachi	,, 21, 1633	335
F. Manconi, John Andrew ...	Sardinia	Cassari	,, 23, 1635	336
F. Montalto, Michael	Sicily	Neti, Italy	,, 25, 1637	338
F. Mattos, Antony de	Portugal	Brazil	,, 25, 1645	339
F. Mesquita, Ven. James de ...	Portugal	Japan	Nov. 4, 1614	350
F. Massimano, Theodore ...	Italy	Cosenza	,, 11, 1653	358
F. Mangot, Adrian	Belgium	Antwerp	,, 15, 1624	363
F. Moranta, Jerome	Spain	Mexico	,, 19, 1616	366
Martin, Nicholas Schol. ...	Germany	Ingolstadt	,, 21, 1634	369
F. Manareo, Oliver	Belgium	Tournay	,, 28, 1614	376
F. Maus, John	Belgium	Bruges	,, 28, 1621	377
F. Metella, John	Portugal	Ceylon	Dec. 6, 1616	385
F. Martinez, Emmanuel ...	Spain	Philippines	,, 12, 1626	391
F. Monticl, John	Italy	Mindanao, Philipp.	,, 13, 1655	392
Montalto, Diego Coad. ...	America	Chili	,, 14, 1621	393
F. Mustoni, Mark Antony ...	Italy	Forli	,, 15, 1589	394
Merle, John de Schol. ...		Ashaffenbourg	,, 16.	396
F. Matheó, Claude	France	Ancona	,, 24, 1587	403
F. Montoya, John de	Spain	Potosi, Peru	,, 30.	409

N.

NAME.	COUNTRY.	PLACE OF DEATH.	DAY AND YEAR.	PAGE.
F. Nobile, Robert de	Italy	Meliapor	Jan. 16, 1656	18
Nobile, Robert Cardinal de *Schol.*	Italy	Rome	,, 17, 1559	19
F. Nunez, Louis		Messina	,, 30, 1576	33
F. Nove Chaupenois, Anne di		Canada	Feb. 2, 1646	38
F. Neville, Francis	England	England	,, 25, 1679	64
F. Nadasi, John	Hungary	Vienna	March 3, 1679	71
F. Nadal, Jerome		Rome	April 3, 1580	99
F. Navarola, John Paul	Italy	Rome	May 18, 1597	153
Neri, Emmanuel *Coad.*	Italy	Klaussenburg	June 9, 1603	178
F. Netterville, Robert	Ireland	Drogheda	,, 15, 1649	184
Nicholas, Brother *Coad.*	Poland	Stockholm	,, 28, 1610	200
F. Nugüez, Leonard	Portugal	Western Ocean	,, 30, 1554	202
F. Neuville, Charles Frey de	France	St. Germain	July 13, 1774	217
Nottin, Philip *Coad.*	Belgium	Utrecht	,, 14, 1638	217
Nicofori, Thomas *Coad.*	Japan	Nangasachi	,, 22, 1633	226
F. Nickel, Goswin *General*	Germany	Rome	,, 31, 1664	236
F. Noyelle, Philip de	France		Aug. 6, 1628	243
F. Nugnez, Melchior	Portugal	Goa	,, 10, 1752	247
Nichesole, Lælius *Schol.*	Italy	Novellara	,, 17, 1583	256
Naves, John *Coad.*	Spain	Gerona	,, 27, 1605	266
F. Nolhuc, Antony	France	Avignon	Oct. 19, 1791	333
F. Nacaura, Julian	Japan	Nangasachi	,, 21, 1633	334
F. Nuza, Ven. Aloysius la	Sicily	Palermo	,, 21, 1656	335
F. Navarro, Blessed Peter Paul	Italy	Ximabara	Nov. 1, 1622	347
F. Neville, Edmund	England	England	,, 9, 1648	355
F. Nugent, Nicholas	Ireland	Oporto	,, 22, 1656	370
F. Noyelle, Charles de *General*	Belgium	Rome	Dec. 11, 1686	390
F. Nugnez, John	Portugal	Goa	,, 20, 1562	399
Nacaxima, Blessed Michael *Schol.*	Japan	Nangasachi	,, 25, 1628	404
F. Nugnez, John	Portugal	Lisbon	,, 29, 1616	407

O.

F. Oviedo, Francis de		Alcala	Feb. 9, 1651	46
F. Oller, Raphael	Spain	Majorca	,, 19, 1621	58
F. Otelli, Jerome		Sicily	March 4.	71
F. Ogilvie, John	Scotland	Glasgow	,, 10, 1615	75
F. Orunnius, Andrew Ortiz	Biscay	Peru	,, 28.	93
F. Ozonio, Gaspar		Paraguay	April 1, 1639	97
F. Oldcorne, Edward	England	Worcester	,, 7, 1606	103
Oliveri, Antony *Coad.*		Palermo	May 8, 1576	140
F. Onneking, Conrad	Germany	Mayence	,, 12, 1607	145
F. Orlandini, Nicholas	Italy	Rome	,, 17, 1606	152
F. Oleskiewiez, Bartholomew	Lithuania	Pultowa	June 16, 1650	185

Index.—O, P.

NAME.	COUNTRY.	PLACE OF DEATH.	DAY AND YEAR.	PAGE.
F. Oviedo, Ven. Andrew *Patriarch*	Spain	Abyssinia	June 29, 1580	201
Ortunez, John *Schol.*	Spain	Salamanca	July 28.	233
Ota, Blessed Augustine *Schol.*	Japan	Ikinosima, Japan	Aug. 10, 1622	248
F. Otazo, Francis de	Spain	Huete, Spain	,, 16, 1622	254
F. Olave, Martin	Spain	Rome	,, 17, 1556	255
F. Olivarez, Bernard	Belgium	Tournay	,, 22, 1556	260
F. Orsini, Alexander *Cardinal*	Italy	Bracciano	,, 22, 1626	260
F. Ochoia, Michael	Spain	Syracuse	Oct. 1, 1575	309
Onate, Dominic de *Coad.*	Spain	Cozorla	,, 4, 1596	313
F. Orimbello, Angelo	Italy	Bologna	,, 7, 1630	317
F. Ortega, Emmanuel	Portugal	La Plata	,, 21.	335
Onizucca, Blessed Peter *Schol.*	Japan	Ximabara	Nov. 1, 1622	347
Ovando, Alphonsus *Schol.*	Spain	Lima	,, 6, 1614	352
Owen, Nicholas (Little John) *Coad.*	England	London	,, 12, 1606	358
F. Orosco, Diego de		Mexico	,, 18, 1616	365
F. Oliva, John Paul *General*	Genoa	Rome	,, 26, 1681	374
F. Orsini, Julius	Italy	Placenza	Dec. 9, 1620	389
Ortega, Lawrence *Coad.*	Spain	Placenza	,, 16, 1644	396
Ortolano, Francis *Coad.*	Spain	Cagliari	,, 20, 1623	400
F. Oppel, Bernard	Moravia	Prague	,, 29, 1651	408

P.

NAME	COUNTRY	PLACE OF DEATH	DAY AND YEAR	PAGE
F. Pelletier, John		Toulouse	Jan. 1, 1654	1
F. Puellas, Diego		Gandia	,, 4, 1576	5
F. Pinto, Francis		Brazil	,, 11, 1608	12
F. Paz, James Alvarez de		Potosi, Peru	,, 17, 1620	19
F. Paranympho, Gaspar	Sicily	Naro, Sicily	,, 23, 1624	25
F. Peckham, Robert	England	England	,, 25, 1621	27
F. Ponte, Bernard de		Naples	,, 27, 1644	29
F. Paliola, Francis	Italy	Mindanao, Philipp.	,, 29, 1648	31
F. Pujol, John	France	Avignon	,, 30, 1633	32
F. Pasquale, Julius	Italy	Guadaloupe	Feb. 1, 1632	36
F. Ponce, John	Spain	Cuidad Real	,, 1, 1606	36
F. Perin, Leonard	France	Besançon	,, 10, 1638	46
F. Ponte, Ven. Louis da	Spain	Valladolid	,, 16, 1624	54
F. Petkoroski, Gaspar	Poland	Cracow	,, 16, 1612	54
F. Prado, Jerome de		Manilla	,, 17, 1605	56
Prescott, Cuthbert Stephen *Coad.*	England	London	,, 20, 1647	60
F. Pavone, Francis		Naples	,, 24, 1637	63
F. Posevianus, Anthony	Italy	Ferrara	,, 26, 1611	65
F. Perez, Antony		Spain	March 2, 1649	69
F. Pond, Thomas	England	England	,, 5, 1615	72
F. Planterose, Robert		Hesdin, France	,, 9, 1655	75
F. Pasman, — *Cardinal*		Presburg	,, 19, 1637	85
F. Perez, Francis		Antwerp	,, 22, 1655	88
F. Pepper, John	Scotland	Terregles, Scotland	,, 24, 1810	89

Index—P. 431

NAME.	COUNTRY.	PLACE OF DEATH.	DAY AND YEAR.	PAGE.
F. Paez, Stephen		Lima	March 26, 1613	91
F. Paterno, Ferdinand ...		Catania, Sicily	,, 26, 1604	91
F. Pisquedda, Salvator ...	Sardinia	Sassari, Sardinia	,, 27, 1624	92
F. Persons, Robert	England	Rome	April 15, 1610	112
F. Paez, Ven. Gaspar ...	Portugal	Abyssinia	,, 25, 1635	124
F. Pereira, Ven. John ...	Portugal	Abyssinia	,, 25, 1635	124
F. Padial, Ven. Emmanuel ...		Granada	,, 27, 1725	127
F. Page, Francis	England	London	,, 29, 1602	129
F. Ponceot, Claude	France	Le Puy	,, 30, 1609	130
F. Potier, Gabriel		Caen	May 9, 1655	141
F. Polo, Bartholomew ...	Spain	Quito	,, 10, 1649	141
F. Petre, Edward	England	Watten	,, 15, 1699	148
F. Paez, Peter	Spain	Abyssinia	,, 20, 1622	156
F. Parricios, John Sebastian ...	Spain	Peru	,, 21, 1612	156
Parneso, John *Coad.* ...		Cracow	,, 29, 1638	166
F. Pallavicini, Sforza *Cardinal*	Italy	Rome	June 4, 1667	173
Perez, Michael *Coad.* ...		Seville	,, 6, 1649	175
F. Piccolomini, Francis *General*	Italy	Rome	,, 17, 1651	186
F. Poncet, Joseph	France	Martinique	,, 18, 1657	188
F. Pacecho, Blessed Francis ...		Nangasachi	,, 20, 1626	190
F. Pinamonti, John Peter ...	Italy	Orta, Lombardy	,, 24, 1703	194
F. Pignatelli, Lucius	Italy	Naples	,, 28, 1656	199
F. Papebrack, Daniel		Antwerp	,, 28, 1714	200
F. Poso, Ildephonsus à ...	Spain	Gusco, Peru	,, 29, 1606	200
F. Pierre, William		Moulins	,, 30, 1561	202
F. Paregard, Francis	France	Tonquin	July 5, 1695	208
F. Pescatore, John	Italy	Naples	,, 7, 1591	210
F. Poraecky, Thomas	Lithuania	Pultowa	,, 9, 1653	212
F. Pequet, Peter	France	Carpentras	,, 11, 1591	214
F. Pallavicini, Julio	Italy	Genoa	,, 11, 1657	215
F. Paesman, Gerard		Utrecht	,, 20, 1638	224
F. Piña, Balthasar de	Spain	Lima	,, 29, 1611	234
F. Platus, Jerome	Milan	Rome	Aug. 14, 1591	252
F. Perez, John	Spain	Peru	,, 24, 1609	262
Pozzo, Andrew *Coad.* ...	Italy	Vienna	,, 31, 1709	270
F. Pinto, Bl. Anthony Yxida ...	Japan	Nangasachi	Sept. 3, 1632	275
Paro, Charles de *Schol.* ...		Ghent	,, 5, 1621	278
F. Pimentel, Francis	Portugal	Tonquin	,, 5, 1675	278
F. Pongracz, Ven. Stephen ...	Hungary	Cassau, Transylvania	,, 7, 1639	281
F. Parisot, John	France	Verdun	,, 9, 1651	283
Paz, Andrew		Coast of Brazil	,, 14, 1591	290
F. Pe-cho, Bernardino ...	China	Jafantapa, E. Indies	,, 15, 1628	291
F. Pirez, Vasco	Portugal	Lisbon	,, 21, 1590	298
F. Pineda, Michael	Japan	Nangasachi	,, 22, 1633	299
F. Paumbgartner, Tobias ...	Germany	Augsburg	,, 26, 1627	303
F. Pereunin, Dominic ...	France	Pekin	,, 27, 1741	305
F. Pereira, Bernard	Portugal	Abyssinia	,, 28, 1625	305
F. Pardos, Francis	Spain	Lerena, Spain	Oct. 2, 1677	316
F. Paradinas, Bonaventure ...	Spain	Monaco	,, 5, 1595	315
F. Peralta, John	Spain	Toledo	,, 7, 1588	317
F. Pasqual, Nicholus		Indian Ocean	,, 11, 1555	322
F. Pedelongo, John	Italy	Naples	,, 11, 1569	322

NAME.	COUNTRY.	PLACE OF DEATH.	DAY AND YEAR.	PAGE.
F. Pennant, Francis Philip	Belgium	Huy	Oct. 13, 1653	325
F. Puche, Francis	Spain	Philippines	,, 15, 1650	327
F. Pompon, Ignatius		Lyons	,, 15, 1628	327
Peter —— Schol.	Japan	Nangasachi	,, 21, 1633	335
F. Plozzins, Blasius	Poland	Kalisch	,, 22, 1634	336
F. Pisa, Januarius		Aquila	,, 28, 1656	343
F. Passoki, Lawrence	Silesia	Germany	Nov. 2, 1642	348
F. Ponce, Aloysius	Spain	Granada	,, 2, 1611	348
F. Pinas, Anthony	Portugal	Evora	,, 3, 1608	349
F. Petris, Francis de	Italy	Tchao-tche	,, 5, 1593	350
F. Paez, Stephen	Spain	Lima	,, 5, 1613	350
F. Piccio, Bernardin	Italy	Tivoli	,, 8, 1612	354
F. Pretere, William de	Belgium	Antwerp	,, 10, 1626	357
F. Palmio, Benedict	Italy	Ferrara	,, 14, 1598	360
F. Pignatelli, Ven. Joseph Mary	Spain	Rome	,, 15, 1811	361
F. Perez, Bartholomew	Spain	Villagarcia	,, 24, 1621	373
F. Padilla, Anthony de	Spain	Valladolid	,, 29, 1611	377
F. Palao, Ferdinand de Castro	Spain	Medina	Dec. 1, 1633	381
F. Polingotti, Louis	Italy	Ceylon	,, 6, 1616	385
Prato, Alphonsus de Coad.	Spain	Salamanca	,, 8, 1559	388
F. Petaux, Denis	France	Paris	,, 11, 1652	391
F. Piwnichi, Nicholas	Prussia	Dantzic	,, 15, 1631	395
F. Pelinga, George	Moravia	Glattow, Bohemia	,, 17, 1648	397
F. Polanco, John	Spain	Rome	,, 21, 1577	401
F. Perrin, Charles Joseph		Liege	,, 23, 1767	403
F. Pollieni, Nicholas	Savoy	France	,, 28, 1623	407

Q.

F. Quiros, Louis	Florida	North America	Feb. 3, 1571	39

R.

NAME.	COUNTRY.	PLACE OF DEATH.	DAY AND YEAR.	PAGE.
Rocha, Vincent de Schol.		Evora	Jan. 4, 1610	4
F. Ruiz, John		Madrid	,, 9, 1556	10
F. Ramirez, Jerome		Mexico	,, 12, 1621	14
Renart, Edmund Coad.		Liege	,, 31, 1643	34
F. Ruiz, Jerome	Spain	Lima	Feb. 2, 1592	38
F. Riviere, Simon	France	France	,, 7, 1610	44
F. Renesse, John de		Namur, Belgium	,, 11.	47
F. Rodriguez, Christopher	Portugal	Naples	,, 12, 1581	48
Rion, Paul Coad.	Japan	Manilla	,, 17, 1615	56
F. Rodriguez, Alphonsus	Spain	Seville	,, 21, 1616	61
F. Robe, John	Scotland	Douay	March 13, 1633	79
F. Reginald, Valerian	Burgundy	Dole, Burgundy	,, 14, 1623	80
F. Ruiz, Diego		Seville	,, 15, 1532	82

NAME.	COUNTRY.	PLACE OF DEATH.	DAY AND YEAR.	PAGE.
F. Roche, James		Cahors, France	March 18, 1633	84
F. Rubini, Antony	Italy	Japan	,, 22, 1643	87
F. Romero, Peter		Paraguay	,, 22, 1645	87
Rodes, Francis *Schol.*		Valencia	,, 31, 1621	96
F. Ripari, Anthony		Paraguay	April 1, 1639	97
F. Rabi, Justin		Cracow	,, 1, 1612	97
F. Regi, Charles	France	Amiens	,, 4, 1626	100
F. Ramirez, John		Alcala	,, 4, 1586	100
Rosner, Daniel *Coad.*	Germany	Germany	,, 18, 1630	117
F. Ruffino, Albert	Italy	Reggio, Italy	,, 22, 1651	122
F. Ripalda, John Martinez de	Spain	Madrid	,, 26, 1648	126
F. Rho, James	Italy	Pekin	,, 27, 1638	126
F. Roberti, Venusto	Italy	Parma	May 4, 1630	136
F. Ruggieri, Michael	Italy	Salerno	,, 11, 1607	143
F. Ricci, Matthew	Italy	Pekin	,, 11, 1610	143
F. Roseffe, Gregory	Germany	Augsburg	,, 15, 1623	149
F. Rodrigo, Peter	Spain	Toledo	,, 29.	166
Ruiz, James *Coad.*	Spain	Majorca	June 1, 1601	169
F. Ribera, John de	Spain	Manilla	,, 5, 1622	173
F. Rosmer, Paul	Belgium	Grätin, Styria	,, 8, 1664	177
F. Rastell, John	England	Ingolstadt	,, 15, 1600	184
Rinxei or Binxei, Bl. Peter *Schol.*	Japn	Nangasachi	,, 20, 1626	190
F. Riccioli, John Baptist	Italy	Bologna	,, 25, 1671	196
F. Ramos, John Francis		Carmona, Andalusia	,, 27, 1719	198
F. Realino, Ven. Bernardine	Italy	Lecce, Apulia	July 2, 1616	204
F. Riswig, Theodore	Belgium	Neustadt	,, 4, 1624	207
Ruiz, Louis *Coad.*	Spain	Alcala	,, 5, 1599	208
F. Ribellio, John		Evora	,, 14, 1602	218
F. Rodriguez, Simon	Portugal	Lisbon	,, 15, 1579	219
F. Ribera, John	Spain	Cali, America	,, 19, 1649	223
F. Reyno, Michael de		Madrid	,, 20, 1604	225
F. Rose, William	France	Czestokoff, Poland	,, 25, 1657	230
Renée, Brother	France	America	Aug. 5.	242
F. Raulino, Francis	Italy	Parma	,, 13, 1657	251
F. Romano, Charles		Gonsano, Sicily	,, 16, 1624	254
F. Rubiola, Jerome	Spain	Sienna	,, 21, 1571	259
F. Ribera, Nugnez	Portugal	Amboyna, E. Indies	,, 22, 1549	260
F. Rasles, Sebastian	France	Canada	,, 23, 1724	262
F. Rocher, Peter Guérin du	France	Paris	Sept. 2, 1792	274
F. Rocher, Francis Guérin du	France	Paris	,, 2, 1792	274
F. Ragueneau, —	France	Paris	,, 3, 1680	276
F. Raimondo Vincent	Italy	Catania	,, 4, 1637	276
F. Rudomina, Andrew	Lithuania	China	,, 5, 1631	277
F. Ribera, Christopher		Burgos	,, 9, 1599	284
Riocan, Thomas *Coad.*	Japan	Cocyra, Japan	,, 9, 1633	284
F. Rho, John	Italy	Rome	,, 10, 1661	285
F. Richeaume, Louis		Bourdeaux	,, 15, 1625	292
F. Ribadeneira, Peter	Spain	Madrid	,, 22, 1611	299
F. Rosweyde, Herbert	Belgium	Antwerp	Oct. 5, 1629	315
F. Rhem, James	Germany	Ingolstadt	,, 12, 1618	324
F. Romeo, Sebastian	Italy	Rome	,, 13, 1574	324

DDD

Index.—R, S.

NAME.	COUNTRY.	PLACE OF DEATH.	DAY AND YEAR.	PAGE.
F. Rongère, William de la	France	Rennes	Oct. 14.	326
F. Rico, John	Spain	Urgel	,, 18, 1605	331
F. Ronsillo, Francis	Spain	Coast of Gallicia	,, 19, 1596	332
F. Richter, Samuel	Moravia	Brünn	,, 22, 1648	336
Russell, Ralph *Schol.*	England	Liège	,, 23, 1634	336
F. Rosillo, Francis	Spain	Upon the British Sea	,, 28, 1596	342
Rodriguez, Blessed Alphonsus	Spain	Majorca	,, 31, 1617	345
F. Raynand, Theophilus	France	Lyons	,, 31, 1663	345
F. Rhodes, Alexander de	France	Persia	Nov. 5, 1660	351
F. Rodriguez, Alphonsus	Spain	Paraguay	,, 15, 1618	362
F. Retz, Francis *General*	Prague	Rome	,, 19, 1750	367
F. Ricci, Lawrence *General*	Florence	Rome	,, 24, 1775	371
F. Ribera, Francis	Spain	Salamanca	,, 24, 1601	372
Raflinghem, Ignatius de *Coad.*	Belgium	Tournay	Dec. 7, 1621	387
F. Reggio, Vincent	Italy	Palermo	,, 16, 1614	396
F. Roder, Matthew	Tyrol	Munich	,, 22, 1634	402
F. Regis, St. John Francis	France	La Louvesc	,, 31, 1640	409

S.

NAME	COUNTRY	PLACE OF DEATH	DAY AND YEAR	PAGE
F. Sanchez, Gabriel		Philippines	Jan. 1, 1617	2
F. Schacht, Henry	Germany	Hamburg, Germany	,, 2, 1654	2
Silva, Edward de *Schol.*	Portugal	Jacnseo, Japan	,, 5, 1564	6
F. Scannacca, Joseph		Palermo	,, 8, 1627	9
F. Swihowski, Wenceslaus	Bohemia	Harasdowitz, Bohem.	,, 8, 1610	9
F. Stanihurst, William	Belgium	Brussels	,, 10, 1663	11
F. Schatelinch, Jodocus	Belgium	Louvain	,, 21, 1658	23
F. Schott, Andrew	Belgium	Antwerp	,, 23, 1629	25
F. Salian, James	France	Paris	,, 23, 1640	25
Soier, Ignatius *Schol.*	Germany	Ingolstadt	,, 26, 1647	28
F. Susa, Salvator		Bivona	,, 29, 1619	31
F. Sales, James de		Aubenas, France	Feb. 7, 1593	43
Saltemouche, William *Coad.*		Aubenas	,, 7, 1593	43
F. Segura, John Bapt.	Spain	Florida, America	,, 8, 1571	44
F. Salmeron, Alphonsus	Spain	Naples	,, 13, 1585	49
F. Sucquet, Anthony	Belgium	Paris	,, 15, 1626	52
F. Skarsinski, George	Poland	Pultowa	,, 17, 1611	56
F. Silva, Francis de	Spain	Seville	,, 18, 1673	58
F. Sanchez, James		Seville	,, 19, 1688	58
F. Serrano, James	Spain	Frezenal, Spain	,, 19, 1680	59
Sanga, Mathias	Japan	Manilla	,, 24, 1615	63
Saito, Andrew *Coad.*	Japan	Manilla	,, 28, 1615	66
F. Southwell, Robert	England	London	March 3, 1595	70
F. Samaniego, James		Peru	,, 7, 1626	74
F. Saile, Thomas		Brussels	,, 8, 1625	74
F. Sewall, Nicholas	America	Worcester, England	,, 14, 1834	80
F. Sylveria, Ven. Gonzales	Portugal	Monomotapa, Africa	,, 15, 1561	81
F. Saller, Adam		Münster	,, 24, 1630	89

NAME.	COUNTRY.	PLACE OF DEATH.	DAY AND YEAR.	PAGE.
F. Sands, John	Belgium	Germany	March 30, 1622	94
F. Sommal, Henry	Belgium	Valenciennes	,, 30, 1619	94
F. Strunica, Diego		Peru	April 10.	108
F. Saredo, Francis de		Spain	,, 13, 1657	111
F. Soldi, —		Japan	,, 18, 1609	116
Spinosa, John Bapt. *Coad.*	Spain	America	,, 21, 1624	119
F. Stibigk, Andrew	Prussia	Brunsberg, Prussia	,, 21, 1669	119
F. Surin, John Joseph	France	Bourdeaux	,, 21, 1665	120
F. Slostowski, John	Poland	Jaroslaw, Poland	,, 25, 1651	125
Schacher, Christian *Coad.*	Germany	Munich	,, 26, 1615	126
F. St. Jure, John Bapt.	France	Paris	,, 30, 1657	130
F. San Domingo, Martin de	Spain	Compostello	May 1, 1593	132
Silva, da Edward *Schol.*	Portugal	Japan	,, 2, 1564	133
F. Sotomayor, James de		Cadiz	,, 4, 1571	136
F. Suarez, John Francis	France	Toulouse	,, 7, 1627	139
F. Sanchez, Thomas		Spain	,, 19, 1610	154
F. Serrarier, Nicolas	France	Mayence	,, 20, 1609	155
Sevilla, John *Coad.*		Granada	,, 20, 1607	156
F. Scott, Gaspar	Germany	Würtzburg	,, 22, 1666	158
F. Sager, Charles	France	Tournon	,, 24, 1596	160
F. Salasar, Nicholas de		Seville	,, 25, 1649	161
F. Stanney, Thomas	England	St. Omers	,, 29, 1617	165
F. Suarez, James	Spain	Murcia	June 1, 1566	169
F. Sibilla, Angelo	Sicily	Messina	,, 3, 1577	172
F. Sanchez, Bartholomew	Spain	Bubayeni, Philipp.	,, 7, 1642	175
F. Spinola, Andrew	Italy	Naples	,, 10, 1588	178
F. Spotech, Christopher	Poland	Sweden	,, 14, 1601	183
Sandamantaza, Bl. Gaspar *Coad.*	Japan	Nangasachi	,, 20, 1626	190
F. Sandée, Maximilian	Belgium	Cologne	,, 21, 1656	191
Saa, Andrew *Schol.*	Portugal	Coimbra	,, 22, 1612	192
F. Scribani, Charles	Belgium	Antwerp	,, 24, 1629	194
Sarabias, Diego *Coad.*		Valencia	,, 27, 1558	298
Salazar, Diego Lopez de *Schol.*	America	Chili	,, 30.	202
F. Saura, Bartholomew de	Spain	Manilla	July 9, 1631	212
F. Sannois, Denis	Belgium	St. Omers	,, 10, 1612	214
F. Sanchez, Peter	Spain	Mexico	,, 16, 1609	220
F. Sanchez, Blasius	Spain	Sicily	,, 17, 1577	221
F. Stitz, James		Constance	,, 19, 1611	224
Suarez, Michael *Coad.*	France	Avignon	,, 23, 1598	227
F. Sequeira, Antony		Evora	,, 23, 1585	227
F. Sonciet, John Bapt.	Belgium	Salonica	,, 23, 1733	227
F. Savedra, Peter de	Spain	Alcala	,, 24, 1572	228
F. Smigletz, Martin	Poland	Kalisch	,, 26, 1618	230
Salumbrino, Augustine *Coad.*		Lima	Aug. 2, 1642	239
F. Serpe, Gaspar Maurice	Portugal	Mauritania	,, 4, 1578	240
F. Sanguinot, Charles	France	Bourdeaux	,, 7, 1571	244
F. Sarmiento, Sebastian	Spain	Burgos	,, 8, 1643	245
F. Shobach, Augustine	Moravia	East Indies	,, 9, 1684	247
F. Schafili, Albert		Palermo	,, 10, 1704	248
F. Soto, Thomas de	Spain	Spain	,, 20, 1600	258
F. Sluyskens, James	Flanders	Holland	,, 23, 1651	261

NAME.	COUNTRY.	PLACE OF DEATH.	DAY AND YEAR.	PAGE.
F. Syrwid, Constantine	Lithuania	Wilna	Aug. 23, 1631	262
F. Schall, John Adam	Germany	Pekin	„ 25, 1666	264
F. Stredonitz, Martin	Silesia	Brunn	„ 26, 1649	264
Stopelli, Peter *Coad.*	Italy	Milan	Sept. 3, 1601	275
F. Strada, Damian	Italy	Rome	„ 6, 1649	279
F. Spinola, Blessed Charles	Italy	Nangasachi	„ 10, 1622	285
Sampo, Blessed Peter *Schol.*	Japan	Nangasachi	„ 10, 1622	285
F. Sanchez, Michael	Spain	Marchena	„ 12, 1637	288
Schiesa, Louis *Schol.*	Italy	Como	„ 13, 1630	289
F. Suffren, John	France	Flushing, Zealand	„ 15, 1641	291
F. Sanchez, John	Spain	Valencia	„ 18, 1617	295
F. Sibilla, Angelo	Italy	Calatagirone	„ 21, 1611	298
F. Suarez, Francis	Spain	Lisbon	„ 25, 1617	302
F. Scarga, Peter	Poland	Cracow	„ 27, 1612	304
F. Sirmond, James	France	Paris	Oct. 7, 1651	318
F. Straub, Adam	Germany	Straubingen	„ 10, 1634	321
Silva, Jerome de *Coad.*	Portugal	Lisbon	„ 14, 1639	326
Sopp, John *Schol.*	Germany	Trêves	„ 16, 1588	328
F. Schorick, George	Germany	Baden	„ 20, 1573	333
Soria, John de *Coad.*	Spain	Seville	„ 23, 1647	337
F. See, John le	France	Rouen	„ 24, 1626	337
F. Strada, Francis	Spain	Toledo	„ 26, 1584	339
F. Sousa, Antony de	Portugal	Nangasachi	„ 26, 1633	340
F. Sylworst, John	Belgium	Mentz	„ 30, 1620	344
F. Sanivan, Melchior de	Spain	Seville	Nov. 3, 1609	349
F. Suffren, Anthony	France	Cambrai	„ 10, 1623	356
F. Streidt, Philip	Bohemia	Brünn	„ 12, 1643	359
F. Santa Cruz, Roche Gonzalez de	America	Paraguay	„ 15, 1618	362
F. Sanchez, Gaspar	Spain	Madrid	„ 16, 1629	363
F. Stull, Daniel	Belgium	Friesland	„ 16, 1651	364
F. Santaren, Ferdinand	Spain	Tenerapa, Mexico	„ 20, 1616	368
F. Soldano, Mark	Italy	Prague	„ 23, 1613	371
F. Sanchez, John Bapt.	Spain	Rome	„ 26, 1572	375
Saulx, Mathias de la *Coad.*	Belgium	Douay	„ 27, 1617	375
F. Segneri, Ven. Paul	Italy	Rome	„ 29, 1694	378
Salazar, Peter de	Spain	Lima	Dec. 4, 1613	384
F. Staroscirski, Stephen	Poland	Choynetz	„ 5, 1656	385
F. Segneri, Paul (the younger)	Italy	Rome	„ 8, 1694	388
Schmidt, Peter *Coad.*	Germany	Münster	„ 10, 1655	390
F. Savier, Andrew	Austria	China	„ 12, 1660	392
F. Suffren, John		Flushing	„ 13, 1641	393
F. Spinelli, Peter Antony	Italy	Rome	„ 14, 1615	394
F. Sacchini, Francis	Italy	Rome	„ 16, 1624	396
F. Suarez, John	Spain	Alcala	„ 17, 1625	397
F. Schaller, Sebastian	Germany	Ingolstadt	„ 18, 1648	398
F. Ségand, William de	France	Paris	„ 19, 1748	399
Sosa, John *Schol.*	Portugal	Brazil	„ 24, 1554	403
F. Sa, Emmanuel	Portugal	Arona	„ 30, 1596	408
F. Stremos, John	Portugal	Evora	„ 30, 1600	409
Scaglione, Marcellus *Coad.*	Italy	Messina	„ 31, 1630	410

T.

NAME.	COUNTRY.	PLACE OF DEATH.	DAY AND YEAR.	PAGE.
F. Torres, Jerome	Spain	Munich	Jan. 9, 1611	10
F. Tylkowsky, Albert	Poland	Warsaw	„ 14, 1695	16
Tai-chieu, Mancien *Coad.*	Japan	Macao, Japan	„ 20, 1615	22
F. Tucci, Stephen	Sicily	Rome	„ 27, 1597	28
F. Tanner, Mathias	Bohemia	Prague	Feb. 8, 1692	45
F. Tablares, Peter	Spain		March 6, 1565	73
F. Torres, Francis		Messina	„ 7, 1625	74
F. Terentius John	Germany	Pekin	„ 13, 1630	79
Tibald, John *Coad.*		Rome	„ 16, 1626	83
F. Terry, James	Scotland	Rome	„ 20, 1597	86
Terres, Vas *Schol.*	Portugal	Oporto	„ 22, 1547	88
F. Tollenaire, John		Antwerp	April 3, 1643	99
F. Tavora, George		Coimbra	„ 5, 1599	102
Thenens, John *Coad.*	Belgium	Louvain	May 13, 1610	147
F. Tanner, Adam	Tyrol	Tyrol	„ 25, 1632	162
Truoska, Wenceslaus *Coad.*		Bohemia	„ 31, 1739	168
F. Tonéra, James	Spain	Manresa	June 5, 1627	174
F. Torres, Blessed Baltassar de	Spain	Nangasachi	„ 20, 1626	190
Toxo, Blessed Michael *Schol.*	Japan	Nangasachi	„ 20, 1626	190
F. Turner, Anthony	England	London	„ 30, 1679	201
F. Tapia, Gonsalvo de	Spain	Roborosa, S. America	July 10, 1594	213
F. Tausch, Caspar	Prussia	Prague	„ 26, 1646	230
Tensier, Br. Adam		Klausenburg	Aug. 5, 1586	242
F. Tyszkiewicz, George	Poland	Cracow	„ 14, 1625	252
F. Tennier, Florence	Belgium	Chatêlet	„ 31, 1629	270
F. Tzugi, Blessed Thomas	Japan	Nangasachi	Sept. 6, 1627	279
F. Toleto, Francis *Cardinal*	Spain	Rome	„ 14, 1596	289
F. Teller, John	France	Rome	„ 17, 1599	294
F. Trinkel, Zachary	Hungary	Presburg	„ 18, 1665	295
F. Thelen, Godfrey	Germany	Upon the Rhine	„ 25, 1620	302
F. Todor, Stephen	Bohemia	Nissa	„ 27, 1633	305
F. Tacusima, James Antony	Japan	Sciki, Japan	„ 30, 1633	307
F. Torres, Cosmo de	Spain	Isle of Xiqui, Japan	Oct. 2, 1570	310
F. Tolgsdorff, Ertman	Prussia	Wenden, Livonia	„ 4, 1620	312
F. Tocuum, Xystus	Japan	Nangasachi	„ 9, 1633	320
F. Trebosie, William	France	Toulouse	„ 14, 1621	326
F. Torres, Michael de	Spain	Alcala	„ 24, 1593	338
F. Tarsia, Francis	Italy	Caltagirone	„ 22, 1622	345
F. Trigault, Nicholas	Belgium	Nankin	Nov. 14, 1628	361
F. Tovar, Ferdinand de	America	America	„ 16, 1616	363
F. Torres, Francis de	Spain	Rome	„ 21, 1584	369
F. Terzo, John Andrew		Naples	„ 25, 1613	374
F. Teinzer, John	Germany	Osnaburg	„ 30, 1630	379
F. Teller, Godfrey	Belgium	Brisac, Alsace	Dec. 2, 1635	382
F. Torres, Antony de	Spain	Palencia	„ 15, 1595	395
F. Torres, John de	Spain	Granada	„ 19, 1610	398

U.

NAME.	COUNTRY.	PLACE OF DEATH.	DAY AND YEAR.	PAGE.
F. Ubierna, Francis de	...	Almonacid, Spain	Jan. 9, 1623	10
F. Ujoysky, Ven. Th. de Rupniew	Poland	Wilna	Aug. 1, 1689	238
F. Urrea, Michael de	Spain	Peru	,, 28, 1597	266
F. Urtaso, Martin Xavier	Spain	Paraguay	Dec. 1614	382
F. Urteaga, Peter de	Spain	Seville	,, 30, 1644	409

V.

NAME	COUNTRY	PLACE OF DEATH	DAY AND YEAR	PAGE
F. Villareggio, Alexander	...	Ceuta, Mexico	Jan. 11, 1580	12
F. Valignani, Alexander	Italy	Macao	,, 20, 1606	22
F. Verbiest, John	Belgium	Pekin	,, 20, 1688	22
Vega, Peter de *Coad.*	Spain	America	Feb. 1, 1619	36
F. Valli, Paul	...	Punchal, East Indies	,, 5, 1552	41
F. Vitelleschi, Mutius *General.*	Italy	Rome	,, 9, 1645	45
F. Villalobos, John	America	Peru	March 5, 1630	72
Valditaro, Bartholomew *Schol.*	Italy	Messina	,, 25, 1619	90
F. Villalobos, John de	France	Peru	,, 29, 1654	94
Vayle, Gabriel *Schol.*	Spain	Ripoll, Spain	,, 29.	94
F. Vanderbergen, Francis	...	Antwerp	April 1, 1598	97
F. Vitorez, Diego San	Spain	Isle of St. John	,, 6, 1672	103
F. Vagnoni, Alphonsus	Piedmont	China	,, 9, 1640	106
F. Valentia, Gregory de	Spain	Naples	,, 25, 1603	125
F. Visconti, Ignatius *General*	Milan	Rome	May 4, 1755	135
F. Villanova, Francis de	Spain	Alcala	,, 5, 1557	137
F. Villalpandos, John Bapt.	Spain	Rome	,, 22, 1608	158
F. Vragonitz, Peter	Croatia	Zagrabe	June 3, 1617	171
F. Vieyrea, Ven. Sebastian	Portugal	Yendi, Japan	,, 6, 1634	174
F. Valesi, Dominic	Italy	Krems	,, 9, 1615	178
F. Vasia, Gabriel	Spain	Gerona, Spain	,, 11, 1607	180
F. Viverez, Christopher	Peru	La Paz, Peru	,, 13, 1661	182
F. Venegas, Melchior de	America	Chili	,, 19, 1641	189
Veley, Claude *Coad.*	Belgium	Cambrai	,, 22, 1610	192
F. Vasée, John	Flanders	Paraguay	,, 23, 1623	193
F. Vogler, John George	Germany	Würtsburg	,, 26, 1625	196
F. Vicine, Arnold	France	Annecy, Savoy	July 7, 1596	211
F. Villasante, John de	...	Oviedo	,, 12, 1599	216
F. Vieyra, Antony	...	San Salvador	,, 18, 1697	222
F. Viola, Claude	France	Bar-le-duc	,, 29, 1632	234
F. Vecchia, Barnabas la	Italy	Bivona	Aug. 19, 1614	257
F. Villar Peter	Spain	Tarragona	,, 31, 1604	270
F. Vazin, John	Germany	Wratislaw, Silesia	Sept. 8, 1653	282
F. Vasquez, Gabriel	Spain	Alcala	,, 23, 1604	300
F. Varsewitch, Stanislaus	Poland	Cracow	Oct. 3, 1591	311
F. Venusti, Peter	Italy	Bivona	,, 19, 1564	332

NAME.	COUNTRY.	PLACE OF DEATH.	DAY AND YEAR.	PAGE.
F. Vallier, George	Spain	On the British Sea	Oct. 28, 1596	342
Verloyn, Thomas *Coad.*	Belgium	Antwerp	„ 29, 1625	344
F. Verviau, Gerard		Douay	Nov. 1, 1618	348
F. Valdivia, Louis de	Spain	Valladolid	„ 5, 1642	351
F. Velasquez, John Anthony	Spain	Madrid	„ 6, 1669	352
Vas, Alphonsus *Schol.*	Portugal	Coimbra	„ 9, 1553	356
Valentino, Angelo *Coad.*	Italy	Lecce	„ 10.	357
F. Valle, John de		Mexico	„ 18, 1616	366
Viconti, Louis *Schol.*	Italy	Milan	Dec. 11, 1612	391
F. Valdivia, Martin de Aranda	Spain	Chili	„ 14, 1621	393
F. Vecchi, Horatio	Italy	Chili	„ 14, 1621	393
F. Vallière, James de	France	West India Isles	„ 19, 1650	399
Vasserot, James *Coad.*	France	Carpentras	„ 26, 1628	405

W.

NAME.	COUNTRY.	PLACE OF DEATH.	DAY AND YEAR.	PAGE.
Wilson, Andrew *Schol.*	England	St. Omers	Jan. 15, 1634	17
F. Worthington, John	England	England	„ 25, 1652	27
Werden, Henry *Coad.*	Germany	Hildeheim	Feb. 22, 1656	62
F. Warlich, John	Germany	Glatz, Germany	March 27, 1653	92
F. Weston, William	England	Valladolid	April 9, 1615	106
F. Walpole, Henry	England	York	„ 17, 1595	115
F. Wippermann, Simon	Germany	Osnaburg, Germany	„ 25, 1619	125
F. Weltheim, William	Germany	Luxembourg	May 1, 1636	132
F. Woynicz, Gaspar	Poland	Poland	„ 5, 1642	137
F. Wiglocki, Albert	Poland	Jaroslaw, Poland	„ 17, 1647	152
F. Wright, Peter	England	London	„ 19, 1651	153
F. Walsh, James	Ireland	Waterford	June 4, 1650	172
F. Wisoski, Simon	Russia	Cracow	„ 12, 1622	181
F. Wiecz, James	Poland	Cracow	„ 26.	197
F. Waring (*alias* Barrow) Wm.	England	London	„ 30, 1679	201
F. Wujeck, James	Poland	Cracow	July 27, 1597	232
F. Wishaw, Cornelius	Flanders	Loretto	Aug. 25, 1559	263
F. Warsewich, Stanislaus	Poland	Cracow	Oct. 11, 1591	323
F. Worthington, Laurence	England	Lorraine	„ 19, 1637	331
F. Weguelin, Balthasar	Germany	Constance	„ 20, 1635	333
F. Woysza, Stanislaus	Poland	Posen	„ 20, 1655	333
F. Werner Thomas	Germany	Mt. St. Gothard	Dec. 15, 1654	394
F. White, Andrew	England	London	„ 27, 1656	406

X.

NAME.	COUNTRY.	PLACE OF DEATH.	DAY AND YEAR.	PAGE.
Ximenes, John *Coad.*	Spain	Saragossa	Feb. 24, 1579	63
F. Xavier, Jerome	Spain	Goa	June 17, 1617	187
Xingutke (or Chinsuche) Bl. Paul *S*	Japan	Nangasachi	,, 20, 1626	190
Xumpo, Blessed Michael	Japan	Japan	Sept. 10, 1622	285
Xucan, Michael *Catech.*	Japan	Ximoxima, Japan	Oct. 6, 1628	316
F. Ximenes, Peter	Spain	Militch, Germany	Nov. 29, 1633	378
F. Xavier, St. Francis	Spain	I. of Sancian, China	Dec. 2, 1552	381

Y.

Yovenez, James de *Coad.*	Spain	Granada	Jan. 22, 1585	23
F. Yuki, Diego	Japan	Japan	Feb. 8, 1636	44
Yama, John *Catech.*	Japan	Japan	Sept. 8, 1633	283
Yama, John *Coad.*	Japan	Yendi, Japan	,, 22, 1637	299
Yamomoto, Denis *Coad.*	Japan	Cocyra, Japan	,, 28, 1633	305

Z.

F. Zara, Jerome de		Seville	Jan. 27, 1600	29
F. Zuniga, John de		Lima	Feb. 2, 1577	37
F. Zanoni, Bernardine		Genoa	March 29, 1620	94
F. Zucchi, Nicolas	Italy	Rome	May 21, 1670	157
F. Zola, Blessed John Bapt.	Italy	Nangasachi	June 20, 1626	190

www.ingramcontent.com/pod-product-compliance
Lightning Source LLC
Chambersburg PA
CBHW032138010526
44111CB00035B/605